Focus Edition
Unofficial Quantitative Review 2023

Title : Focus Edition Unofficial Quantitative Review 2023

Language : English

Editor's Name : CL Editorial Team

Typeset & Published by :

Career Launcher Infrastructure (P) Ltd.

A-45, Mohan Cooperative Industrial Area, Near Mohan Estate Metro Station, New Delhi - 110044

Marketed by :

G.K. Publications (P) Ltd.

Plot No. 9A, Sector-27A, Mathura Road, Faridabad, Haryana-121003

ISBN : 978-93-56812-78-9

Printer's Details : Printed in India, New Delhi.

Foreword

Welcome to the "GMAT Focus Edition - Unofficial Quantitative Review 2023" book - a comprehensive and specialized resource designed to sharpen your skills and elevate your performance on the Graduate Management Admission Test (GMAT).

The GMAT is a gateway to countless opportunities in the world of business and management. It demands not only a solid grasp of fundamental concepts but also the ability to apply that knowledge strategically. The book has been meticulously crafted to provide you with precisely what you need - a focused and expertly curated collection of content to maximize your potential on this critical exam.

In this book, you will find a streamlined and potent selection of practice questions, thoughtfully organized to cover Quantitative and Data Insight sections of the GMAT Focus Edition. Each question has been handpicked to represent the diverse array of challenges you are likely to encounter on test day.

Recognizing that time is a valuable asset in your preparation, this edition emphasizes efficiency. As you progress through these pages, you will find that every question, every explanation, and every strategy has been fine-tuned to provide the most impactful learning experience.

The authors of the "GMAT Unofficial Quantitative Review" are experts in their fields, each with a deep understanding of the GMAT and a passion for helping aspiring business leaders like you to succeed. They have poured their expertise and dedication into crafting a resource that goes beyond the norm, guiding you through each question with clarity and precision.

While this book is a powerful tool, it is only one part of your journey. Your success on the GMAT will also depend on your commitment, perseverance, and the belief that you have what it takes to excel. Embrace the challenges presented within these pages, and let each question be an opportunity to refine your thinking, hone your skills, and push the boundaries of your abilities.

Remember that the GMAT is not just about achieving a score; it is a stepping stone toward your dreams and aspirations. Embrace the process of learning, celebrate every step forward, and allow this experience to shape you into the future leader you envision.

As you embark on this transformative journey, know that you are not alone. Countless individuals have faced the GMAT before you, and many more will follow. Let the "GMAT Quantitative Review" be your ally, guiding you with expertise and encouragement as you navigate the path to success.

On behalf of the authors and the entire team behind this book, I extend my best wishes for your GMAT preparation. May your dedication, hard work, and focus on excellence propel you toward a bright and prosperous future.

Best Wishes!

Content

Introduction to the GMAT

Introduction to GMAT

The GMAT (Graduate Management Admission Test) is a standardized exam that is used to assess the readiness of prospective students for graduate-level business programs. The exam evaluates various skills that are important for success in a business school, such as Data insight, quantitative reasoning, and verbal reasoning. The GMAT is accepted by thousands of graduate-level business programs worldwide, and it is typically taken by individuals who are seeking admission to MBA (Master of Business Administration) programs or other business-related master's degree programs. The exam is administered in English, and it is offered year- round at test centers around the world.

The GMAT score is used in admission decisions by more than 7,000 graduate management programs, at approximately 2,300 graduate business schools worldwide. It helps you gauge, and demonstrate to schools, your academic potential for success in graduate-level management studies.

Let's start with the basics. The GMAT is, among other things, an endurance test. It is a computerized test, consisting of 135 minutes of multiple-choice math, verbal, and data insights questions.

Taking the GMAT helps you stand out in the admissions process; and demonstrate your readiness and commitment to pursuing graduate management education. Schools use GMAT scores to help them select the most-qualified applicants because they know that candidates who take the GMAT are serious about earning a graduate business degree; and it's a proven predictor of a student's ability to succeed in his or her chosen program.

Format of GMAT

The GMAT exam is designed to assess the critical reasoning and data literacy skills that are essential for success in business school and beyond.

The GMAT has three sections:

- **Quantitative Reasoning:** This section tests your ability to solve math problems using a variety of methods, including basic arithmetic, algebra and data analysis.
- **Verbal Reasoning:** This section tests your ability to read critically and understand complex text. It includes questions that test your reasoning and reading comprehension skills.
- **Data Insights:** This section tests your ability to interpret and analyze data. It includes questions that test your ability to understand graphs, charts, and tables.

Each section of the GMAT is 45 minutes long, for a total test time of 2 hours and 15 minutes. There is one optional 10-minute break after the Quantitative Reasoning section.

The scores for the GMAT are reported on a scale of 205 to 805, with a 10-point increment. The scores for each section are also reported separately.

The GMAT is a valuable tool for students who are preparing for business school. It can help you assess your strengths and weaknesses in the critical reasoning and data literacy areas, and it can give you a good idea of how you would perform on the actual GMAT exam.

Here is a table summarizing the format of the GMAT:

Section	Time	Number of Questions
Quantitative Reasoning	45 minutes	21 questions
Verbal Reasoning	45 minutes	23 questions
Data Insights	45 minutes	20 questions

Section Order

The GMAT allows you to choose the order in which you take the three sections. You can choose to take the Quantitative Reasoning section first, the Verbal Reasoning section first, or the Data Insights section first.

There are a few factors to consider when choosing your section order. First, you should consider your strengths and weaknesses. If you are stronger in quantitative reasoning, you may want to take that section first. If you are stronger in verbal reasoning, you may want to take that section first.

Second, you should consider your timing. If you know that you tend to get tired towards the end of the exam, you may want to take the Data Insights section first, as it is the shortest section.

Finally, you should consider your personal preference. Some people prefer to start with the section that they are most confident in, while others prefer to start with the section that they are least confident in.

Here are some tips for choosing your section order:

- Consider your strengths and weaknesses. If you are stronger in quantitative reasoning, you may want to take that section first. If you are stronger in verbal reasoning, you may want to take that section first.

- Consider your timing. If you know that you tend to get tired towards the end of the exam, you may want to take the Data Insights section first, as it is the shortest section.

- Consider your personal preference. Some people prefer to start with the section that they are most confident in, while others prefer to start with the section that they are least confident in.

Ultimately, the best way to choose your section order is to experiment and see what works best for you. Try taking a practice test with different section orders and see how you do.

Quantitative Aptitude

Chapter 1

Number Properties

Number Properties is a topic that is tested in the Quantitative Reasoning section of the GMAT. It is a broad topic that covers various concepts related to numbers, such as prime numbers, divisibility, fractions, decimals, integers, and their properties.

Here are some key concepts related to Number Properties that you should be familiar with for the GMAT:

- **Prime numbers :** A prime number is a positive integer greater than 1 that has no positive integer divisors other than 1 and itself.
- **Divisibility :** An integer a is divisible by an integer b if there exists an integer c such that a = bc. For example, 15 is divisible by 3, since $15 = 3 \times 5$.
- **Factors :** A factor of an integer a is any integer that divides a without leaving a remainder. For example, the factors of 12 are 1, 2, 3, 4, 6, and 12.
- **Multiples :** A multiple of an integer a is any integer that is the product of a and another integer. For example, the multiples of 3 are 3, 6, 9, 12, and so on.
- **Even and odd numbers :** An even number is an integer that is divisible by 2 without leaving a remainder, while an odd number is an integer that is not divisible by 2 without leaving a remainder.
- **Fractions and decimals :** Fractions represent a part of a whole, while decimals represent a number that has been divided by a power of 10.

Divisibility Rules

If there is no remainder when integer x is divided by integer y, then x is said to be divisible by y. Put another way, divisible means you can evenly divide the bigger number by the smaller number. For example, 10 is divisible by 5.

Some useful divisibility rules are mentioned below:

Divisibility rule for 2 : A number is divisible by 2 if its unit's digit is even. For example, 138 is divisible by 2 as unit digit is even, which is 8, whereas 1,234,567 is odd, as 7 is odd.

Divisibility rule for 3 : A number is divisible by 3 if the sum of its digits is divisible by 3. For example, 4,317 is divisible by 3 because $4 + 3 + 1 + 7 = 15$ and 15 is divisible by 3.

Divisibility rule for 4 : A number is divisible by 4 if its last two digits is divisible by 4. For example, 1,728 is divisible by 4 because 28 is divisible by 4, but 25,618 is not divisible by 4 because 18 is not divisible by 4

Divisibility rule for 5 : A number is divisible by 5 if its unit's digit is divisible by 5. For example, 75 and 80 are divisible by 5, but 77 and 83 are not.

Divisibility rule for 6 : A number is divisible by 6 if the number is divisible by both 2 and 3. If the unit's digit is even and the sum of the digits divisible by 3, then the number is divisible by 6. For example, 48 is divisible by 6 since it is divisible by 2 (it ends with an 8, which is even) AND by 3 (4 + 8 = 12, which is divisible by 3).

Divisibility rule for 8 : A number is divisible by 8 if its last three digits compose a three-digit number that is itself divisible by 8. For example, 23,456 is divisible by 8 because 456 is divisible by 8, whereas 23,556 is not divisible by 8 because 556 is not divisible by 8.

Divisibility rule for 9 : A number is divisible by 9 if the sum of its digits is divisible by 9. For example, 4,185 is divisible by 9 since the sum of its digits is 4 + 1 + 8 + 5 = 18, which is divisible by 9.

Divisibility rule for 10 : A number is divisible by 10 if its units digit is zero. For example, 670 is divisible by 10, but 675 is not.

Divisibility rule for 11 : A number is divisible by 11 if the difference between the sum of its odd-placed digits and the sum of its even-placed digits is divisible by 11. For example, 5,181 is divisible by 11 because (5 + 8) - (1 + 1) = 11, which is divisible by 11

Divisibility rule for 12 : Rule of 3 and 4 both; i.e. if sum of digits divisible by 3 and the last two digits divisible by 4, then the number is divisible by 12. For example, 1,732 is divisible by both 3 and 4, hence divisible by 12

Example : Is the integer 7,256 divisible by 8?

Solution : To determine whether 7,256 is divisible by 8, we need to check whether its last three digits are divisible by 8, as per the divisibility rule for 8. The last three digits of 7,256 are 256, which is divisible by 8 since it is a multiple of 8. Therefore, 7,256 is divisible by 8.

Answer : Yes.

Example : Is the integer 4,809 divisible by 3?

Solution : To determine whether 4,809 is divisible by 3, we need to check whether the sum of its digits is divisible by 3, as per the divisibility rule for 3. The sum of the digits of 4,809 is 4 + 8 + 0 + 9 = 21, which is divisible by 3. Therefore, 4,809 is divisible by 3.

Answer : Yes.

Remainders

If an integer cannot be divided evenly by another integer, the integer that is left over at the end of division is called the remainder. Thus, remainders must be integers.

Example : When 7 is divided by 2, remainder is 1.

Every division has four parts :

1. The dividend is the number being divided. In 7 ÷ 2, the dividend is 7.

2. The divisor is the number that is dividing. In 7 ÷ 2, the divisor is 2.

3. The quotient is the number of times that the divisor goes into the dividend completely. The quotient is always an integer. In 7 ÷ 2, the quotient is 3 because 2 goes into 7 three (1) times completely.

4. The remainder is what is left over if the dividend is not divisible by the divisor. In 7 ÷ 2, the remainder is 1.

Note : A remainder is always smaller than the divisor.

Example : 17 divided by 3 is 5 with a remainder of 2.

The relation between dividend, divisor, quotient and remainder is :

Dividend = divisor × Quotient + Remainder

Example :

100 divided by 3 is 33 remainder 1, since 100 = (33)(3) + 1.

100 divided by 25 is 4 remainder 0, since 100 = (4)(25) + 0.

80 divided by 100 is 0 remainder 80, since 80 = (0)(100) + 80.

The remainder r is 0 if and only if dividend is evenly divisible by divisor.

Example : Since 32 divided by 8 yields a remainder of 0, 32 is divisible by 8. So 8 is a divisor or factor of 32, and 32 is a multiple of 8.

Example : What is the remainder when 3^{17} is divided by 7?

Solution: To find the remainder when 3^{17} is divided by 7, we can use the concept of cyclicity of remainders. Since the divisor is 7, we need to find the remainders when 3 is divided by 7, 3^2 is divided by 7, 3^3 is divided by 7, and so on, until we identify a pattern.

3^1 divided by 7 leaves a remainder of 3.

3^2 divided by 7 leaves a remainder of 2.

3^3 divided by 7 leaves a remainder of 6.

3^4 divided by 7 leaves a remainder of 4.

3^5 divided by 7 leaves a remainder of 5.

3^6 divided by 7 leaves a remainder of 1.

3^4 divided by 7 leaves a remainder of 3. ...

We can see that the remainders repeat in a pattern of length 6. Therefore, we can find the remainder when 3^{17} is divided by 7 by dividing the exponent 17 by 6, which gives a quotient of 2 and a remainder of 5. This means that the remainder when 3^{17} is divided by 7 is the same as the remainder when 3^5 is divided by 7.

3^5 divided by 7 leaves a remainder of 5, as we can see from the pattern above.

Therefore, the remainder when 3^{17} is divided by 7 is 5.

Answer : 5.

Factors and Multiples

Multiples

Multiples are numbers that can be obtained by multiplying a given number by any integer. For example, the multiples of 3 are 3, 6, 9, 12, 15, and so on.

Multiples are an important concept that is tested on the GMAT, particularly in the areas of number properties and algebra.

Example : What is the sum of all the even multiples of 7 that are less than 100?

(a) 392

(b) 294

(c) 394

(d) 492

(e) 494

Solution : To solve this question, we need to find the even multiples of 7 that are less than 100 and add them up. We can do this by multiplying 7 by each even integer from 2 to 14 (since 7 times 16 is greater than 100):

Even multiples of 7 : 14, 28, 42, 56, 70, 84, 98

Sum of even multiples of 7 : $14 + 28 + 42 + 56 + 70 + 84 + 98 = 392$

Therefore, the answer is (a) 392

Factors

The factors, or divisors, of a number are the positive integers that divide the given number without a remainder (or a remainder of 0).

An integer, x, is a factor of another integer, y, if y is divisible by x. So, in other words, y = nx, where y, n and x are all integers.

The positive factors of 60 are 1, 2, 3, 4, 5, 6, 10, 12, 15, 20, 30, and 60.

Important points :

- 1 and (–1) are divisors of every integer.
- Every integer is a divisor of itself.
- Every integer is a divisor of 0, except, by convention, 0 itself.

Here are some important rules:

- If x is a factor of y and y is a factor of z, then x is a factor of (y+z).
- If x is a factor of y and y is a factor of z, then x is a factor of z.
- If x is a factor of y and y is a factor of x, then or x = y or x = – y.

Example : What is the sum of the factors of 48?

(a) 60

(b) 78

(c) 96

(d) 124

(e) 144

Solution : To find the sum of the factors of 48, we first need to determine all the factors of 48. We can do this by finding the prime factorization of 48:

$$48 = 2^4 \times 3^1$$

To find all the factors, we need to determine all possible combinations of the prime factors. For example, the factors of 48 include 1, 2, 3, 4, 6, 8, 12, 16, 24, and 48.

The sum of these factors is :

$$1 + 2 + 3 + 4 + 6 + 8 + 12 + 16 + 24 + 48 = 124$$

Therefore, the answer is (d) 124

Finding Number of factors

Let $n = a^p \times b^q \times c^r$, where a, b and c are prime factors of n and p, q and r are their powers.

The number of factors of n will be expressed by the formula $(p + 1)(q + 1)(r + 1)$.

Example : How many positive factors does 540 have?

(a) 12

(b) 16

(c) 18

(d) 20

(e) 24

Solution : To solve this question, we need to determine how many positive integers divide evenly into 540. We can do this by finding the prime factorization of 540:

$$540 = 2^2 \times 3^3 \times 5$$

To find the number of factors, we can count the number of ways to choose exponents for each prime factor, and then multiply those counts together.

Number of factors of 540 = $(2 + 1) \times (3 + 1) \times (1 + 1) = 24$

Therefore, the answer is (e) 24.

HCF / LCM

HCF / GCD (Highest Common Factor / Greatest Common Divisor)

The greatest common divisor (GCD), also known as the greatest common factor (GCF), or highest common factor (HCF), of two or more non-zero integers, is the largest positive integer that divides the numbers without a remainder.

Example : the greatest common divisor of 30 and 75 is 15. This is because the positive divisors of 30 are 1, 2, 3, 5, 6, 10, 15, and 30, and the positive divisors of 75 are 1, 3, 5, 15, 25, and 75. Thus, the common positive divisors of 30 and 75 are 1, 3, 5, and 15, and the greatest of these is 15.

To find the HCF / GCD, you will need to do prime-factorization. Then, multiply the common factors (pick the lowest power of the common factors)

Example : To find HCF of 4 and 6

Solution : Prime factorisation of 4 is 2^2

Prime factorisation of 6 is 2×3

Lowest power of 2 is 1 and lowest power of 3 is 1, hence HCF is $2^1 \times 3^1 = 2 \times 3 = 6$

Example : HCF of 63 and 72

$63 = 7 \times 3 \times 3 = 3^2 \times 7$

$72 = 2 \times 2 \times 2 \times 3 \times 3 = 2^3 \times 3^2$

$HCF = 3^2 = 9$

Important points :

- Every common divisor of a and b is a divisor of HCF (a, b).
- $a \times b = HCF(a, b) \times LCM(a, b)$

Example : What is the highest common factor (HCF) of 72 and 90?

(a) 3

(b) 6

(c) 9

(d) 12

(e) 18

Solution : To solve this question, we need to find the factors of both 72 and 90, and then identify the highest factor that is common to both. First, we can find the prime factorizations of 72 and 90:

$72 = 2^3 \times 3^2$

$90 = 2^1 \times 3^2 \times 5$

To find the HCF, we need to identify the lowest power of the prime numbers involved. In this case, the only prime factor that appears in both is 2, with the lowest power of 2 being 2^1 and lowest power of 3 is 3^2. The highest common factor of 72 and 90 is therefore $2^1 \times 3^2 = 18$.

Option (e) is correct.

LCM (Least Common Multiple)

The least common multiple of two nonzero integers a and b is the least positive integer that is a multiple of both a and b.

Example : Least common multiple of 30 and 75 is 150. This is because the positive multiples of 30 are 30, 60, 90, 120, 150, 180, 210, 240, 270, 300, etc., and the positive multiples of 75 are 75, 150, 225, 300, 375, 450, etc.

Thus, the common positive multiples of 30 and 75 are 150, 300, 450, etc., and the least of these is 150.

LCM of two numbers ranges: Larger no $\leq$ LCM $\leq$ Product of two Numbers

To find the LCM, you will need to do prime-factorization. Then multiply all the factors (pick the highest power of the common factors).

Example : LCM of 24 and 36

24 : $2 \times 2 \times 2 \times 3$

36 : $2 \times 2 \times 3 \times 3$

LCM : $2 \times 2 \times 2 \times 3 \times 3 = 72$

Example : What is the smallest positive integer that is a multiple of 9 and a multiple of 14?

(a) 54

(b) 126

(c) 162

(d) 252

(e) 378

Solution : To solve this question, we need to find the LCM (least common multiple) of 9 and 14. We can do this by listing out the multiples of each number and finding the first one they have in common:

Multiples of 9 : 9, 18, 27, 36, 45, 54, 63, 72, 81, 90, 99, 108, 117, 126, 135, 144, 153, 162, 171, 180, 189, 198, 207, 216, 225...

Multiples of 14 : 14, 28, 42, 56, 70, 84, 98, 112, 126, 140, 154, 168, 182, 196, 210, 224, 238, 252, 266, 280, 294, 308, 322, 336, 350...

The first multiple that they have in common is 126, so the answer is (b) 126.

Example : What is the least common multiple (LCM) of 12, 18, and 30?

(a) 180

(b) 360

(c) 540

(d) 720

(e) 900

Solution : To solve this question, we need to find the prime factorizations of all three numbers and then identify the smallest number that contains all the factors with their highest power. The prime factorizations of 12, 18, and 30 are:

$12 = 2^2 \times 3^1$

$18 = 2 \times 3^2$

$30 = 2 \times 3^1 \times 5^1$

To find the LCM, we need to take the highest power of each prime factor that appears in any of the three numbers. In this case, we need to take 2^2 (the highest power of 2), 3^2 (the highest power of 3), and 5^1 (the only power of 5). Multiplying these together, we get :

$\text{LCM} = 2^2 \times 3^2 \times 5^1 = 180$

Therefore, the answer is (a) 180.

Positive and Negative

Some GMAT questions gives importance on whether the numbers involved are positive or negative. These properties are especially important when Picking Numbers on a Data Sufficiency question. If both positives and negatives are permissible for a given question, make sure to check for both possibilities.

A positive number is a real number that is greater than zero.

A negative number is a real number that is smaller than zero.

Zero is not positive, nor negative.

Properties of Positive and Negative :

Multiplication :

positive $\times$ positive = positive

positive $\times$ negative = negative

negative $\times$ negative = positive

Division :

positive / positive = positive

positive / negative = negative

negative / negative = positive

Properties of Zero

Adding or subtracting zero from a number does not change the number.

Example : $12 \times 0 = 0$

Division by zero is undefined.

Properties of 1 and –1

Multiplying or dividing a number by 1 does not change the number.

Multiplying or dividing a number by – 1 changes the sign.

The sum of a number and – 1 times that number is equal to zero.

The reciprocal of a number between 0 and 1 is greater than the number itself.

Example : The reciprocal of $\frac{2}{3}$ is $\frac{3}{2}$.

Decimals

The decimal number system is based on representing numbers using powers of 10. The place value of each digit corresponds to a power of 10. For example, the digits of the number 7,532.418 have the following place values.

Thousands		Hundreds	Tens	Ones of Units		Tenths	Hundredths	Thousandths
7	,	5	3	2	.	4	1	8

$$7{,}532.418 = 7(1{,}000) + 5(100) + 3(10) + 2(1) + \frac{4}{10} + \frac{1}{100} + \frac{8}{1000}$$

In scientific notation, a decimal is expressed as a number with only one nonzero digit to the left of the decimal point, multiplied by a power of 10. To convert a number expressed in scientific notation to regular decimal notation, move the decimal point by the number of places equal to the absolute value of the exponent on the 10. Move the decimal point to the right if the exponent is positive and to the left if the exponent is negative.

Example : In scientific notation, 231 is written as 2.31×10^2, and 0.0231 is written as 2.31×10^{-2}.

To multiply decimals, multiply the numbers as if they were integers and then insert the decimal point in the product so that the number of digits to the right of the decimal point equals the sum of the numbers of digits to the right of the decimal points in the numbers being multiplied, the multiplicands.

Example : If $0.75x = 2.25$, what is the value of x?

(a) 1

(b) 2

(c) 3

(d) 4

(e) 5

Solution : To solve this question, we can start by isolating x on one side of the equation. We can do this by dividing both sides of the equation by 0.75:

$$0.75x = 2.25$$

$$x = \frac{2.25}{0.75}$$

$$x = 3$$

Therefore, the answer is (c) 3.

Problem Solving

1. A straight wire one centimetre in length was cut into smaller pieces by cutting on every third and fourth. Which of the following is the range of all the lengths of smaller wire pieces, in centimetre?

   (*a*) $\frac{1}{6}$ and $\frac{1}{4}$ only

   (*b*) $\frac{1}{4}$ and $\frac{1}{3}$ only

   (*c*) $\frac{1}{6}, \frac{1}{4}$, and $\frac{1}{3}$

   (*d*) $\frac{1}{12}, \frac{1}{6}$, and $\frac{1}{4}$

   (*e*) $\frac{1}{12}, \frac{1}{6}$, and $\frac{1}{3}$

2. All 7 students of a class received their scores on math test. All of them got at least a score of 1. At most three of the students received the same score, and no two of the remaining students got the same score. What is the least possible sum of the scores of the seven students?

   (*a*) 7

   (*b*) 13

   (*c*) 17

   (*d*) 22

   (*e*) 28

3. In an increasing sequence of 12 consecutive integers, the sum of the first 6 integers is 594. What is the sum of the last 6 integers in the sequence?

   (*a*) 630

   (*b*) 625

   (*c*) 620

   (*d*) 615

   (*e*) 610

4. Kevin has an odd number of cards with him. All his cards are either white or green. He placed all his cards on the table alternating between white and green. If the first card is white, and the total number of cards is x, how many of cards were white?

   (*a*) $\frac{(x+1)}{2}$

   (*b*) $\frac{(x-1)}{2}$

   (*c*) $\left(\frac{x}{2}\right)+1$

   (*d*) $\left(\frac{x}{2}\right)-1$

   (*e*) $\left(\frac{x}{2}\right)$

5. If w, x, y, and z are prime factors of 3315 such that $w < x < y < z$, then what is the value of y?

   (*a*) 3

   (*b*) 5

   (*c*) 11

   (*d*) 13

   (*e*) 17

6. If m is a multiple of 18, but not a multiple of 12, which of the following CANNOT be an integer?

   (*a*) $\frac{m}{6}$

   (*b*) $\frac{m}{7}$

   (*c*) $\frac{m}{8}$

   (*d*) $\frac{m}{26}$

   (*e*) $\frac{m}{81}$

7. If x and y are integers such that $1 < x < y$, then which of the following CANNOT be a multiple of either x or y?

I. $x - 1$

II. $y - 1$

III. $xy - 1$

(a) I only

(b) II only

(c) III only

(d) I and II only

(e) I, II and III

8. When a number is divided by 10,000, the remainder is 41. What is the remainder when the same number is divided by 1,000?

(a) 0

(b) 1

(c) 4

(d) 21

(e) 41

9. If $x = 0.9999$, $y = \sqrt{0.9999}$, and $z = (0.9999)^2$, which of the following is correct?

(a) $x > y > z$

(b) $x > z > y$

(c) $y > x > z$

(d) $y > z > x$

(e) $z > x > z$

10. If $5p + 13q = 61$; where p and q are positive integers, what is the value of pq?

(a) 2

(b) 10

(c) 12

(d) 14

(e) Cannot be determined

11. If $x = 85n$, and $y = 95n$, where n is prime, what is the greatest common factor of x and y ?

(a) 5

(b) n

(c) $5n$

(d) $1{,}615n$

(e) $1{,}615n^2$

12. How many numbers from 4 to 501, inclusive are NOT divisible by 7?

(a) 69

(b) 70

(c) 71

(d) 427

(e) 428

13. If a and b are positive integers, which of the following can be the remainder of $\frac{a}{b}$, if $\frac{a}{b} = 3.75$?

(a) 1

(b) 2

(c) 4

(d) 8

(e) 12

14. What is the units digit of

$(13^{49} \times 12^{49}) + (17^{39} \times 25^{34})$?

(a) 1

(b) 2

(c) 3

(d) 6

(e) 9

15. How many even numbers between 1 and 400 are divisible by 17 but not by 11 ?

(*a*) 9

(*b*) 10

(*c*) 11

(*d*) 12

(*e*) 20

16. A shopkeeper sold his first 50 books at the price of \$60 per book and the rest at \$50 per book. If he collected \$25,000 at the end of the day, how many books did he sell?

(*a*) 270

(*b*) 310

(*c*) 440

(*d*) 490

(*e*) 520

17. What is the value of $6 + |-3 - (12 - (-8 + 12))|$?

(*a*) 12

(*b*) 14

(*c*) 16

(*d*) 17

(*e*) 19

18. If $A = 12! + 14! + 6$, which of the following numbers is NOT a factor of A?

(*a*) 1

(*b*) 2

(*c*) 3

(*d*) 5

(*e*) 6

19. John has 18 pencils, 27 erasers, and 45 sharpeners. He wants to distribute these items among a few students such that each student gets the same number of pencils, erasers, and sharpeners. How many items does each student get if John wishes to distribute the items to the maximum number of students?

(*a*) 3

(*b*) 9

(*c*) 10

(*d*) 45

(*e*) 90

20. How many numbers that are squares of prime numbers have the sum of their factors equal to 133 ?

(*a*) One

(*b*) Two

(*c*) Three

(*d*) Eleven

(*e*) Twelve

Answer Key

1. (*d*)
2. (*c*)
3. (*a*)
4. (*a*)
5. (*d*)
6. (*c*)
7. (*e*)
8. (*c*)
9. (*c*)
10. (*d*)
11. (*c*)
12. (*d*)
13. (*e*)
14. (*a*)
15. (*b*)
16. (*d*)
17. (*d*)
18. (*d*)
19. (*c*)
20. (*a*)

Answer Explanations

1. (d)

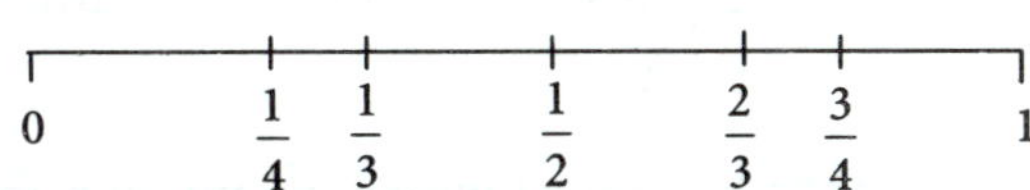

The markings represent the points at which the wire is cut. As the wire is cut at 5 points, 6 pieces are cut. Possible lengths

$$\left(\frac{1}{4}\right) - 0 = \frac{1}{4}$$

$$\left(\frac{1}{3}\right) - \left(\frac{1}{4}\right) = \frac{1}{12}$$

$$\left(\frac{1}{2}\right) - \left(\frac{1}{3}\right) - \frac{1}{6}$$

$$\left(\frac{2}{3}\right) - \left(\frac{1}{2}\right) = \frac{1}{6}$$

$$\left(\frac{3}{4}\right) - \left(\frac{2}{3}\right) = \frac{1}{12}$$

$$1 - \left(\frac{3}{4}\right) = \frac{1}{4}$$

2. (c) To determine the least possible sum of the seven scores, the smallest possible scores should be given to each score. Let the three students.who received the same score, get a score of 1 each. Let the fourth student gets a score of 2, fifth student gets a score of 3, sixth student gets a score of 4, and the seventh student gets a score of 5.

Hence, the total sum of the scores = 1 + 1 + 1 + 2 + 3 + 4 + 5 = 17

Hence, the answer is (c).

3. (a) Let the first six number be $(x + 1)$, $(x + 2)$, $(x + 3)$, $(x + 4)$, $(x + 5)$ and $(x + 6)$.

So, the last six numbers will be $(x + 7)$, $(x + 8)$, $(x + 9)$, $(x + 10)$, $(x + 11)$, and $(x + 12)$.

Sum of the first six numbers is $6x + 21$

Sum of the last six numbers is $6x + 57$

Difference between the two sums

$$= (6x + 57) - (6x + 21) = 36$$

Hence, the sum of the last six numbers will be 594 + 36 = 630

The answer is (a).

4. (a) Since there is an odd number of cards and the first card is white, the last card must be white. Hence, there is one more white card than green cards.

If the number of white cards is w, then the number of green cards is $w - 1$.

So, the total number of cards is $w + (w - 1)$.

$\Rightarrow \quad w + (w - 1) = x$

$\Rightarrow \quad 2w - 1 = x$

$\Rightarrow \quad 2w = x + 1$

$\Rightarrow \quad w = \dfrac{(x+1)}{2}$

The answer is (a).

5. (d) $3315 = 3 \times 5 \times 13 \times 17$

Hence, the four prime numbers are 3, 5, 13, and 17.

As y is the second greatest of the four numbers, y = 13

The answer is (d).

6. (c) Minimum possible value of m is 18 as m is multiple of 18.

$18 = 2 \times 3 \times 3$

Hence, m must have at least one 2 and two 3s.

Also, m is not a multiple of 12.

$12 = 2 \times 2 \times 3$

Hence, m must have less than two 2s.

$\Rightarrow$ m has exactly one 2.

(*a*) If m = 18, then $\frac{m}{6}$ is an integer.

(*b*) If $m = 18 \times 7$, then $\frac{m}{7}$ is an integer.

(*c*) For $\frac{m}{8}$ to be an integer, m must have at least three 2s, which is not allowed.

(*d*) If $m = 18 \times 13$, then $\frac{m}{26}$ is an integer.

(*e*) If $m = 18 \times 9$, then $\frac{m}{81}$ is an integer.

The answer is (c).

7. (e) A multiple is always greater than equal to divisor.

x – 1 is smaller than both x and y, hence, it CANNOT be the multiple of either x or y.

Hence, I must be among the answer choices.

So, eliminate (A), (C), and (D)

Also, xy is a multiple of both x and y, hence, xy – 1 CANNOT be a multiple of either x or y.

Hence, the answer is (e).

8. (c) Say the number is where is the quotient, a positive integer. Since is divisible by 1,000, the question comes down to whether 41 is divisible by 1,000. Since 41 is not divisible by 1,000, the remainder would be 41 only.

9. (c) Note that the base number 0.9999, is less than 1. Remember that...

(1) n^{th} root of a number less than 1 is always greater than the number itself; so $0.9999 < \sqrt{0.9999}$.

(2) Squares, cubes, and other high value powers of a number less than 1 are always smaller than the number itself; so, $0.9999 > (0.9999)^2$.

It means that $z < x < y$.

Opposite is true for a number greater than 1.

You may take a convenient number.

Say $x = \frac{1}{4}, y = \sqrt{\frac{1}{4}}, \& z = \left(\frac{1}{4}\right)^2$.

Thus, $x = \frac{1}{4}, y = \frac{1}{2}, \& z = \frac{1}{16}$.

Thus, $z < x < y$.

10. (d) Looking at the linear equation $5p + 13q = 61$, we may presume that the values of *p* and *q* are indeterminable as there are two unknown variables and only one equation is given; however, it is not so. We have the second condition given in the question: '*p* and *q* are positive integers'. Let's make use of it.

The equation $5p + 13q = 61$ can be written as $p = \frac{61-13q}{5}$. Since *p* is a positive integer, (61 – 13q) must be divisible by 5. Let us plug in some positive integers for *q*, and see for what value of q, (61 – 13q) is a multiple of 5.

For q = 1, $p = \frac{61-13\times1}{5} = \frac{48}{5}$ (not an integer); So, we discard the probable value of q as 1.

For q = 2, $p = \frac{61-13\times2}{5} = \frac{35}{5} = 7$ (an integer); So, we take the value of q as 2, and p would be 7 and $pq = 7 \times 2 = 14$.

There is no need to check further as the value of pq would be a finite number; however, for your curiosity, we find that for

$q = 3$, $p = \frac{61-13\times3}{5} = \frac{22}{5}$ (not an integer).

For *q* = 4, $p = \frac{61-13\times4}{5} = \frac{9}{5}$ (not an integer). There is no need to deep dive as for larger values of q, p would be negative. So, we get $pq = 7 \times 2 = 14$.

11. **(c)** Greatest common factor among numbers is also called HCF or GCD. The question asks us to find out the HCF of $85n$ and $95n$. Since $85n = 17 \times 5 \times n$ and $95n = 19 \times 5 \times n$ have '5' and 'n' common, the HCF would be $5 \times n = 5n$ or the greatest common factor of x and y is '$5n$'.

Alternatively,

$x = 17 \times 5 \times n;$

$y = 19 \times 5 \times n;$

HCF = 5n (Common between x and y)

The answer is $5n$.

12. **(d)** There are a total of ([501 – 4) + 1] = 498 numbers under consideration.

The first number, within 4 and 501, divisible by 7 is 7, and the last number is 497.

So, there are total of $\left[\frac{497-7}{7}+1\right] = 71$ numbers divisible by 7.

So, the total numbers, not divisible by 7 from 4 to 501 = 498 – 71 = 427.

13. **(e)** So, we have $\frac{a}{b} = 3.75$.

Thus, $a = 3.75b = 3b + 0.75b$

$$a = 3b + \frac{3b}{4}$$

Given a and b are positive integers, and since for the fraction $\frac{3b}{4}$, 3 and 4 are co-prime to each other, b must be a multiple of 4. So, the reminder for $\frac{a}{b}$ must be a multiple of 3. Or, the set of remainders would be {3, 6, 9, 12, ..., 150, ...}.

For example: Say, $\frac{a}{b} = 3.75 = \frac{15}{4}$. Reminder = 3; however, say, $\frac{a}{b} = 3.75 = \frac{750}{200}$. Reminder = 150.

Among the options, only 12 is the multiple of 3, therefore, the remainder could be 12.

14. **(a)** The units digit of 13^{49} is the same as that of 3^{49}; it is governed by the digit at the units place.

The same logic works for the other numbers too.

Thus, the question is equivalent to finding the units digit of $(3^{49} \times 2^{49}) + (7^{39} \times 5^{34})$.

Since the exponents of 3 and 2 are the same, we can write $3^{49} \times 2^{49}$ as $(3 \times 2)^{49} = 6^{49}$

We know that the units digit of 6 raised to any positive integer exponent is always 6.

Similarly, for $7^{39} \times 5^{34}$, we observe that 7^{39} is odd and 5^{34} has units digit of 5 (since the 5 raised to any positive integer exponent is always 5).

Thus, the units digit of $(7^{39} \times 5^{34})$ is essentially an odd number multiplied with 5, which is always 5, irrespective of any odd number being multiplied to.

Hence, the units digit of $(13^{49} \times 12^{49}) + (17^{39} \times 25^{34})$ is the units digit of the sum of 6 and 5, equals to 1.

15. **(b)** Since we need even numbers divisible by '17', we should look at numbers

$17 \times 2, 17 \times 4, 17 \times 6, 17 \times 8, 17 \times 10 ...$

The last number, less than 400, divisible by '17' is $391 = 17 \times 23$

Since we need even numbers, the last multiple of '17' would be

$17 \times (23 - 1) = 17 \times 22.$

Thus, the required set of numbers: $17 \times 2, 17 \times 4, 17 \times 6, 17 \times 8, ... 17 \times 22$, i.e., 11 numbers

However, we do not want numbers divisible by '11'.

In the above set, there is only one multiple of '11' i.e. 17×22

Thus, we need to exclude it.

Hence, the number of required numbers = $11 - 1 = 10$.

16. **(d)** Let number of books sold by the shopkeeper = n

Total sum collected

= Sum collected from 50 books + Sum collected from the remaining books

$\Rightarrow$ $25{,}000 = 50 \times 60 + (n - 50) \times 50$

$\Rightarrow$ $25{,}000 = 3{,}000 + 50n - 2{,}500$

$50n = 25{,}000 - 500$

$n = 490$ books

17. **(d)** $6 + |-3 - (12 - (-8 + 12))|$

$= 6 + |-3 - (12 - 4)|$

$= 6 + |-3 - 8| = 6 + |-11|$

$= 6 + 11$

$= 17$

18. **(d)** We can write $12! + 14! + 6$ as (1.2.3.4.5.6 ... 12) + (1.2.3.4.5.6 ...12.13.14) + (1.2.3).

Thus, each term of A : 12!, 14!, and 6 is divisible by 1, 2, 3 and 6; thus, the correct answer is 5 as the third term of A, 6, is not divisible by 5.

19. **(c)** The maximum number of students among whom the items can be distributed would be the HCF of 18, 27 and 45 = 9. HCF – Highest Common Factor-implies that John cannot have a greater common factor from them (18, 27, and 45) compared to itself, i.e., 9.

Thus, John can distribute these items to a maximum of 9 students so that each student gets the same number of items.

In such an event, each student gets $\frac{18}{9} = 2$ pencils; $\frac{27}{9} = 3$ erasers; and $\frac{45}{9} = 5$ sharpeners.

Thus, each student gets $2 + 3 + 5 = 10$ items.

20. **(a)** Let the number (s) be a^2, where a is a prime number.

The factors of a^2 are 1, a and a^2.

Thus, we have

$1 + a + a^2 = 133$

$\Rightarrow$ $a + a^2 = 132$

$\Rightarrow$ $a^2 + a - 132 = 0$

$\Rightarrow$ $a^2 + 12a - 11a - 132 = 0$

$\Rightarrow$ $a(a + 12) - 11(a + 12) = 0$

$\Rightarrow$ $(a - 11)(a + 12) = 0$

$\Rightarrow$ $a = 11$ or -12

Since a is a prime number, we have a = 11

Hence, we have only one such number.

You may cross check this. For $a^2 = 121$, we have factors 1, 11, & 121, and their sum $= 1 + 11 + 121 = 133$.

Data Sufficiency

1. What is the remainder when x is divided by 20?

   I. x is a multiple of 2.

   II. x is a multiple of 5.

   (*a*) Statement (I) ALONE is sufficient but statement (II) ALONE is not sufficient.

   (*b*) Statement (II) ALONE is sufficient but statement (I) ALONE is not sufficient.

   (*c*) BOTH statements TOGETHER are sufficient, but NEITHER statement ALONE is sufficient.

   (*d*) EACH statement ALONE is sufficient.

   (*e*) Statements (I) and (II) TOGETHER are not sufficient.

2. Is $\frac{x}{9}$ an integer?

   I. $\frac{x}{909909}$ is an integer.

   II. $\frac{x}{567}$ is an integer.

   (*a*) Statement (I) ALONE is sufficient but statement (II) ALONE is not sufficient.

   (*b*) Statement (II) ALONE is sufficient but statement (I) ALONE is not sufficient.

   (*c*) BOTH statements TOGETHER are sufficient, but NEITHER statement ALONE is sufficient.

   (*d*) EACH statement ALONE is sufficient.

   (*e*) Statements (I) and (II) TOGETHER are not sufficient.

3. How many of the three positive different integers X, Y and Z are divisible by 7?

   I. The product of X, Y and Z is divisible by 3, but only Z in divisible by 21.

   II. Each of the three positive integers is divisible by 3, but only Z is divisible by 21.

   (*a*) Statement (I) ALONE is sufficient but statement (II) ALONE is not sufficient.

   (*b*) Statement (II) ALONE is sufficient but statement (I) ALONE is not sufficient.

   (*c*) BOTH statements TOGETHER are sufficient, but NEITHER statement ALONE is sufficient.

   (*d*) EACH statement ALONE is sufficient.

   (*e*) Statements (I) and (II) TOGETHER are not sufficient.

4. Sapna runs a friendship club on the 10th floor of a multi-storeyed building. The left in this building has a different stop sequence on different days of the week. On which days of the week should Sapna keep her club open, if the club members visit the club only on those days when the lift stops at the 10th floor?

   I. The lift stops on only odd-numbered floors on Monday, Tuesday and Wednesday.

   II. The lift stops on floors divisible by 3 or 5 on Thursday and Friday.

   (*a*) Statement (I) ALONE is sufficient but statement (II) ALONE is not sufficient.

   (*b*) Statement (II) ALONE is sufficient but statement (I) ALONE is not sufficient.

   (*c*) BOTH statements TOGETHER are sufficient, but NEITHER statement ALONE is sufficient.

   (*d*) EACH statement ALONE is sufficient.

   (*e*) Statements (I) and (II) TOGETHER are not sufficient.

5. If $P > Q$, what is the value of P and Q?

I. LCM of P and Q is 42 and HCF of P and Q is 6.

II. Product of P and Q is 1764.

(a) Statement (I) ALONE is sufficient but statement (II) ALONE is not sufficient.

(b) Statement (II) ALONE is sufficient but statement (I) ALONE is not sufficient.

(c) BOTH statements TOGETHER are sufficient, but NEITHER statement ALONE is sufficient.

(d) EACH statement ALONE is sufficient.

(e) Statements (I) and (II) TOGETHER are not sufficient.

6. If both Sonu and Mohit started running simultaneously, find the distance traveled by Sonu.

I. Sonu and Mohit are running towards each other and their speeds are in the ratio 1 : 4 respectively.

II. Sonu and Mohit were initially separated by a distance of 420 m in a straight road, and finally they were together.

(a) Statement (I) ALONE is sufficient but statement (II) ALONE is not sufficient.

(b) Statement (II) ALONE is sufficient but statement (I) ALONE is not sufficient.

(c) BOTH statements TOGETHER are sufficient, but NEITHER statement ALONE is sufficient.

(d) EACH statement ALONE is sufficient.

(e) Statements (I) and (II) TOGETHER are not sufficient.

7. If a, b and c are digits, is $(a + b + c)$ a multiple of 9?

[A digit can be one of the integers 0, 1, 2, 3, 4, 5, 6, 7, 8, 9.]

I. The three digit number abc is a multiple of 9.

II. $[(a \times b) + c]$ is a multiple of 9.

(a) Statement (I) ALONE is sufficient but statement (II) ALONE is not sufficient.

(b) Statement (II) ALONE is sufficient but statement (I) ALONE is not sufficient.

(c) BOTH statements TOGETHER are sufficient, but NEITHER statement ALONE is sufficient.

(d) EACH statement ALONE is sufficient.

(e) Statements (I) and (II) TOGETHER are not sufficient.

8. If X and Y, both are 2-digit integers, is $\frac{(X - Y)}{9}$ an integer?

I. X and Y have the same two digits, but in reverse order.

II. The tens' digit of X is 2 more than the units' digit, and the tens' digit of Y is 2 less than the units' digit.

(a) Statement (I) ALONE is sufficient but statement (II) ALONE is not sufficient.

(b) Statement (II) ALONE is sufficient but statement (I) ALONE is not sufficient.

(c) BOTH statements TOGETHER are sufficient, but NEITHER statement ALONE is sufficient.

(d) EACH statement ALONE is sufficient.

(e) Statements (I) and (II) TOGETHER are not sufficient.

9. How many books does Gautam have?

I. No. of books Gautam has is less than the square root of 100.

II. The number of books Gautam has, is divisible by both 2 and 3.

(*a*) Statement (I) ALONE is sufficient but statement (II) ALONE is not sufficient.

(*b*) Statement (II) ALONE is sufficient but statement (I) ALONE is not sufficient.

(*c*) BOTH statements TOGETHER are sufficient, but NEITHER statement ALONE is sufficient.

(*d*) EACH statement ALONE is sufficient.

(*e*) Statements (I) and (II) TOGETHER are not sufficient.

10. X, Y, Z are three different positive odd integers. Is (X + Z) divisible by 8?

I. $Y - X = 4$

II. $Z - Y = 4$

(*a*) Statement (I) ALONE is sufficient but statement (II) ALONE is not sufficient.

(*b*) Statement (II) ALONE is sufficient but statement (I) ALONE is not sufficient.

(*c*) BOTH statements TOGETHER are sufficient, but NEITHER statement ALONE is sufficient.

(*d*) EACH statement ALONE is sufficient.

(*e*) Statements (I) and (II) TOGETHER are not sufficient.

11. Four points a, y, x, and b are on the number line such that $a < y < x < b$. What is the value of $\frac{(b-y)}{(y-a)}$?

I. x is halfway between a and b

II. y is halfway between a and x

(*a*) Statement (I) ALONE is sufficient but statement (II) ALONE is not sufficient.

(*b*) Statement (II) ALONE is sufficient but statement (I) ALONE is not sufficient.

(*c*) BOTH statements TOGETHER are sufficient, but NEITHER statement ALONE is sufficient.

(*d*) EACH statement ALONE is sufficient.

(*e*) Statements (I) and (II) TOGETHER are not sufficient.

12. M and N are two-digit numbers, what is the sum of M + N?

I. M and N have the same digits.

II. M and N have the same digits, but in reverse order.

(*a*) Statement (I) ALONE is sufficient but statement (II) ALONE is not sufficient.

(*b*) Statement (II) ALONE is sufficient but statement (I) ALONE is not sufficient.

(*c*) BOTH statements TOGETHER are sufficient, but NEITHER statement ALONE is sufficient.

(*d*) EACH statement ALONE is sufficient.

(*e*) Statements (I) and (II) TOGETHER are not sufficient.

13. Is $O < x < 1$?

I. $x^2 \leq x$

II. $x^3 < 0$

(*a*) Statement (I) ALONE is sufficient but statement (II) ALONE is not sufficient.

(*b*) Statement (II) ALONE is sufficient but statement (I) ALONE is not sufficient.

(*c*) BOTH statements TOGETHER are sufficient, but NEITHER statement ALONE is sufficient.

(*d*) EACH statement ALONE is sufficient.

(*e*) Statements (I) and (II) TOGETHER are not sufficient.

14. What is the value of the two-digit integer x?

I. The sum of the digits of x is 5.

II. x is divisible by 5.

(a) Statement (I) ALONE is sufficient but statement (II) ALONE is not sufficient.

(b) Statement (II) ALONE is sufficient but statement (I) ALONE is not sufficient.

(c) BOTH statements TOGETHER are sufficient, but NEITHER statement ALONE is sufficient.

(d) EACH statement ALONE is sufficient.

(e) Statements (I) and (II) TOGETHER are not sufficient.

15. Is $xy < 8$?

I. $x < 2$ and $y < 4$

II. $x^2 < 4$ and $y^2 < 16$

(a) Statement (I) ALONE is sufficient but statement (II) ALONE is not sufficient.

(b) Statement (II) ALONE is sufficient but statement (I) ALONE is not sufficient.

(c) BOTH statements TOGETHER are sufficient, but NEITHER statement ALONE is sufficient.

(d) EACH statement ALONE is sufficient.

(e) Statements (I) and (II) TOGETHER are not sufficient.

16. If a and b are positive single digit integers, is $3(10^a) + b$ divisible b 9 ?

I. $a = 4$

II. $b = 6$

(a) Statement (I) ALONE is sufficient but statement (II) ALONE is not sufficient.

(b) Statement (II) ALONE is sufficient but statement (I) ALONE is not sufficient.

(c) BOTH statements TOGETHER are sufficient, but NEITHER statement ALONE is sufficient.

(d) EACH statement ALONE is sufficient.

(e) Statements (I) and (II) TOGETHER are not sufficient.

17. If a and b are integers, is $a + b + ab$ an odd number?

I. a is an even number

II. $a + b$ is an odd number

(a) Statement (I) ALONE is sufficient but statement (II) ALONE is not sufficient.

(b) Statement (II) ALONE is sufficient but statement (I) ALONE is not sufficient.

(c) BOTH statements TOGETHER are sufficient, but NEITHER statement ALONE is sufficient.

(d) EACH statement ALONE is sufficient.

(e) Statements (I) and (II) TOGETHER are not sufficient.

18. If x, y, and z are positive integers such that $x^3 y^5 = z$, what is the value of x ?

I. $z = 1944$

II. $y = 3$

(a) Statement (I) ALONE is sufficient but statement (II) ALONE is not sufficient.

(b) Statement (II) ALONE is sufficient but statement (I) ALONE is not sufficient.

(c) BOTH statements TOGETHER are sufficient, but NEITHER statement ALONE is sufficient.

(d) EACH statement ALONE is sufficient.

(e) Statements (I) and (II) TOGETHER are not sufficient.

19. If x, y, and z are integers, is xyz divisible by 6?

I. xyz is a multiple of 3

II. x, y, and z are consecutive

(*a*) Statement (I) ALONE is sufficient but statement (II) ALONE is not sufficient.

(*b*) Statement (II) ALONE is sufficient but statement (I) ALONE is not sufficient.

(*c*) BOTH statements TOGETHER are sufficient, but NEITHER statement ALONE is sufficient.

(*d*) EACH statement ALONE is sufficient.

(*e*) Statements (I) and (II) TOGETHER are not sufficient.

20. How many of the 10 consecutive integers are multiples of 7?

I. When the greatest of the 10 integers is divided by 7, the remainder is 3

II. The median of the 10 integers is 12.5

(*a*) Statement (I) ALONE is sufficient but statement (II) ALONE is not sufficient.

(*b*) Statement (II) ALONE is sufficient but statement (I) ALONE is not sufficient.

(*c*) BOTH statements TOGETHER are sufficient, but NEITHER statement ALONE is sufficient.

(*d*) EACH statement ALONE is sufficient.

(*e*) Statements (I) and (II) TOGETHER are not sufficient.

21. When $4^a + 1$ is divided by 5, what is the remainder?

I. a is an odd number

II. a is a multiple of 3

(*a*) Statement (I) ALONE is sufficient but statement (II) ALONE is not sufficient.

(*b*) Statement (II) ALONE is sufficient but statement (I) ALONE is not sufficient.

(*c*) BOTH statements TOGETHER are sufficient, but NEITHER statement ALONE is sufficient.

(*d*) EACH statement ALONE is sufficient.

(*e*) Statements (I) and (II) TOGETHER are not sufficient.

22. If x and y are prime numbers, what is the value of x?

I. $x^3 y^2$ is an even number

II. y is an odd number

(*a*) Statement (I) ALONE is sufficient but statement (II) ALONE is not sufficient.

(*b*) Statement (II) ALONE is sufficient but statement (I) ALONE is not sufficient.

(*c*) BOTH statements TOGETHER are sufficient, but NEITHER statement ALONE is sufficient.

(*d*) EACH statement ALONE is sufficient.

(*e*) Statements (I) and (II) TOGETHER are not sufficient.

23. If a and b are integers, is a + b an odd number?

I. $b = 7a + 3$

II. $b = 2a - 7$

(*a*) Statement (I) ALONE is sufficient but statement (II) ALONE is not sufficient.

(*b*) Statement (II) ALONE is sufficient but statement (I) ALONE is not sufficient.

(*c*) BOTH statements TOGETHER are sufficient, but NEITHER statement ALONE is sufficient.

(*d*) EACH statement ALONE is sufficient.

(*e*) Statements (I) and (II) TOGETHER are not sufficient.

24. What is the value of a + b + 1 ?

I. $a^3 + b^3 + 1 = 3ab$

II. $a^2 - 2ab + b^2 > 0$

(a) Statement (I) ALONE is sufficient but statement (II) ALONE is not sufficient.

(b) Statement (II) ALONE is sufficient but statement (I) ALONE is not sufficient.

(c) BOTH statements TOGETHER are sufficient, but NEITHER statement ALONE is sufficient.

(d) EACH statement ALONE is sufficient.

(e) Statements (I) and (II) TOGETHER are not sufficient.

25. If $a > 1$, is $M > N$? (M and N are positive numbers.)

I. $M = (a - 1)(a^2 + a + 1)$

and $N = (a + 1)(a^2 - a + 1)$

II. $M = a \times N$

(a) Statement (I) ALONE is sufficient but statement (II) ALONE is not sufficient.

(b) Statement (II) ALONE is sufficient but statement (I) ALONE is not sufficient.

(c) BOTH statements TOGETHER are sufficient, but NEITHER statement ALONE is sufficient.

(d) EACH statement ALONE is sufficient.

(e) Statements (I) and (II) TOGETHER are not sufficient.

26. a, b and c are 3 digits of a number 'abc', which is a multiple of 3.

Find (a + b + c).

I. a = 3, b = 4

II. c is an odd number.

(a) Statement (I) ALONE is sufficient but statement (II) ALONE is not sufficient.

(b) Statement (II) ALONE is sufficient but statement (I) ALONE is not sufficient.

(c) BOTH statements TOGETHER are sufficient, but NEITHER statement ALONE is sufficient.

(d) EACH statement ALONE is sufficient.

(e) Statements (I) and (II) TOGETHER are not sufficient.

27. If a, b and c are consecutive integers, in increasing order, what is the value of a?

I. $b = a + c$

II. $ac = -1$

(a) Statement (I) ALONE is sufficient but statement (II) ALONE is not sufficient.

(b) Statement (II) ALONE is sufficient but statement (I) ALONE is not sufficient.

(c) BOTH statements TOGETHER are sufficient, but NEITHER statement ALONE is sufficient.

(d) EACH statement ALONE is sufficient.

(e) Statements (I) and (II) TOGETHER are not sufficient.

28. What is the average of 3 consecutive odd integers?

I. One of the integers is –1.

II. The sum of 2 of the integers is 4.

(a) Statement (I) ALONE is sufficient but statement (II) ALONE is not sufficient.

(b) Statement (II) ALONE is sufficient but statement (I) ALONE is not sufficient.

(c) BOTH statements TOGETHER are sufficient, but NEITHER statement ALONE is sufficient.

(d) EACH statement ALONE is sufficient.

(e) Statements (I) and (II) TOGETHER are not sufficient.

29. If $n = p + r$, where n, p and r are positive integers and n is odd, is $p = 2$?

I. p and r are prime numbers.

II. $r \neq 2$

(a) Statement (I) ALONE is sufficient but statement (II) ALONE is not sufficient.

(b) Statement (II) ALONE is sufficient but statement (I) ALONE is not sufficient.

(c) BOTH statements TOGETHER are sufficient, but NEITHER statement ALONE is sufficient.

(d) EACH statement ALONE is sufficient.

(e) Statements (I) and (II) TOGETHER are not sufficient.

30. If p is an integer between 10 and 100, what is the value of p?

I. One of p's digits is 3 more than the other, and sum of its digits is 9.

II. $p < 50$

(a) Statement (I) ALONE is sufficient but statement (II) ALONE is not sufficient.

(b) Statement (II) ALONE is sufficient but statement (I) ALONE is not sufficient.

(c) BOTH statements TOGETHER are sufficient, but NEITHER statement ALONE is sufficient.

(d) EACH statement ALONE is sufficient.

(e) Statements (I) and (II) TOGETHER are not sufficient.

31. A, B, C are positive but unequal integers and $A < B < C$. Is $C - A$ even?

I. $A \times B \times C$ is odd.

II. $AB + BC + CA$ is even.

(a) Statement (I) ALONE is sufficient but statement (II) ALONE is not sufficient.

(b) Statement (II) ALONE is sufficient but statement (I) ALONE is not sufficient.

(c) BOTH statements TOGETHER are sufficient, but NEITHER statement ALONE is sufficient.

(d) EACH statement ALONE is sufficient.

(e) Statements (I) and (II) TOGETHER are not sufficient.

32. A two-digit number is mistakenly written in the reversed order of the digits. The difference between original number and reversed number is divisible by 9. What is the original two-digit number?

I. The digits of the number are odd.

II. The sum of the digits of the number is divisible by 16.

(a) Statement (I) ALONE is sufficient but statement (II) ALONE is not sufficient.

(b) Statement (II) ALONE is sufficient but statement (I) ALONE is not sufficient.

(c) BOTH statements TOGETHER are sufficient, but NEITHER statement ALONE is sufficient.

(d) EACH statement ALONE is sufficient.

(e) Statements (I) and (II) TOGETHER are not sufficient.

33. Is X an even integer? [Where 'n' and 'p' are integers.]

I. $X = (n + p)^2$

II. $X = 2n + 10p$

(a) Statement (I) ALONE is sufficient but statement (II) ALONE is not sufficient.

(b) Statement (II) ALONE is sufficient but statement (I) ALONE is not sufficient.

(c) BOTH statements TOGETHER are sufficient, but NEITHER statement ALONE is sufficient.

(d) EACH statement ALONE is sufficient.

(e) Statements (I) and (II) TOGETHER are not sufficient.

34. is p divisible by 35?

I. p is divisible by 15.

II. p is divisible by 14.

(a) Statement (I) ALONE is sufficient but statement (II) ALONE is not sufficient.

(b) Statement (II) ALONE is sufficient but statement (I) ALONE is not sufficient.

(c) BOTH statements TOGETHER are sufficient, but NEITHER statement ALONE is sufficient.

(d) EACH statement ALONE is sufficient.

(e) Statements (I) and (II) TOGETHER are not sufficient.

35. If $Ax = Bx$, is $A = B$?

I. $A + x = B + x$

II. x is a non-negative integer

(a) Statement (I) ALONE is sufficient but statement (II) ALONE is not sufficient.

(b) Statement (II) ALONE is sufficient but statement (I) ALONE is not sufficient.

(c) BOTH statements TOGETHER are sufficient, but NEITHER statement ALONE is sufficient.

(d) EACH statement ALONE is sufficient.

(e) Statements (I) and (II) TOGETHER are not sufficient.

36. Is $\frac{49}{x}$ an integer?

I. x is an odd integer

II. $10 < x < 20$

(a) Statement (I) ALONE is sufficient but statement (II) ALONE is not sufficient.

(b) Statement (II) ALONE is sufficient but statement (I) ALONE is not sufficient.

(c) BOTH statements TOGETHER are sufficient, but NEITHER statement ALONE is sufficient.

(d) EACH statement ALONE is sufficient.

(e) Statements (I) and (II) TOGETHER are not sufficient.

37. Is the product of 14 integers in Set negative?

I. Set L has at most 7 negative integers.

II. Set L has at least 7 positive integers.

(a) Statement (I) ALONE is sufficient but statement (II) ALONE is not sufficient.

(b) Statement (II) ALONE is sufficient but statement (I) ALONE is not sufficient.

(c) BOTH statements TOGETHER are sufficient, but NEITHER statement ALONE is sufficient.

(d) EACH statement ALONE is sufficient.

(e) Statements (I) and (II) TOGETHER are not sufficient.

38. If $x = \frac{a}{b}$, is x an integer?

I. a is a multiple of 10.

II. b is a divisor of 10.

(a) Statement (I) ALONE is sufficient but statement (II) ALONE is not sufficient.

(b) Statement (II) ALONE is sufficient but statement (I) ALONE is not sufficient.

(c) BOTH statements TOGETHER are sufficient, but NEITHER statement ALONE is sufficient.

(d) EACH statement ALONE is sufficient.

(e) Statements (I) and (II) TOGETHER are not sufficient.

39. If z is a positive integer, what is the remainder when z is divided by 4?

I. The remainder when z is divided by 8 is 2.

II. The remainder when z is divided by 12 is 6.

(*a*) Statement (I) ALONE is sufficient but statement (II) ALONE is not sufficient.

(*b*) Statement (II) ALONE is sufficient but statement (I) ALONE is not sufficient.

(*c*) BOTH statements TOGETHER are sufficient, but NEITHER statement ALONE is sufficient.

(*d*) EACH statement ALONE is sufficient.

(*e*) Statements (I) and (II) TOGETHER are not sufficient.

40. Is the number of divisors of a^4 greater than the number of divisors of b^2 ?

I. b = 4

II. a = 3.

(*a*) Statement (I) ALONE is sufficient but statement (II) ALONE is not sufficient.

(*b*) Statement (II) ALONE is sufficient but statement (I) ALONE is not sufficient.

(*c*) BOTH statements TOGETHER are sufficient, but NEITHER statement ALONE is sufficient.

(*d*) EACH statement ALONE is sufficient.

(*e*) Statements (I) and (II) TOGETHER are not sufficient.

Answer Key

1. (*e*)	**11.** (*c*)	**21.** (*a*)	**31.** (*a*)
2. (*d*)	**12.** (*a*)	**22.** (*c*)	**32.** (*e*)
3. (*b*)	**13.** (*b*)	**23.** (*a*)	**33.** (*b*)
4. (*e*)	**14.** (*c*)	**24.** (*c*)	**34.** (*c*)
5. (*a*)	**15.** (*b*)	**25.** (*d*)	**35.** (*e*)
6. (*c*)	**16.** (*b*)	**26.** (*c*)	**36.** (*b*)
7. (*a*)	**17.** (*b*)	**27.** (*d*)	**37.** (*e*)
8. (*a*)	**18.** (*a*)	**28.** (*c*)	**38.** (*c*)
9. (*c*)	**19.** (*b*)	**29.** (*c*)	**39.** (*d*)
10. (*c*)	**20.** (*d*)	**30.** (*c*)	**40.** (*c*)

Answer Explanations

1. (e) Neither statements I and II alone nor taken together can give remainder as remainder will vary according to the numbers.

   The answer is (e).

2. (d) From statement I, since x is divisible by 909909 and 909909 is divisible by 9.

   ∴ x is also divisible by 9.

   Hence statement I alone is sufficient.

   From statement II, since x is divisible by 567 which is also divisible by 9.

   ∴ x is also divisible by 9.

   Hence statement II alone is also sufficient.

   The answer is (d).

3. (b) From statement I, Only Z is divisible by 21, we cannot conclude that X and Y cannot be divisible by 7.

   Hence, statement I alone is not sufficient.

   From statement II - Since, each of X, Y and Z is divisible by 3 and only Z is divisible by 21, so only Z is divisible by 7.

   Hence, statement II alone is sufficient.

   The answer is (b).

4. (e) Combining both statements, we cannot find the days because we don't have data on Saturday and Sunday.

   The answer is (e).

5. (a) From statement I, since HCF and LCM of P and Q are 6 and 42 respectively, so each of them must be greater than or equal to 6 and less than or equal to 42.

   Product of P and Q = LCM × HCF

   $= 42 \times 6 = 252.$

   By factorizing, the value of P and Q must be 42 and 6.

   From statement II,

   Product of P and Q = 1764.

   Multiple values of P and Q are possible.

   Hence, statement II alone is not sufficient.

   The answer is (a).

6. (c) From statement I, only ratio of their speed is given, nothing can be said about the distance.

   Hence, statement I alone is not sufficient.

   From statement II, the initial distance between them was 420 m and finally they meet to each other. But in which direction they travelled to meet other is not given.

   Hence, statement II alone is also not sufficient.

   Using both the statements together, we can say that distance travelled by Sonu

   $$= \frac{1}{5} \times 420 = 84\text{m}.$$

   The answer is (c).

7. (a) The three digit number abc is $(100 \times a) + (10 \times b) + c$. If abc is a multiple of 9, then there is an integer k such that $9k = (100 \times a) + (10 \times b) + c$. Divide this equation by 9 and you have

   $$k = \left(\frac{100}{9} \times a\right) + \left(\frac{10}{9} \times b\right) + \frac{c}{9}$$

   $$= \left(11a + \frac{a}{9}\right) + \left(b + \frac{b}{9}\right) + \frac{c}{9}$$

   $$= 11a + b + \left(\frac{a}{9} + \frac{b}{9} + \frac{c}{9}\right)$$

$= 11a + b + \frac{a+b+c}{9}$

[Or if number is multiple of 9 its sum of digits has to be multiple of 9].

Hence, statement I alone is sufficient.

Statement II is not sufficient since choosing a = 0 = b and c = 9 makes II valid and (a + b + c) is 9 but choosing a = 4 = b and c = 2 also makes II valid with (a + b + c) equal to 10.

Hence, statement II alone is not sufficient.

The answer is (a).

8. (a) From statement I, it follows that if X = 10a + b, then Y = 10b + a (where a and b are each digits from 1 to 9)

$X - Y = 10a + b - (10b + a) = 9(a - b)$

$\therefore \quad \frac{(X-Y)}{9} = a - b$, which is an integer.

Even if a = b, that is when our numbers are 55, 66, 77 or any other such number, $\frac{(X-Y)}{9} = 0$, which is still an integer.

Hence, statement I alone is sufficient.

From statement II, consider the example if X = 53 and Y = 35, then X – Y = 18, which is divisible by 9; however, if X = 53 and Y = 46, then X – Y = 7, which is not divisible by 9.

Hence, statement II alone is not sufficient.

The answer is (a).

9. (c) From statement I, Number of books < 10.

Hence, statement I alone is not sufficient.

From statement II, Number of books = 6, 12, 18 and so on.

Hence, statement II alone is also not sufficient.

Combining both statement, we get number of books = 6.

The answer is (c).

10. (c) Neither of the statements independently gives the answers.

Combining the two we have the information that Z > Y > X and the difference between Z and X is 8. So X + Z = 2X + 8. For this to be divisible by 8, X must be a multiple of 4 (or) an even number, which violates the condition given.

The answer is (c).

11. (c) **Considering statement (I) alone :**

$x = \frac{(a+b)}{2}$

No information about y

INSUFFICIENT Eliminate AD

Considering statement (II) alone :

$y = \frac{(a+x)}{2}$

No information about b

INSUFFICIENT Eliminate B

Considering both the statements together :

$x = \frac{(a+b)}{2}$ and $y = \frac{(a+x)}{2}$

$\Rightarrow \quad y = \frac{(3a+b)}{4}$

So,

$$\frac{(b-y)}{(y-a)} = \{b - \left(\frac{(3a+b)}{(4)}\right)\}\{\left(\frac{(3a+b)}{(4)}\right) - a\}$$

$$= \frac{\{4b - (3a+b)\}}{\{(3a+b) - 4a)\}} = \frac{3(b-a)}{3(b-a)} = 1$$

Sufficient The answer is (c).

12. (a) **Considering statement (I) alone :**

If M = 12 and N = 21, then M + N = 12 + 21 = 33

if M = 31 and N = 13, then M + N = 31 + 13 = 44

INSUFFICIENT Eliminate AD

Considering statement (II) alone :

If $M = 12$ and $N = 21$, then $M + N = 12 + 21 = 33$

If $M = 31$ and $N = 13$, then $M + N = 31 + 13 = 44$

INSUFFICIENT Eliminate B

Considering both the statements together :

If $M = 12$ and $N = 21$, then $M + N = 12 + 21 = 33$

If $M = 31$ and $N = 13$, then $M + N = 31 + 13 = 44$

Insufficient The answer is (e).

13. (b) **Considering statement (I) alone :**

if $x = 0$, then $x^2 \leq x$. Is $0 < x < 1$? No

If $x = 0.5$, then $x^2 \leq x$. Is $0 < x < 1$? Yes INSUFFICIENT Eliminate AD

Considering statement (II) alone :

If x3 < 0, then $x < 0$

SUFFICIENT The answer is (b).

14. (c) **Considering statement (I) alone :**

x can be 14, 41, 50 and many others.

INSUFFICIENT Eliminate AD

Considering statement (II) alone :

x can be 10, 15, 20 and many more, INSUFFICIENT Eliminate B

Considering both the statements together :

Possible values of x are 14, 23, 32, 41, and 50.

Only 50 is a multiple of 5.

SUFFICIENT The answer is (c)

15. (b) **Considering statement (I) alone :**

If $x = 1$ and $y = 3$, then $xy < 8$. Yes

If $x = -3$ and $y = -4$, then $xy > 8$. No

INSUFFICIENT Eliminate AD

Considering statement (II) alone :

If $x^2 < 4$ and $y^2 < 16$, then $-2 < x < 2$ and $-4 < y < 4$

Hence, $-8 < xy < 8$

SUFFICIENT The answer is (b).

16. (b) For a number to be divisible by 9, the sum of the digits must be divisible by 9.

Possible values for $3(10^a) = 30$ or 300 or 3000 or 30000 or any such number with 0s at the end.

Hence, the sum of digits of $3(10^a) + b$ would be $3 + b$

As b is a single digit number, $3 + b$ would be divisible by 9 if $b = 6$

Considering statement (I) alone :

if $a = 4$, then $3(10^a) + b = 30000 + b$

Hence, the sum of digits is $3 + b$

If $b = 1$, then $3(10^a) + b$ is not divisible by 9

If $b = 6$, then $3(10^a) + b$ is divisible by 9

INSUFFICIENT Eliminate AD

Considering statement (II) alone :

If $b = 6$, then $3(10^a) + b$ would be any number such as $30 + 6$ or $300 + 6$ or $3000 + 6$ or any such number. Hence, the sum of the digits will always be 9, which is divisible by 9.

SUFFICIENT The answer is (b).

17. (b) For $a + b + ab$ to be odd, either all a, b, and ab must be odd or exactly one of the three must be odd.

Considering statement (I) alone :

If a is even, then ab is also even.

Let b also be even.

Then $a + b + ab = \text{even} + \text{even} + \text{even} = \text{even}$

If a is even, then ab is also even.

Let b be odd.

Then a + b + ab = even + odd + even = odd

INSUFFICIENT Eliminate AD

Considering statement (II) alone :

If a + b is odd, then only of the two – a or b – is odd.

If a is odd and b is even, then ab is even.

Hence, a + b + ab = odd + even + even = odd

If a is even and b is odd, then ab is even.

Hence, a + b + ab = even + odd + even = odd

SUFFICIENT The answer is (b).

18. (a) If (C) look like the obvious answer, be more careful.

Considering statement (I) alone :

If z = 1944, then $x^3y^5 = 1944$

$1944 = 2^3 3^5$

Hence, $x^3y^5 = 2^3 3^5$

So, x = 2 and y = 3

SUFFICIENT Eliminate BCE

Considering statement (II) alone :

If y = 3, there still are 2 unknowns and only equation.

INSUFFICIENT The answer is (a)

19. (b) A number is divisible by 6 only if the number is divisible by both 2 and 3.

Considering statement (I) alone :

If xyz is an even multiple of 3, then it is divisible by both 2 and 3 and hence, by 6.

If xyz is an odd multiple of 3, then it is not divisible by both 2 and 3 and hence, is not divisible by 6. INSUFFICIENT Eliminate AD

Considering statement (II) alone :

If x, y, and z are consecutive integers, then xyz is a multiple of both 2 and 3, hence, 6.

SUFFICIENT The answer is (b).

20. (d) **Considering statement (I) alone :**

The largest number of the list could be 10 or 17 or 24 or any other number that leaves a remainder of 3 when the number is divided by 7.

If the greatest number in the list is 10, then the list is as follows: 1, 2, 3, 4, 5, 6, 7, 8, 9, 10. Only one of these numbers is divisible by 7. If the greatest number in the list is 17, then the list is as follows: 8, 9, 10, 11, 12, 13, 14, 15, 16, 17.

Only one of these numbers is divisible by 7.

SUFFICIENT Eliminate BCE.

Considering statement (II) alone :

If the median of 10 consecutive integers is 12.5, then the two numbers must be 12 and 13.

Hence, the list of numbers is 8, 9, 10, 11, 12, 13, 14, 15, 16, and 17.

Only one of these numbers is divisible by 7.

SUFFICIENT The answer is (d).

21. (a) **Considering statement (I) alone :**

If a is odd, then 4^a is a number that ends in 4 always. Hence, $4^a + 1$ will always end in 5. Any number that ends in 5 is always divisible by 5 i.e it leaves a remainder of 0.

SUFFICIENT Eliminate BCE

Considering statement (II) alone :

If a = 3, then $4^a + 1$ is 64 + 1 = 65. It leaves a remainder of 0 when divided by 5.

If a = 6, then $4^a + 1$ is 4096 + 1 = 4097. It leaves a remainder of 2 when divided by 5.

INSUFFICIENT The answer is (a)

22. (c) **Considering statement (I) alone :**

If x^3y^2 is an even number, then at least one of x or y is an even number. But, no information about either of the numbers.

INSUFFICIENT Eliminate AD

Considering statement (II) alone :

No information about x.

INSUFFICIENT Eliminate B

Considering both the statements together :

If x^3y^2 is an even number and y is an odd number, then x must be an even prime number.

Hence, the value of x is 2.

SUFFICIENT The answer is (c)

23. (a) **Considering statement (I) alone :**

If a is even, then b is odd. Hence, a + b is odd

If a is odd, then b is even. Hence, a + b is odd.

SUFFICIENT Eliminate BCE

Considering statement (II) alone :

If a is even, then b is odd. Hence, a + b is odd

If a is odd, then b is odd. Hence, a + b is even.

INSUFFICENT The answer is (a).

24. (c) From statement I, we can say that either $a + b + 1 = 0$ or $a = b = 1$.

Hence, statement I alone is not sufficient.

From statement II, $a^2 - 2ab + b^2 > 0 \Rightarrow (a - b)^2 > 0 \Rightarrow a \neq b$

Hence, statement II alone is also not sufficient.

Using both the statements, we get that

$a + b + 1 = 0$

The answer is (c).

25. (d) **From statement I :** $M = a^3 - 1$ and $N = a^3 + 1$

$\Rightarrow$ N > M (if a > 1, then $a^3 + 1 > a^3 - 1$).

Hence, statement I alone is sufficient.

From statement II : M = a N

$\Rightarrow \dfrac{M}{N} = a > 1$

$\Rightarrow$ M > N.

Hence, statement II alone is also sufficient.

The answer is (d).

26. (c) From statement I, a = 3, b = 4

For 'abc' to be divisible by 3, a + b + c should be divisible by 3. Thus, 'c' can be 2, 5, 8

Hence statement I alone is not sufficient.

From statement II, nothing is given about a and b.

Hence statement II alone is also not sufficient.

Using both the statements together, we get a = 3, b = 4 and c = 5.

The answer is (c).

27. (d) From statement I, a + 1 = a + a + 2

$\therefore$ a = –1

Hence statement I alone is sufficient.

From statement II, a (a + 2) = – 1

$\therefore$ a = –1

Hence statement II alone is also sufficient.

The answer is (d).

28. **(c)** From statement I, we get

a − 2	a	a + 2
(−1)	1	3
−3	(−1)	1
−5	−3	(−1)

All 3 cases we get '−1'

So we do not know what the average.

Hence statement I alone is not sufficient.

From statement II, we can say that the numbers are

−1, 1, 3 or 1, 3, 5.

Hence statement II alone is also not sufficient.

Using both the only possibility is −1, 1, 3 and hence we can find the average.

The answer is (c).

29. **(c)** Since n is odd, it follows that either p is odd and r is even or p is even and r is odd.

From statement I, with the fact that 2 is the only even prime number, it can be concluded that p = 2 or r = 2; but additional information is needed to decide which one of these two alternative holds.

Hence, statement I alone is not sufficient.

From statement II, $r \neq 2$. But this alone is not sufficient.

By combining both we can find the value of p.

The answer is (c).

30. **(c)** Let X and Y (X > Y) are the digits of p.

From statement I,

X = Y + 3 and X + Y = 9, by solving we get X = 3 and Y = 6. There are two possible values of numbers 36 and 63.

Hence, statement I alone is not sufficient.

From statement II, it is not sufficient because it only say that p is less than 50.

Hence, statement II alone is also not sufficient.

By combining both we can say that p = 36.

The answer is (c).

31. **(a)** From statement I, since $A \times B \times C$ is odd, so each of A, B and C is odd.

So, C − A = even. (odd − odd = even)

Hence, statement I alone is sufficient.

From statement II, it can be deduced that at least two among A, B, C, are even. So the value of C − A may be even or odd.

Hence statement II alone is not sufficient.

The answer is (a).

32. **(e)** From statement I, multiple values of the number are possible.

Hence statement I alone is not sufficient.

From statement II, the possible values of the number are possible and 97 and 79.

Hence statement II alone is also not sufficient.

Even using both the statements together, we do not get any unique value of the digits of the number. The number can be 79 or 97.

The answer is (e).

33. **(b)** As even integer is an integer divisible by 2.

From statement I, n + p may be even or not, depending upon value of p and n.

Hence, statement I alone is not sufficient.

From statement II, Since 2n + 10p

= 2(n + 5p).

$X^2 = 4(n + p)^2$ which is even.

Hence, statement II alone is sufficient.

The answer is (b).

34. **(c)** For p to be divisible by 35, p must be divisible by each prime factor of 35. The prime factor s of 35 are 5 and 7.

Question rephrased: Is p divisible by 3 and 7 both?

Let's see each statement one by one.

Considering Statement (I) alone:

Since p is divisible by 15, p must be divisible by each prime factor of 15, i.e., 3 and 5. However, we are not certain that p is divisible by 7, too. Insufficient.

Hence, eliminate A/D.

Considering Statement (II) alone

Since p is divisible by 14, p must be divisible by each prime factor of 14, i.e., 2 and 7. However, we are not certain that p is divisible by 5, too. Insufficient.

Hence, eliminate B.

Statement (I) and (II) together:

From Statement 1, we know that p is divisible by 5 and from Statement 2, we know that p is divisible by 7. Sufficient.

The correct answer is Option (c).

35. **(e)** Given that $Ax = bx$, it seems that it is self-sufficient to conclude that A = B. We can divide both sides by x and get A = B. However, it is not so. What if $x = 0$? In that case, A & B need not necessarily be equal.

Example : $3 \times 0 = 4 \times 0$. So, the question boils down to whether $x \neq 0$.

Let's see each statement one by one.

Considering Statement (I) alone :

Given that $A + x = B + x$, we can cancel x from both sides and get A = B. However, $x = 0$ is still a possible value. Insufficient.

Hence, eliminate A/D.

Considering Statement (II) alone :

The information means that x can be 0 or a positive integer. x = 0 is still a possible vale. Insufficient.

Hence, eliminate B.

Statements (I) and (II) together :

Even both statements together are insufficient.

The correct answer is Option (e).

36. **(b)** $\frac{49}{x}$ can be an integer only if x is one among $\pm 1, \pm 7$ or ± 49, i.e., x is a factor of 49.

Considering Statement (I) alone :

Knowing that x is an odd number is not sufficient since x can be $\pm1, \pm3, \pm7, \pm11, \pm49$, etc. This statement alone is not sufficient.

Hence, eliminate A/D.

Considering Statement (II) alone :

Given that $10 < x < 20$, we know that x lies between 10 and 20. $\frac{49}{x}$ cannot be an integer since $\frac{49}{x}$ can be an integer only if $x = \pm1$, ±7 or ± 49.

Hence this statement alone is sufficient.

Hence, eliminate C/E.

The answer is (b).

37. **(e)** For the product of 14 integers to be negative, no integer must be equal to 0, and there must be an odd number of negative integers in the list because even number of integers makes the product positive.

Let's see each statement one by one.

Considering Statement (I) alone :

Set L has at the most 7 negative integers.

This statement alone is not sufficient because we do not know whether there is an integer 0 in the set and whether there are an odd or even number of negative integers.

Statement 1 alone is not sufficient.

Hence, eliminate A/D.

Considering Statement (II) alone :

Set L has at least 7 positive integers.

Again, this statement alone is not sufficient because we do not know whether there is an integer 0 in the set and whether there are an odd or even number of negative integers.

Statement 2 alone is not sufficient.

Hence, eliminate B.

Considering Statement (I) and (II) together:

Let us take two cases to analyze.

(1) There are 7 negative, and 7 positive integers. It means the product would be negative. The answer is Yes.

(2) There are 6 negative, and 8 positive integers. It means the product would be positive. The answer is No.

Since we do not get the unique answer, statements (I) and (II) together are not sufficient.

The answer is (e).

38. (c) **Considering Statement (I) alone :**

We are not given any information about b; for example, if a = 10 and b is 3, then x is not an integer; however, if a = 10, and b is 2, then x is an integer. No unique value.

Hence Statement (I) alone is not sufficient.

Considering Statement (II) alone :

Statement (II) alone is also insufficient because of no information about a.

Take a couple of test values.

Case 1 : Say a = 35; since b is a divisor of 10, let us assume b = 2. We get $x = \frac{a}{b} = \frac{35}{2}$, not an integer.

Case 2 : Say a = 40, and b = 2, then $x = \frac{a}{b} = \frac{40}{2} = 20$, an integer

We do not get a unique answer, hence Statement 2 alone is not sufficient

Hence, eliminate B.

Statements (I) and (II) together :

In the light of both statements, Case 1 discussed in Statement (II) in not applicable; thus, x must be an integer. Sufficient.

The answer is (c).

39. (d) **Considering Statement (I) alone :**

Statement 1 implies that z = 8a + 2, where a is a positive integer. Since 8a is divisible by 4, the remainder of (8a + 2) when divided by 4 will be 2. Statement (I) alone is sufficient.

Hence, eliminate B/C/E.

Considering Statement (II) alone :

Statement (II) implies that z = 12a + 6 $\Rightarrow$ z = 12a + 4 + 2. Since 12a and 4 are divisible by 4, the remainder of [(12a + 4) + 2] will be 2. Statement (II) alone is also sufficient.

Hence, eliminate A.

The answer is (d).

40. (c) Let us first understand the counting of divisors of any number, say, p^n.

Case1: If p is a prime number, then the number of divisor of, $p^n = (n + 1)$

Case 2: If p is a composite number, say, p = st; where s and t are prime numbers. thus, $p^n = s^n t^n$, then the number of divisors of, $p^n = (n + 1)^2$

Considering Statement (I) alone:

Statement 1 tells us only about the value of b and is therefore insufficient. Let's take two cases.

- **Case 1 :** Say

  a = 2; the number of divisors of

  a^4 (=2^4) = 4 + 1 = 5.

  The number of divisors of

  b^2 (=4^2 = 2^4) = 4 + 1 = 5. The answer is No.

- **Case 2 :** Say

  a = 4; the number of divisors of a^4 (= 4^4 = 2^8) = 8 + 1 = 9.

  The number of divisors of

  b^2 (= 4^2 = 2^4) = 4 + 1= 5. The answer is Yes.

No unique answer. Insufficient.

Hence, eliminate A/D

Considering Statement (II) alone :

Statement 2 only tells us about a and is therefore insufficient. Let's take two cases.

- **Case 1 :** Say

  b = 9; the number of divisors of a^4 (=3^4) = 4 + 1 = 5.

  The number of divisors of

  b^2 (= 9^2 = 3^4) = 4 + 1 = 5. The answer is No.

- **Case 2 :** Say

  b = 1; the number of divisors of

  a^4 (=3^4) = 4 + 1 = 5.

  The number of divisors of b^4 (= 1^2 = 1) = 1.

  The answer is Yes.

  No unique answer. Insufficient.

Hence, eliminate B.

Considering Statements (I) and (II) together:

Both statements combined are sufficient as we know the values of both a and b.

In DS questions, it is not necessary to calculate the answer if you are satisfied that you will get the unique answer.

For the sake of your curiosity, let's calculate the answer.

- Number of divisors of a^4 (= 3^4) = 4 + 1 = 5
- Number of divisors of b^2 (= 4^2 = 2^4) = 4 + 1 = 5

We see that the number of divisors of a^4 is equal, not greater than the number of divisors of b^2. The answer is No - a unique answer. Sufficient.

The answer is (c).

Chapter 2

Arithmetic

Most of the Quantitative questions you will see on the GMAT involve arithmetic to some extent. The GMAT frequently increases the difficulty level of questions by combining various topics, such as absolute value, inequalities, exponents, and fractions, and often incorporating these topics into questions that involve algebra, geometry, or proportions.

This chapter will guide you through the basics and give you practice applying arithmetic concepts to GMAT questions ranging from the simple to the most advanced.

Classification of Numbers

Numbers can be classified into various categories based on their properties and characteristics. Here are some common classifications of numbers:

- **Real numbers :** These are all the rational and irrational numbers combined. Every number on the number line is a real number.
- **Rational numbers :** These are numbers that can be expressed as a ratio of two integers, i.e., numbers that can be written in the form a/b, where a and b are integers and b is not equal to zero. For example, $\frac{1}{2}, \frac{3}{4}, -\frac{2}{3}$, etc. are all rational numbers.
- **Natural numbers :** These are the counting numbers 1, 2, 3, 4, 5, ... and so on.
- **Whole numbers :** These are the natural numbers and zero (0), i.e., 0, 1, 2, 3, 4, 5, ... and so on.
- **Integers :** These are the whole numbers and their negatives, i.e., ..., -3, -2, -1, 0, 1, 2, 3, ... and so on.
- **Irrational numbers :** These are numbers that cannot be expressed as a ratio of two integers, and they have non-repeating, non-terminating decimal expansions. Examples of irrational numbers include pi (π) and the square root of 2.

Real Numbers

All numbers on the number line. All of the numbers on the GMAT are real.

The set of real numbers consists of all rational numbers and all irrational numbers.

The real numbers include all integers, fractions, and decimals. The set of real numbers can be represented by a number line called the real number line.

Real numbers can be positive, negative, or zero. They can be expressed as either a terminating decimal (such as 0.5, –1.75, or 3.0) or a non-terminating, non-repeating decimal (such as pi, the square root of 2, or 0.33333...)

Integers

All of the numbers with no fractional or decimal parts: in other words, all multiples of 1. Negative numbers and 0 are also integers.

The integers are the numbers 1, 2, 3, and so on, together with their negatives, −1, −2, −3, . . . , and 0. Thus, the set of integers is {. . . . , −3, −2, −1, 0, 1, 2, 3, . . .}.

The positive integers are greater than 0, the negative integers are less than 0, and 0 is neither positive nor negative. When integers are added, subtracted, or multiplied, the result is always an integer

Here are some general facts regarding multiplication of integers.

- The product of two positive integers is a positive integer.
- The product of two negative integers is a positive integer.
- The product of a positive integer and a negative integer is a negative integer.

Rational Numbers

All of the numbers that can be expressed as the ratio of two integers (all integers and fractions).

A fraction is a number $\frac{a}{b}$, of the form where a and b are integers and $b \neq 0$. The integer a is called the numerator of the fraction, and b is called the denominator.

For example, $\frac{-7}{5}$ is a fraction in which is the numerator is −7 and 5 is the denominator Such numbers are also called rational numbers.

Irrational Numbers

All real numbers that are not rational, both positive and negative. All the numbers that can be written as non-terminating, nonrepeating decimals are non-rational, so they are called the "irrationals". Examples would be square root of two or the number pi.

Root 2 is 1.41421356237. . . , and it can be shown that this decimal does not terminate or repeat.

Another example is 0.010110111011110111110. . . , which has groups of consecutive 1's separated by a 0, where the number of 1's in each successive group increases by one. Since these two decimals do not terminate or repeat, they are not rational numbers. Such numbers are called irrational numbers.

Few properties of Real Numbers

- $a + b = b + a$
- $a \times b = b \times a$
- $(a + b) + c = a + (b + c)$
- $(a \times b) \times c = a \times (b \times c)$
- $a\,(b + c) = ab + bc$
- $1 \times a = a$
- $\frac{a}{1} = a$
- $a \times 0 = 0$
- $a + 0 = a$
- $\frac{a}{a} = 1$ (excluding 0)
- $a + (-b) = a - b$
- $a - (-b) = a + b$
- $(a) \times (b) = ab$
- $(-a) \times (-b) = ab$
- $\frac{(a)}{(b)} = \frac{a}{b}$
- $\frac{(-a)}{(-b)} = \frac{a}{b}$
- $(-a) \times (b) = -ab$
- $(a) \times (-b) = -ab$
- $\frac{(-a)}{(b)} = \frac{-a}{b}$
- $(a) \times (-b) = -ab$

Odd/Even Numbers

The terms odd and even apply only to integers.

Odd numbers are integers that are not divisible by 2. An odd number is an integer of the form $n = 2k + 1$, where k is an integer.

Even numbers are integers that are evenly divisible by 2, i.e., divisible by 2 without any remainder. An even number is an integer of the form $n = 2k$, where k is an integer.

Odd and even numbers may be negative; 0 is an even number.

Rules for Odds and Evens

Odd ± Odd = Even	Odd × Odd = Odd
Even ± Even = Even	Even × Even = Even
Odd ± Even = Odd	Odd + Even = Even

Division of two integers can result into an even/odd integer or a fraction.

Example : If the product of two consecutive even numbers is 168, what is the sum of these two numbers?

Solution : Let's start by using algebra to represent the two consecutive even numbers:

Let x be the smaller even number.

Then x + 2 is the next even number, since it is two more than x.

Now we can use the given information to write an equation :

The product of these two numbers is 168, so we have: $x(x + 2) = 168$

To solve for x, we can first simplify the equation by expanding the product on the left-hand side:

$$x^2 + 2x = 168$$

Next, we can rearrange the terms to get a quadratic equation in standard form:

$$x^2 + 2x - 168 = 0$$

We can factor this quadratic equation as follows:

$$(x - 12)(x + 14) = 0$$

From this factorization, we see that there are two possible solutions:

$x = 12$, which gives $x + 2 = 14$

$x = -14$, which gives $x + 2 = -12$

We can eliminate the negative solution, since we are looking for two consecutive even numbers. Therefore, the two numbers are 12 and 14.

To check that these are indeed the correct numbers, we can verify that their product is 168:

$$12 \times 14 = 168$$

Finally, we can find the sum of these two numbers:

$$12 + 14 = 26$$

Therefore, the sum of the two consecutive even numbers whose product is 168 is 26.

Prime Numbers

A Prime number is a natural number with exactly two distinct natural number divisors: 1 and itself. In other words, a prime number has no positive integer divisors other than 1 and itself.

Therefore, 1 is not a prime, since it only has one divisor, namely 1. The number 2 is the first prime number and the only even prime.

A number $n > 1$ is prime if it cannot be written as a product of two factors a and b, both of which are greater than 1 then $n = ab$.

The GMAT expects test takers to recognize the prime numbers up to 50. They are 2, 3, 5, 7, 11, 13, 17, 19, 23, 29, 31, 37, 41, 43, and 47.

Note :

- Only positive numbers can be primes.
- There are infinitely many prime numbers.
- All prime numbers except 2 and 5 end in 1, 3, 7 or 9
- All prime numbers above 3 are of the form $6n - 1$ or $6n + 1$, because all other numbers are divisible by 2 or 3.
- Any nonzero natural number can be factored into primes, written as a product of primes or powers of primes.

Prime Factorization

The prime factorization of a number is the expression of the number as the product of its prime factors. No matter how you factor a number, its prime factors will always be the same.

Any nonzero natural number can be factored into primes, written as a product of primes or powers of primes.

Example : $36 = 6 \times 6 = 2 \times 3 \times 2 \times 3 = 2^2 \times 3^2$

$12 = (2)(2)(3) = (2^2)(3)$

$14 = (2)(7)$

$81 = (3)(3)(3)(3) = 3^4$

$338 = (2)(13)(13) = (2)(13^2)$

$800 = (2)(2)(2)(2)(2)(5)(5) = (2^5)(5^2)$

$1{,}155 = (3)(5)(7)(11)$

Note :

If n is a positive integer greater than 1, then there is always a prime number p with $n < p < 2n$.

An integer greater than 1 that is not a prime number is called a composite number. The first ten composite numbers are 4, 6, 8, 9, 10, 12, 14, 15, 16, and 18.

Example : Find the prime factorization of 72.

Solution : To find the prime factorization of 72, we can start by dividing it by the smallest prime number, which is 2 :

$$72 \div 2 = 36$$

Now we have 36, which is an even number and can be divided by 2 again:

$$36 \div 2 = 18$$

Continuing in this way, we can divide by 2 repeatedly until we can no longer do so:

$$18 \div 2 = 9$$

At this point, we cannot divide by 2 anymore, so we need to try the next smallest prime number, which is 3:

$$9 \div 3 = 3$$

Now we have 3, which is a prime number, so we have found the prime factorization of 72:

$$72 = 2 \times 2 \times 2 \times 3 \times 3$$

Therefore, the prime factorization of 72 is $2 \times 2 \times 2 \times 3 \times 3$, which can also be written as $2^3 \times 3^2$

Example : What is the largest prime factor of 84?

Solution : To find the prime factors of 84, we can start by dividing it by 2, since it is even:

$$84 \div 2 = 42$$

Now we have an even number, so we can divide it by 2 again:

$$42 \div 2 = 21$$

21 is odd, so it is not divisible by 2. We can now try dividing it by the next smallest prime number, which is 3:

$$21 \div 3 = 7$$

7 is a prime number, so we have found all the prime factors of 84. They are 2, 2, 3, and 7.

To find the largest prime factor, we can simply look at the list of prime factors and choose the largest one, which is 7.

Therefore, the largest prime factor of 84 is 7.

Percentages

GMAT questions will often require that you convert among percents, decimals, fractions, and ratios.

percent is just another word for "per one hundred."

The term percent means per hundred, or hundredths. Percents are ratios that are often used to represent parts of a whole, where the whole is considered as having 100 parts.

1 percent means 1 part out of 100 parts, or $\frac{1}{100}$

32 percent means 32 parts out of 100 parts, or $\frac{32}{100}$

50 percent means 50 parts out of 100 parts, or $\frac{1}{2}$

Note : that the part is the numerator of the ratio and the whole is the denominator. Percents are often written with the % symbol; fractional and decimal equivalents are often used as well but without the % symbol

Example : If the whole is 20 and the part is 13, you can find the percent as follows.

$$\frac{\text{Part}}{\text{whole}} = \frac{13}{20} = 0.65 = 65\%$$

To make a percent from a decimal or fraction, multiply by 100%. Since 100% means 100 hundredths, or 1, multiplying by 100% will not change the number.

Example : $0.17 = 0.17 \times 100\% = 17\%$

To drop a percent, divide by 100%. Once again, dividing by 100%, which is equivalent to 1, will not change the number.

Example : $32\% = 0.32$

Example : 15 is 60% of what number?

Solution : Use the decimal equivalent of 60%. Because 60% of some number z is 15, multiply z by the decimal equivalent of 60%, or 0.6.

$$0.6z = 15$$

$$z = 25$$

Example : A store is having a 20% off sale on all items. If a dress originally costs \$50, what is the sale price?

Solution : To find the sale price, we need to subtract the discount from the original price:

Discount = 20% of \$50 = 0.20 × \$50 = \$10

Sale price = Original price – Discount = \$50 – \$10 = \$40

Therefore, the sale price of the dress is \$40.

Common Fraction-to-Percent Equivalents

$\frac{1}{20} = 5\%$	$\frac{1}{11} = 9\frac{1}{11}\%$	$\frac{1}{10} = 10\%$	$\frac{1}{9} = 11\frac{1}{9}\%$
$\frac{1}{8} = 12\frac{1}{2}\%$	$\frac{1}{6} = 16\frac{2}{3}\%$	$\frac{1}{5} = 20\%$	$\frac{1}{4} = 25\%$
$\frac{1}{3} = 33\frac{1}{3}\%$	$\frac{1}{2} = 50\%$	$10\% = \frac{1}{10}$	$12\frac{1}{2}\% = \frac{1}{8}$

$16\frac{2}{3}\% = \frac{1}{6}$ $20\% = \frac{2}{10} = \frac{1}{5}$ $25\% = \frac{2}{8} = \frac{1}{4}$ $33\frac{1}{3}\% = \frac{2}{6} = \frac{1}{3}$

$30\% = \frac{3}{10}$ $37\frac{1}{2}\% = \frac{3}{8}$ $50\% = \frac{3}{6} = \frac{1}{2}$ $40\% = \frac{4}{10} = \frac{2}{5}$

$50\% = \frac{4}{8} = \frac{2}{4} = \frac{1}{2}$ $66\frac{2}{3}\% = \frac{4}{6} = \frac{2}{3}$ $50\% = \frac{5}{10} = \frac{1}{2}$ $62\frac{1}{2}\% = \frac{5}{8}$

$83\frac{1}{3}\% = \frac{5}{6}$ $60\% = \frac{6}{10} = \frac{3}{5}$ $75\% = \frac{6}{8} = \frac{3}{4}$ $70\% = \frac{7}{10}$

$87\frac{1}{2}\% = \frac{7}{8}$ $80\% = \frac{8}{10} = \frac{4}{5}$ $90\% = \frac{9}{10}$ $100\% = \frac{10}{10} = 1$

Percentage Change

When dealing with percent increase and percent decrease, always be careful to put the amount of increase or decrease over the original whole, not over the new whole

General formula for percent increase or decrease, (percent change):

$$\text{Percent Change} = \frac{(\text{Final} - \text{Original}) \times 100\%}{\text{Original}} = \frac{(\text{Change})}{(\text{Original})} \times 100\%$$

When a quantity changes from an initial positive amount to another positive amount, for example, an employee's salary that is raised, you can compute the amount of change as a percent of the initial amount. This is called percent change. If a quantity increases from 600 to 750, then the percent increase is found by dividing the amount of increase, 150, by the base, 600

Example : The price of a book increased from $20 to $25. What is the percentage change in price?

Solution : To find the percentage change, we need to first find the difference between the old and new prices, and then divide that difference by the old price. We can express this as a formula:

$$\text{Percentage change} = \frac{(\text{new price} - \text{old price})}{\text{old price}} \times 100\%$$

Plugging in the values given in the problem, we get :

$$\text{Percentage change} = \frac{(\$25 - \$20)}{\$20} \times 100\% = \frac{\$5}{\$20} \times 100\% = 0.25 \times 100\% = 25\%$$

Therefore, the percentage change in the price of the book is 25%. This means that the price increased by 25% from its original value of $20.

Interest

Interest rate questions rely on three important pieces of information: (1) the principal, or the amount initially invested; (2) the interest rate, or the rate at which the investment grows; and (3) the time period during which the investment accrues interest.

Simple Interest

Simple interest = Principal x Interest rate × Time, where "principal" is the starting amount and "rate" is the interest rate at which the money grows per a given period of time (**note :** express the rate as a decimal in the formula).

$$V = P\left(1 + \frac{rt}{100}\right)$$

Simple interest is based only on the initial deposit, which serves as the amount on which interest is computed, called the principal, for the entire time period. If the amount P is invested at a simple annual interest rate of r percent, then the value V of the investment at the end of t years is given by the formula

Example : If $8,000 is invested at 6% simple annual interest, how much interest is earned after 3 months?

Solution : Since the annual interest rate is 6%, the interest for 1 year is (0.06)($8,000) = $480. There are 12 months in a year, so the interest earned in 3 months is $\left(\frac{3}{12}\right)(\$480) = \$120$.

Example : John borrowed $5,000 from a bank for 3 years at an annual interest rate of 6%. How much interest will he pay at the end of the 3 years?

Solution : The formula for simple interest is:

Interest = Principal × Rate × Time, where Principal is the initial amount borrowed, Rate is the interest rate per year, and Time is the duration of the loan in years.

Plugging in the values given in the problem, we get :

Interest = \$5,000 x 0.06 x 3 = \$900

Therefore, John will pay \$900 in interest at the end of the 3-year period.

Compound Interest

In the case of compound interest, interest is added to the principal at regular time intervals, such as annually, quarterly, and monthly. Each time interest is added to the principal, the interest is said to be compounded. After each compounding, interest is earned on the new principal, which is the sum of the preceding principal and the interest just added. If the amount P is invested at an annual interest rate of r percent, compounded annually, then the value V of the investment at the end of t years is given by the formula :

Final Amount = Principal × [1 + (interest/c)]^{nt}

where n is the number of times compounded and t is the number of years

Example : If \$10,000 is invested at 10% annual interest, compounded semiannually, what is the balance after 1 year?

Solution : Since the interest is compounded semi-annually (every 6 months), the interest rate for each 6-month period is 5%, which is half of the 10% annual rate. Thus, the balance after the first 6 months would be 10,000 + (10,000)(0.05) = \$10,500. For the second 6-month period, the interest is calculated on the \$10,500 balance at the end of the first 6-month period. Thus, the balance after 1 year would be 10,500 + (10,500)(0.05) = \$11,025.

The balance after one year can also be expressed as $10{,}000\left(1+\frac{0.1}{2}\right)^2$ dollars.

Example : Mary invests \$10,000 in a savings account that pays 4% interest compounded annually. How much money will she have after 5 years?

Solution : The formula for compound interest is:

$$A = P\left(1+\frac{r}{n}\right)^{nt}$$

where A is the final amount, P is the initial principal, r is the annual interest rate, n is the number of times the interest is compounded per year, and t is the number of years.

Plugging in the values given in the problem, we get:

$$A = \$10{,}000\left(1 + \frac{0.04}{1}\right)^{(1 \times 5)}$$

$$A = \$10{,}000(1.04)^5$$

Ratio

A ratio is a comparison of two quantities by division.

The ratio of one quantity to another is a way to express their relative sizes, often in the form of a fraction, where the first quantity is the numerator and the second quantity is the denominator.

For example, if there are 2 apples and 3 oranges in a basket, we can say that the ratio of the number of apples to the number of oranges is $\frac{2}{3}$ or that it is 2 to 3 or that it is 2:3. Like fractions, ratios can be reduced to lowest terms.

Example : Joe is 16 years old and Mary is 12. The ratio of Joe's age to Mary's age is 16 to 12.

A ratio represents the proportional relationship between quantities or numbers. A ratio can compare either a part to another part or a part to a whole.

Example : The ratio of domestic sales to foreign sales of a certain product is 3 : 5. Then the ratio of the domestic sales to total sales is 3 : 8

One type of ratio can readily be converted to the other only if all the parts together equal the whole and there is no overlap among the parts.

Some GMAT questions deal with ratios that have three or more terms. Always represent them with colons (e.g., $x : y : z$).

Example : If the ratio of men to women to children in a room is 4:3:2, then

Ratio of men : total people = 4 : 9

Ratio of women : total people = 3 : 9 = 1 : 3

Ratio of children : total people = 2 : 9

A proportion is an equation relating two ratios; for example, $\frac{9}{12}=\frac{3}{4}$. To solve a problem involving ratios, you can often write a proportion and solve it by cross multiplication.

Important Points:

If $\frac{a}{b}=\frac{c}{d}$, then:

- **Invertendo :** $\frac{b}{a}=\frac{d}{c}$
- **Alternendo :** $\frac{a}{c}=\frac{b}{d}$
- **Componendo :** $\frac{(a+b)}{b}=\frac{(c+d)}{d}$
- **Dividendo :** $\frac{(a-b)}{b}=\frac{(c-d)}{d}$

Example : A recipe calls for a ratio of 3 cups of flour to 2 cups of sugar. If you want to make the recipe with 6 cups of flour, how much sugar do you need?

Solution : We can use proportions to solve this problem. If we know that the ratio of flour to sugar is 3:2, we can set up the following proportion:

3 cups flour / 2 cups sugar = 6 cups flour / x cups sugar

where x is the unknown amount of sugar needed.

Cross-multiplying, we get :

3 cups flour x x cups sugar = 6 cups flour x 2 cups sugar

Simplifying, we get :

$$3x = 12$$

$$x = 4$$

Therefore, if you want to make the recipe with 6 cups of flour, you need 4 cups of sugar.

Rate and Work

Most rate problems involve conversions from one rate to another. These are best handled by multiplying the various rates so that measurements cancel.

Rate is defined as the amount of work done in a given amount of time.

When a job involves two or more people, then we can add their individual rates, but not the Time.

Combined work questions present you with information about different people or machines that can perform the same job in different amounts of time.

When dealing with multiple rates, be sure to express rates in equivalent units. If a person takes A hours to complete a job, and a second person takes B hours to complete the same job. If both of them work together (at their respective rates), then time required (T) to complete the same job is given as:

$$\frac{1}{T} = \frac{1}{A} + \frac{1}{B}$$

or,

$$T = \frac{AB}{(A+B)}$$

Example : If John can complete a job in 6 hours and Jack can complete the same job in 4 hours, how long will it take them to complete the job if they work together?

Solution : We can use the formula :

Rate × Time = Work, where Rate is the work done per unit of time, Time is the duration of work, and Work is the total amount of work that needs to be done.

Let's assume that the total work is 1 unit. Then we can find the individual rates of John and Jack:

John's rate = $\frac{1}{6}$ units per hour Jack's rate = $\frac{1}{4}$ units per hour

If they work together, their combined rate is the sum of their individual rates:

Combined rate = John's rate + Jack's rate = $\frac{1}{6} + \frac{1}{4} = \frac{5}{12}$ units per hour

Now we can use the formula again to find the time it takes for them to complete the job together:

$$\text{Rate} \times \text{Time} = \text{Work}$$

$$\left(\frac{5}{12}\right) \times \text{Time} = 1$$

$$\text{Time} = \frac{12}{5} \text{ hours}$$

Therefore, it will take John and Jack 2.4 hours, or 2 hours and 24 minutes, to complete the job if they work together.

Example : A group of 6 workers can complete a construction project in 12 days. How many workers are needed to complete the same project in 8 days?

Solution : Let's start by finding the total amount of work required for the project. If a group of 6 workers can complete the project in 12 days, then their combined rate is : $\frac{1}{12}$ of the project per day per worker

Multiplying by the number of workers, we get the rate for the group: $6 \times \frac{1}{12} = \frac{1}{2}$ of the project per day

So, the amount of work required for the project is 1.

Now, we can use the formula :

Amount of work = Rate × Time × Number of workers

To find how many workers are needed to complete the project in 8 days.

Since we want to complete the same amount of work in a shorter time, we need to increase the rate. Let's call the new number of workers needed "x". The rate for this new group is:

$x \times \text{Rate per worker} = \frac{x}{2}$ of the project per day

The time is 8 days, so we can set up the equation:

$$1 = \left(\frac{x}{2}\right) \times 8$$

Simplifying, we get:

$$x = 4$$

Therefore, we need 4 workers to complete the same construction project in 8 days.

Speed Time Distance

The GMAT often uses scenarios involving multi-part journeys in order to ask questions about "average rates."

$$\text{Distance} = \text{Speed} \times \text{Time}$$

$$\text{Speed} = \frac{\text{Distance}}{\text{Time}}$$

$$\text{Time} = \frac{\text{Distance}}{\text{Speed}}$$

For any multi-part journey,

$$\text{Average Speed} = \frac{\text{Total distance traveled}}{\text{Total time taken}}$$

Example : If a car travels at an average speed of 70 kilometers per hour for 4 hours, how many kilometers does it travel?

Solution : Since distance = rate × time, simply multiply 70 km/hour × 4 hours. Thus, the car travels 280 kilometers in 4 hours.

Example : A car travels 240 km in 4 hours. What is the average speed of the car?

Solution : We can use the formula : $\text{Speed} = \frac{\text{Distance}}{\text{Time}}$ to find the average speed of the car.

Plugging in the given values, we get : $\text{Speed} = \frac{240}{4}$ km/hours = 60 km/hour

Therefore, the average speed of the car is 60 km/hour.

Relative speed

The concept of relative speed can appear in some GMAT questions, particularly in problem-solving questions related to rates and time.

It's important to remember that in relative speed problems, you need to pay attention to the direction of the movement, as well as the speed. When two objects are moving in opposite directions, you need to add their speeds to find their relative speed. When two objects are moving in the same direction, you need to subtract their speeds to find their relative speed.

Overall, understanding the concept of relative speed and knowing how to apply it to different types of problems can be a useful skill to have for the GMAT.

Example : Two trains are traveling towards each other on parallel tracks. Train A is traveling at a speed of 50 km/hour and train B is traveling at a speed of 60 km/hour. If the distance between the trains is 500 km, how long will it take for the two trains to meet?

Solution : Since the two trains are traveling towards each other, we need to find their relative speed. To do this, we add their speeds:

Relative speed = Speed of train A + Speed of train B = 50 km/hour + 60 km/hour = 110 km/hour

Now we can use the formula :

$$\text{Distance} = \text{Speed} \times \text{Time}$$

To find the time it takes for the two trains to meet. Let's call this time "t". Since the trains are moving towards each other, the combined distance they cover is the sum of their initial distances:

Distance = Distance of train A + Distance of train B = 500 km + 500 km = 1000 km

Plugging in the values, we get:

$$1000\text{ km} = 110\text{ km/hour} \times t$$

Solving for "t", we get:

t = 9.09 hours (rounded to two decimal places)

Therefore, it will take approximately 9.09 hours for the two trains to meet

Problem Solving

1. Jack has 80 pens out of which 45 percent are blue. He must purchase 82 new pens, how many of them must be blue such that he has 50 percent of all the pens after the purchase?

   (*a*) 36

   (*b*) 45

   (*c*) 50

   (*d*) 55

   (*e*) 51

2. A trader makes a profit equal to the selling price of 12 articles on selling 84 articles. What is the percentage profit?

   (*a*) 25

   (*b*) 14.28

   (*c*) 16.67

   (*d*) 20

   (*e*) 12.5

3. The salary of A is 20% more than the salary of B, which in turn is 25% more than the salary of C. By what percent is the salary of C less than the salary of A?

   (*a*) 33.33

   (*b*) 40

   (*c*) 47.5

   (*d*) 50

   (*e*) 30

4. Helix University declared its annual results and it followed a trend that first 2500 results had m% distinction holders and the rest had n% of them. If 3700 results yielded 788 distinction holders and 5000 results yielded 1100 distinction holders, find the value of 'n'.

   (*a*) 18

   (*b*) 20

   (*c*) 22

   (*d*) 24

   (*e*) 26

5. Adam incurred a loss by selling a TV set for Rs. 4,280. Bob earned a profit by the same percentage when he sold a similar TV set for Rs. 4,720. At what price (in Rs.) should the TV set be sold to make a profit of $16\frac{2}{3}\%$?

   (*a*) 5250

   (*b*) 4950

   (*c*) 5400

   (*d*) 5512

   (*e*) 5521

6. Nancy sold his ipod to Trixy at a loss of 12%. After using it for a few days, Trixy sold it off to her friend, Megan at a profit of 20%. Had Megan bought it directly from Nancy spending the same amount, what would have been the profit for Nancy?

   (*a*) 1.2%

   (*b*) 4.2%

   (*c*) 5.6%

   (*d*) 8%

   (*e*) 6.5

7. Sam went to the shop with Rs. 300 to buy flour. The price of flour has fallen down by 15%, so he could buy an extra of 3 kg. What was the approximate original price of one kilo flour?

(*a*) Rs. 15

(*b*) Rs. 17.65

(*c*) Rs. 20.25

(*d*) Rs. 13.04

(*e*) Rs. 16.15

8. A trader, who has 90 units of an article, makes a profit equals the cost price of 12 units of the article on selling 50 units of it. If the profit made on selling the rest of units of the article equals the cost price of 10 units, then what is the percentage profit of the trader?

(*a*) 55.55

(*b*) 24.44

(*c*) 23.33

(*d*) 22.22

(*e*) 25.22

9. A container contains a mixture of wine and water in the ratio 1 : 3. What percentage of the mixture should a butler replace with another mixture that contains wine and water in the ratio 3 : 1 in order to make 100% profit by selling the resultant mixture at the price of the pure wine ? (Assume the cost price of water is negligible)

(*a*) 20

(*b*) 25

(*c*) 50

(*d*) 100

(*e*) 75

10. The ratio of the speeds of top three position holders in a marathon is 2 : 4 : 5. Find the ratio of their respective ratio of time to speed.

(*a*) 10 : 5 : 4

(*b*) 100 : 25 : 16

(*c*) 10 : 25 : 16

(*d*) 20 : 12 : 9

(*e*) 25 : 16 : 20

11. A 30% milk-water solution is mixed with another n% milk-water solution to get a 45% final solution. Every five parts of this solution has two parts of 30% milk-water solution. What is the value of 'n' ?

(*a*) 48

(*b*) 52

(*c*) 55

(*d*) 67.5

(*e*) 50

12. Prakash and Ajay started a business with initial investments in the ratio of 2 : 5 respectively. After 4 months, Ajay pulled out of the business and 2 months later, Niraj joined it by investing 40% less than Ajay. At the end of the year, they made a profit of Rs. 46,500. What is the share of profit for Ajay?

(*a*) Rs. 18,000

(*b*) Rs. 16,500

(*c*) Rs. 15,000

(*d*) Rs. 13,500

(*e*) Rs. 18,500

13. A milkman mixes milk and water in the ratio 9 : 1 respectively and sells the mixture at the cost price of milk. But while selling the mixture, he uses a measurement of 950 ml instead of 1 liter. If water comes free of cost, then the percentage profit made by the milkman is

(*a*) 16.37

(*b*) 17.37

(*c*) 17.96

(*d*) 16.96

(*e*) 14.28

14. The ratio of two numbers is 5 : 6. If the ratio becomes 4 : 5 on subtracting 3 from both the numbers, what is the absolute difference between the two numbers?

(*a*) 1

(*b*) 2

(*c*) 4

(*d*) 5

(*e*) 3

15. A, B and C started a business in partnership, with an investment of Rs. 60,000 by each. B withdrew one-third of his capital after four months, whereas C withdrew two-thirds of his capital after eight months. At the end of the year, the profit share of C was Rs. 2,100. What was the total amout (in Rs.) of profit in the business at the end of the year?

(*a*) 6600

(*b*) 9900

(*c*) 7200

(*d*) 6900

(*e*) 6500

16. A shopkeeper mixed two varieties of tea costing Rs. 280 per kg and Rs. 360 per kg. If he sells the mixture at Rs. 330 per kg by making 10% profit, then what is the quantity of tea costing Rs. 280 per kg in the mixture of 68 kg?

(*a*) 17 kg

(*b*) 34 kg

(*c*) 48 kg

(*d*) 51 kg

(e) 46 kg

17. A container contains 10 liters of water-milk solution, with water and milk in the ratio 2 : 3. X liters of the solution is taken out and replaced with X + 2 liters of water. If the ratio of water to milk in the resulting solution is 3 : 2, then find the value of X.

(*a*) 4

(*b*) 1

(*c*) 3

(*d*) 2

(*e*) 5

18. Raghu invests a sum of money with the bank at a certain rate of simple interest. He receives a sum of Rs. 645 at the end of the fourth year and Rs. 690 at the end of the fifth year. Find the amount invested by him.

(*a*) Rs. 465

(*b*) Rs. 500

(*c*) Rs. 555

(*d*) Rs. 180

(*e*) Rs. 395

19. A man purchases 11 pencils for Rs. 10 and sells 10 pencils for Rs. 11. How much profit or loss does he make?

(*a*) 11.33%

(*b*) 11%

(*c*) 21%

(*d*) 9.09%

(*e*) 25%

20. A timber merchant uses a weight of 950 g for weighing 1 kg of timber. If he gives a discount of 5% on the marked price which is 20% more than his cost price, then the percentage profit made by the merchant is

(*a*) 25

(*b*) 20

(*c*) 22

(*d*) 21

(*e*) $16\frac{2}{3}$

21. A sum of Rs. 20,000 is invested in three schemes, which offer simple interest at rates (in p.a.) of 2%, 3% and 4% respectively, in the ratio 5 : 8 : 7. What is the effective annual rate of interest?

(*a*) 3%

(*b*) 3.1%

(*c*) 3.2%

(*d*) 2.9%

(*e*) 2.5%

22. A milkman mixes water and milk in the ratio 2 : 23 and sells the mixture at Rs. 48/liter. If the cost price of milk and water is Rs. 48/liter and Rs. 10/liter respectively, the percentage profit made by the milkman is

(*a*) 6.23

(*b*) 6.76

(*c*) 6.33

(*d*) 6.50

(*e*) 5.00

23. A shopkeeper mixes Basmati rice costing Rs. 28/kg and Sabarmati rice costing Rs. 32/kg in the ratio 5 : 3. What must be the marked price per kg of the mixture, so that the shopkeeper gains 10% even after allowing a discount of 2%?

(*a*) Rs. 32.50

(*b*) Rs. 33.50

(*c*) Rs. 33.11

(*d*) Rs. 32.00

(*e*) Rs. 35.00

24. Three vessels A, B and C, whose capacities are in ratio 3 : 4 : 5 are full up to the brim with alcohol-water solution of concentration 40%, 55% and 75% respectively. If the contents of the three vessels are poured into a new vessel D, then find the concentration of alcohol in D.

(*a*) 50%

(*b*) 56%

(*c*) 59.6%

(*d*) 66%

(*e*) 62.5%

25. A, B and C together started a joint venture. The amount invested by A was one-third of the amount invested by B and the amount invested by C was half of the amount invested by B. B withdrew the amount invested by him after some time. If the profit at the end of year was distributed in the ratio 2 : 4 : 3, then after how many months did B withdraw his investment?

(*a*) 6

(*b*) 3

(*c*) 8

(*d*) 2

(*e*) 5

26. What is the value of the ratio of the larger value of x and the smaller value of x if $x^2 - 3\sqrt{x} + 2 = 0$?

(a) $\frac{2}{1}$

(b) $\frac{3}{1}$

(c) $\frac{4}{1}$

(d) $\frac{9}{2}$

(e) $\frac{5}{1}$

27. A 90-ml mixture of water and spirit is prepared and left outside for a fixed time; 30 ml of the mixture is evaporated. If 10 ml of only water is left outside, 2 ml of water evaporates at the same time, and if 10 ml of only spirit is left outside, 6 ml of spirit evaporates at the same time. What is the ratio of water to spirit by volume in the mixture?

(a) 1 : 2

(b) 1 : 4

(c) 2 : 3

(d) 1 : 1

(e) 2 : 1

28. At company X, one-tenth of the male staff and one-fourth of the female staff play sports. If the number of males is half that of females, what fraction of the staff plays sports?

(a) $\frac{1}{3}$

(b) $\frac{1}{4}$

(c) $\frac{1}{5}$

(d) $\frac{1}{6}$

(e) $\frac{1}{7}$

29. If a factory worker rejects 0.07% of spanners as defective, how many spanners does he examine to reject 700 spanners?

(a) 7

(b) 49

(c) 100

(d) 10,000

(e) 1,000,000

30. If a sum of money becomes four times of itself in 15 years, what is the simple rate of interest per annum?

(a) 10%

(b) 20%

(c) 22%

(d) 25%

(e) 30%

31. On sunny days, 10 equally efficient laborers can build a 100-meter-long wall in 5 days; a company ordered them to build a 220-meter-long wall. If a laborer can perform 10% faster on a cloudy day as compared to a sunny day, how many equally efficient laborers are required to complete this job in 5 cloudy days?

(a) 10

(b) 20

(c) 22

(d) 40

(e) 50

32. If a and b are positive integers and c and d are negative integers, and each of them ends with the digit 2, what is the units digit of $(a + b + c + d)$?

(a) 0

(b) 1

(c) 2

(d) 3

(e) 4

33. If a decimal number 65.4n7 rounded to the nearest tenth is less than 65.5, how many values can n take?

(*a*) Two

(*b*) Three

(*c*) Four

(*d*) Five

(*e*) Six

34. If n is even, which of the following CANNOT be odd?

I. $4n + 9$

II. $5n - 4$

III. $5n^4 + 3$

(*a*) I only

(*b*) II only

(*c*) III only

(*d*) I and II

(*e*) All three

35. If n is an even integer, which of the following is an odd integer?

(*a*) $n^2 + 4$

(*b*) $5n^2 - 5$

(*c*) $3n^3 - 4$

(*d*) $3n - 4$

(*e*) $5n^2 + 4$

36. A 90-ml mixture of water and spirit is prepared and left outside for a fixed time; 30 ml of the mixture is evaporated. If 10 ml of only water is left outside, 2 ml of water evaporates at the same time, and if 10 ml of only spirit is left outside, 6 ml of spirit evaporates at the same time. What is the ratio of water to spirit by volume in the mixture?

(*a*) 1 : 2

(*b*) 1 : 4

(*c*) 2 : 3

(*d*) 1 : 1

(*e*) 2 : 1

37. At company X, one-tenth of the male staff and one-fourth of the female staff play sports. If the number of males is half that of females, what fraction of the staff plays sports?

(*a*) $\frac{1}{3}$

(*b*) $\frac{1}{4}$

(*c*) $\frac{1}{5}$

(*d*) $\frac{1}{6}$

(*e*) $\frac{1}{7}$

38. What is the value of $\sqrt{11}$ percent of $11\sqrt{11}$?

(*a*) 0.121

(*b*) 1.1

(*c*) 1.21

(*d*) 1.331

(*e*) 11

39. If a factory worker rejects 0.07% of spanners as defective, how many spanners does he examine to reject 700 spanners?

(*a*) 7

(*b*) 49

(*c*) 100

(*d*) 10,000

(*e*) 1,000,000

40. If a sum of money becomes four times of itself in 15 years, what is the simple rate of interest per annum?

(*a*) 10%

(*b*) 20%

(*c*) 22%

(*d*) 25%

(*e*) 30%

41. Simple interest on a certain sum for 5 years at 5% per annum is one-fourth of the compound interest on $10,000 for 3 years at 10% per annum. What is the sum put on simple interest?

(*a*) $3,331

(*b*) $4,000

(*c*) $4,444

(*d*) $5,000

(*e*) $5,555

42. How many numbers between 10 and 10,000 have the digit '6' in the units place and the digit '3' in the tens place?

(*a*) 91

(*b*) 99

(*c*) 100

(*d*) 191

(*e*) 999

43. A book seller increased the price of a book by 40%. If he sold the book at a discount of 20%, what was his actual profit percentage?

(*a*) 10%

(*b*) 12%

(*c*) 22%

(*d*) 20%

(*e*) 40%

Answer Key

1. (*b*)	12. (*c*)	23. (*c*)	34. (*b*)
2. (*c*)	13. (*d*)	24. (*c*)	35. (*b*)
3. (*a*)	14. (*e*)	25. (*c*)	36. (*e*)
4. (*d*)	15. (*d*)	26. (*c*)	37. (*c*)
5. (*a*)	16. (*d*)	27. (*e*)	38. (*c*)
6. (*c*)	17. (*d*)	28. (*c*)	39. (*e*)
7. (*b*)	18. (*a*)	29. (*e*)	40. (*b*)
8. (*b*)	19. (*c*)	30. (*b*)	41. (*a*)
9. (*c*)	20. (*b*)	31. (*b*)	42. (*c*)
10. (*b*)	21. (*b*)	32. (*a*)	43. (*b*)
11. (*c*)	22. (*b*)	33. (*d*)	

Answer Explanations

1. (b) Number of blue pens before purchase

$$= 45\% \times 80 = 36$$

Total number of pens after purchase

$$= 80 + 82 = 162$$

Number of blue pens out of the total pens

$$= 50\% \times 162 = 81$$

Number of blue pens required from the purchase

$$= 81 - 36 = 45$$

The correct answer is option (b)

2. (c) Let the selling price of one article be Rs. x.

Hence, the percentage profit

$$= \frac{12x}{84x - 12x} \times 100 = 16.67.$$

3. (a) Let salary of A, B, C be a, b, c

$$a = 1.2\,b = \frac{6}{5} \times b$$

$$b = 1.25\,c = \frac{5}{4} \times c$$

$$\text{so, } a = \frac{6}{5} \times \frac{5}{4} \times c = \frac{3}{2} \times c$$

$$\frac{a}{c} = \frac{3}{2}$$

means if $a = 3$ then $c = 2$

c is less than a by $\frac{1}{3}$ or 33.3%

Option (a) is correct.

4. (d) The two equations can be written as m% of 2500 + n% of

$$(3700 - 2500) = 788$$

$$\Rightarrow \quad 25m + 12n = 788 \quad \text{...(i)}$$

and m% of 2500 + n% of (5000 – 2500)

$$= 1100$$

$$\Rightarrow \quad 25m + 25n = 1100 \quad \text{...(ii)}$$

Subtracting (i) from (ii), we get

$$13n = 312$$

$$\Rightarrow \quad n = 24.$$

5. (a) Let the cost price of the TV set be Rs. x.

It is given that:

Loss percentage for Govind = Profit percentage for Bob

$$\Rightarrow \frac{x - 4280}{x} = \frac{4720 - x}{x}$$

$$\Rightarrow x = \frac{4280 + 4720}{2} = 4500$$

Therefore, cost price of the TV set

$$= \text{Rs. } 4{,}500$$

To earn a profit of $16\frac{2}{3}\%$, selling price of the TV set

$$= 4500 + 16\frac{2}{3}\% \text{ of } 4500 = \text{Rs. } 5{,}250.$$

6. (c) Let the CP of the ipod be Rs. 100.

Then SP of the ipod for Nancy = CP for Trixy = Rs. 88

Again, CP of the ipod for Megan = SP for Trixy = 1.2×88 = Rs. 105.6

In case, Megan had bought the ipod directly from Nancy, the profit for Nancy

$$= \frac{105.6 - 100}{100} \times 100 = 5.6\%$$

7. (b) Since the price of flour has decreased by 15%, so Sam saved 15% of Rs. 300 = Rs. 45.

With this savings, he bought 3 kilos of flour.

$\therefore$ New price of 1 kilo of flour = Rs. 15

Therefore, original price of 1kg of flour

$$= \frac{15}{0.85} \approx \text{Rs. } 17.65.$$

8. **(b)** Let the cost price of 90 units of article be Rs. 90.

Selling price of 90 units of article

= Selling price of 50 units of article + Selling price of 40 units of article

= 62 + 50 = Rs. 112.

The profit percentage

$$= \frac{112-90}{90} \times 100 = 24.44.$$

9. **(c)** In order to make a profit of 100%, quantity of wine in the resultant mixture should be twice of the initial quantity, which means ratio of wine and water in the resultant mixture will be 1 : 1.

Let the required percent be k.

$$\therefore \quad \frac{1 \times \left(\frac{100-k}{100}\right) + 3 \times \left(\frac{k}{100}\right)}{3 \times \left(\frac{100-k}{100}\right) + 1 \times \left(\frac{k}{100}\right)} = \frac{1}{1}$$

$\Rightarrow$ k = 50.

10. **(b)** Let the distance be LCM (2,4, 5) i.e. 20 units. Therefore, the respective ratio of the time taken by them = 10 : 5 : 4.

Hence, the ratio $= \frac{10}{2} : \frac{5}{4} : \frac{4}{5} = 100 : 25 : 16.$

11. **(c)** **Using allegation :**

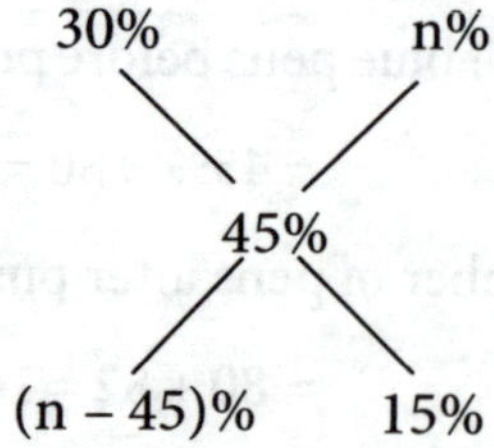

i.e 2 : 3

Therefore, $\frac{n-45}{15} = \frac{2}{3}$ or n = 55.

12. **(c)** Let the initial investments of Prakash and Ajay be Rs. 2k and Rs. 5k respectively.

Total investment of Prakash = 12 × 2k

= Rs. 24k

Ajay = 4 × 5k = Rs. 20k

Niraj = 6 × 0.6 × 5k = Rs. 18k

$\therefore$ Ratio of profit sharing for Prakash, Ajay and Niraj

= 24 : 20 : 18 = 12 : 10 : 9

Therefore, Ajay's share of profit

$$= \frac{10}{12+10+9} \times 46500$$

= Rs. 15,000.

13. **(d)** Let the total volume of the mixture be 10x litres. The profit percentage

$$= \frac{\frac{1000}{950} \times 10x - 9x}{9x} \times 100 \approx 16.96$$

14. **(e)** Let the two numbers be 5x and 6x.

$$\therefore \quad \frac{5x-3}{6x-3} = \frac{4}{5}$$

$\Rightarrow$ x = 3.

Hence, the absolute difference = 18 – 15 = 3

15. (d) Let the total profit be Rs. x.

The ratio of investments of A, B and C

= (60000 × 12) : (60000 × + 40000 × 8) : (60000 × 8 + 20000 × 4)

= 9 : 7 : 7.

$$\therefore \quad \frac{7}{9+7+7} \times x = 2100$$

$$\Rightarrow \quad x = 6900.$$

16. (d) Let the quantity of tea costing Rs. 280 per kg in the mixture be x kg.

$$\text{Cost price of the mixture} = \frac{330}{1.1} = \text{Rs. } 300$$

$$\frac{x \times 280 + (68 - x) \times 360}{68} = 300$$

$$\Rightarrow \quad x = 51.$$

17. (d) The volume of the new solution

= 10 + 2 = 12 liters

The quantity of water in the new solution

$$= \frac{2}{5} \times 10 - \frac{2}{5} X + (x+2) = 12 \times \frac{3}{5}$$

$$\Rightarrow \quad X = 2$$

18. (a) Simple interest on Rs. 645 for 1 year

= 690 – 645 = Rs. 45

Simple interest for 4 years

= 45 × 4 = Rs. 180

∴ Principal = 645 – 180 = Rs. 465.

19. (c) Suppose the person bought 11 × 10 pencils.

$$\text{CP of 110 pencils} = \frac{10}{11} \times 110 = \text{Rs. } 100$$

$$\text{SP of 110 pencils} = \frac{10}{11} \times 110 = \text{Rs. } 121$$

$$\therefore \text{ percentage profit} = \frac{121 - 100}{100} \times 100 = 21\%.$$

20. (b) Let the CP of timber be Rs. 1000/kg.

Actual CP for the timber merchant = Rs. 950 (since he uses a false weight of 950 gm)

Marked price = 1.2 × 1000 = Rs. 1200

$$\text{SP} = 1200\left(1 - \frac{5}{100}\right) = \text{Rs. } 1140$$

Profit = Rs. 1140 – 950 = Rs. 190

$$\text{Profit percentage} = \frac{190}{950} \times 100 = 20.$$

21. (b) The amounts invested at the rates of 2%, 3% and 4% come out to be Rs. 5000, Rs. 8000 and Rs. 7000 respectively. Total interest earned

$$= \left(\frac{5000 \times 2 \times 1}{100} + \frac{8000 \times 3 \times 1}{100} + \frac{7000 \times 4 \times 1}{100}\right)$$

= Rs. 620

Hence, the effective rate of interest

$$= \frac{620 \times 100}{20000} = 3.1\% \text{ p.a.}$$

22. (b) Since the ratio of water and milk in the mixture is 2 : 23, their respective percentages will be 8% and 92%. Cost price of 1 liter adulterated milk

= (0.92 × 48 + 0.08 × 10) = Rs. 44.96

Selling price = Rs. 48

Hence, profit percentage

$$= \frac{3.04}{44.96} \times 100 = 6.76\%$$

23. **(c)** Average price of mixture

$$= \frac{28 \times 5 + 32 \times 3}{8} = \text{Rs.}29.5/\text{kg}.$$

The selling price, in order to gain 10% must be $29.5 \times 1.1 = \text{Rs. } 32.45$

Let the marked price be Rs x/kg.

$\Rightarrow \quad 0.98 \times x = 32.45$

$\Rightarrow \quad x = 33.11.$

24. **(c)** Let the capacities of the vessels be 3, 4 and 5 litres respectively.

$\Rightarrow$ The concentration of alcohol in vessel D

$$= \frac{3 \times 40 + 4 \times 55 + 5 \times 75}{3 + 4 + 5} = \frac{715}{12} = 59.6\%$$

25. **(c)** The amounts invested by A, B and C are in the ratio 2 : 6 : 3.

Let the number of months after which B withdrew his amount be x.

$\therefore \quad 2 \times 12 : 6 \times x : 3 \times 12 = 2 : 4 : 3$

$\Rightarrow \quad x = 8.$

26. **(c)** This is indeed a quadratic equation, though it does not look like one as we do not see a squared term; however, the equation can be solved by applying the concept of quadratic equation.

Say $\sqrt{x} = y$, then the equation becomes $y^2 - 3y + 2 = 0$. It is a quadratic equation. Let's solve this.

$y^2 - 3y + 2 = 0$

$y^2 - 2y - y + 2 = 0$

$y(y - 2) - 1(y - 2) = 0$

$(y - 2)(y - 1) = 0$

So, $y = 2$ or 1.

$\sqrt{x} = 2$ or 1

$x = 4$ or 1

Thus, the ratio of the larger value of x and the smaller value of x $= \frac{4}{1}$.

27. **(e)** Let w be the volume of water and s be the volume of spirit in the mixture; thus, $w + s = 90$.

2 ml of water evaporates out of 10ml at the given time;

$\Rightarrow$ evaporated water percentage

$= 20\% = 0.2.$

Hence, from the mixture of 90 ml, water evaporated $= 0.2w$ ml.

Also, 6 ml of spirit evaporates out of 10 ml at the given time;

$\Rightarrow$ evaporated spirit percentage $= 60\% = 0.6.$

So, the volume of spirit evaporated $= 0.6s$ ml.

Now we have,

$0.2w + 0.6s = 30$; given that the evaporated mixture volume is 30 ml.

We also know that $w + s = 90$.

Solving the above two simultaneous equations, we get $s = 30$ and $w = 60$

$\Rightarrow \quad w : s = 2 : 1$

The correct answer is Option (e).

28. **(c)** Since the number of male staff is half that of female staff, it means that 2M = F.

Let us assume that the total number of staff is 300. Therefore, the number of male staff = 100 and the number of female staff = 200. We chose 300 because it is a convenient figure; you may choose any number.

Number of male staff that play sports

$$= \frac{100}{10} = 10$$

Number of female staff that play sports

$$= \frac{200}{4} = 50$$

Total staff that play sports = 10 + 50 = 60

The fraction of the staff that play sports

$$= \frac{60}{300} = \frac{1}{5}$$

29. **(e)** Say, the worker examines x number of spanners.

So, 0.07% of $x = 700$

$$\Rightarrow \quad x = \frac{700}{0.07\%} = \frac{700}{\frac{0.07}{100}}$$

$$= \frac{700 \times 100}{0.07} = 1{,}000{,}000 \text{ spanners.}$$

30. **(b)** Let the sum P be \$100, so it becomes A = Amount = 4 × \$100 = \$400 in $t = 15$ years

Thus, SI = 400 – 100 = \$300

We know that $SI = \frac{p \times r \times t}{100}$

$$\Rightarrow \quad r = \frac{SI \times 100}{P \times t}$$

$$r = \frac{300 \times 100}{100 \times 15} = 20\%$$

31. **(b)** On sunny days, 10 laborers can build a 100-meter-long wall in 5 days.

Therefore, one laborer can build $\frac{100}{10}$

= 10-meter-long wall in 5 days.

If a laborer can perform 10% faster on a cloudy day, then he can build 10 × 1.1 = 11 meter long wall in 5 days.

Number of laborers required to build a 220-meter-long wall in 5 cloudy days

$$= \frac{220}{11} = 20$$

32. **(a)** The integers a, b, c, and d can have any number of digits; however, for this question, it is not important to know how many digits each integer has as while adding the integers, we first add units digits, so the addition of unit digits of a, b, c, and d would be $2 + 2 + (-2) + (-2) = 4 - 4 = 0$.

Alternatively, you can assume some values for a, b, c, and d. Say $a = 2{,}452$, $b = 32$, $c = -82$, and $d = -2$. It is clear that the units digit of the sum of a, b, c, and d would be 0.

The correct answer is Option (a).

33. **(d)** Note that n must be less than '5' for if n were '5' or greater than 5, the tenth digit '4' of the number 65.4n7 would be rounded off to '5' ('4' is increased by 1) and the number would be '25.5'.

So, to keep the number less than '65.5', the set of values of n = {0, 1, 2, 3, 4}. So n can have five values.

Note that we must not start rounding off from the right-most digit, i.e., '7'. Had you done this way, since '7' is greater than '5', you would round up n to $(n + 1)$. Thus, the set of values of n + 1 = {0, 1, 2, 3, 4} and the set of values of n = {0, 1, 2, 3}. So n would have four values, which is incorrect.

The correct answer is Option (d).

34. **(b)** The question is if **n** is even, which of the following CANNOT be odd?

Results of the product of Even and Odd numbers

- Even × Even = Even
- Even × Odd = Even
- Odd × Odd = ODD

It must be noted that if there is only one even number, the product is even; whereas, if the product of two numbers is Odd, then both the numbers must be Odd.

Let us look at the options one by one.

1. $4n + 9$: In this option, 4 and n are even, whereas 9 is odd.

   So, $4n + 9$ = even × even + odd = even + odd = odd.

   Thus, $(4n + 9)$ is an odd number.

II. $5n - 4$: In this option, 4 and n are even, whereas 5 is odd.

   So, $5n - 4$ = odd × even – even = even – even = even.

   Thus, $(5n - 4)$ is an even number. **correct answer.**

III. $5n^4 + 3$: In this option, n is even, whereas 5 and 3 are odd. Any positive exponent of an even number is also an even.

   So, $5n^4 + 3$ = odd × even + odd

   = even + odd = odd.

   Thus, $(5n^4 + 3)$ is an odd number.

The correct answer is Option (b).

35. **(b)** The efficient approach to solve this question is by assuming a convenient value for the even integer n. Say $n = 2$. You may also choose 0; note 0 is an even number.

Let's take each option one by one by plugging-in the value of $n = 2$. You may even choose 0.

(*a*) $n^2 + 4 \Rightarrow 2^2 + 4 = 4 + 4 = 8$, an even number

(*b*) $5n^2 - 5 \Rightarrow 5 \times 2^2 - 5 = 20 - 5 = 15$, an odd number : correct answer

(*c*) $3n^3 - 4 \Rightarrow 3 \times 2^3 - 4 = 24 - 4 = 20$, an even number

(*d*) $3n - 4 \Rightarrow 3 \times 2 - 4 = 6 - 4 = 2$, an even number

(*e*) $5n^2 + 4 \Rightarrow 5 \times 2^2 + 5 = 20 + 4 = 24$. an even number

The correct answer is Option (b).

36. **(e)** Let w be the volume of water and s be the volume of spirit in the mixture; thus, $w + s = 90$.

2 ml of water evaporates out of 10ml at the given time;

⇒ evaporated water percentage

$$= 20\% = 0.2.$$

Hence, from the mixture of 90 ml, water evaporated = $0.2w$ ml.

Also, 6 ml of spirit evaporates out of 10 ml at the given time;

⇒ evaporated spirit percentage

$$= 60\% = 0.6.$$

So, the volume of spirit evaporated

$$= 0.6s \text{ ml}.$$

Now we have,

$0.2w + 0.6s = 30$; given that the evaporated mixture volume is 30 ml.

We also know that $w + s = 90$.

Solving the above two simultaneous equations, we get $s = 30$ and $w = 60$

$\Rightarrow \quad w : s = 2 : 1.$

37. **(c)** Since the number of male staff is half that of female staff, it means that 2M = F.

Let us assume that the total number of staff is 300. Therefore, the number of male staff = 100 and the number of female staff = 200. We choose 300 because it is a convenient figure; you may choose any number.

Number of male staff that play sports

$$= \frac{100}{10} = 10$$

Number of female staff that play sports

$$= \frac{200}{4} = 50$$

Total staff that play sports = 10 + 50 = 60

The fraction of the staff that play sports

$$= \frac{60}{300} = \frac{1}{5}$$

38. **(c)** We have to get the value of $\sqrt{11}$ percent of $11\sqrt{11}$.

$\sqrt{11}$ percent of $11\sqrt{11} = \sqrt{11}$ % of $11\sqrt{11}$

$$\frac{\sqrt{11} \times 11\sqrt{11}}{100} = \frac{11^2}{100} = 1.21$$

39. **(e)** Say, the worker examines x number of spanners.

So, 0.07% of $x = 700$

$$\Rightarrow \quad x = \frac{700}{0.07\%} = \frac{700}{\frac{0.07}{100}}$$

$$= \frac{700 \times 100}{0.07} = 1{,}000{,}000 \text{ spanners.}$$

40. **(b)** Let the sum P be \$100, so it becomes A

= Amount = 4 × \$400 in $t = 15$ years

Thus, SI = 400 – 100 = \$300

We know that $SI = \frac{p \times r \times t}{100}$

$$\Rightarrow \quad r = \frac{SI \times 100}{P \times t}$$

$$r = \frac{300 \times 100}{100 \times 15}$$

$$r = 20\%.$$

41. **(a)** Let's first compute compound interest.

We know that $CI = P\left[\left(1 + \frac{r}{100}\right)^n - 1\right]$;

where CI = Compound interest;
P = Principal (Sum); r = Rate of interest; n = Number of compounding (time)

$$CI = 10{,}000\left[\left(1 + \frac{10}{100}\right)^3 - 1\right]$$

$$= 10{,}000\left[\left(\frac{11}{10}\right)^3 - 1\right]$$

$$= 10{,}000\left[\frac{1{,}331}{1{,}000} - 1\right]$$

$$= 10{,}000\,[1.331 - 1]$$

$$CI = 10{,}000 \times 0.331 = \$3{,}331$$

So, Simple interest = $\frac{1}{4}$ of Compound interest

We know that $SI = \frac{p \times r \times t}{100}$; where SI = Simple interest; P = Principal (Sum); r = Rate of interest; n = time (in years)

$$SI = \frac{P \times 5 \times 5}{100} = \frac{1}{4} \times 3{,}331$$

P = \$3,331, upon simplification.

42. **(c)** There is only 'one' two-digit number having the digit '6' in the units place and the digit '3' in the tens place, i.e., 36.

Of the three-digit numbers with the units and tens digits 6 and 3, respectively, the hundreds digit may be chosen from '1' to '9' in 9 ways. Thus, there are 'nine' such three-digit numbers.

Of the four-digit numbers with the units and tens digits 6 and 3, respectively, the thousands digit may be chosen from '1' to '9' in 9 ways and the hundreds digit may be chosen from '0' to '9' in 10 ways. Total number of ways of choosing the two digits. Thus, there are 90 such four-digit numbers.

There is no five-digit number having the digit '6' in the unit's place and the digit '3' in the tens place since the last number is 10,000, which is the least possible five-digit number.

Thus, we have such numbers.

43. **(b)** Let x be the initial price of a book.

After the 40% increase, the new price would be $\left(x+\frac{40}{100}\times x\right)=1.4x$.

After discount, the price would be

$1.4x - 1.4x \times \left(\frac{20}{100}\right)$

or $1.4x \times (1 - 0.2) = 1.12x$.

Therefore, the actual profit percentage

$$=\left[\frac{(1.12x-x)}{x}\right]\times 100\% = 12\%.$$

Data Sufficiency

1. If m and n are both greater than 0, what is the value of m?

   I. m is 200% of n.

   II. $m \times n = z^2$, where z is a positive integer.

   (a) Statement (I) ALONE is sufficient but statement (II) ALONE is not sufficient.

   (b) Statement (II) ALONE is sufficient but statement (I) ALONE is not sufficient.

   (c) BOTH statements TOGETHER are sufficient, but NEITHER statement ALONE is sufficient.

   (d) EACH statement ALONE is sufficient.

   (e) Statements (I) and (II) TOGETHER are not sufficient.

2. If x and y are positive and $\frac{x}{y}$ is greater than 110 percent, is x greater than 35?

   I. $y > 35$

   II. $x = 10 + y$

   (a) Statement (I) ALONE is sufficient but statement (II) ALONE is not sufficient.

   (b) Statement (II) ALONE is sufficient but statement (I) ALONE is not sufficient.

   (c) BOTH statements TOGETHER are sufficient, but NEITHER statement ALONE is sufficient.

   (d) EACH statement ALONE is sufficient.

   (e) Statements (I) and (II) TOGETHER are not sufficient.

3. Which one is greater in a stationary shop: the total number of pens and pencils, or the number of sharpeners?

   I. The ratio of the number of sharpeners to the number of pens to the number of pencils in the shop is 33 : 17 : 21.

   II. The total number of sharpeners, pens, and pencils in the shop is 142.

   (a) Statement (I) ALONE is sufficient but statement (II) ALONE is not sufficient.

   (b) Statement (II) ALONE is sufficient but statement (I) ALONE is not sufficient.

   (c) BOTH statements TOGETHER are sufficient, but NEITHER statement ALONE is sufficient.

   (d) EACH statement ALONE is sufficient.

   (e) Statements (I) and (II) TOGETHER are not sufficient.

4. What is the number of type 2 widgets produced if the total number of widgets produced is 20,000?

   I. If the number of type 1 widgets produced is higher by 10% and that of type 2 is lower by 6%, the total production remains the same.

   II. The ratio in which type 1 and type 2 are produced is 2 : 3.

   (a) Statement (I) ALONE is sufficient but statement (II) ALONE is not sufficient.

   (b) Statement (II) ALONE is sufficient but statement (I) ALONE is not sufficient.

   (c) BOTH statements TOGETHER are sufficient, but NEITHER statement ALONE is sufficient.

   (d) EACH statement ALONE is sufficient.

   (e) Statements (I) and (II) TOGETHER are not sufficient.

5. What is the profit percentage made by the shopkeeper?

   I. Selling price of 100 eggs is Rs. 120.

   II. Cost price is two-thirds of the selling price.

   (a) Statement (I) ALONE is sufficient but statement (II) ALONE is not sufficient.

   (b) Statement (II) ALONE is sufficient but statement (I) ALONE is not sufficient.

   (c) BOTH statements TOGETHER are sufficient, but NEITHER statement ALONE is sufficient.

(*d*) EACH statement ALONE is sufficient.

(*e*) Statements (I) and (II) TOGETHER are not sufficient.

6. Steve's running speed is what percent of his walking speed?

I. Steve takes 40 minutes to walk from his home to the office and return home running.

III. Steve takes 30 minutes to run from his home to the office and return home running.

(*a*) Statement (I) ALONE is sufficient but statement (II) ALONE is not sufficient.

(*b*) Statement (II) ALONE is sufficient but statement (I) ALONE is not sufficient.

(*c*) BOTH statements TOGETHER are sufficient, but NEITHER statement ALONE is sufficient.

(*d*) EACH statement ALONE is sufficient.

(*e*) Statements (I) and (II) TOGETHER are not sufficient.

7. Amy travels from Stop X to Stop Y, and Betty travels from Stop Y to Stop X. At what time do they meet on the way?

I. Amy starts at 10:00 am, and Betty starts at 1 : 00 pm.

II. Amy takes 10 hours to reach Stop Y, and Betty takes 5 hours to reach Stop X.

(*a*) Statement (I) ALONE is sufficient but statement (II) ALONE is not sufficient.

(*b*) Statement (II) ALONE is sufficient but statement (I) ALONE is not sufficient.

(*c*) BOTH statements TOGETHER are sufficient, but NEITHER statement ALONE is sufficient.

(*d*) EACH statement ALONE is sufficient.

(*e*) Statements (I) and (II) TOGETHER are not sufficient.

8. A car leaves City A at 1:00 p.m. and travels towards City B at a speed of 100 kilometers per hour. Another car leaves City A after some time. At what time will the second car overtake the first?

I. The distance between the cities is 400 kilometers, and the second car leaves at 2:00 p.m.

II. The distance between the cities is 400 kilometers, and speed of the second car is 1.5 times that of the first.

(*a*) Statement (I) ALONE is sufficient but statement (II) ALONE is not sufficient.

(*b*) Statement (II) ALONE is sufficient but statement (I) ALONE is not sufficient.

(*c*) BOTH statements TOGETHER are sufficient, but NEITHER statement ALONE is sufficient.

(*d*) EACH statement ALONE is sufficient.

(*e*) Statements (I) and (II) TOGETHER are not sufficient.

9. A and B start from their homes at the same time, move at their respective uniform speeds towards each other, and meet at Point X. If A were late by t minutes, they would have met at Point Y. What is the value of t?

I. A and B move at speeds of 6 kilometers per hour and 12 kilometers per hour, respectively.

II. The distance between the points X and Y is 1.2 kilometers.

(*a*) Statement (I) ALONE is sufficient but statement (II) ALONE is not sufficient.

(*b*) Statement (II) ALONE is sufficient but statement (I) ALONE is not sufficient.

(*c*) BOTH statements TOGETHER are sufficient, but NEITHER statement ALONE is sufficient.

(*d*) EACH statement ALONE is sufficient.

(*e*) Statements (I) and (II) TOGETHER are not sufficient.

10. How long would it take 7 men and 3 women to paint a wall with dimensions of 30 feet by 80 feet, if all men and all women work at their respective uniform rates?

I. Fifteen men can paint a wall with dimensions of 15 feet by 90 feet in 9 hours.

II A 20-square-foot wall can be painted by two men in 1 hour or by one women in 2 hours.

(*a*) Statement (I) ALONE is sufficient but statement (II) ALONE is not sufficient.

(*b*) Statement (II) ALONE is sufficient but statement (I) ALONE is not sufficient.

(*c*) BOTH statements TOGETHER are sufficient, but NEITHER statement ALONE is sufficient.

(*d*) EACH statement ALONE is sufficient.

(*e*) Statements (I) and (II) TOGETHER are not sufficient.

11. If pq and r are even, is $(p + r)$ even?

I. q is even.

II. p and q are integers.

(*a*) Statement (I) ALONE is sufficient but statement (II) ALONE is not sufficient.

(*b*) Statement (II) ALONE is sufficient but statement (I) ALONE is not sufficient.

(*c*) BOTH statements TOGETHER are sufficient, but NEITHER statement ALONE is sufficient.

(*d*) EACH statement ALONE is sufficient.

(*e*) Statements (I) and (II) TOGETHER are not sufficient.

12. Steve's running speed is what percent of his walking speed?

I. Steve takes 40 minutes to walk from his home to the office and return home running.

II. Steve takes 30 minutes to run from his home to the office and return home running.

(*a*) Statement (I) ALONE is sufficient but statement (II) ALONE is not sufficient.

(*b*) Statement (II) ALONE is sufficient but statement (I) ALONE is not sufficient.

(*c*) BOTH statements TOGETHER are sufficient, but NEITHER statement ALONE is sufficient.

(*d*) EACH statement ALONE is sufficient.

(*e*) Statements (I) and (II) TOGETHER are not sufficient.

13. Amy travels from Stop X to Stop Y, and Betty travels from Stop Y to Stop X. At what time do they meet on the way?

I. Amy starts at 10:00 am, and Betty starts at 1:00 pm.

II. Amy takes 10 hours to reach Stop Y, and Betty takes 5 hours to reach Stop X.

(*a*) Statement (I) ALONE is sufficient but statement (II) ALONE is not sufficient.

(*b*) Statement (II) ALONE is sufficient but statement (I) ALONE is not sufficient.

(*c*) BOTH statements TOGETHER are sufficient, but NEITHER statement ALONE is sufficient.

(*d*) EACH statement ALONE is sufficient.

(*e*) Statements (I) and (II) TOGETHER are not sufficient.

14. The bill for a Dutch dinner was shared equally among friends. What was the bill amount for the Dutch dinner?

I. Each of them paid $21.

II. If there were one more friend at the dinner, each would have paid $20.

(*a*) Statement (I) ALONE is sufficient but statement (II) ALONE is not sufficient.

(*b*) Statement (II) ALONE is sufficient but statement (I) ALONE is not sufficient.

(*c*) BOTH statements TOGETHER are sufficient, but NEITHER statement ALONE is sufficient.

(*d*) EACH statement ALONE is sufficient.

(*e*) Statements (I) and (II) TOGETHER are not sufficient.

15. A car leaves City A at 1:00 p.m. and travels towards City B at a speed of 100 kilometers per hour. Another car leaves City A after some time. At what time will the second car overtake the first?

I. The distance between the cities is 400 kilometers, and the second car leaves at 2:00 p.m.

II. The distance between the cities is 400 kilometers, and speed of the second car is 1.5 times that of the first.

(*a*) Statement (I) ALONE is sufficient but statement (II) ALONE is not sufficient.

(*b*) Statement (II) ALONE is sufficient but statement (I) ALONE is not sufficient.

(*c*) BOTH statements TOGETHER are sufficient, but NEITHER statement ALONE is sufficient.

(*d*) EACH statement ALONE is sufficient.

(*e*) Statements (I) and (II) TOGETHER are not sufficient.

16. If *s* is a positive integer, is *s* a prime number?

I. $\frac{21}{s}$ is an integer.

II. $\frac{47}{s}$ is an integer.

(*a*) Statement (I) ALONE is sufficient but statement (II) ALONE is not sufficient.

(*b*) Statement (II) ALONE is sufficient but statement (I) ALONE is not sufficient.

(*c*) BOTH statements TOGETHER are sufficient, but NEITHER statement ALONE is sufficient.

(*d*) EACH statement ALONE is sufficient.

(*e*) Statements (I) and (II) TOGETHER are not sufficient.

17. What is the present age of Jasmine?

I. The ratio of the present ages of Jasmine and Katy is 2:3.

II. The sum of the present ages of Jasmine and Katy is 40 years.

(*a*) Statement (I) ALONE is sufficient but statement (II) ALONE is not sufficient.

(*b*) Statement (II) ALONE is sufficient but statement (I) ALONE is not sufficient.

(*c*) BOTH statements TOGETHER are sufficient, but NEITHER statement ALONE is sufficient.

(*d*) EACH statement ALONE is sufficient.

(*e*) Statements (I) and (II) TOGETHER are not sufficient.

18. A and B start from their homes at the same time, move at their respective uniform speeds towards each other, and meet at Point X. If A were late by *t* minutes, they would have met at Point Y. What is the value of *t*?

I. A and B move at speeds of 6 kilometers per hour and 12 kilometers per hour, respectively.

II. The distance between the points X and Y is 1.2 kilometers.

(*a*) Statement (I) ALONE is sufficient but statement (II) ALONE is not sufficient.

(*b*) Statement (II) ALONE is sufficient but statement (I) ALONE is not sufficient.

(*c*) BOTH statements TOGETHER are sufficient, but NEITHER statement ALONE is sufficient.

(*d*) EACH statement ALONE is sufficient.

(*e*) Statements (I) and (II) TOGETHER are not sufficient.

19. How long would it take 7 men and 3 women to paint a wall with dimensions of 30 feet by 80 feet, if all men and all women work at their respective uniform rates?

I. Fifteen men can paint a wall with dimensions of 15 feet by 90 feet in 9 hours.

II. A 20-square-foot wall can be painted by two men in 1 hour or by one woman in 2 hours.

(*a*) Statement (I) ALONE is sufficient but statement (II) ALONE is not sufficient.

(*b*) Statement (II) ALONE is sufficient but statement (I) ALONE is not sufficient.

(*c*) BOTH statements TOGETHER are sufficient, but NEITHER statement ALONE is sufficient.

(*d*) EACH statement ALONE is sufficient.

(*e*) Statements (I) and (II) TOGETHER are not sufficient.

20. John and Christian invested their money in a bank at 10% interest rate per annum. By how much, in dollars, Christian's investment was greater than John's investment?

I. After one year Christian earned $50 more than John.

II. If the interest rate were 12%, Christian would have earned $60 more than John.

(*a*) Statement (I) ALONE is sufficient but statement (II) ALONE is not sufficient.

(*b*) Statement (II) ALONE is sufficient but statement (I) ALONE is not sufficient.

(*c*) BOTH statements TOGETHER are sufficient, but NEITHER statement ALONE is sufficient.

(*d*) EACH statement ALONE is sufficient.

(*e*) Statements (I) and (II) TOGETHER are not sufficient.

21. To cover a particular distance, a man calculated that he would arrive on time if he traveled the first half of the distance at 20 miles per hour and the remaining half at a greater speed. What is the total distance the man traveled?

I. The man traveled the second half of the distance at 40 miles per hour and reached his destination on time.

II. Had the man traveled the second half of the distance at 30 miles per hour, he would have reached his destination 15 minutes late.

(*a*) Statement (I) ALONE is sufficient but statement (II) ALONE is not sufficient.

(*b*) Statement (II) ALONE is sufficient but statement (I) ALONE is not sufficient.

(*c*) BOTH statements TOGETHER are sufficient, but NEITHER statement ALONE is sufficient.

(*d*) EACH statement ALONE is sufficient.

(*e*) Statements (I) and (II) TOGETHER are not sufficient.

Answer Key

1. (*e*)	**7.** (*c*)	**13.** (*c*)	**19.** (*b*)
2. (*a*)	**8.** (*c*)	**14.** (*c*)	**20.** (*d*)
3. (*a*)	**9.** (*c*)	**15.** (*c*)	**21.** (*c*)
4. (*d*)	**10.** (*b*)	**16.** (*c*)	
5. (*b*)	**11.** (*e*)	**17.** (*c*)	
6. (*c*)	**12.** (*c*)	**18.** (*c*)	

Answer Explanations

1. (e) **Considering statement 1 alone :**

$m = 200\% \times n$

$m = 2n$

Not sufficient to get the single numerical value of m.

Eliminate A/D

Considering statement 2 alone :

$m \times n = z^2$, where z is a positive integer

Not sufficient to get the single numerical value of m

Eliminate B.

Considering statement 1 & 2 together :

Since from statement (1) $m = 2n$ then from statement (2) $2n \times n = z^2$

$2n^2 = z^2$

Taking square root on both sides

Hence, $z = \sqrt{2} \times n$

We still cannot get the single numerical value of m. Insufficient.

Eliminate C.

The correct answer is option (e)

2. (a) It is given that $\frac{x}{y} > 1.1$

As y is positive, $x > 1.1y$

Considering statement 1 alone :

when $y > 35, x > 35$

Sufficient

Eliminate B/C/E

Considering statement 2 alone :

$x = 10 + y$

x could be greater than or less than 35.

Insufficient

The correct answer is option (a)

3. (a) **Considering statement 1 alone :**

The ratio of the number of sharpeners to the number of pens to the number of pencils in the shop is 33 : 17 : 21

So, the number of sharpeners are 33x, number of pens are 17x and number of pencils are 21x, where x is an integer

Hence, the total number of pens and pencils $= 17x + 21x = 38x$

The number of sharpeners are 33x

Sufficient

Eliminate B/C/E

Considering statement 2 alone :

The total number of sharpeners, pens, and pencils in the shop is 142.

Total number of three items is only given which is not sufficient to answer the question. Insufficient

The correct answer is option (a)

4. (d) Let the number of type 2 widgets produced be x. The number of type 2 widgets produced = 200 – x. From statement I,

$$(20000 - x) \times \frac{10}{100} = x \times \frac{6}{100}$$

$$\Rightarrow 2000 - \frac{x}{10} = \frac{3x}{50}$$

$\Rightarrow 2000 = \frac{8}{50}x$

$\Rightarrow x = \frac{2000 \times 50}{8} = 150 \times 50 = 12500.$

Hence, statement I alone is sufficient. From statement II, type 2 widgets

$= 20000 \times \frac{3}{5} = 4000 \times 3 = 12000.$

Hence, statement II alone is also sufficient.

The answer is (d).

5. (b) From statement I, nothing is given about the cost price. Hence statement I alone is not sufficient.

From statement II,

$CP = \frac{2}{3}\ SP$

$\Rightarrow \quad SP = 1.5\ CP$

Profit percentage is 50.

Hence statement II alone is sufficient.

The answer is (b).

6. (c) Let the time Steve takes to walk from his home to office be w minutes.

Let the time Steve takes to run from his home to office be r minutes.

Considering Statement 1 alone :

$r + w = 40$ ...(i)

Since the individual values of r and w are not known, the answer cannot be determined. – Insufficient

Hence, eliminate A/D.

Considering Statement 2 alone :

$r + r = 30$

$\Rightarrow \quad r = 15$ ...(ii)

However, there is no information about w. – Insufficient

Hence, eliminate B.

Considering Statements 1 and 2 together :

Using (i) and (ii):

$w = 40 - 15 = 25$ ...(iii)

Thus, the ratio of Steve's running and walking speeds is inverse of the times taken while running and walking, respectively (since the distance is constant)

$= 25 : 15 = 5 : 3$

Thus, the required percent

$= \frac{5}{3} \times 100\% = 166.7\%$ – Sufficient

The answer is (c).

7. (c) **Considering Statement 1 alone :**

There is no information about the ratio of the speeds of Amy and Betty. – Insufficient

Hence, eliminate A/D.

Considering Statement 2 alone :

There is no information about the times Amy and Betty start their respective journeys.- Insufficient

Hence, eliminate B.

Considering statements 1 and 2 together :

We know that the ratio of the times taken by Amy and Betty to cover the same distance

$= 10 : 5 = 2 : 1$

Thus, the ratio of the speeds of Amy and Betty is the inverse of the ratio of their speeds as the distance is constant.

$= 1 : 2$

Let us assume the speeds of Amy and Betty to be x miles per hour and $2x$ miles per hours.

Thus, the distance between the stops X and Y = $10 \times x = 10x$ miles or $5 \times 2x = 10x$ miles.

Since Amy started 3 hours before Berry, the distance covered by Amy from 10:00 am to 1:00 pm

Since Amy started 3 hours before Betty, the distance covered by Amy from 10:00 am to 1:00 pm

$$= 3 \times x = 3x \text{ miles}$$

Thus, the remaining distance

$$= 10x - 3x = 7x \text{ miles}$$

At 1:00 pm, both Amy and Betty are traveling towards each other.

Thus, their relative speed = $x + 2x = 3x$ miles per hour; relative speed would the sum of their speeds as they are traveling in opposite directions. Thus, time taken to meet

$$= \frac{7x}{3x} = 2.33 \text{ hours}$$

$$= 2 \text{ hours } 20 \text{ minutes}$$

Thus, the meeting time is 2 hours 20 minutes past 1:00 pm, i.e., 3:20 pm. – Sufficient.

The answer is (c).

8. (c) Let the first car be X and the second car be Y.

Speed of Car X is 100 kmph

The question asks us to find the time when Car Y overtakes Car X.

To answer this, we need to know the speed of Y and the time it departs from City A.

Let's see each statement one by one.

Considering Statement 1 alone :

Statement 1 only gives the time of departure of Y from City A, hence this statement alone is not sufficient.

Hence, eliminate A/D.

Considering Statement 2 alone :

Statement 2 only gives the speed of Y, which is $1.5 \times 100 = 150$ kmph, but not departure time; hence this statement alone is not sufficient.

Hence, eliminate B.

Considering statements 1 and 2 together :

Since Statement 1 gives the departure time of Car Y and Statement 2 gives its speed, statements 1 and 2 together are sufficient. There is no need to calculate the answer as this is a DS question.

For the sake of completeness, let's compute the time.

Since both cars are moving in the same direction, their relative speed = 150 – 100 = 50 kmph. Since Car Y departed after 1 hour, it has to cover = $1 \times 100 = 100$ kilometers (Distance covered by Car X in 1 hour) at a speed of 50 kmph. Thus, Car Y will take $\frac{100}{50} = 2$ hours to overtake Car X.

The answer is (c).

9. (c) Let us assume that A and B meet at 12:00 at Point X.

Since A was late by *t* minutes, we need to find out the time when A would reach X. The difference between this time and 12:00 would give us the value of *t*.

Considering Statement 1 alone :

We have no information about the position of the new meeting point, Y, with respect to the earlier meeting point, X. – Insufficient

Hence, eliminate A/D

Considering Statement 2 alone :

We have no information about the speeds of A and B. - Insufficient

Hence, eliminate B.

Considering statements 1 and 2 together :

We know that Y is 1.2 km away from X (Y is closer to A than to X since A was late).

Since B was on time, he must have reached X at 12:00 (actual meeting time).

Time taken by B to travel 1.2 km to reach point Y

$= \frac{1.2}{12} = 0.1$ hours = 6 minutes.

Thus, B reaches Y at 12:06 pm.

Since A and B meet at point Y, A was also at Y at 12:06 pm.

Time taken by A to cover 1.2 km to reach X

$= \frac{1.2}{6} = 0.2$ hours = 12 minutes.

Thus, A reaches X at 12:06 + 12 min.

= 12:18 pm.

Thus, we observe that A reaches X 18 minutes later than when he was supposed to reach.

Thus, we have $t = 18$ - Sufficient.

The answer is (c).

10. (b) **Considering Statement 1 alone :**

There is no information about the working rate of women. So, this is insufficient.

Hence, eliminate A/D.

Considering Statement 2 alone :

We have

An area painted by 2 men in 1 hour is the same as that painted by 1 woman in 2 hours. Thus, the efficiencies of men and women are the same.

Thus, we have

To paint the 20 square feet wall, 2 men take 1 hour

Thus, to paint (30 × 80) or 2,400 square feet wall, time taken by 2 men

$$= \frac{1}{20} \times 2{,}400 = 120 \text{ hours}$$

So, the question : *How long would 7 men and 3 women take to paint a wall having dimensions 30 feet by 80 feet? becomes...*

How long would (7 + 3 = 10) men take to paint a wall having dimensions of 2,400 square feet?

Note: Working rate of one man = Working rate of one women

Thus, to paint 2,400 square feet, time taken by 10 men

$$= 120 \times \frac{2}{10} = 24 \text{ hours – Sufficient}$$

Hence, eliminate C/E.

The answer is (b).

11. (e) Given that r is even, we can write the question as : Is (p + even) even?

It will depend on the nature of p; if p is even, (p + even) would be even, else not even (odd or fraction).

From the information pq = even we cannot ascertain that p is even or odd. p can have any value even/odd/fraction. Let's see.

1. $p = \frac{1}{2}$ & $q = 4 \Rightarrow pq = \frac{1}{2} \times 4 = 2$, even
2. $p = 1$ & $q = 4 \Rightarrow pq = 1 \times 4 = 4$, even
3. $p = 2$ & $q = 4 \Rightarrow pq = 2 \times 4 = 8$, even

Question rephrased : Is p even?

Let's see each statement one by one.

Considering Statement 1 alone :

All the three cases discussed above are applicable; p can be even, odd, or fraction. Insufficient.

Hence, eliminate A/D.

Considering Statement 2 alone :

Case 2 and 3 discussed above are applicable; p can be even or odd. Insufficient.

Hence, eliminate B.

Statements 1 and 2 together :

Even both statements together are insufficient. Case 2 and 3 discussed above are applicable; p can be even or odd.

The correct answer is Option (e).

12. (c) Let the time Steve takes to walk from his home to office be w minutes.

Let the time Steve takes to run from his home to office be r minutes.

Considering Statement 1 alone :

$r + w = 40$ ...(i)

Since the individual values of r and w are not known, the answer cannot be determined. – Insufficient

Hence, eliminate A/D.

Considering Statement 2 alone :

$r + r = 30$

$\Rightarrow \quad r = 15$ ...(ii)

However, there is no information about w. - Insufficient

Hence, eliminate B.

Considering statements 1 and 2 together :

Using (i) and (ii):

$w = 40 - 15 = 25$ ...(iii)

Thus, the ratio of Steve's running and walking speeds is inverse of the times taken while running and walking, respectively (since the distance is constant)

$= 25 : 15 = 5 : 3$

Thus, the required percent

$= \frac{5}{3} \times 100\% = 166.7\%$ - Sufficient

The answer is (c).

13. (c) **Considering Statement 1 alone :**

There is no information about the ratio of the speeds of Amy and Betty. – Insufficient

Hence, eliminate A/D.

Considering Statement 2 alone :

There is no information about the times Amy and Betty start their respective journeys.- Insufficient

Hence, eliminate B.

Considering statements 1 and 2 together :

We know that the ratio of the times taken by Amy and Betty to cover the same distance $= 10 : 5 = 2 : 1$

Thus, the ratio of the speeds of Amy and Betty is the inverse of the ratio of their speeds as the distance is constant. $= 1 : 2$

Let us assume the speeds of Amy and Betty to be x miles per hour and $2x$ miles per hour.

Thus, the distance between the stops X and Y $= 10 \times x = 10x$ miles or $5 \times 2x = 10x$ miles. Since Amy started 3 hours before Betty, the distance covered by Amy from 10:00 am to 1:00 pm $= 3 \times x = 3x$ miles

Thus, the remaining distance $= 10x - 3x = 7x$ miles at 1:00 pm, both Amy and Betty are traveling towards each other.

Thus, their relative speed $= x + 2x = 3x$ miles per hour; relative speed would the sum of their speeds as they are traveling in opposite directions

Thus, time taken to meet

$= \frac{7x}{3x} = 2.33$ hours = 2 hours 20 minutes

Thus, the meeting time is 2 hours 20 minutes past 1:00 pm, i.e., 3:20 pm. – Sufficient.

The answer is (c).

14. (c) Say k friends had the dinners, sharing equally.

Considering Statement 1 alone:

Bill of the dinner = $\$21k$ ...(i)

However, the value of k is unknown. - Insufficient

Hence, eliminate A/D.

Considering Statement 2 alone:

Bill of the dinner = $\$20\,(k+1)$ ...(ii)

However, the value of k is unknown. -Insufficient.

Hence, eliminate B.

Statement 1 and 2 together:

From (i) and (ii), we have

$21k = 20\,(k+1)$

$k = 20$

The bill amount = $21k = 21 \times 20$

= $420 – sufficient.

The answer is (c).

15. (c) Let the first car be X and the second car be Y.

Speed of Car X is 100 kmph

The question asks us to find the time when Car Y overtakes Car X.

To answer this, we need to know the speed of Y and the time it departs from City A.

Let's see each statement one by one.

Considering Statement 1 alone:

Statement 1 only gives the time of departure of Y from City A, hence this statement alone is not sufficient.

Hence, eliminate A/D.

Considering Statement 2 alone:

Statement 2 only gives the speed of Y, which is $1.5 \times 100 = 150$ kmph, but not departure time; hence this statement alone is not sufficient.

Hence, eliminate B.

Considering Statements 1 and 2 together:

Since Statement 1 gives the departure time of Car Y and Statement 2 gives its speed, statements 1 and 2 together are sufficient. There is no need to calculate the answer as this is a DS question.

For the sake of completeness, let's compute the time.

Since both cars are moving in the same direction, their relative speed = 150 – 100 = 50 kmph. Since Car Y departed after 1 hour, it has to cover = $1 \times 100 = 100$ kilometers (Distance covered by Car X in 1 hour) at a speed of 50 kmph. Thus, Car Y will take $\frac{100}{50} = 2$ hours to overtake Car X.

The answer is (c).

16. (c) **Considering Statement 1 alone:**

If $\frac{21}{s}$ is an integer, s can be any factor of 21 : 1, 3, 7, or 21. While 3 and 7 are prime numbers, 1 and 21 are not. No unique answer. This statement is insufficient.

Hence, eliminate A/D.

Considering Statement 2 alone :

If $\frac{47}{s}$ is an integer, s can be any factor of 47: 1, or 47. While 47 is a prime number, 1 is not. No unique answer. This statement is insufficient.

Hence, eliminate B.

Considering statements 1 and 2 together :

s = 1 is the only common value for both statements; a unique value; hence both statements together are sufficient.

The answer is (c).

17. (c) **Considering statements 1 alone:**

Given : $\frac{\text{Jasmine's age}}{\text{Katty's age}} = \frac{2}{3}$

For any ratio based problems, we take the ratio as follows:

Let Jasmine's age = $2k$ and Katty's age = $3k$

We cannot say anything about Jasmine's age since $2k$ can be anything say 2, 4, 6, 8, etc.

This statement alone is not sufficient.

Considering Statement 2 alone :

Sum of present ages = 40

Jasmine's age could be anything. This statement alone is not sufficient.

Hence, eliminate B.

Considering Statement 1 and 2 together :

From Statement 1, Jasmine's age = $2k$ and Katty's age = $3k$

From Statement 2, sum of ages = 40

Hence, $2k + 3k = 40 \Rightarrow 5k = 40 \Rightarrow k = 8$

Jasmine's age = $2k = 16$

Statements 1 and 2 together are sufficient.

The answer is (c).

18. (c) Let us assume that A and B meet at 12:00 at Point X.

Since A was late by t minutes, we need to find out the time when A would reach X. The difference between this time and 12:00 would give us the value of t.

Considering Statement 1 alone :

We have no information about the position of the new meeting point, Y, with respect to the earlier meeting point, X. - Insufficient

Hence, eliminate A/D.

Considering Statement 2 alone :

We have no information about the speeds of A and B. - Insufficient

Hence, eliminate B.

Considering statements 1 and 2 together :

We know that Y is 1.2 km away from X (Y is closer to A than to X since A was late).

Since B was on time, he must have reached X at 12:00 (actual meeting time).

Time taken by B to travel 1.2 km to reach point Y = $\frac{1.2}{12}$ = 0.1 hours = 6 minutes.

Thus, B reaches Y at 12:06 pm.

Since A and B meet at point Y, A was also at Y at 12:06 pm.

Time taken by A to cover 1.2 km to reach X = $\frac{1.2}{6}$ = 0.2 hours = 12 minutes.

Thus, A reaches X at 12:06 + 12 min. = 12:18 pm.

Thus, we observe that A reaches X 18 minutes later than when he was supposed to reach.

Thus, we have $t = 18$ - Sufficient

The answer is (c).

19. (b) **Considering Statement 1 alone :**

There is no information about the working rate of women. So, this is insufficient.

Hence, eliminate A/D.

Considering Statement 2 alone :

We have

An area painted by 2 men in 1 hour is the same as that painted by 1 woman in 2 hours.

Thus, the efficiencies of men and women are the same.

Thus, we have

To paint the 20 square feet wall, 2 men take 1 hour

Thus, to paint (30 × 80) or 2,400 square feet wall, time taken by 2 men

$= \frac{1}{20} \times 2{,}400 = 120$ hours.

Thus, to paint 2,400 square feet, time taken by 10 men

$= 120 \times \frac{2}{10} = 24$ hours - Sufficient

Hence, eliminate C/E.

The answer is (b).

20. (d) Let $\$x$ be the amount of money invested by Christian and $\$y$ be the money invested by John. We have to find out the value of $\$(x - y)$.

Considering Statement 1 alone :

$\Rightarrow$ 10% of x – 10% of $y = 50$

$\Rightarrow 0.1x - 0.1y = 50$

$\Rightarrow x - y = 500$; Christian's investment was greater than John's by $500.

Statement 1 alone is sufficient. The correct answer would be between A/D.

Considering Statement 2 alone :

$\Rightarrow$ 12% of x – 12% of $y = 60$

$\Rightarrow 0.12x - 0.12y = 60$;

$\Rightarrow x - y = 500$; Christian's investment was greater than John's by $500.

Statement 2 alone is also sufficient.

The answer is (d).

21. (c) Let the total distance be $2d$ miles.

Time taken to cover d miles at 20 miles per hour $= \frac{d}{20}$ hours

Considering Statement 1 alone :

Time taken to cover the remaining d miles at 40 miles per hour

$= \frac{d}{40}$ hours

However, there is no information regarding the actual time taken. - Insufficient

Hence, eliminate A/D.

Considering Statement 2 alone :

We know that if the man traveled the remaining distance at 30 miles per hour, he would have reached his destination 15 minutes or $\frac{1}{4}$ hours late.

Time taken to cover the remaining d miles at 30 miles per hour

$= \frac{d}{30}$ hours.

However, there is no information regarding the actual time taken. - Insufficient

Hence, eliminate B.

Considering statements 1 and 2 together :

$$\frac{d}{30} - \frac{d}{40} = \frac{1}{4}$$

$\Rightarrow d = 30$

Thus, the total distance

$= 2d = 60$ miles. – Sufficient.

The answer is (c).

Chapter 3

Algebra

Algebra is a significant component of the GMAT, which tests your ability to solve problems using algebraic concepts. Here are some important topics in algebra that are frequently tested on the GMAT:

- **Linear equations and inequalities :** You should be able to solve linear equations and inequalities, graph them on a coordinate plane, and use them to solve word problems.
- **Quadratic equations :** You should be able to solve quadratic equations using the quadratic formula, factoring, and completing the square.
- **Functions :** You should be able to understand the concept of a function and evaluate functions for specific inputs.
- **Exponents and radicals :** You should be able to simplify expressions with exponents and radicals, and solve equations involving them.
- **Absolute value :** You should be able to work with absolute values and solve equations and inequalities that involve them.

It's important to note that these topics are not exhaustive, and there may be other algebraic concepts that are tested on the GMAT. Additionally, some GMAT questions may involve more than one algebraic concept, so it's important to be able to recognize when to use different algebraic tools to solve a problem.

Linear Equations

Linear Equations are equations in which all the variables are raised to the first power. To solve such an equation, you'll need to perform operations on both sides of the equation in order to get the variable you're solving for alone on one side.

A linear equation is an equation involving one or more variables in which each term in the equation is either a constant term or a variable multiplied by a coefficient. None of the variables are multiplied together or raised to a power greater than 1. For example, $2x + 1 = 7x$ and $10x - 9y - z = 3$ are linear equations, but $x + y^2 = 0$ and $xz = 3$ are not.

Here are some examples of linear equations:

$3x + 2 = 11$

$5y - 7 = 3y + 11$

$2z + 4 = 10 - 3z$

$0.5a - 1 = 2.5$

$-2b + 3 = -7b - 1$

Example : Find the value of x in the equation $3x - 5 = 7$.

Solution : We can solve for x by isolating it on one side of the equation. To do this, we'll add 5 to both sides of the equation to get:

$$3x - 5 + 5 = 7 + 5$$

Simplifying, we get:

$$3x = 12$$

Now we can isolate x by dividing both sides of the equation by 3:

$$\frac{3x}{3} = \frac{12}{3}$$

Simplifying, we get:

$$x = 4$$

Therefore, the value of x that satisfies the equation $3x - 5 = 7$ is 4.

There are two ways of solving the equation: Substitution method and elimination method.

Substitution Method

The substitution method is one way to solve a system of linear equations. In this method, we solve one of the equations for one variable in terms of the other variable, and then substitute that expression into the other equation. This creates a new equation with only one variable, which can be solved. Once we find the value of one variable, we can use that value to solve for the other variable.

Here's an example of how to solve a system of linear equations using the substitution method:

1. Solve the first equation for one variable in terms of the other. For example, if the equations are:

$$2x + 3y = 7$$

$$4x - y = 1$$

   We can solve the second equation for y :

$$y = 4x - 1$$

2. Substitute the expression we just found for the variable into the other equation. In this case, we substitute $y = 4x - 1$ into the first equation:

$$2x + 3(4x - 1) = 7$$

3. Simplify the equation and solve for the variable:

$$2x + 12x - 3 = 7$$

$$14x = 10$$

$$x = \frac{10}{14} = \frac{5}{7}$$

4. Use the value we just found for x to find the value of y. We can use either of the original equations to do this. Let's use the second equation:

$$4x - y = 1$$

$$4\left(\frac{5}{7}\right) - y = 1$$

$$y = 4\left(\frac{5}{7}\right) - 1$$

$$y = \frac{15}{7} - \frac{7}{7}$$

$$y = \frac{8}{7}$$

So the solution to the system of linear equations is $x = \frac{5}{7}, y = \frac{8}{7}$.

Example : Solve the system of equations using the substitution method:

$$2x + y = 10\, x - y = 4$$

Solution : To use the substitution method, we need to solve one of the equations for one of the variables, and then substitute the resulting expression into the other equation. Let's solve the second equation for "y":

$$x - y = 4$$

$$y = x - 4$$

Now we can substitute this expression for "y" into the first equation:

$$2x + y = 10$$

$$2x + (x - 4) = 10$$

Simplifying, we get :

$$3x - 4 = 10$$

Adding 4 to both sides, we get:

$$3x = 14$$

Dividing both sides by 3, we get:

$$x = 4.67$$

Now that we know the value of x, we can substitute it back into the expression we found for "y":

$$y = x - 4$$

$$y = 4.67 - 4$$

$$y = 0.67$$

Therefore, the solution to the system of equations is:

$$x = 4.67$$

$$y = 0.67$$

Elimination Method

The elimination method is another way to solve a system of linear equations. In this method, we add or subtract the equations in such a way that one variable is eliminated, and then we solve for the other variable. We can then substitute the value we found into one of the equations to solve for the other variable.

Here's an example of how to solve a system of linear equations using the elimination method:

1. Rewrite the equations in standard form:

$$2x + 3y = 7$$

$$4x - y = 1$$

2. Multiply one or both equations by a constant to make the coefficients of one of the variables opposite in sign. In this case, we can multiply the second equation by 3 to make the coefficient of y in both equations opposite:

$$2x + 3y = 7$$

$$12x - 3y = 3$$

3. Add the equations to eliminate one of the variables:

$$2x + 3y = 7 \text{ and } 12x - 3y = 3$$

$$14x = 10$$

4. Solve for the remaining variable:

$$14x = 10$$

$$x = \frac{10}{14} = \frac{5}{7}$$

5. Substitute the value we just found for x into one of the original equations to find the value of the other variable. Let's use the first equation:

$$2x + 3y = 7$$

$$2\left(\frac{5}{7}\right) + 3y = 7$$

$$\frac{10}{7} + 3y = 7$$

$$3y = 7 - \frac{10}{7}$$

$$3y = \frac{49}{7} - \frac{10}{7}$$

$$3y = \frac{39}{7}$$

$$y = \frac{13}{7}$$

So the solution to the system of linear equations is $x = \frac{5}{7}, y = \frac{13}{7}$.

Types of Solutions

If a system of linear equations is given as:

$$a_1x + b_1y + c_1 = 0$$

$$a_2x + b_2y + c_2 = 0$$

There are three types of solutions possible for this pair of linear equations:

- **Unique solution :** It means only one point (x, y) will satisfy both the equations. So the graph for the system of linear equations will be intersecting lines. Unique solution is possible when $\frac{a_1}{a_2} \neq \frac{b_1}{b_2}$
- **Infinite solutions :** It means all points (x, y) satisfies either of the equations. So the graph for the system of linear equations will be coincident lines. This is possible when $\frac{a_1}{a_2} = \frac{b_1}{b_2} = \frac{c_1}{c_2}$
- **No solution :** It means that these equations have no point in common. So the graph for the system of linear equations will be parallel lines. This type of solution is possible when $\frac{a_1}{a_2} = \frac{b_1}{b_2} \neq \frac{c_1}{c_2}$

Quadratic Equations

A quadratic equation is a polynomial equation of degree 2, which means that the highest power of the variable in the equation is 2. The general form of a quadratic equation is:

$ax^2 + bx + c = 0$, where a, b, and c are constants and x is the variable.

To solve a quadratic equation, we need to find the values of x that satisfy the equation.

We can use the quadratic formula to find the solutions of a quadratic equation. The quadratic formula is:

$$x = \frac{\left(-b \pm \sqrt{(b^2 - 4ac)}\right)}{2a}$$

where the symbol ± means "plus or minus", and the square root is only defined for non-negative values.

To use the quadratic formula, we first need to identify the values of a, b, and c in the quadratic equation. Then, we substitute those values into the formula to find the values of x.

Example, consider the quadratic equation:

$$2x^2 + 3x - 5 = 0$$

Here, a = 2, b = 3, and c = -5. Substituting these values into the quadratic formula, we get:

$$\frac{\left(-3 \pm \sqrt{(3^2 - 4(2)(-5))}\right)}{2(2)}$$

Simplifying this expression, we get:

$$x = \frac{\left(-3 \pm \sqrt{49}\right)}{4}$$

$$x = \frac{(-3 \pm 7)}{4}$$

So, the solutions of the quadratic equation $2x^2 + 3x - 5 = 0$ are:

$$x = \frac{(-3+7)}{4} = \frac{1}{2}$$

Example : Solve the quadratic equation $2x^2 + 3x - 5 = 0$ using the quadratic formula.

Solution : The quadratic formula is:

$\dfrac{\left(-b \pm \sqrt{(b^2 - 4ac)}\right)}{2a}$, where a, b, and c are the coefficients of the quadratic equation $ax^2 + bx + c = 0$.

Using this formula, we can find the solutions to the given quadratic equation.

First, we identify the coefficients :

$$a = 2$$

$$b = 3$$

$$c = -5$$

Now we can substitute these values into the quadratic formula and simplify:

$$x = \frac{\left(-b \pm \sqrt{(b^2 - 4ac)}\right)}{2a}$$

$$x = \frac{\left(-3 \pm \sqrt{(3^2 - (4)(2)(-5))}\right)}{2(2)}$$

$$x = \frac{\left(-3 \pm \sqrt{(49)}\right)}{4x}$$

$$x = \frac{(-3 \pm 7)}{4}$$

So the solutions to the quadratic equation are:

$$x = \frac{(-3+7)}{4} = \frac{1}{2}$$

$$x = \frac{(-3-7)}{4} = -\frac{5}{2}$$

Therefore, the solutions to the quadratic equation $2x^2 + 3x - 5 = 0$ are $x = \frac{1}{2}$ and $x = -\frac{5}{2}$

Splitting the Middle Term

Splitting the middle term is a method used to factorize quadratic expressions of the form $ax^2 + bx + c$, where a, b, and c are constants.

The method involves finding two numbers whose sum is equal to b, the coefficient of the x-term, and whose product is equal to a times c, the product of the first and last coefficients. We then rewrite the quadratic expression as a sum of two terms using these two numbers, and then factorize the expression by grouping the terms.

Here are the steps to use the splitting the middle term technique to factorize a quadratic expression:

1. Write the quadratic expression in the standard form $ax^2 + bx + c$.
2. Identify the values of a, b, and c.
3. Find two numbers whose sum is equal to b, the coefficient of the x-term, and whose product is equal to a times c, the product of the first and last coefficients.
4. Rewrite the quadratic expression as a sum of two terms, using the two numbers found in step 3.
5. Factorize each of the two terms separately.
6. Rearrange the terms to obtain the factorized form of the quadratic expression.

Lets understand with an example:

Factorise : $2x^2 + 7x + 3$.

1. Write the quadratic expression in the standard form $ax^2 + bx + c : 2x^2 + 7x + 3$.
2. Identify the values of a, b, and c : $a = 2, b = 7, c = 3$.
3. Find two numbers whose sum is equal to b, the coefficient of the x-term, and whose product is equal to a times c, the product of the first and last coefficients. In this case, we need to find two numbers whose sum is 7 and whose product is $2 \times 3 = 6$. The two numbers are 6 and 1.

4. Rewrite the quadratic expression as a sum of two terms, using the two numbers found in step 3:

$$2x^2 + 7x + 3 = 2x^2 + 6x + x + 3$$

5. Factorize each of the two terms separately:

$$2x^2 + 6x = 2x(x + 3)\ x + 3 = 1(x + 3)$$

6. Rearrange the terms to obtain the factorized form of the quadratic expression:

$$2x^2 + 7x + 3 = (2x + 1)(x + 3)$$

Therefore, the quadratic expression $2x^2 + 7x + 3$ can be factorized as $(2x + 1)(x + 3)$ using the splitting the middle term method.

Example : Factor the quadratic expression $x^2 + 5x + 6$ using the method of splitting the middle term.

Solution : To factor the expression $x^2 + 5x + 6$ using the method of splitting the middle term, we need to find two numbers that multiply to 6 and add to 5. Those numbers are 2 and 3. Therefore, we can rewrite the expression as:

$$x^2 + 2x + 3x + 6$$

Now we can group the terms as follows:

$$(x^2 + 2x) + (3x + 6)$$

We can factor out the greatest common factor from each group:

$$x(x + 2) + 3(x + 2)$$

Notice that both groups have a factor of $(x + 2)$. We can factor this out:

$$(x + 2)(x + 3)$$

Therefore, the factored form of the quadratic expression $x^2 + 5x + 6$ is $(x + 2)(x + 3)$.

Discriminant Formula & Nature of Roots

The discriminant is a formula used to determine the nature of the roots of a quadratic equation. The quadratic equation is of the form $ax^2 + bx + c = 0$, where a, b, and c are constants.

The discriminant formula is given by:

$$D = b^2 - 4ac$$

If the discriminant is positive (i.e., $b^2 - 4ac > 0$), then the quadratic equation has two distinct real roots.

If the discriminant is zero (i.e., $b^2 - 4ac = 0$), then the quadratic equation has one real root.

If the discriminant is negative (i.e., $b^2 - 4ac < 0$), then the quadratic equation has two imaginary roots.

The discriminant formula can also be used to find the roots of a quadratic equation

Using the quadratic formula :

$$\frac{\left(-b \pm \sqrt{(b^2 - 4ac)}\right)}{2a}$$

If the discriminant is positive, then the square root in the quadratic formula is a positive real number, so the equation has two distinct real roots. If the discriminant is zero, then the square root is zero, so the equation has one real root, which is repeated. If the discriminant is negative, then the square root is an imaginary number, so the equation has two complex conjugate roots.

The roots of the quadratic equation is generally denoted by α and β.

where, $\alpha = \frac{\left(-b + \sqrt{D}\right)}{2a}$ and, $\beta = \frac{\left(-b - \sqrt{D}\right)}{2a}$

Sum & Product of Roots

The sum of the roots of a quadratic equation of the form $ax^2 + bx + c = 0$ can be found using the following formula:

Sum of roots $= -\frac{b}{a}$

Here, "a", "b", and "c" are the coefficients of the quadratic equation.

For example, consider the quadratic equation $2x^2 + 5x - 3 = 0$.

The sum of the roots can be found using the formula:

Sum of roots $= -\frac{b}{a}$

Substituting the coefficients into the formula, we get:

Sum of roots $= -\frac{5}{2}$

Therefore, the sum of the roots of the quadratic equation $2x^2 + 5x - 3 = 0$ is $-\frac{5}{2}$.

Product of roots = $\frac{c}{a}$

Here, "a", "b", and "c" are the coefficients of the quadratic equation.

For example, consider the quadratic equation $2x^2 + 5x - 3 = 0$.

The product of the roots can be found using the formula:

Product of roots = $\frac{c}{a}$

Substituting the coefficients into the formula, we get:

Product of roots = $\frac{(-3)}{2}$

Therefore, the product of the roots of the quadratic equation $2x^2 + 5x - 3 = 0$ is $\frac{-3}{2}$.

Inequality

In the context of the GMAT (Graduate Management Admission Test), inequality typically refers to mathematical inequalities, which are used to express relationships between two values that are not equal.

The GMAT often tests students' abilities to solve and manipulate inequalities, particularly in the Quantitative section of the exam.

Inequalities can be represented using symbols such as < (less than), > (greater than), ≤ (less than or equal to), and ≥ (greater than or equal to). To solve inequalities on the GMAT, you typically need to isolate the variable on one side of the inequality sign and determine the range of values that satisfy the inequality.

Example, if you are given the inequality $3x - 5 > 7$, you would start by adding 5 to both sides to isolate the variable:

$$3x - 5 + 5 > 7 + 5$$

$$3x > 12$$

Then, you would divide both sides by 3 to solve for x:

$$x > 4$$

This tells you that the range of values for x that satisfy the inequality is all numbers greater than 4.

When you multiply or divide an inequality by a negative number on both sides, the inequality sign changes!!

Inequalities can involve variables and are similar to equations, except that the two sides are related by one of the inequality signs instead of the equality sign used in equations. For example, the inequality $4x - 1 \leq 7$ is a linear inequality in one variable, which states that "$4x - 1$ is less than or equal to 7."

When the same constant is added to or subtracted from both sides of an inequality, the direction of the inequality is preserved and the new inequality is equivalent to the original.

When both sides of the inequality are multiplied or divided by the same nonzero constant, the direction of the inequality is preserved if the constant is positive but the direction is reversed if the constant is negative. In either case, the new inequality is equivalent to the original.

Example : Solve the inequality $2x - 5 > 7$.

Solution : To solve the inequality $2x - 5 > 7$, we need to isolate "x" on one side of the inequality symbol. We can do this by adding 5 to both sides of the inequality:

$$2x - 5 + 5 > 7 + 5$$

Simplifying, we get:

$$2x > 12$$

Now we can isolate "x" by dividing both sides of the inequality by 2:

$$\frac{2x}{2} > \frac{12}{2}$$

Simplifying, we get:

$$x > 6$$

Therefore, the solution to the inequality $2x - 5 > 7$ is $x > 6$. This means that any value of "x" that is greater than 6 will satisfy the inequality

Absolute Value / Modulus

In mathematics, the absolute value (or modulus) of a real number is the non-negative value of that number without regard to its sign. It is denoted by two vertical bars on either side of the number.

For example, the absolute value of 5 is written as $|5|$, which is equal to 5, and the absolute value of -3 is written as $|-3|$, which is also equal to 3.

More formally, if x is a real number, then its absolute value is defined as:

$$|x| = \{x, \text{ if } x >= 0; -x, \text{ if } x < 0\}$$

The absolute value of a number represents its distance from zero on the number line. For instance, |5| represents the distance of 5 units from zero on the number line, while |–3| represents the distance of 3 units from zero, in the opposite direction.

Here are some examples of absolute value:

|5| = 5 The absolute value of 5 is 5 since 5 is a positive number.

|–3| = 3 The absolute value of –3 is 3 since the distance of –3 units from zero on the number line is 3 units in the opposite direction.

|0| = 0 The absolute value of 0 is 0 since 0 is equidistant from both positive and negative numbers on the number line.

|4 – 7| = |–3| = 3 The absolute value of the difference between 4 and 7 is 3 since the distance between 4 and 7 units on the number line is 3 units in the opposite direction.

|–2.5| = 2.5 The absolute value of –2.5 is 2.5 since 2.5 is the distance of 2.5 units from zero on the number line.

Example : Solve the inequality $\frac{(3x+1)}{(2x-3)} \leq 2$.

Solution : To solve the inequality $\frac{(3x+1)}{(2x-3)} \leq 2$, we need to isolate "x" on one side of the inequality symbol.

First, we can simplify the left-hand side of the inequality by multiplying both sides by the denominator (2x – 3):

$$\frac{(3x+1)}{(2x-3)} \leq 2$$

$$(3x+1) \leq 2(2x-3)$$

Simplifying, we get:

$$3x + 1 \leq 4x - 6$$

Now we can isolate "x" by subtracting 3x and adding 6 to both sides of the inequality:

$$3x + 1 - 3x + 6 \leq 4x - 6 - 3x + 6$$

Simplifying, we get:

$$7 \leq x$$

Therefore, the solution to the inequality $\frac{(3x+1)}{(2x-3)} \leq 2$ is $x \geq 7$. This means that any value of "x" that is greater than or equal to 7 will satisfy the inequality

Exponents / Radicals

An exponent is a mathematical operation that indicates how many times a number or variable should be multiplied by itself. The exponent is represented as a superscript number to the right of the base number or variable. For example, in the expression 2^3, 2 is the base and 3 is the exponent.

The exponent tells you how many times the base should be multiplied by itself. In the example above, 2^3 means 2 multiplied by itself three times, which is equal to $2 \times 2 \times 2 = 8$.

Exponents can also be written using negative numbers and fractions. When an exponent is negative, it indicates that the base should be divided by itself the number

of times specified by the absolute value of the exponent. For example, $\frac{1}{(2^3)} = \frac{1}{8}$.

When an exponent is a fraction, it represents a root of the base. For example, $2^{(1/2)}$ represents the square root of 2, which is approximately 1.414. Similarly, $2^{(1/3)}$ represents the cube root of 2, which is approximately 1.259.

When negative numbers are raised to powers, the result may be positive or negative.

For example, $(-3)^2 = (-3)(-3) = 9$, while $(-3)^5 = (-3)(-3)(-3)(-3)(-3) = -243$.

Important Points :

- For all nonzero numbers a, $a^0 = 1$.
- The expression 0^0 is undefined.
- For all nonzero numbers a, $a^{-1} = \frac{1}{a}$.
- If n is an even integer, then $(-1)^n = 1$.
- If n is an odd integer, then $(-1)^n = -1$.

Few exponents' rules are stated below :

$a^p \times a^q = a^{(p+q)}$	$\sqrt{a} \times \sqrt{b} = \sqrt{(ab)}$
$\frac{a^p}{a^q} = a^{(p-q)}$	$\frac{\sqrt{a}}{\sqrt{b}} = \sqrt{\frac{a}{b}}$
$(a^p)^q = a^{pq}$	$x\sqrt{a} + y\sqrt{a} = (x+y)\sqrt{a}$
$a^p \times b^p = (ab)^p$	$\sqrt{x} = x^{\frac{1}{2}}$
$x^0 = 1$	$x^{-a} = \frac{1}{x^a}$

Example : Simplify the expression $\frac{(2^{(3x+2)}) \times 8^{(x-1)}}{(16^{(x+1)})}$

Solution : We can start by rewriting 8 and 16 in terms of powers of 2:

$$8 = 2^3 \; 16 = 2^4$$

Substituting these values into the expression, we get:

$$\frac{\left(2^{(3x+2)} \times 2^{(3(x-1))}\right)}{(2^{(4(x+1))})}$$

Simplifying, we get:

$$\frac{2^{(3x+2+3x-3)}}{2^{(4x+4)}}$$

Combining like terms, we get:

$$\frac{2^{(6x-1)}}{2^{(4x+4)}}$$

Now we can use the rule of exponents that states $a^{(m-n)} = \frac{a^m}{a^n}$ to simplify the expression:

$$\frac{2^{(6x-1)}}{2^{(4x+4)}} = \frac{2^{(6x-1-(4x+4))}}{2^{(2x-5)}}$$

Therefore, the simplified form of the expression $\frac{\left(2^{(3x+2)} \times 8^{(x-1)}\right)}{\left(16^{(x+1)}\right)}$ is $2^{(2x-5)}$

Arithmetic Progression

An arithmetic progression (AP) is a sequence of numbers in which each term after the first is obtained by adding a constant value to the preceding term. This constant value is called the common difference of the AP. In other words, an arithmetic progression is a sequence of numbers where the difference between any two consecutive terms is the same.

Example : find the 10th term and sum of first terms of the following sequence of numbers: 2, 5, 8, 11, 14, ...

This is an arithmetic progression because the common difference between any two consecutive terms is 3. The first term of the sequence is 2, and each subsequent term is obtained by adding 3 to the previous term.

The nth term of an arithmetic progression can be found using the following formula:

$$a_n = a_1 + (n - 1)d$$

where a_n is the nth term of the AP, a_1 is the first term, d is the common difference, and n is the position of the term in the sequence.

The sum of the first n terms of an arithmetic progression can be found using the following formula:

$$S_n = \left(\frac{n}{2}\right)(a_1 + a_n)$$

where S_n is the sum of the first *n* terms, a_1 is the first term, a_n is the nth term, and n is the number of terms in the sequence.

Here is an example of an arithmetic progression :

2, 5, 8, 11, 14, 17, 20, 23, 26, 29, ...

In this sequence, the common difference between any two consecutive terms is 3. The first term of the sequence is 2, and each subsequent term is obtained by adding 3 to the previous term.

Using the formulas for arithmetic progressions, we can find the nth term and the sum of the first *n* terms of this sequence. For example:

- The 10th term of the sequence is $a_{10} = a_1 + (10 - 1)d = 2 + 9 \times 3 = 29$.
- The sum of the first 7 terms of the sequence is

$$S_7 = \left(\frac{7}{2}\right)(a_1 + a_7) = \left(\frac{7}{2}\right)(2 + 20) = 77.$$

Example : Find the 10th term of an arithmetic sequence where the first term is 3 and the common difference is 4.

Solution : To find the 10th term of an arithmetic sequence, we can use the formula: $a_n = a_1 + (n - 1)d$, where a_n is the nth term, a_1 is the first term, *n* is the term number, and d is the common difference.

Substituting the values given in the problem, we get:

$$a_{10} = 3 + (10 - 1)4$$

Simplifying, we get:

$$a_{10} = 3 + 36$$

$$a_{10} = 39$$

Therefore, the 10th term of the arithmetic sequence is 39

Example : The sum of the first 10 terms of an arithmetic sequence is 145 and the sum of the next 5 terms is 90. Find the first term and the common difference of the sequence.

Solution : Let's denote the first term of the arithmetic sequence as "a" and the common difference between consecutive terms as "d". We know that the sum of the first 10 terms is 145, so we can use the formula for the sum of an arithmetic series to get:

$$S_{10} = \left(\frac{10}{2}\right)(2a + (10\text{-}1)d) = 145$$

Simplifying, we get:

$$5(2a + 9d) = 145$$

$$2a + 9d = 29 \text{ (Equation 1)}$$

Similarly, we can use the sum of the next 5 terms (which is given as 90) and the formula for the sum of an arithmetic series to get:

$$S_{15} = \left(\frac{15}{2}\right)(2a + (15\text{-}1)d) = 235$$

Simplifying, we get :

$$15a + 105d = 470 \text{ (Equation 2)}$$

Now we can solve this system of equations to find the values of "a" and "d". First, we can use Equation 1 to solve for "a" in terms of "d":

$$a = \frac{(29 - 9d)}{2}$$

Substituting this expression for "a" into Equation 2, we get:

$$15\left[\frac{(29-9d)}{2}\right]+105d=470$$

Simplifying, we get :

$$-45d+435=0$$

$$d=9$$

Substituting this value of "d" back into Equation 1 to solve for "a", we get:

$$2a+9(9)=29$$

$$2a=-58$$

$$a=-29$$

Therefore, the first term of the arithmetic sequence is -29 and the common difference between consecutive terms is 9

Functions

The GMAT often tests students' abilities to understand and apply mathematical functions, particularly in the Quantitative section of the exam.

The domain of a function is the set of all possible input values for which the function is defined. In other words, it is the set of all x-values that can be plugged into the function to obtain a valid output.

For example, consider the function $f(x)=\frac{1}{(x-2)}$. The denominator of this function cannot be equal to zero, so $x-2$ cannot be equal to zero. Therefore, the domain of the function is all real numbers except $x=2$.

The range of a function is the set of all possible output values that the function can produce. In other words, it is the set of all y-values that are obtained when the function is evaluated at all possible x-values in its domain.

For example, consider the function $f(x)=x^2$. To find the range of this function, we can analyze the behavior of the function as x varies.

Some common types of functions that are tested on the GMAT include:

- Linear functions: Functions of the form $f(x)=mx+b$, where m and b are constants.
- Quadratic functions: Functions of the form $f(x)=ax^2+bx+c$, where a, b, and c are constants.
- Exponential functions: Functions of the form $f(x)=ab^x$, where a and b are constants.

Example : Let f(x) = 2x – 1 and g(x) = x^2. Find the value of f(g(3)).

Solution : To find f(g(3)), we need to first find the value of g(3). Since g(x) = x^2, we have:

$$g(3) = 3^2 = 9$$

Now we can use this value to find f(g(3)). Since f(x) = 2x – 1, we have:

$$f(g(3)) = f(9) = 2(9) - 1 = 17$$

Therefore, f(g(3)) = 17

Example : Let f(x) = 2x + 3 and g(x) = x^2 – 5. Find the value of (f of g)(2).

Solution : To find the value of (f of g)(2), we need to first find the value of g(2), and then use that value to find the value of f(g(2)). Since g(x) = x^2 – 5, we have:

$$g(2) = 2^2 - 5 = -1$$

Now we can use this value to find f(g(2)). Since f(x) = 2x + 3, we have:

$$f(g(2)) = f(-1) = 2(-1) + 3 = 1$$

Therefore, (f of g)(2) = f(g(2)) = 1.

Problem Solving

1. For what value of x is $|x - 4| + 1$ less than zero?

   (a) 0

   (b) 1

   (c) 3

   (d) 4

   (e) There is no such value of x

2. $|-x| \geq 5$ and $xy^2 < 0$, which of the following is a possible value of x?

   (a) –6

   (b) –3

   (c) –1

   (d) 0

   (e) 6

3. If $|x| + |y| > |x + y|$, then which of the following must be true?

   (a) $y < 0$

   (b) $x > 0$

   (c) $y > 0$

   (d) $xy > 0$

   (e) $xy < 0$

4. If $|x + 3| = 5$ and $|y + 5| = 3$, then what is the greatest possible value of x + y?

   (a) –16

   (b) –10

   (c) 6

   (d) 0

   (e) 10

5. If $xy < 0$, and $\frac{a}{x} + \frac{b}{y} < xy$, then which of the following must be true?

   (a) $ax + by < (xy)^2$

   (b) $ax + by < 1$

   (c) $ax + by > (xy)^2$

   (d) $a + b > xy$

   (e) $ax > -by$

6. The first three terms of an arithmetic sequence are 20, 23, and 26. What is the 70th term of the sequence?

   (a) 69

   (b) 127

   (c) 207

   (d) 227

   (e) 272

7. The sequence S is defined by $S_n = 3(S_{n-1}) - 2$ for each integer n^3 2. If S1 = 2, what is the value of S5?

   (a) 2

   (b) 4

   (c) 10

   (d) 28

   (e) 82

8. If $\frac{2^2 < x}{(2^6 - 2^4)} < 2^3$, which of the following is x?

   (a) 8

   (b) 16

   (c) 128

   (d) 232

   (e) 600

9. If $5^k - 5^{k+1} + 5^{k-1} = 5^k \times m$, what is the value of m?

(a) $\frac{-19}{5}$

(b) $\frac{-5}{19}$

(c) 0

(d) $\frac{5}{19}$

(e) $\frac{19}{5}$

10. Which of the following is greater than 10^5?

(a) 2^{13}

(b) 2^{14}

(c) 2^{15}

(d) 2^{16}

(e) 2^{17}

11. If $-2 < x < 4$ and $-3 < y < 2$, then which of the following must be true for $x - y$?

(a) $-4 < x - y > 2$

(b) $1 < x - y < 7$

(c) $1 < x - y < 4$

(d) $-4 < x - y < 2$

(e) $-4 < x - y < 7$

12. If $|x + 3| > 5$, what are the possible values of x?

(a) $-5 < x < 5$

(b) $-3 > x$ and $x > 3$

(c) $-8 < x < 2$

(d) $x < -8$ and $x > 2$

(e) $-3 < x < 3$

13. How many integer integer values satisfy $|x| > 3$?

(a) 0

(b) 1

(c) 3

(d) 5

(e) Infinitely many

14. An art class of 20 students took a final exam and ten of the students scored between 78 and 86 in the exam. If s is defined as the scores of the ten students, which of the following describes values of s?

(a) $|s - 82| = 4$

(b) $|s + 82| = 4$

(c) $|s - 82| < 4$

(d) $|s - 82| > 4$

(e) $|s + 82| > 4$

15. If $0 < x < 1$, which of the following must be true?

I. $x^7 < x^5$

II. $x^7 + x^6 < x^5 + x^4$

III. $x^6 + x^7 < x^4 + x^5$

(a) None of the above

(b) I only

(c) II only

(d) I and II only

(e) I, II, and III

16. Sandy estimates that there are p pens in a box. Many who knows the actual number of pens in the box, notes that the actual number, n, is within 10 pens (inclusive) of Sandy's estimate. Which of the following inequalities represents the relationship between Sandy's estimate and the actual number of pens in the box?

(*a*) $n + 10 \leq p \leq n - 10$

(*b*) $p - 10 \leq n \leq p + 10$

(*c*) $n \leq p \leq 10n$

(*d*) $\frac{p}{10} \leq n \leq 10p$

(*e*) $10 - p \leq n \leq 10 + p$

17. If $7^{4x} = 49$, what is possible value of $(7^{x-1})^2$?

(*a*) 49

(*b*) 21

(*c*) 7

(*d*) $\frac{1}{7}$

(*e*) $\frac{1}{49}$

18. In a sequence, $a_{n+1} = 2 \times a_n$. If $a_7 - a_6 = 96$, then what is the value of a_7?

(*a*) 48

(*b*) 96

(*c*) 98

(*d*) 192

(*e*) 198

19. If $x = 2^{y+1}$, then in terms of x, 4^y is

(*a*) x

(*b*) $\frac{x}{2}$

(*c*) x^2

(*d*) $\frac{x^2}{2}$

(*e*) $\frac{x^2}{4}$

20. If $(32)^{\frac{1}{x}} = 2^{5x}$, then what is the value of x?

(*a*) –1

(*b*) 1

(*c*) Both (a) & (b)

(*d*) 0

(*e*) Cannot be determined

21. The sum of the first three terms of an arithmetic progression is 30 and their product is 750. Find the 5th term of the A.P?

(*a*) 25

(*b*) –5

(*c*) 25 or –5

(*d*) –10

(*e*) 10

22. The midpoints of the sides of a square of length 15m are joined to form another square. Midpoints of the newly formed square are joined to form another square and the process continues indefinitely. Find the sum of the areas (in m^2) of all the squares.

(*a*) 60

(*b*) 225

(*c*) 450

(*d*) 600

(*e*) 900

23. If $(24)^{4(4+x)} = \frac{(16)^{8-x}}{(81)^{3x-y}}$, then find the value

(*a*) –1

(*b*) 0

(*c*) 1

(*d*) –2

(*e*) 2

24. $x^2 \times y^3 = 147$, where x and y are positive real numbers. Find the minimum value of 6x + 7y.

(*a*) 35

(*b*) 70

(*c*) $5\sqrt{7}$

(*d*) 49

(*e*) 40

25. The number of detergent cakes product by a machine increased by 400 every month. Total number of detergent cakes produced by the machine in 2 years is 153600. What is the number of detergent cakes produced by the machine in 8th month?

(*a*) 4600

(*b*) 4400

(*c*) 5000

(*d*) 5200

(*e*) 4800

26. $(x-2)^2 + (x-1)^2 + x^2 + (x+1)^2 + (x+2)^2 = ?$

(*a*) $5x^2$

(*b*) $5x^2 + 10$

(*c*) $x^2 + 10$

(*d*) $5x^2 + 6x + 10$

(*e*) $5x^2 - 6x + 10$

27. If x is directly proportional to y. If x = 8 then y = 2, what is x when y = 4?

(*a*) 10

(*b*) 16

(*c*) 32

(*d*) 64

(*e*) 128

28. In a class of 12 students, there are three times as many girls as boys. How many girls are there in the class?

(*a*) 3

(*b*) 4

(*c*) 6

(*d*) 8

(*e*) 9

29. The sum of the square of a number and its reciprocal is thrice the difference of the square of the number and its reciprocal. How many different rational value(s) of the number is/are possible?

(*a*) 1

(*b*) 2

(*c*) 3

(*d*) 4

(*e*) 0

30. What is the number that is one-third of two-fifth of three quarters of 760?

(*a*) 114

(*b*) 86

(*c*) 76

(*d*) 38

(*e*) 95

31. Milind bought 3 apples, 4 bananas and 7 guavas together for Rs. 86. Had he bought 13 guavas, 6 apples and 7 bananas together, it would have coasted him Rs. 164. Find the cost of 5 bananas, 4 apples and 9 guavas together.

(*a*) 104

(*b*) 112

(*c*) 125

(*d*) 150

(*e*) 115

32. There are some mangoes with Panchu and Chhakku. If Chhakku were to give 20 mangoes to Panchu, Panchu would have twice as many mangoes as left with Chhakku; whereas if Panchu were to give 40 mangoes to Chhakku, Chhakku would have thrice as many mangoes as left with Panchu. The number of mangoes with Chhakku is

(*a*) 76

(*b*) 60

(*c*) 72

(*d*) 68

(*e*) 80

33. Find the smallest root of the equation

$$2x^3 + 5x^2 + 3x = 0$$

(*a*) 0

(*b*) –1

(*c*) –2

(*d*) $-\frac{3}{2}$

(*e*) 1

34. If $x^2 < x$, then what can be the value of x?

(*a*) 2

(*b*) 1

(*c*) $\frac{23}{5}$

(*d*) $\frac{5}{23}$

(*e*) –2

35. If $-6 \le a \le 5$ and $8 \le b \le 11$, what is the least possible value of $|a - b|$?

(*a*) –17

(*b*) –2

(*c*) 0

(*d*) 3

(*e*) 17

36. If $5x - 7 \ge 3x + 9$ which of the following must be true?

(*a*) $x < 7$

(*b*) $x > 7$

(*c*) $x < 8$

(*d*) $x > 8$

(*e*) $x > 9$

37. If $|x| > 5$, which of the following CANNOT be the value of x?

(*a*) 6

(*b*) 12

(*c*) 1

(*d*) –6

(*e*) –8

38. If 'x' is a real number and $\frac{9}{x-6} > -x$, find the range of 'x'.

(*a*) $x \in [0, 6]$

(*b*) $x \in (9, \infty)$

(*c*) $x \in (6, \infty)$

(*d*) $x \in (3, \infty)$

(*e*) $x \in (4, \infty)$

39. If x and y are two integers such that $-3 < x < 8$ and $-5 < y < 4$, then find the least possible value of $8x - x(2-4y)$.

(a) 0

(b) –70

(c) –36

(d) 70

(e) 36

40. A function is defined as $f(x) = \dfrac{x^2 - 5x + 6}{x^2 + 9x + 20}$.

If $f(x) < 0$, find the range of x.

(a) $(-5,-4)\cup(2,3)$

(b) $[-5,-4]\cup(2,3)$

(c) $[-5,-4]\cup(2,4)$

(d) $[-5,-4]\cup[2,3]$

(e) None of these

41. If $|x-2| = 9$ and $|y+9| = 8$, then find the minimum possible value of xy. [where, x and y are real numbers]

(a) –11

(b) –207

(c) –187

(d) –154

(e) None of these

42. Given that $a < b < c$ and a, b, and c are all positive, consider the following inequalities:

I. $\dfrac{ab}{c} > b + a$

II. $a - b < b - c$

III. $\dfrac{b}{a} < \dfrac{c}{b}$

Which of the following inequalities is always true?

(a) I Only

(b) II Only

(c) I and III

(d) II and III

(e) None of these

43. What is the value of n, if the sum of consecutive odd numbers from 1 to n equals 256?

(a) 17

(b) 27

(c) 29

(d) 31

(e) 33

44. What is the value of the ratio of the larger value of x and the smaller value of x if $x^2 - 3\sqrt{x} + 2 = 0$?

(a) $\dfrac{2}{1}$

(b) $\dfrac{3}{1}$

(c) $\dfrac{4}{1}$

(d) $\dfrac{9}{2}$

(e) $\dfrac{5}{1}$

45. What is the value of x if $-6x^{\frac{1}{4}} + x^{\frac{1}{2}} + 9 = 0$?

(a) 3

(b) 9

(c) 27

(d) 81

(e) 243

46. If [x] is the greatest integer less than or equal to x, what is the vallue of [−2.1] + [2.7] + [6.3]?

(a) 1

(b) 2

(c) 3

(d) 4

(e) 5

47. If $x^2 - xy = -6$, $y^2 + xz = 12$, $z^2 + 26$, and $xy + xz - yz = 5$, what is the value of $x^2 + y^2 + z^2$?

(a) 8

(b) 13

(c) 27

(d) 32

(e) 30

48. A showroom has a few bikes, cars, and buses. The number of bikes and cars is three times the number of buses. There are more cars than bikes or buses. If cars and bikes together have a total of 100 tries and horns, how many bikes are there in the showroom? (Assume that each car has one horn and four tires, and each bike one horn and two tires.)

(a) 5

(b) 8

(c) 10

(d) 14

(e) 17

49. If $a = \sqrt{17} + \sqrt[3]{9} + \sqrt{2}$, which of the following must be true?

(a) $a > 7$

(b) $6 < a < 7$

(c) $|a| < 5$

(d) $a < -7$

(e) $|a| < 6$

50. If $a^3 - a^2 - a + 1 = 0$, how many unique values does a have?

(a) None

(b) One

(c) Two

(d) Three

(e) Four

51. Which of the following inequalities correctly expresses the inequality $\frac{5x-1}{-6} \le \frac{1-2x}{3}$?

(a) $x \ge -1$

(b) $x \ge 1$

(c) $-1 \le x \le 1$

(d) $x \le 0$

(e) $x \ge 0$

52. If $6 < x < 12$ and $y = x + 4$, what is the maximum possible integer value of $(x + y)$?

(a) 22

(b) 24

(c) 26

(d) 27

(e) 28

53. If $f(x) = 4x - 7$, for what values of x, does $4f(x) - 3 = f(2x - 6)$?

(*a*) 0

(*b*) $\frac{1}{2}$

(*c*) 1

(*d*) $\frac{3}{2}$

(*e*) 2

54. If $f(x) = x(x + 3)$, what is the value of $f(f(x))$?

(*a*) $x(x + 3)$

(*b*) $[X(x + 3)]^2$

(*c*) $x(x + 3)(x^2 + 3x + 3)$

(*d*) $x(x + 3)(x + 4x)$

(*e*) $x(x + 3)(x + 6x)$

55. If $\frac{x}{2} - \frac{y}{3} = -4$ and $x - \frac{y}{2} + 7 = 0$, what is the value of xy?

(*a*) –24

(*b*) –12

(*c*) 12

(*d*) 14

(*e*) 24

56. Aunt Mary is giving chocolates to each of her nephews and nieces. She has 40 chocolates. If Jack gets 4 more than Katherine, Bob gets 12 fewer than Susanne, and Susanne gets 4 more than Jack, and Katherine gets 4 more than Bob, how many chocolates does Katherine get?

(*a*) 2

(*b*) 4

(*c*) 6

(*d*) 8

(*e*) 10

57. If $f(a) = f(a^3)$, which of the following must be true?

(*a*) $f(9) = [f(3)]^2$

(*b*) $f(27) = f(3)$

(*c*) $f(3) = -f(81)$

(*d*) $f(1) = 9f(-1)$

(*e*) $f(0) = 1$

58. What is the sum of the series 1 + 2 + 3 ... ... + 199?

(*a*) 10,500

(*b*) 19,200

(*c*) 25,452

(*d*) 19,900

(*e*) 20,100

Answer Key

1. (*e*)
2. (*a*)
3. (*e*)
4. (*d*)
5. (*c*)
6. (*d*)
7. (*e*)
8. (*d*)
9. (*a*)
10. (*e*)
11. (*d*)
12. (*d*)
13. (*e*)
14. (*c*)
15. (*e*)
16. (*b*)
17. (*d*)
18. (*d*)
19. (*e*)
20. (*c*)
21. (*c*)
22. (*c*)
23. (*b*)
24. (*a*)
25. (*a*)
26. (*b*)
27. (*b*)
28. (*e*)
29. (*e*)
30. (*c*)
31. (*b*)
32. (*d*)
33. (*d*)
34. (*d*)
35. (*d*)
36. (*e*)
37. (*c*)
38. (*c*)
39. (*b*)
40. (*a*)
41. (*c*)
42. (*e*)
43. (*d*)
44. (*c*)
45. (*d*)
46. (*e*)
47. (*c*)
48. (*c*)
49. (*a*)
50. (*c*)
51. (*a*)
52. (*d*)
53. (*a*)
54. (*c*)
55. (*a*)
56. (*d*)
57. (*b*)
58. (*d*)

Answer Explanations

1. (e) Minimum possible value of $|x - 4|$ is 0.

Hence, minimum possible value of $|x - 4| + 1$ is $0 + 1 = 1$.

So, the answer is (e).

2. (a) If you picked (e), you fell for a trap.

If $xy^2 < 0$, then $x < 0$

Eliminate answer choices (d) and (e).

If $x = -1$, then $|-x| = |-(-1)| = 1$, which is not more than 5.

If $x = -3$, then $|-x| = |-(-3)| = 3$, which is not more than 5.

If $x = -6$, then $|-x| = |-(-6)| = 6$, which is more than 5.

Hence, the answer is (a).

3. (e) Let $x = 3$ and $y = 2$, then $|x| + |y| = |3| + |2| = 5$ and $|x + y| = |3 + 2| = 5$.

So, $x > 0$ and $y > 0$ doesn't work.

Let $x = 3$ and $y = -2$, then $|x| + |y| = |3| + |-2| = 5$ and $|x + y| = |3 - 2| = 1$.

So, $x > 0$ and $y < 0$ works. Hence, $xy < 0$.

Let $x = -3$ and $y = 2$, then $|x| + |y| = |-3| + |2| = 5$ and $|x + y| = |-3 + 2| = 1$.

So, $x < 0$ and $y > 0$ works.

Let $x = -3$ and $y = -2$, then $|x| + |y| = |-3| + |-2| = 5$ and $|x + y| = |-3 - 2| = 5$.

So, $x < 0$ and $y < 0$ doesn't work. Hence, $xy < 0$.

The answer is (e).

4. (d) If $|x + 3| = 5$, then $x = 2$ or -8

If $|y + 5| = 3$, then $x = -2$ or -8

Hence, there are four possible values of $x + y$.

If $x = 2$ and $y = -2$, then $x + y = 0$

If $x = 2$ and $y = -8$, then $x + y = -6$

If $x = -8$ and $y = -2$, then $x + y = -10$

If $x = -8$ and $y = -8$, then $x + y = -16$

Hence, the answer is (d)

5. (c) If $\frac{a}{x} + \frac{b}{y} < xy$, then $\frac{ax + by}{xy} < xy$

As $xy < 0$, multiplying it will change the sign

$\Rightarrow ax + by > (xy)^2$

The answer is (c)

6. (d) In a arithmetic sequence, each term increases or decreases by a constant difference.

n^{th} term of an AP $= a + (n - 1)d$

Here, $a = 20$, $n = 70$, and $d = 3$

So, 70th term of the AP $= 20 + (70 - 1)3$

$= 20 + 207$

$= 227$

The answer is (d)

7. (e) $S2 = 3S1 - 2 = 3 \times 2 - 2 = 4$

$S3 = 3S2 - 2 = 3 \times 4 - 2 = 10$

$S4 = 3S3 - 2 = 3 \times 10 - 2 = 28$

$S5 = 3S4 - 2 = 3 \times 28 - 2 = 82$

The answer is (e)

8. **(d)** $\dfrac{2^2 < x}{(2^6 - 2^4) < 2^3}$

$\dfrac{2^2 < x}{(2^4 - (2^2 - 1) < 2^3}$

$\dfrac{2^2 < x}{(2^4 \times 3) < 2^3}$

$\dfrac{2^6 < x}{3 < 2^7}$

Only $\dfrac{232}{3}$ is between 2^6 and 2^7

So, the answer is (d).

9. **(a)** $5^k - 5^{k+1} + 5^{k-1} = 5^k \times m$

$5^k(1 - 5 + \dfrac{1}{5}) = 5^k \times m$

$-4 + \dfrac{1}{5} = m$

$m = -\dfrac{19}{5}$

The correct answer is (a).

10. **(e)** The answer is (a).

$10^5 = 10^3 \times 10^2$

(a) $2^{13} = 2^{10} \times 2^3$

$2^{10} > 10^3$, but $2^3 < 10^2$.

(b) $2^{14} = 2^{10} \times 2^4$

$2^{10} > 10^3$, but $2^4 < 10^2$.

(c) $2^{15} = 2^{10} \times 2^5$

$2^{10} > 10^3$, but $2^5 < 10^2$.

(d) $2^{16} = 2^{10} \times 2^6$

$2^{10} > 10^3$, but $2^6 < 10^2$.

(e) $2^{17} = 2^{10} \times 2^7$

$2^{10} > 10^3$, and $2^7 < 10^2$

So, $2^{17} > 10^5$.

Hence, the answer is (e).

11. **(d)** To solve questions asking about the range, it is a good idea to consider all possible values for all the variables.

There could be 4 possibilities.

1. $x = -2$ and $y = -3 \Rightarrow x - y = -2 - (-3) = 1$
2. $x = 4$ and $y = -3 \Rightarrow x - y = 4 - (-3) = 7$
3. $x = -2$ and $y = 2 \Rightarrow x - y = -2 - 2 = -4$
4. $x = 4$ and $y = 2 \Rightarrow x - y = 4 - 2 = 2$

Range means minimum value and maximum value

From the possible values above, the minimum value is–4 and the maximum value is 7

Hence, $-4 < x - y < 7$

So, the answer is (d).

12. **(d)** If $|x + 3| > 5$, then

Case 1 : If $x + 3 > 0$, then

$x + 3 > 5$

$\Rightarrow \quad x > 2 \quad$ ...(i)

Case II : If $x + 3 < 0$, then

$x + 3 < -5$

$x < -8 \quad$ ...(ii)

Hence, the answer is (d)

13. **(e)** If $|x| > 3$, then $x > 3$ or $x < -3$.

Hence, there are infinitely many integers that work for $|x| > 3$.

The answer is (e)

14. **(c)** The ten students scored between 78 and 86. So, $78 < s < 86$.

So, we can eliminate answer choice (a) and (b).

Now, we need to simplify the other two answer choices.

If $|s - 82| < 4$, then

$-4 < s - 82 < 4$

$78 < s < 86$

Hence, the answer is (c).

15. **(e)** If $0 < x < 1$, then $x > x^2 > x^3 > x^4$.......

Hence, $x^7 < x^5$

Eliminate (A) and (C)

As $x^7 < x^5$ and $x^6 < x^4$, then $x^7 + x^6 < x^5 + x^4$ Eliminate (B)

Same way III also works.

The answer is (e).

16. **(b)** Sandy's estimate is p

His estimate is within 10 pens of the actual number

The actual number is n

Hence, $p - 10 \le n \le p + 10$

The answer is (b).

17. **(d)** We need to find value of $(7^{x-1})^2 = (7^{2x-2})^2$

$= 7^{2x} \times 7^{-2} = \dfrac{7^{2x}}{7^2}$ It is given

$7^{4x} = 49$

Taking square root on both the sides.

$7^{2x} = +$ or $-$ 7 (but, -7 is not possible as options are positive)

Hence, value of $\dfrac{7^{2x}}{7^2} = \dfrac{7}{7^2} = \dfrac{1}{7}$

The correct answer is option (d).

18. **(d)** It is given that,

$a_{n+1} = 2 \times a_n$.

when $n = 6$; $a_7 = 2 \times a_6$

Substituting this value in $a_7 - a_6 = 96$

$2 \times a_6 - a_6 = 96$

$a_6 = 96$

As $a_7 = 2 \times a_6 = 2 \times 96 = 192$

The correct answer is option (d).

19. **(e)** $x = 2^{y+1}$,

$x = 2^y \times 2^1$

$2^y = \dfrac{x}{2}$

$4^y = \dfrac{x^2}{4}$

The correct answer is option (e).

20. **(c)** $(32)^{\frac{1}{x}} = 2^{5x}$,

$(2^5)^{\frac{1}{x}} = 2^{5x}$,

$(2^5)^{\frac{5}{x}} = 2^{5x}$,

Hence, $\dfrac{5}{x} = 5x$

$x^2 = 1$

$x = 1$ or -1

The correct answer is option (c).

21. (c) Let the three terms of the arithmetic progression be

(a – d), a and (a + d)

$\therefore \quad a - d + a + a + d = 30$

$\Rightarrow \quad a = 10$

Also, $(a - d) \times a \times (a + d) = 750$

$\Rightarrow \quad 10^2 - d^2 = 75$

$\Rightarrow \quad d = 5 \text{ or } -5$

Hence, $t_5 = 10 + 3 \times 5 \text{ or } 10 + 3 \times (-5)$

$\Rightarrow \quad t_5 = 5 \text{ or } -5$

The correct answer is option (c).

22. (c)

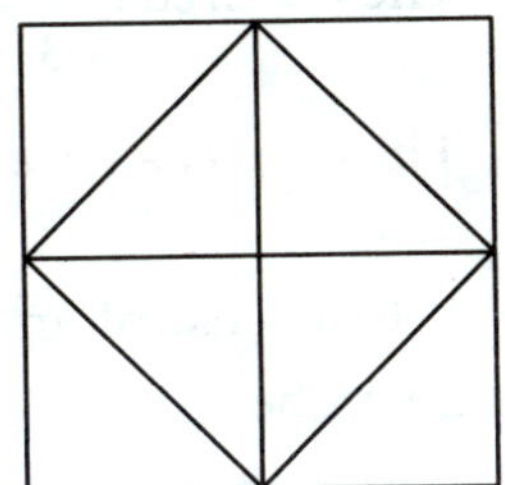

Area of inner square will be half of the immediate outer square.

$$= 15 \times 15\left(1 + \frac{1}{2} + \frac{1}{4} + \frac{1}{8} + ...\right)$$

$$= \frac{225}{1 - \frac{1}{2}} = 450$$

Hence, the required area = 450 m^2.

The correct answer is option (c).

23. (b) $2^{48+12x} \times 3^{16+4x} = 2^{32-4x} \times 3^{4y-12x}$

$\Rightarrow \quad 48 + 12x = 32 - 4x$

$\Rightarrow \quad x = -1$

$\therefore \quad 16 - 4 = 4y + 12$

$\Rightarrow \quad y = 0.$

24. (a) The minimum value of 6x + 7y can be found by using A.M ³ G.M. inequality.

$$\therefore \frac{\frac{6x}{2} + \frac{6x}{2} + \frac{7y}{3} + \frac{7y}{3} + \frac{7y}{3}}{5} \geq \left(\frac{6x}{2} \cdot \frac{6x}{2} \cdot \frac{7y}{3} \cdot \frac{7y}{3} \cdot \frac{7y}{3}\right)^{\frac{1}{5}}$$

$$\Rightarrow 6x + 7y \geq 5\left(3^2 . \frac{7^3}{3^3} x^2 y^3\right)^{\frac{1}{5}}$$

$$\Rightarrow 6x + 7y \geq 5\left(\frac{343}{3} .147\right)^{\frac{1}{5}}$$

$$\Rightarrow 6x + 7y \geq 35$$

Hence, the minimum value of expression is 35.

The correct answer is option (a).

25. (a) The number of detergent cakes product every month

will form an arithmetic progression.

Let 'a' be the number of detergent cakes produced by the machine in the first month.

∴ First term = a and common difference, d = 400

2 years = 24 months

$$S_n = \frac{n}{2}[2a + (n-1)d]$$

$$\Rightarrow \quad 153600 = \frac{24}{2}[2a + (24-1)400]$$

$$\Rightarrow \quad a = 1800$$

$$T_n = a + (n-1)d$$

Where T_n is the number of detergent cakes produced in n^{th} month.

$\therefore \quad T_5 = 4600.$

The correct answer is option (a).

26. (b) $(x-2)^2+(x-1)^2+x^2+(x+1)^2+(x+2)^2$

Using the formulas:

$(a+b)^2 = a^2+b^2+2ab$, and

$(a-b)^2 = a^2+b^2-2ab$

$(x^2-2x-2x+4)+(X^2-1x-1x+1)(x^2)$

$+(x^2+1x+1x+1)$

$+(x^2+2x+2x+4)$

Simplifying:

$(x^2+4)+(x^2+1)+(x^2)+(x^2+1)+(x^2+4)$

Hence, $5x^2+10$

The correct answer is option (b)

27. (b) When x is directly proportional to y, it means that x = ny, where n is a constant

Or In other words, $\frac{x}{y}=n$, where n is a constant.

Hence, $\frac{x_1}{y_1}=\frac{x_2}{y_2}$

Plugging in values:

$\frac{8}{2}=\frac{x_2}{4}$

$x_2 = 16$

The correct answer is option (b).

28. (e) Let, number of boys be m

Number of girls = 3m

Note that we are solving for 3m

Note that we are solving for 3m

3m + m = 12

4m = 3

3m = 9

The correct answer is option (e).

29. (e) Let the number be x.

$\therefore \quad x^2+\frac{1}{x}=3\left(x^2-\frac{1}{x}\right)$

or $\quad x^2+\frac{1}{x}=3\left(\frac{1}{x}-x^2\right)$

$\Rightarrow \quad x^3+1=3x^3-3$ or $x^3+1=3-3x^2$

$\Rightarrow \quad x=\sqrt[3]{2}$ or $x=\sqrt[3]{\frac{1}{2}}$

Hence, no rational value of the number is possible for the given condition.

The correct answer is option (e)

30. (c) The required is $\frac{1}{3}\times\frac{2}{5}\times\frac{3}{4}\times 760 = 76.$

The correct answer is option (c)

31. (b) Let the cost of an apple, a banana and a guava be

Rs. a, Rs. b and Rs. g respectively.

According to given question,

$3a+4b+7g=86$ ...(i)

$6a+7b+13g=164$ ...(ii)

Subtracting (ii) from (i), we get

$3a+3b+6g=78$

or $a+b+2g=26$ ...(iii)

Adding (i) and (iii), we get

$4a+5b+9g=112$

Therefore, cost of 5 bananas, 4 apples and 9 guavas is Rs. 112.

The correct answer is option (b)

32. (d) Let the number of mangoes with Panchu and Chhakku be x and y respectively.

$\therefore \quad x + 20 = 2(y - 20)$

$\Rightarrow \quad x - 2y = -60 \quad ...(i)$

and, $\quad 3(x - 40) = y + 40$

$\Rightarrow \quad 3x - y = 160 \quad ...(ii)$

Solving (i) and (ii), we get, $x = 76$ and $y = 68$.

The correct answer is option (d)

33. (d) $2x^2 + 5x^2 + 3x = x(2x + 3)(x + 1) = 0$

$\Rightarrow x = 0, -1 -\frac{3}{2}$

Hence, the smallest root is $-\frac{3}{2}$.

The correct answer is option (d)

34. (d) $x^2 < x$

$x^2 - x < 0$

$x(x - 1) < 0$

Zeros of the upward parabola (as the coefficient of x^2 is positive) are 0 and 1.

Hence, $x(x - 1)$ is less than 0 when $0 < x < 1$

The correct answer is option (d)

35. (d) Try each of the four extremes for value of $|a - b|$

$|-6 - 8| = 14$

$|-6 - 11| = 17$

$|5 - 8| = 3$

$|5 - 11| = 6$

Hence, $3 \leq |a - b| \leq 17$

The correct answer is option (d)

36. (e) $5x - 7 \geq 3x + 9$

Simplifying :

$2x \geq 16$

$x \geq 8$

(e) is correct

The correct answer is option (e)

37. (c) If $|x| > 5$, then $x > 5$ or $x < -5$

Therefore, x cannot be 1

The correct answer is option (c)

38. (c) $\frac{9}{x-6} > -x$

$\Rightarrow \quad \frac{9}{x-6} + x > 0$

$\Rightarrow \quad \frac{9 + x^2 - 6x}{x-6} > 0$

$\Rightarrow \quad \frac{(x-3)^2}{(x-6)} > 0 \quad ...(i)$

Since numerator is a square, therefore, it is always positive.

To satisfy (i), $x > 6$

The correct answer is option (c)

39. (b) $8x - x(2 - 4y) = 6x + 4xy = 2x(3 + 2y)$

$= 2 \times 7 \times [3 + 2 \times (-4)] = -70.$

The correct answer is option (b)

40. (a) $\frac{x^2 - 5x + 6}{x^2 + 9x + 20} < 0$

$\Rightarrow \quad \frac{(x-2)(x-3)}{(x+4)(x+5)} < 0$

$\Rightarrow \quad \frac{(x-2)(x-3)(x+4)(x+5)}{(x+4)^2(x+5)^2} < 0$

$\Rightarrow \quad (x - 2)(x - 3)(x + 4)(x + 5) < 0$

$\Rightarrow \quad x \in (-5, -4) \cup (2, 3)$

The correct answer is option (a)

41. (c) $|x-2|=9$

$\therefore \quad x-2=\pm 9$

$\therefore \quad x=11 \text{ or } x=-7$

$|x+9|=8$

$\therefore \quad y+9=\pm 8$

$\therefore \quad y=-1 \text{ or } y=-17$

$\therefore$ Minimum possible value of xy

$= 11\times(-17) = -187$

The correct answer is option (c)

42. (e) I. ab > cb + ca. Not true

II. 2b > a + c. Not necessarily true

Take a - 9, b = 3 and c = 1

III. Similarly $b^2 > ac$ is not necessarily true.

The correct answer is option (e)

43. (d) Consecutive odd integers from 1: 1, 3, 5, 7, 9,....

We see that there is a constant gap of '2' between consecutive terms of the above series and hence, it constitutes an arithmetic progression.

The sum of terms is given as:

$$\left[\frac{\text{First term} + \text{Last term}}{2}\right] \times (\text{Number of terms})$$

In the above arithmetic progression, the first term is '1' and the last term is 'n'.

Since we start with '1' (an odd number) and end with 'n', another odd number, the number of terms in the series $= \frac{n-1}{2}+1 = \frac{n+1}{2}$; (for example: for the series: 1, 3, 5, 7, 0; the number of terms $= \frac{9-1}{2}+1 = 5$)

Thus, we have

$$\left[\frac{\text{First term} + \text{Last term}}{2}\right] \times (\text{Number of terms}) = \text{Sum}$$

$$\left(\frac{1+n}{2}\right) \times \left(\frac{n+1}{2}\right) = 256$$

$$\Rightarrow \left(\frac{n+1}{2}\right)^2 = 256$$

$$\Rightarrow \frac{n+1}{2} = 16$$

$$\Rightarrow n = 31$$

The correct answer is Option (d).

44. (c) This is indeed a quadratic equation, though it does not look like one as we do not see a squared term; however, the equation can be solved by applying the concept of quadratic equation.

Say $\sqrt{x} = y$, then the equation becomes $y^2 - 3y + 2 = 0$. It is a quadratic equation. Let's solve this.

$$y^2 - 3y + 2 = 0$$

$$y^2 - 2y - y + 2 = 0$$

$$y(y-2) - 1(y-2) = 0$$

$$(y-2)(y-1) = 0$$

So, $y = 2$ or 1.

$$\sqrt{x} = 2 \text{ or } 1$$

$$x = 4 \text{ or } 1$$

Thus, the ratio of the larger value of x and theh smaller value of $x = \frac{4}{1}$.

The correct answer is option (c)

45. **(d)** This is indeed a quadratic equation, though it does not look like one as we do not see a squared term: however, the equation can be solved by applying the concept of a quadratic equation.

Say $x^{\frac{1}{4}} = y$, then the equation becomes $-6y + y^2 + 9 = 0$. It is a quadratic equation.

Let's solve this.

$$y^2 - 6y + 9 = 0$$
$$y^2 - 2 \times 3 \times y + 3^2 = 0$$
$$(y - 3)^2 = 0$$

So, $y = 3$

$\Rightarrow$ $x^{\frac{1}{4}} = y = 3$

$$x = 3^4 = 81$$

The correct answer is option (d)

46. **(e)** Set of integers less than –2.1 are {–3, –4, –5,...}; among them, the greatest is –3, so, [–2.1] = –3.

Similarly, set of integers less than 2.7 are {2, 1, 0, –1,...}; among them, the greatest is 2, so, [2.7] = 2.

Similarly, set of integers less than 6.3 are {6, 5, 4,...}; among them, the greatest is 6, so, [6.3] = 6.

So, (–2.1] + [2.7] + [6.6] = –3 + 2 + 6 = 5.

The correct answer is option (e)

47. **(c)** Simply add three equations, we get $x^2 - yz + y^2 + xz + z^2 + xy = 32$

$\Rightarrow$ $(x^2 + y^2 + z^2) + (xy + xz - yz) = 32$

Replace the value of $xy + xz - yz = 5$ in the equation, we get

$$(x^2 + y^2 + z^2) + 5 = 32$$

$\Rightarrow$ $x^2 + y^2 + z^2 = 27$

The correct answer is option (c)

48. **(c)** Let x be the number of bikes, y the number of cars, and z the number of buses.

Total numbers of tires and horns

= Number of horns in bikes and cars

+ Number of tires in bikes

+ Number of tires in cars

$\Rightarrow$ $100 = 1 \times (x + y) + 2 \times x + 4 \times y$

$\Rightarrow$ $100 = 3x + 5y$

$\Rightarrow$ $100 - 5y = 3x$

$\Rightarrow$ $5(20 - y) = 3x$

We see that on the left-hand side, we have 5, a prime number; similarly, on the right-hand side, we have another 3, a prime number. For the equality to hold true, (20 – y) must be a multiple of 3, and x must be a multiple of 5. Also, it is given that y > x, picking a few numbers, we get two pairs of probable values of x, and y: (5, 17) and (10, 14).

Also given that $(x + y) = 3z$;

If we plug in x = 5, and y = 17 in $(x + y) = 3z$, we get $5 + 17 = 3z = 22 \Rightarrow z = \frac{22}{3}$, not an integer.

The number of buses must be an integer. This pair of values is not possible. If we plug in x = 10, and y = 14 in $(x + y) = 3z$, we get $10 + 14 = 3z \Rightarrow z = 8$, in integer. This pair of values is possible.

Therefore, only the second pair will work. So, x = number of bikes = 10.

The correct answer is option (c)

49. **(a)** So, we are given that $a = \sqrt{17} + \sqrt[3]{9} + \sqrt{2}$. Note that $\sqrt{17}$ will be slightly greater than 4, which is the square root of the nearest perfect square number (16) to 17. Similarly, the cube root of 9 will be slightly greater than 2, which is the cube root of the nearest perfect cube number (8) to 9. And the square root of 2 will be slightly greater than 1.

Since a is the sum of these three numbers, i.e., (number greater than 4) + (number greater than 2) + (number greater than 1), it must be bigger than 7.

$[a > \{(4 + 2 + 1) = 7\}]$

The correct answer is option (a)

50. (c) We have $a^3 - a^2 - a + 1 = 0$

$\Rightarrow \quad a^2(a - 1) - 1(a - 1) = 0$

$(a - 1)(a^2 - 1) = 0$

$(a - 1)(a - 1)(a + 1) = 0$

$\Rightarrow \quad a = \pm 1$

There are only two possible values of a : 1 and –1. The answer is: "Two." Seeing a cubic equation, one must not jump to a conclusion that the variable will necessarily have three values.

The correct answer is option (c)

51. (a) So, we have $\frac{5x - 1}{-6} \le \frac{1 - 2x}{3}$.

$\frac{5x - 1}{-6} \le \frac{1 - 2x}{3}$ can be written as

$-\frac{5x}{6} + \frac{1}{6} \le \frac{1}{3} - \frac{2x}{3}$

$-\frac{5x}{6} + \frac{2x}{3} \le \frac{1}{3} - \frac{1}{6}$

$\frac{-5x + 4x}{6} \le \frac{2 - 1}{6}$

$\Rightarrow -x \le 1$; cancelling 6 from both the sides and simplifying

$\Rightarrow x \ge -1$; multiplying both sides by –1.

Notes the sign reversal of the inequality; when a negative number is multiplied or divided, the inequality reverses its sign.

The correct answer is option (a)

52. (d) We know that $6 < x < 12$ and $y = x + 4$.

$x + y = x + x + 4 = 2x + 4$; so basically, we have to calculate the maximum possible value of $(2x + 4)$.

$6 < x < 12$ can be written as $12 < 2x < 24$ and then as $(12 + 4) < (2x + 4) < (24 + 4)$

$\Rightarrow 16 < 2x + 4 < 28 \Rightarrow 16 < x + y < 28.$

It is clear that the maximum possible integer value of $(x + y)$ would be 27.

Had you done in the following way, the answer would be wrong.

The greatest possible integer value of $x = 11$, and the greatest possible integer value of $y = 11 + 4 = 15$, then the answer would been $11 + 15 = 26$, which would have been wrong. We must not assume that x and y are integers. They are real numbers.

The correct answer is option (d)

53. (a) Since $f(x) = 4x - 7$, we have $f(2x - 6) = 4 \times (2x - 6) - 7 = 8x - 24 - 7 = 8x - 31$; by replacing x with $2x - 6$ in $f(x) = 4x - 7$.

Now, $4f(x) - 3 = f(2x - 6) \Rightarrow 4 \times (4x - 7) - 3 = 16x - 31$; substituting the values of $f(x) = 4x - 7$.

Again, $4f(x) - 3 = f(2x - 6)$, substituting the value of $4f(x) - 3$ and $f(2x - 6)$

We get $16x - 31 = 8x - 31 \Rightarrow 8x = 0 \Rightarrow x = 0.$

The correct answer is option (a)

54. **(c)** Replacing the value of f(x) for x, we get f(f(x))

= [x (x + 3)] × [{x(x + 3) + 3} = x(x + 3) $(x^2 + 3x + 3)$: The correct answer is C.

Alternate approach

Plug in any value for x; say, x = 2 ⇒ f(x) = x(x + 3)

$\Rightarrow f(x) = 2 \times (2 + 3) = 10.$

Hence, $f(f(x)) = f(x)\,(f(x) + 3) = 10 \times (10 + 3) = 130.$

Now, plug in x = 2 in the options; only option (c) equals 130, correct answer.

The disadvantage of this approach is that you might have to try all the options to match 130. It may consume more time.

The correct answer is option (c)

55. **(a)** So, for the given two linear equations $\frac{x}{2} - \frac{y}{3} = -4$ and $x - \frac{y}{2} + 7 = 0,$ we have to find out the values of x and y to get the value of xy.

Let's name the two equations.

$$\frac{x}{2} - \frac{y}{3} = -4 \qquad ...(1)$$

$$x - \frac{y}{2} + 7 = 0 \qquad ...(ii)$$

Let's multiply equation (2)by $-\frac{1}{2}$ and transposing 7 other side. We get

$$\frac{x}{2} - \frac{y}{3} = -4 \qquad ...(1)$$

$$-\frac{x}{2} + \frac{y}{4} = \frac{7}{2} \qquad ...(2)$$

Adding the two equations, we get

$$\frac{x}{2} - \frac{y}{3} - \frac{x}{2} + \frac{y}{4} = -4 + \frac{7}{2}$$

$$-\frac{y}{3} + \frac{y}{4} = -\frac{1}{2}$$

$$-\frac{y}{12} = -\frac{1}{2}$$

$$y = 6$$

Let's plug-in the value of y in equation (1) to get the value of x.

$$\frac{x}{2} - \frac{6}{3} = -4 \qquad ...(1)$$

$$\frac{x}{2} - 4 + 2 = -2$$

$$x = -4$$

So, $xy = -4 \times 6 = -24$

The correct answer is option (a)

56. **(d)** We use the initial letter of each name to represent the number of chocolates each kid gets.

Therefore,

- J = K + 4
- B = S – 12
- S = J + 4
- K = B + 4

We have four simultaneous equations with four variables. It may be time-consuming to solve this question by the traditional approach. The optimum approach is to plug in the values from the options. But which option should you try first? If you start plugging in from options (a), (b), (c) onwards, then you may lose more time in case the answer is (d) or (e).

The best way to plug-in is to try option (b), and then (d). It is called the B/D plug-in approach for problem solving questions. Under this approach, the values in the options must be arranged in ascending order from options (a) through (e).

Option (b) : If K = 4; J = 8' S = 12; B = 0. This option cannot be the answer as total number of candies, 4 + 8 + 12 + 0 = 24, not equal to 40. As 24 < 40, it means that the answer must be greater than 4, hence answer must not be option A or B. Let's try option (d).

Option (d) : If K = 8; J = 12; S = 16; B = 4. This option is the correct answer as the total number of chocolates, 8 + 12 + 16 + 4 = 40 = actual total number of chocolates.

The advantage with B/D plugging in approach is that if the value in Option (d) had been less than 40, then Option (e) must be the correct answer. We must not calculate the value for option (e); whereas, if the value in Option (d) had been more than 40, then option (c) must be the correct answer. So, merely by trying with only two option values (b & d), we can cover all the five options.

The correct answer is option (d)

57. (b) Since we only know one property of the function but not the actual function, the absolute value can't be evaluated.

Let us see each option one by one. Note this is a must be true question; thus, the correct option must be true for all values.

(a) $f(9) = f(9^3) = f(729)$;

$f(3) = f(3^3) = f(27)$;

$[f(3)]^2 = [f(27)]^2$

f(729) may or may not be equal to $[f(27)]^2$.

Hence, option (a) is discarded.

(b) $f(27) = f(3)$

$f(3) = f(3^3) = f(27)$

Hence, the correct answer is option (b).

(c) $f(3) = -f(81)$

We know that f(3) is f(27), but f(3) may or may not be equal to – f(81).

Hence, option (c) is discarded.

(d) $f(1) = 9f(-1)$

f(1) may or may not be equal to 9f(–1).

Hence, option (d) is discarded.

(e) f(0) = 1 may or may not be true as we don't know the absolute value of the function.

Hence, option (e) is discarded.

58. (d) Given numbers are in arithmetic series as the difference between the numbers is constant (=1). The sum of the arithmetic series is given by $\frac{n}{2} \times$ (first term + last term)

Total number of terms = 199

Sum of arithmetic series

$$\frac{199}{2} \times (199 + 1) = 19{,}900$$

Data Sufficiency

1. Is $|x| > |y|$?

   1. $x > y$
   2. $y < 0$

   (*a*) Statement (1) ALONE is sufficient but statement (2) ALONE is not sufficient.

   (*b*) Statement (2) ALONE is sufficient but statement (1) ALONE is not sufficient.

   (*c*) BOTH statements TOGETHER are sufficient, but NEITHER statement ALONE is sufficient.

   (*d*) EACH statement ALONE is sufficient.

   (*e*) Statements (1) and (2) TOGETHER are not sufficient.

2. What is the value of x?

   1. $4|x - 4| = 16$
   2. x is a non-negative integer.

   (*a*) Statement (1) ALONE is sufficient but statement (2) ALONE is not sufficient.

   (*b*) Statement (2) ALONE is sufficient but statement (1) ALONE is not sufficient.

   (*c*) BOTH statements TOGETHER are sufficient, but NEITHER statement ALONE is sufficient.

   (*d*) EACH statement ALONE is sufficient.

   (*e*) Statements (1) and (2) TOGETHER are not sufficient.

3. Does $x = 2$?

   1. x is an integer.
   2. $-x|x| \geq 4$

   (*a*) Statement (1) ALONE is sufficient but statement (2) ALONE is not sufficient.

   (*b*) Statement (2) ALONE is sufficient but statement (1) ALONE is not sufficient.

   (*c*) BOTH statements TOGETHER are sufficient, but NEITHER statement ALONE is sufficient.

   (*d*) EACH statement ALONE is sufficient.

   (*e*) Statements (1) and (2) TOGETHER are not sufficient.

4. Is $x > y$?

   1. $|x| > |y|$
   2. $x + y > 0$

   (*a*) Statement (1) ALONE is sufficient but statement (2) ALONE is not sufficient.

   (*b*) Statement (2) ALONE is sufficient but statement (1) ALONE is not sufficient.

   (*c*) BOTH statements TOGETHER are sufficient, but NEITHER statement ALONE is sufficient.

   (*d*) EACH statement ALONE is sufficient.

   (*e*) Statements (1) and (2) TOGETHER are not sufficient.

5. Is $|x| > |y|$?

   1. $x + y > 0$
   2. $x > y$

   (*a*) Statement (1) ALONE is sufficient but statement (2) ALONE is not sufficient.

   (*b*) Statement (2) ALONE is sufficient but statement (1) ALONE is not sufficient.

   (*c*) BOTH statements TOGETHER are sufficient, but NEITHER statement ALONE is sufficient.

   (*d*) EACH statement ALONE is sufficient.

   (*e*) Statements (1) and (2) TOGETHER are not sufficient.

6. Is $x > y$?

   1. $|x| + |y| > |x + y|$
   2. $|x| > |y|$

(*a*) Statement (1) ALONE is sufficient but statement (2) ALONE is not sufficient.

(*b*) Statement (2) ALONE is sufficient but statement (1) ALONE is not sufficient.

(*c*) BOTH statements TOGETHER are sufficient, but NEITHER statement ALONE is sufficient.

(*d*) EACH statement ALONE is sufficient.

(*e*) Statements (1) and (2) TOGETHER are not sufficient.

7. Is $x > 0$?

1. $|x|y > x|y|$

2. $xy < 0$

(*a*) Statement (1) ALONE is sufficient but statement (2) ALONE is not sufficient.

(*b*) Statement (2) ALONE is sufficient but statement (1) ALONE is not sufficient.

(*c*) BOTH statements TOGETHER are sufficient, but NEITHER statement ALONE is sufficient.

(*d*) EACH statement ALONE is sufficient.

(*e*) Statements (1) and (2) TOGETHER are not sufficient.

8. If $x > |y| > z$, then which of the following must be true?

I. $x + y > 0$

II. $y + z > 0$

III. $x + y > |y| + z$

(*a*) None of the above

(*b*) I only

(*c*) I and II only

(*d*) III only

(*e*) I, II, and III

9. What is the value of x?

1. $x = -|x|$

2. $x^2 = 9$

(*a*) Statement (1) ALONE is sufficient but statement (2) ALONE is not sufficient.

(*b*) Statement (2) ALONE is sufficient but statement (1) ALONE is not sufficient.

(*c*) BOTH statements TOGETHER are sufficient, but NEITHER statement ALONE is sufficient.

(*d*) EACH statement ALONE is sufficient.

(*e*) Statements (1) and (2) TOGETHER are not sufficient.

10. If $a + b + c > 0$, is $a > 1$?

1. $a > b + c + 1$

2. $b + c + 1 < 0$

(*a*) Statement (1) ALONE is sufficient but statement (2) ALONE is not sufficient.

(*b*) Statement (2) ALONE is sufficient but statement (1) ALONE is not sufficient.

(*c*) BOTH statements TOGETHER are sufficient, but NEITHER statement ALONE is sufficient.

(*d*) EACH statement ALONE is sufficient.

(*e*) Statements (1) and (2) TOGETHER are not sufficient.

11. Is $|x - 50| < |70 - x|$?

1. $70 - x > x - 50$

2. $x < 60$

(*a*) Statement (1) ALONE is sufficient but statement (2) ALONE is not sufficient.

(*b*) Statement (2) ALONE is sufficient but statement (1) ALONE is not sufficient.

(*c*) BOTH statements TOGETHER are sufficient, but NEITHER statement ALONE is sufficient.

(*d*) EACH statement ALONE is sufficient.

(*e*) Statements (1) and (2) TOGETHER are not sufficient.

12. How many cards does Adam have currently?

1. If Adam receives three more cards from his friend then he will have at least 20 cards.
2. If Adam gives three of his cards to a friend, then Adam will have fewer than 15 cards.

(*a*) Statement (1) ALONE is sufficient but statement (2) ALONE is not sufficient.

(*b*) Statement (2) ALONE is sufficient but statement (1) ALONE is not sufficient.

(*c*) BOTH statements TOGETHER are sufficient, but NEITHER statement ALONE is sufficient.

(*d*) EACH statement ALONE is sufficient.

(*e*) Statements (1) and (2) TOGETHER are not sufficient.

13. Roger has 25 pens and 30 erasers. What is the total cost of the 25 pens and 30 erasers?

1. The price of each pen is 3 times the cost of each eraser.
2. The total cost of one pen and 2 erasers in $5.

(*a*) Statement (1) ALONE is sufficient but statement (2) ALONE is not sufficient.

(*b*) Statement (2) ALONE is sufficient but statement (1) ALONE is not sufficient.

(*c*) BOTH statements TOGETHER are sufficient, but NEITHER statement ALONE is sufficient.

(*d*) EACH statement ALONE is sufficient.

(*e*) Statements (1) and (2) TOGETHER are not sufficient.

14. If $3x + 5y = 17$, what is the value of x?

1. y is a positive integer
2. $x = 4y$

(*a*) Statement (1) ALONE is sufficient but statement (2) ALONE is not sufficient.

(*b*) Statement (2) ALONE is sufficient but statement (1) ALONE is not sufficient.

(*c*) BOTH statements TOGETHER are sufficient, but NEITHER statement ALONE is sufficient.

(*d*) EACH statement ALONE is sufficient.

(*e*) Statements (1) and (2) TOGETHER are not sufficient.

15. In a sequence of terms $a_n = 3 \times a_{n-1}$, where, n is an integer greater than 1, what is the value of a_4?

1. $a_1 = 3$
2. $\frac{a_2}{a_n} = 3^{10}$

(*a*) Statement (1) ALONE is sufficient but statement (2) ALONE is not sufficient.

(*b*) Statement (2) ALONE is sufficient but statement (1) ALONE is not sufficient.

(*c*) BOTH statements TOGETHER are sufficient, but NEITHER statement ALONE is sufficient.

(*d*) EACH statement ALONE is sufficient.

(*e*) Statements (1) and (2) TOGETHER are not sufficient.

16. What is value of x?

1. $2x - y = 5x + 2y$
2. $2(x - y) = 8 - 2y$

(*a*) Statement (1) ALONE is sufficient but statement (2) ALONE is not sufficient.

(*b*) Statement (2) ALONE is sufficient but statement (1) ALONE is not sufficient.

(*c*) BOTH statements TOGETHER are sufficient, but NEITHER statement ALONE is sufficient.

(*d*) EACH statement ALONE is sufficient.

(*e*) Statements (1) and (2) TOGETHER are not sufficient.

17. What is the value of x?

1. $2x + 5y = 12$
2. $15y = 26 - 6x$

(*a*) Statement (1) ALONE is sufficient but statement (2) ALONE is not sufficient.

(*b*) Statement (2) ALONE is sufficient but statement (1) ALONE is not sufficient.

(*c*) BOTH statements TOGETHER are sufficient, but NEITHER statement ALONE is sufficient.

(*d*) EACH statement ALONE is sufficient.

(*e*) Statements (1) and (2) TOGETHER are not sufficient.

18. If $0 < xy < xz$, is $x < 0$?

1. $z < 0$
2. $y > z$

(*a*) Statement (1) ALONE is sufficient but statement (2) ALONE is not sufficient.

(*b*) Statement (2) ALONE is sufficient but statement (1) ALONE is not sufficient.

(*c*) BOTH statements TOGETHER are sufficient, but NEITHER statement ALONE is sufficient.

(*d*) EACH statement ALONE is sufficient.

(*e*) Statements (1) and (2) TOGETHER are not sufficient.

19. Is $x \neq 1$?

1. $(3x - 2)^2 = x^2$
2. $(3x - 2)^2 = x$

(*a*) Statement (1) ALONE is sufficient but statement (2) ALONE is not sufficient.

(*b*) Statement (2) ALONE is sufficient but statement (1) ALONE is not sufficient.

(*c*) BOTH statements TOGETHER are sufficient, but NEITHER statement ALONE is sufficient.

(*d*) EACH statement ALONE is sufficient.

(*e*) Statements (1) and (2) TOGETHER are not sufficient.

20. If x, y and z are positive, and $x^2 + z^2 = 313$, what is the value of $(y - x - z)$?

1. $y^2 + z^2 = 244$
2. $x^2 + y^2 = 269$

(*a*) Statement (1) ALONE is sufficient but statement (2) ALONE is not sufficient.

(*b*) Statement (2) ALONE is sufficient but statement (1) ALONE is not sufficient.

(*c*) BOTH statements TOGETHER are sufficient, but NEITHER statement ALONE is sufficient.

(*d*) EACH statement ALONE is sufficient.

(*e*) Statements (1) and (2) TOGETHER are not sufficient.

21. What is the value of a?

1. $2a + 3b = 12$
2. $8a + 12b = 48$

(*a*) Statement (1) ALONE is sufficient but statement (2) ALONE is not sufficient.

(*b*) Statement (2) ALONE is sufficient but statement (1) ALONE is not sufficient.

(*c*) BOTH statements TOGETHER are sufficient, but NEITHER statement ALONE is sufficient.

(*d*) EACH statement ALONE is sufficient.

(*e*) Statements (1) and (2) TOGETHER are not sufficient.

22. If $a > 1$, and $b > 1$, is $a > b$?

1. $\sqrt{a} > b$
2. $\sqrt{b} < a$

(*a*) Statement (1) ALONE is sufficient but statement (2) ALONE is not sufficient.

(*b*) Statement (2) ALONE is sufficient but statement (1) ALONE is not sufficient.

(*c*) BOTH statements TOGETHER are sufficient, but NEITHER statement ALONE is sufficient.

(*d*) EACH statement ALONE is sufficient.

(*e*) Statements (1) and (2) TOGETHER are not sufficient.

23. If x is a two-digit number; where a is tens digit and b is units digit, what is the value of x?

1. $a + b = 10$
2. $a - b = 4$

(*a*) Statement (1) ALONE is sufficient but statement (2) ALONE is not sufficient.

(*b*) Statement (2) ALONE is sufficient but statement (1) ALONE is not sufficient.

(*c*) BOTH statements TOGETHER are sufficient, but NEITHER statement ALONE is sufficient.

(*d*) EACH statement ALONE is sufficient.

(*e*) Statements (1) and (2) TOGETHER are not sufficient.

24. If $x = 100^{\frac{b}{a}}$, where $a\ ^1\ 0$, is x an integer?

1. $\frac{b^6}{a^6}$ is an integer
2. $a - 2b = 0$

(*a*) Statement (1) ALONE is sufficient but statement (2) ALONE is not sufficient.

(*b*) Statement (2) ALONE is sufficient but statement (1) ALONE is not sufficient.

(*c*) BOTH statements TOGETHER are sufficient, but NEITHER statement ALONE is sufficient.

(*d*) EACH statement ALONE is sufficient.

(*e*) Statements (1) and (2) TOGETHER are not sufficient.

25. Is $a^5 - b^2 - c^2 < 0$?

1. $ab > 0$
2. $bc > 0$

(*a*) Statement (1) ALONE is sufficient but statement (2) ALONE is not sufficient.

(*b*) Statement (2) ALONE is sufficient but statement (1) ALONE is not sufficient.

(*c*) BOTH statements TOGETHER are sufficient, but NEITHER statement ALONE is sufficient.

(*d*) EACH statement ALONE is sufficient.

(*e*) Statements (1) and (2) TOGETHER are not sufficient.

26. If $a^2 - ab = a^2 - b^2$ what is the value of c such that $a \neq b$?

1. $c = 3 - a$
2. $b = c^3$

(*a*) Statement (1) ALONE is sufficient but statement (2) ALONE is not sufficient.

(*b*) Statement (2) ALONE is sufficient but statement (1) ALONE is not sufficient.

(*c*) BOTH statements TOGETHER are sufficient, but NEITHER statement ALONE is sufficient.

(*d*) EACH statement ALONE is sufficient.

(*e*) Statements (1) and (2) TOGETHER are not sufficient.

27. What is the value of positive integer x?

1. x^3 is a perfect square
2. $x^2 = x$

(*a*) Statement (1) ALONE is sufficient but statement (2) ALONE is not sufficient.

(*b*) Statement (2) ALONE is sufficient but statement (1) ALONE is not sufficient.

(*c*) BOTH statements TOGETHER are sufficient, but NEITHER statement ALONE is sufficient.

(*d*) EACH statement ALONE is sufficient.

(*e*) Statements (1) and (2) TOGETHER are not sufficient.

28. Is $a > b$?

1. $a < b^4$
2. a and b are negative integers.

(*a*) Statement (1) ALONE is sufficient but statement (2) ALONE is not sufficient.

(*b*) Statement (2) ALONE is sufficient but statement (1) ALONE is not sufficient.

(*c*) BOTH statements TOGETHER are sufficient, but NEITHER statement ALONE is sufficient.

(*d*) EACH statement ALONE is sufficient.

(*e*) Statements (1) and (2) TOGETHER are not sufficient.

29. What is the value of the expression $12x^2 + 18y^2$?

1. $x = 3$
2. $3y^2 + 2x^2 = 14$

(*a*) Statement (1) ALONE is sufficient but statement (2) ALONE is not sufficient.

(*b*) Statement (2) ALONE is sufficient but statement (1) ALONE is not sufficient.

(*c*) BOTH statements TOGETHER are sufficient, but NEITHER statement ALONE is sufficient.

(*d*) EACH statement ALONE is sufficient.

(*e*) Statements (1) and (2) TOGETHER are not sufficient.

30. John is 10 years younger than his cousin. How old will John be in 20 years?

1. Five years ago, John's cousin was twice as old as John.
2. If John's cousin were born 5 years earlier, she would, at present, be twice as old as John.

(*a*) Statement (1) ALONE is sufficient but statement (2) ALONE is not sufficient.

(*b*) Statement (2) ALONE is sufficient but statement (1) ALONE is not sufficient.

(*c*) BOTH statements TOGETHER are sufficient, but NEITHER statement ALONE is sufficient.

(*d*) EACH statement ALONE is sufficient.

(*e*) Statements (1) and (2) TOGETHER are not sufficient.

31. What is the value of a?

1. $a^2 - a - 6 = 0$
2. $(a + 5)$ is a prime number

(*a*) Statement (1) ALONE is sufficient but statement (2) ALONE is not sufficient.

(*b*) Statement (2) ALONE is sufficient but statement (1) ALONE is not sufficient.

(*c*) BOTH statements TOGETHER are sufficient, but NEITHER statement ALONE is sufficient.

(*d*) EACH statement ALONE is sufficient.

(*e*) Statements (1) and (2) TOGETHER are not sufficient.

32. If $a + 3|b| = 50$, what is the value b?

1. $3|b| = a - 20$
2. $|b| + \frac{a}{3} = \frac{50}{3}$

(*a*) Statement (1) ALONE is sufficient but statement (2) ALONE is not sufficient.

(*b*) Statement (2) ALONE is sufficient but statement (1) ALONE is not sufficient.

(*c*) BOTH statements TOGETHER are sufficient, but NEITHER statement ALONE is sufficient.

(*d*) EACH statement ALONE is sufficient.

(*e*) Statements (1) and (2) TOGETHER are not sufficient.

33. What is the value of a^3?

1. $a^2 = 3a + 4$
2. $a^3 - 4a^2 = 4 - a$

(*a*) Statement (1) ALONE is sufficient but statement (2) ALONE is not sufficient.

(*b*) Statement (2) ALONE is sufficient but statement (1) ALONE is not sufficient.

(*c*) BOTH statements TOGETHER are sufficient, but NEITHER statement ALONE is sufficient.

(*d*) EACH statement ALONE is sufficient.

(*e*) Statements (1) and (2) TOGETHER are not sufficient.

34. For all integers x, the function f is defined by $f(x) = (c)^{\frac{6}{x}}$, where c is a constant. What is the value of f(1)?

1. $f(2) = 125$
2. $f(3) = 25$

(*a*) Statement (1) ALONE is sufficient but statement (2) ALONE is not sufficient.

(*b*) Statement (2) ALONE is sufficient but statement (1) ALONE is not sufficient.

(*c*) BOTH statements TOGETHER are sufficient, but NEITHER statement ALONE is sufficient.

(*d*) EACH statement ALONE is sufficient.

(*e*) Statements (1) and (2) TOGETHER are not sufficient.

35. Is $x < 0$?

1. $-x = |-x|$
2. $x^2 = 16$

(*a*) Statement (1) ALONE is sufficient but statement (2) ALONE is not sufficient.

(*b*) Statement (2) ALONE is sufficient but statement (1) ALONE is not sufficient.

(*c*) BOTH statements TOGETHER are sufficient, but NEITHER statement ALONE is sufficient.

(*d*) EACH statement ALONE is sufficient.

(*e*) Statements (1) and (2) TOGETHER are not sufficient.

36. Is $x > y^3z$?

1. $wx > yz$
2. $y = 1$

(*a*) Statement (1) ALONE is sufficient but statement (2) ALONE is not sufficient.

(*b*) Statement (2) ALONE is sufficient but statement (1) ALONE is not sufficient.

(*c*) BOTH statements TOGETHER are sufficient, but NEITHER statement ALONE is sufficient.

(*d*) EACH statement ALONE is sufficient.

(*e*) Statements (1) and (2) TOGETHER are not sufficient.

Answer Key

1. (*e*)	**10.** (*b*)	**19.** (*c*)	**28.** (*e*)
2. (*e*)	**11.** (*d*)	**20.** (*c*)	**29.** (*b*)
3. (*a*)	**12.** (*e*)	**21.** (*e*)	**30.** (d)
4. (*c*)	**13.** (*e*)	**22.** (*a*)	**31.** (*c*)
5. (*c*)	**14.** (*b*)	**23.** (*c*)	**32.** (*e*)
6. (*e*)	**15.** (*a*)	**24.** (a)	**33.** (*b*)
7. (*a*)	**16.** (*b*)	**25.** (*e*)	**34.** (*b*)
8. (*b*)	**17.** (*e*)	**26.** (*b*)	**35.** (*c*)
9. (*c*)	**18.** (*d*)	**27.** (*b*)	**36.** (*c*)

Answer Explanations

1. (e) **Considering statement (1) alone :**

Let $x = 3$ and $y = 2$

So, $|x| = 3$ and $|y| = 2$

Is $|x| > |y|$? Yes

Let $x = -2$ and $y = -3$

So, $|x| = 2$ and $|y| = 3$

Is $|x| > |y|$? No

INSUFFICIENT

Eliminate AD.

Considering statement (2) alone :

Let $x = 3$ and $y = -2$

So, $|x| = 3$ and $|y| = 2$

Is $|x| > |y|$? Yes

Let $x = -2$ and $y = -3$

So, $|x| = 2$ and $|y| = 3$

Is $|x| > |y|$? No

INSUFFICIENT

Eliminate B.

Considering both statement together:

Let $x = 3$ and $y = -2$

So, $|x| = 3$ and $|y| = 2$

Is $|x| > |y|$? Yes

Let $x = -2$ and $y = -3$

So, $|x| = 2$ and $|y| = 3$

Is $|x| > |y|$? No

INSUFFICIENT

The answer is (e).

2. (e) **Considering statement (1) alone :**

If $4|x - 4| = 16$, then $|x - 4| = 4$

So, either $x - 4 = 4$ or $x - 4 = -4$

$\Rightarrow \quad x = 8$ of $x = 0$

INSUFFICIENT

Eliminate AD.

Considering statement (2) alone :

If x is non-negative integer, x can take any value greater than equal to 0.

Considering both the statements together:

From statement (1), we get that $x = 0$ or 8.

Statement (2) allows both the values.

INSUFFICIENT

The answer is (e).

3. (a) **Considering statement (1) alone:**

Just knowing that x is an integer doesn't help.

INSUFFICIENT

Eliminate AD.

Considering statement (2) alone :

If $-x|x| \geq 4$, then $x < 0$

If $x < 0$, then $x \neq 2$.

SUFFICIENT The answer is (b).

4. (c) **Considering statement (1) alone:**

Let $x = 3$ and $y = 2$,

then $|x| > |y|$

Is $x > y$? YES

Let $x = -4$ and $y = -3$,

then $|x| > |y|$

Is $x > y$? NO

INSUFFICIENT

Eliminate AD.

Considering statement (2) alone :

If $x + y > 0$, then $x > -y$

Let $x = 2$ and $y = -1$,

then $x > -y$

Is $x > y$? YES

Let $x = 3$ and $y = 4$, then $x > -y$

Is $x > y$? NO

INSUFFICIENT

Eliminate B

Considering both statements together :

Let $x = 3$ and $y = 2$,

then $|x| > |y|$ and also $x > -y$

Is $x > y$? YES

Let $x = 3$ and $y = -2$, then $|x| > |y|$ and also $x > -y$

Is $x > y$? YES

SUFFICIENT

The answer is (c).

5. (c) **Considering statement (1) alone :**

If $x = 2$ and $y = 1$, then $x + y > 0$

Is $|x| > |y|$? YES

If $x = 2$ and $y = 3$, then $x + y > 0$

Is $|x| > |y|$? NO

INSUFFICIENT

Eliminate AD.

Considering statement (2) alone :

If $x = 2$ and $y = 1$, then $x > y$

Is $|x| > |y|$? YES

If $x = 2$ and $y = -3$,

then $x > y$ Is $|x| > |y|$? NO

INSUFFICIENT

Eliminate B.

Considering both statements together:

If $x = 2$ and $y = 1$, then $x + y > 0$ and $x > y$ Is $|x| > |y|$? YES

If $x = 2$ and $y = -1$, then $x + y > 0$ and $x > y$

Is $|x| > |y|$? YES

SUFFICIENT

The answer is (c).

6. (e) **Considering statement (1) alone :**

For $|x| + |y| > |x + y|$, at least one x or y must be negative.

If $x = 3$ and $y = -2$, then $|x| + |y| > |x + y|$

Is $x > y$? YES If $x = -3$ and $y = 2$, then $|x| + |y| > |x + y|$

Is $x > y$? NO

INSUFFICIENT

Eliminate AD.

Considering statement (2) alone :

If $x = 3$ and $y = -2$, then $|x| > |y|$

Is $x > y$? YES If $x = -3$ and $y = 2$, then $|x| > |y|$

Is $x > y$? NO

INSUFFICIENT

Eliminate B.

Considering both statements together :

If $x = 3$ and $y = -2$, then $|x| > |y|$ and $|x| + |y| > |x + y|$

Is $x > y$? YES If $x = -3$ and $y = 2$, then $|x| > |y|$ and $|x| + |y| > |x + y|$

Is $x > y$? NO

INSUFFICIENT

The answer is (e).

7. (a) **Considering statement (1) alone :**

If $x > 0$ and $y > 0$, then $|x|y = x|y|$.

So, both can't be positive.

If $x < 0$ and $y < 0$, then $|x|y = x|y|$.

So, both can't be negative.

If $x < 0$ and $y > 0$, then $|x|y > x|y|$. Is $x > 0$? NO

If $x > 0$ and $y < 0$, then $|x|y < x|y|$.

These values are not allowed.

SUFFICIENT.

Eliminate BCE.

Considering statement (2) alone :

If $xy < 0$, then either can be negative.

INSUFFICIENT

The answer is (a).

8. (b) If $x = 4$, $y = 3$, and $z = 2$, then $x + y > 0$, $y + z > 0$, and $x + y > |y| + z$.

If $x = 4$, $y = -3$, and $z = 2$, then $x + y > 0$, $y + z < 0$, and $x + y < |y| + z$.

Hence, the answer is (b).

9. (c) **Considering statement (1) alone :**

If $x -|x|$, then x can take any negative value.

INSUFFICIENT Eliminate AD

Considering statement (2) alone :

If $x^2 = 9$, then $x = 3$ or -3

INSUFFICIENT

Eliminate B

Considering both statements together:

Only $x = -3$ works for both the statements.

SUFFICIENT

The answer is (c).

10. (b) If $a + b + c > 0$, then $b + c > -a$

Considering statement (1) alone :

If $a > b + c + 1$, then $a > -a + 1$

So, $2a > 1$

Hence, $a > 0.5$

INSUFFICIENT Eliminate AD

Considering statement (2) alone :

If $b + c + 1 < 0$, then $b + c < -1$

If $a + (b + c) > 0$, then $a > 1$

SUFFICIENT The answer is (b).

11. (d) If $x = 60$, then $|x - 50| = |70 - x|$

If $x > 60$, then $|x - 50| > |70 - x|$

If $x < 60$, then $|x - 50| < |70 - x|$

Considering statement (1) alone :

If $70 - x > x - 50$, then $120 > 2x$

$\Rightarrow x < 60$

SUFFICIENT

Eliminate BCE

Considering statement (2) alone :

If $x < 60$, then $|x - 50| < |70 - x|$

SUFFICIENT

The answer is (d).

12. (e) Let the number of cards that Adam have is c.

Considering statement (1) alone :

$c + 3 = 20$

$\Rightarrow c = 17$

INSUFFICIENT

Eliminate AD

Considering statement (2) alone :

$c - 3 \leq 20$

$\Rightarrow c \leq 18$

INSUFFICIENT

Eliminate B

Considering both the statements together :

$17 \leq c \leq 18$

Hence, c can be 17 or 18.

INSUFFICIENT

The answer is (e).

13. (e) Let the cost of each pen be p and the cost of each eraser be *e*.

Considering statement (1) alone :

$p = 3e$

INSUFFICIENT

Eliminate AD

Considering statement (2) alone :

$p + 2e = 5$

INSUFFICIENT

Eliminate B

Considering both the statement together

$p = 3e$ and $p + 2e = 5$

$\Rightarrow 3e + 2e = 5$

$\Rightarrow e = 1$

If $e = 1$, then $p = 3$

INSUFFICIENT

The answer is (e).

14. (b) **Considering statement (1) alone :**

No information about x

INSUFFICIENT

Eliminate AD

Considering statement (2) alone :

If $x = 4y$ and $3x + 5y = 17$, then $3(4) + 5y = 17$

$\Rightarrow y = 1$

If $y = 1$, then $x = 4$

SUFFICIENT

The answer is (b).

15. (a) $a_1 = 3$

The sequence is : 3, 9, 27, 81, ... so the fourth term is 81.

Sufficient. Eliminate B/C/E

Considering statement 2 alone: $\frac{a_2}{a_n} = 3^{10}$

Since we don't know how many terms are there are there in the sequence, value of n cannot be calculated.

Insufficient.

The correct answer is option (a)

16. (b) **Considering statement 1 alone :**

$2x - y = 5x + 2y$

$-3x = 3y$

$x = -y$

Value of x cannot be calculated. Insufficient

Eliminate A/D.

Considering statement 2 alone :

$2(x - y) = 8 - 2y$

$2x - 2y = 8 - 2y$

$2x = 8$

$x = 4$

Sufficient

17. (e) **Considering statement 1 alone :**

$2x + 5y = 12$

As x and y can have infinite values. Statement (1) is insufficient

Eliminate A and D.

Considering statement 2 alone :

$4y = 12 - 6x$

As x and y can have infinite values, Statement (2) is insufficient

Eliminate B.

Considering statement 1 and 2 together:

Now the equations $2x + 5y = 12$

and $6x + 15y = 26$ are equivalent equations.

If we multiply both sides of the equation $3x + 2y = 6$ of Statement (1) by 3, we will obtain the equation $6x + 4y = 12$. Therefore, there is only one equation given.

Hence, we cannot determine value of x. Insufficient

The correct answer is option (e).

18. (d) Since xy is positive, means that signs of both x and y are the same. Similarly, zx is positive means that signs of both x and y are the same.

Considering statement 1 alone :

As z is negative, therefore, x is negative. So, $x < 0$

Sufficient

Eliminate B/C/E.

Considering statement 2 alone :

It is given that $y > z$ and we know from question stem that $xy < xz$.

When both sides of the inequality $y > z$ is multiplied by x, it reverses sign only when x is negative.

So, $x < 0$

Sufficient

The correct answer is option (d).

19. (c) **Considering Statement 1 alone :**

$(3x - 2)^2 = x^2$

$\Rightarrow (3x - 2)^2 - x^2 = 0$

$\Rightarrow \{(3x - 2) - x\}\ \{(3x - 2) + x\} = 0$

$\Rightarrow (2x - 2)\ (4x - 2) = 0$

$\Rightarrow \quad x = 1 \text{ or } \frac{1}{2}$

Thus, we obtain two values of x:1 and $\frac{1}{2}$.

Thus, Statement 1 is not sufficient to answer the question since the answer may be Yes or No.

The correct answer would be among B/C/E.

Considering Statement 2 alone :

$(3x - 2)^2 = x$

$\Rightarrow \quad 9x^2 - 12x + 4 = x$

$\Rightarrow \quad 9x^2 - 13x + 4 = 0$

$\Rightarrow \quad 9x^2 - 9x - 4x + 4 = 0$

$\Rightarrow \quad 9x(x - 1) - 4(x - 1) = 0$

$\Rightarrow \quad (9x - 4)(x - 1) = 0$

$\Rightarrow \quad x = \frac{4}{9}$ or 1.

Thus, we obtain two values of x : 1 or $\frac{4}{9}$.

Thus Statement 2 is not sufficient to answer the question since the answer may be Yes or No.

The correct answer would be between C/E.

Statements 1 and 2 together :

Combining both the statements, we get x = 1.

Hence, we get the answer by combining statements 1 and 2 and the answer is No- a unique answer

The correct answer is Option (c).

20. (c) **Considering Statement 1 alone :**

The statement has only two variables y and z. Hence Statement 1 alone is not sufficient to find the value of (y – x – z).

Hence, eliminate A/D.

Considering Statement 2 alone :

The statement has only two variables x and y. Hence Statement 2 alone is not sufficient to find the value of (y – x – z).

Hence, eliminate B

Statements 1 and 2 together :

If we subtract equation (2): $x^2 + y^2 = 269$ from equation (1): $y^2 + z^2 = 244$, we get $x^2 - z^2 = 25$.

We also have $x^2 + z^2 = 313$. We can solve these two equations to get x and z and then put these values in equations (1) or (2) to find the value of v. We must keep in mind that x, y, & z are positive, so we need not care about the negative values of the variables.

In DS questions, if you are sure of getting the unique value, you need not necessarily calculate the value.

Hence statements 1 and 2 together are sufficient.

The correct answer is Option (c).

21. (e) **Considering Statement 1 alone :**

We cannot find out the unique value of a as the linear equation has two variables. So, it is insufficient. Hence, eliminate A/D.

Considering Statement 2 alone :

As with Statement 1, we cannot find out the unique value of a as the linear equation has two variables. So, it is insufficient.

Hence, eliminate B.

Statement 1 and 2 together :

You may notice that if we simplify (divide both sides by 4) the equation : $8a + 12b = 48$ in Statement 2, we get the equation: $2a + 3b = 12$ in statement 1. Therefore, we do not really have two distinct equations. Indirectly we are provided only one linear equation. We cannot find the unique value of a.

Both statements together are insufficient.

The correct answer is Option (e).

22. (a) **Considering Statement 1 alone :**

Squaring on both sides we get $a > b^2$. Since $b > 1$, we have $b^2 > b$.

$\Rightarrow a > b^2 > b$. Therefore, a will always be greater than b. This statement alone is sufficient.

Hence, eliminate B/C/E.

Considering Statement 2 alone :

Squaring both the sides we get $b < a^2$. Though we can apply the tactic that we applied in Statement 1, we cannot compare a and b. Let's apply for the sake of understanding. Since $a > 1$, we have $a^2 > a$. From $a^2 > a$ and $b < a^2$, we cannot compare a and b.

Alternatively, ...

Take a couple of test values.

Case 1 : Say $a = 4$ and $b = 3$.

We see that $3^3 > 4$, and $a > b$.

The answer is Yes.

Case 2 : Say $a = 2$ and $b = 3$.

We see that $3^3 > 2$, and $a < b$.

The answer is No.

No unique answer, hence, Statement 2 alone is not sufficient.

Hence, eliminate B.

The correct answer is Option (a).

23. (c) **Considering Statement 1 alone :**

So $x = [ab]$, where a and b are tens and units digits, respectively.

Now to know the value of x, we need to know both a and b.

Now $a + b = 10$.

We can't find the unique value of x since there are numerous possibilities x could be 37, 73, 82, 28, etc; x is not unique.

This statement alone is not sufficient.

Hence, eliminate A/D.

Considering Statement 2 alone :

Like Statement 1, we need to know the value of x we need to know the values of a and b.

$a - b = 4$ is not sufficient to find the unique values of a and b.

This statement alone is not sufficient.

Hence, eliminate B.

Considering statements 1 and 2 together :

Now we have,

$a + b = 10$

$a - b = 4$

Solving we have $a = 7, b = 3$. Therefore the value of x is 73.

The answer is (c).

24. (a) **Considering Statement 1 alone:**

$x = 100^{\frac{b}{a}}$ is an integer only if $\frac{b}{a}$ is a non-negative integer or $\frac{1}{2}$.

$\frac{b^6}{a^6}$ is an integer, but $\frac{b}{a}$ not necessarily be.

Let's see a couple of examples.

Case 1 : Say $\frac{b^6}{a^6} = 2^6 \Rightarrow \frac{b}{a} = 2$. The answer is Yes.

Case 2 : Say $\frac{b^6}{a^6} = 2 \Rightarrow \frac{b}{a} = \sqrt[6]{2}$. The answer is No.

No unique answer, hence Statement 1 alone is not sufficient.

Hence, eliminate A/D.

Considering Statement 2 alone :

$a - 2b = 0 \Rightarrow \frac{b}{a} = \frac{1}{2}$

$\Rightarrow x = 100^{\frac{b}{a}} = 100^{\frac{1}{2}} = 10$, an integer

This statement alone is sufficient.

Hence, eliminate C/E.

The answer is (a).

25. (e) We have to find out whether $a^5 - b^2 - c^2 < 0$. We can rewrite it as $a^5 < b^2 + c^2$. Since b and c, each are squared, the right-hand side of the inequality would always be non-negative. The inequality would be true if a is negative. However, if a is positive or 0, the answer would be interminable as i it will then depend on the values of a, b, and c.

Considering Statement 1 alone :

Given $ab > 0$, a and b can be both negative or both positive. We cannot conclude anything about the nature of a. This statement alone is insufficient.

Hence, eliminate A/D.

Considering Statement 2 alone :

Given $bc > 0$. b and c can be both negative or both positive. We cannot conclude anything about the nature of a. This statement alone is insufficient.

Hence, eliminate B.

Considering statements 1 and 2 together :

Even after combining both statements, we cannot conclude anything about the nature of a.

The answer is (e).

26. (b) The term $a^2 - ab = a^2 - b^2$ simplifies to either a = b or $(a - b) = (a + b)(a - b)$

$\Rightarrow a = a + b \Rightarrow b = 0$, Since $a \neq b$, $b = 0$

Considering Statement 1 alone :

We cannot determine the value of c since we don't know the value of a. This statement is insufficient.

Hence, eliminate A/D.

Considering Statement 2 alone :

Since $c^3 = b$, and $b = 0 \Rightarrow c = 0$. This statement is sufficient.

Hence, eliminate C/E

The answer is (b).

27. (b) **Considering Statement 1 alone :**

There are infinite such positive integer values for x that make x^3 a perfect square. For example: 1, 4, 64, etc. If $x^3 = 1$, $x = 1$; 1 is a perfect square. Similarly, if $x^3 = 64$, $x = 4$; 64 is a perfect square. No unique answer for x. This statement is insufficient.

Hence, eliminate A/D.

Considering Statement 2 alone :

$x^2 = x$ is true for $x = 0$ or 1. Since x is positive integer, $x = 1$; a unique answer. This statement is sufficient.

Hence, eliminate C/E.

The answer is (b).

28. (e) **Considering Statement 1 alone :**

If $a < b^4$, we can't determine if a and b are fractions or integers. If say a = 3, and b = 2, $a < b^4 \Rightarrow 3 < 2^4 \Rightarrow 3 < 16$ then a > b. The answer is Yes. If say a = 2, and b = 3, $a < b^4 \Rightarrow 2 < 3^4 \Rightarrow 2 < 81$ then a < b. The answer is No. No unique answer. This statement is insufficient.

Hence, eliminate A/D.

Considering Statement 2 alone :

Again, we don't the values for a and b. This statement is insufficient.

Hence, eliminate B.

Considering Statement 1 and 2 together :

If say a = –3, and b = –2, $< b^4 \Rightarrow -3 < (-2)^4 \Rightarrow -3 < 16$ then a < b. The answer is No. If say a = –2, and b = –2, and b = –2, $a < b^4 \Rightarrow -2\ (-3)^4 \Rightarrow -2 < 81$ then a > b. The answer is Yes. No unique answer. Even both statements together are insufficient.

The answer is (e).

29. (b) **Considering Statement 1 alone:**

Statement 1 gives only the value of x. Hence Statement 1 alone is not sufficient

Hence, eliminate A/D.

Considering Statement 2 alone :

Multiplying $3y^2 + 2x^2 = 14$ by 6 gives $12x^2 + 18y^2 = 84$, which is the same as the expression in the problem. Therefore, the value of the given expression $12x^2 + 18y^2$ is 84.

Hence, Statement 2 alone is sufficient.

Hence, eliminate C/E.

The answer is (b).

30. (d) Let x be the age of John and c be the age of his cousin

$\Rightarrow \quad x = c - 10$

We have to find the value of x + 20.

Considering Statement 1 alone :

This statement implies $2(x - 5) = c - 5$

$2(c - 10 - 5) = c - 5$

$2c - 30 = c - 5$

$c = 25\ \&\ x = 15 \Rightarrow x + 20 = 15 + 20 = 35$

Therefore, Statement 1 alone is sufficient.

Hence, eliminate B/C/E.

Considering Statement 2 alone :

This statement implies that

$c + 5 = 2x = 2(c - 10)$

$c + 5 = 2c - 20$

$c = 25\ \&\ x = 15 \Rightarrow x + 20 = 15 + 20 = 35$

Therefore, Statement 2 alone is also sufficient.

Hence, eliminate C/E.

The answer is (d).

31. (c) **Considering Statement 1 alone:**

On solving the equation $a^2 - a - 6 = 0$

$\Rightarrow (a - 3)(a + 2) = 0.$

a = 3 or –2; no unique value.

This statement alone is Insufficient.

Hence, eliminate A/D.

Considering Statement 2 alone :

Given that (a + 5) is a prime number, multiple values of a are possible (a = –3, –2, 0, 2, 4, 6, 8, 12, etc).

This statement alone is Insufficient.

Hence, eliminate B.

Considering statements 1 and 2 together :

Both statements together imply that $a = -2$: the only common value. Sufficient.

The answer is (c).

32. (e) **Considering Statement 1 alone:**

We can replace the value of $3|b|$ from statement 1 with $a + 3|b| = 50 \Rightarrow a + 3|b| = a + a - 20 = 50 \Rightarrow 2a = 70 \Rightarrow a = 35$.

By replacing the value of $a = 35$ in the statement, we get $3|b| = 35 - 20 = 15 \Rightarrow |b| = 5$ or $b = 5$ or -5. We are able to get the unique value of a, but not of b. Hence, Statement 1 alone in insufficient.

Hence, eliminate A/D.

Considering Statement 2 alone:

Upon multiplying by 3 on both sides, statement 2 becomes $3|b| + = 50$, i.e., the same equation given in the question. Therefore, we have only one equation and two variables. Statement 2 alone is insufficient.

Hence, eliminate B.

Considering statements 1 and 2 together:

Since statement 2 does not add any value to solve the question, even after combining both statements, we cannot get the unique value of b.

The answer is (e).

33. (b) **Considering Statement 1 alone :**

$a^2 = 3a + 4 \Rightarrow 2 - 3a - 4 = 0$

$\Rightarrow a^2 - 4a + a - 4 = 0$

$\Rightarrow a(a - 4) + 1(a - 4) \Rightarrow (a - 4)(a + 1) = 0$

$\Rightarrow a = 4$ or -1. Since a does not have a unique value, a^3 cannot have a unique value. This statement is insufficient.

Hence, eliminate A/D.

Considering Statement 2 alone :

$a^3 - 4a^2 = 4 - a \Rightarrow a^3 - 4a^2 + a - 4 = 0$

$\Rightarrow a^2(a - 4) + 1(a - 4) = 0$

$\Rightarrow (a - 4)(a^2 + 1) \Rightarrow a = 4$, or $a^2 = -1$

$\Rightarrow a = \sqrt{-1}$, an imaginary number. Since in the GMAT, variables are real numbers, $a = \sqrt{-1}$ is discarded.

So $a = 4 \Rightarrow a^3 = 4^3 = 64$, a unique value. This statement is sufficient.

The answer is (b).

34. (b) We are given that $f(x) = (c)^{\frac{6}{x}}$, where c is a constant.

We have to find out the value of f(1).

Considering Statement 1 alone :

Given that $f(2) = 125$

Thus, $f(2) = (c)^{\frac{6}{2}} = c^3 = 125$

$\Rightarrow c = (125)^{\frac{1}{3}} = 5$

Thus, $f(1) = (c)^{\frac{6}{1}} = c^6 - 5^6$ – Sufficient

Hence, eliminate B/C/E.

Considering Statement 2 alone :

Given that $f(3) = 25$

Thus $f(3) = (c)^{\frac{6}{3}} = c^2 = 25$

$\Rightarrow c = (25)^{\frac{1}{2}} = \pm 5$

Thus,

$f(1) = (c)^{\frac{6}{1}} = c^6 (\pm 5)^6 = 5^6$ – Sufficient

The answer is (b).

35. (c) **Considering Statement 1 alone :**

Statement 1 states $-x = |-x|$. Since the right-hand side ($|-x|$) is an absolute value, which is always a non-negative number, for the equality to hold true, the left-hand side must also be a non-negative number.

So, since $-x$ is a non-negative number, x must be a non-positive number. But x may be negative or 0. Hence, statement 1 alone is not sufficient.

Hence, eliminate A/D.

Considering Statement 2 alone :

From statement 2, we get $x = 4$ or -4. Since x can be positive or negative, statement 2 alone isn't sufficient.

Hence, eliminate B.

Considering Statements 1 and 2 together :

From both statements, we get that $x = -4$, the answer is yes. Sufficient.

The answer is (c).

36. (c) **Considering Statement 1 alone :**

Let us rewrite $wx > y^3z$ as $wx > yz\,(y^2)$

If $y^2 \leq 1$, the answer is YES. However, if $y^2 > 1$, then the answer is YES/NO, depending on the value of y^2. Therefore, Statement 1 alone is insufficient.

Hence, eliminate A/D

Considering Statement 2 alone :

Statement 2 only tells us about y and is therefore insufficient.

Hence, eliminate B.

Considering Statements 1 and 2 together:

Both the statements together give us a fixed value of y. i.e. $y = 1$ implies $wx > yz(y^2)$ $= wx > yz\,(1) = wx > yz$

Therefore, both statements together are sufficient.

The answer is (c).

Chapter 4

Coordinate Geometry

Coordinate geometry is a topic that appears frequently on the GMAT. Questions on this topic can range from simple concepts such as finding the coordinates of a point on a plane, to more complex problems involving slopes, distance, and midpoint formulas.

Coordinate Plane

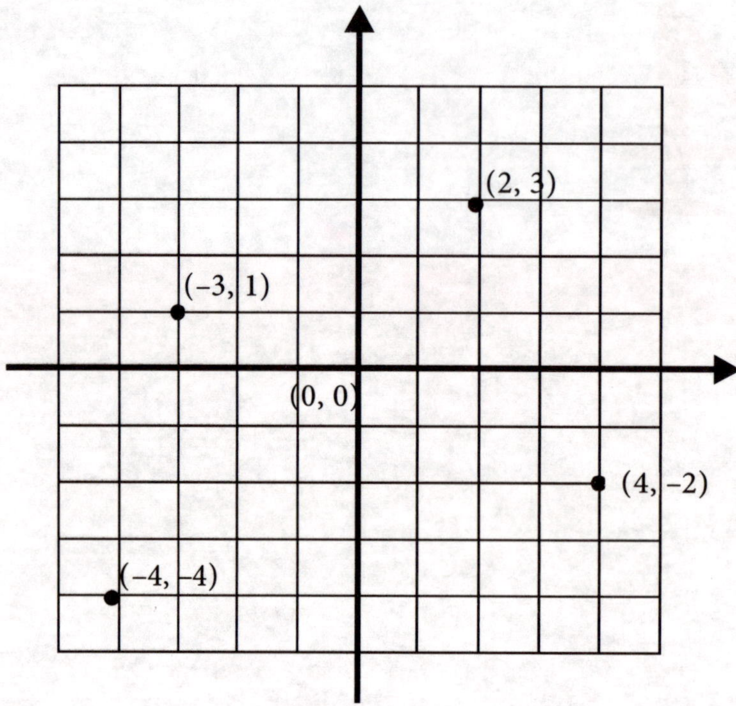

Two real number lines that are perpendicular to each other and that intersect at their respective zero points define a rectangular coordinate system, often called the xy-coordinate system or xy-plane. The horizontal number line is called the x-axis and the vertical number line is called the y-axis. The point where the two axes intersect is called the origin, denoted by O. The positive half of the x-axis is to the right of the origin, and the positive half of the y-axis is above the origin. The two axes divide the plane into four regions called quadrants I, II, III, and IV

Each point P in the xy-plane can be identified with an ordered pair (x, y) of real numbers and is denoted by P(x, y). The first number is called the x-coordinate, and the second number is called the y-coordinate.

Slope

The slope of a line on a coordinate plane tells you how steeply that line goes up or down. If a line gets higher as you move to the right, it has a positive slope. If it goes down as you move to the right, it has a negative slope.

$$m = \frac{(y-b)}{(x-a)}$$

If two lines are parallel, their slopes will be equal

If two lines are perpendicular, their slopes will be negative reciprocal.

Example : What is the slope of the line that contains the points (1, 2) and (4, −5)?

$$\text{Slope} = \frac{(-5-2)}{(4-1)} = -\frac{7}{3}$$

To determine the slope of a line from an equation, put the equation into slope-intercept form: $y = mx + b$, where the slope is m.

The word intercept in "slope-intercept form" is there because b is the value of the y-intercept-the point at which the line crosses the y-axis.

Example : Find the slope of the line passing through the points A(2, 3) and B(5, 7).

Solution : The coordinates of point A are (2, 3) and the coordinates of point B are (5, 7). We can use the slope formula to find the slope of the line passing through the points.

Slope formula : The slope of a line passing through two points with coordinates (x_1, y_1) and (x_2, y_2) is given by:

$$m = \frac{(y_2 - y_1)}{(x_2 - x_1)}$$

Using the slope formula, we have: $m = \frac{(7-3)}{(5-2)} = \frac{4}{3}$

Intercepts

The x-intercept is the point where the line cuts the x-axis. It is found by substituting $y = 0$

The y-intercept is the point where the line cuts the y-axis. It is found by substituting $x = 0$

Distance Formula

To determine the distance between any two points on a coordinate plane, you can use the Pythagorean theorem.

The distance between the points (x, y) and (a, b) is the hypotenuse of a right triangle.

The difference y – b is the measure of the height of the triangle, and the difference x – a is the length of base of the triangle

$$d = \sqrt{\{(x-a)^2 + (y-b)^2\}}$$

Midpoint Formula

The midpoint M between points (x, y) and (a, b) is given by

$$M\left\{\frac{(x+a)}{2}, \frac{(y+b)}{2}\right\}$$

Example : Find the midpoint and distance between the points A(2,3) and B(8,9).

Solution : The coordinates of point A are (2, 3) and the coordinates of point B are (8, 9). We can use the midpoint formula and distance formula to find the midpoint and distance between the points, respectively.

Midpoint formula : The midpoint of a line segment with endpoints (x_1, y_1) and (x_2, y_2) is given by:

$$\left(\frac{(x_1+x_2)}{2}, \frac{(y_1+y_2)}{2}\right)$$

Using the midpoint formula, we have : Midpoint of AB = $\left(\frac{(2+8)}{2}, \frac{(3+9)}{2}\right) = (5,6)$

Therefore, the midpoint of AB is (5,6).

Distance formula : The distance between two points with coordinates (x_1, y_1) and (x_2, y_2) is given by:

$$d = \sqrt{[(x_2-x_1)^2 + (y_2-y_1)^2]}$$

Using the distance formula, we have: Distance between A and B

$$= \sqrt{[(8-2)^2 + (9-3)^2]} = \sqrt{[6^2 + 6^2]} = \sqrt{(72)}$$

Problem Solving

1. On the xy-plane, what is the equation of the line that is a reflection the line $y = -2x - 1$ across the x-axis?

   (a) $y = -2x + 1$

   (b) $y = -2x - 1$

   (c) $y = 2x - 1$

   (d) $y = 2x + 1$

   (e) $y = x + 1$

2. The equation of line p is $y = -x + 2$. If the line is the reflection of the line p over the y-axis, what is the slope of line q?

   (a) -2

   (b) $-\frac{1}{2}$

   (c) 0

   (d) $\frac{1}{2}$

   (e) 1

3. If (b, a) lies in Quadrant III of the xy-coordinate plane, in which quadrant does the point (a, b) lie?

   (a) 1 only

   (b) II only

   (c) III only

   (d) IV only

   (e) Any of the four quadrants

4. Which of the following statements is true for the line that passes through $(-2, 2)$ and $(2, -2)$?

   (a) It crosses the x-axis only

   (b) It crosses the y-axis only

   (c) It has a positive y-intercept.

   (d) It passes through origin (0, 0)

   (e) It has a negative x-intercept and a negative y-intercept.

5. What is the area of the triangular field with the coordinates of the vertices

   $(0, 2)$, $(-2, -2)$ and $(2, -2)$?

   (a) 2

   (b) 4

   (c) 8

   (d) 12

   (e) 16

Answer Key

1. (d)
2. (e)
3. (c)
4. (d)
5. (c)

Answer Explanations

1. (d) A reflection across the x-axis flips all y-coordinates from y to-y and keeps the x-coordinates unchanged Hence, the answer is (d).

2. (e) If you reflect a line over the y-axis, the slope of the new line have the opposite sign of the slope of the oldline. The slope of p is –1, so the slope of q is 1.

3. (c) If (b, a) is in the third quadrant, then b = –ve and a = –ve.

   Hence, (a, b) is also (–ve, –ve).

   So, it should lie in Quadrant III only.

4. (d) The mid-point of (–2, 2) and (2, –2) is

$$\left\{\frac{(+2+2)}{2},\frac{(2-2)}{2}\right\}=0,0$$

   So, it passes through origin.

5. C You may draw a diagram. The vertices of the triangle are A(0, 2), B(–2, –2), and C(2, 2). Thus, the base of the triangle would be BC = |–1| + 2 = 4, and the height would be 2 + –2| = 4.

$$\text{The area of the triangle} = \frac{1}{2}\times\text{base}\times\text{height}$$

$$=\frac{1}{2}\times 4\times 4=8$$

Data Sufficiency

1. What is the angle between line k and line p?

   1. Equation of line k is $y - 5x = 4$.
   2. Line k and line p do not intersect.

   (*a*) Statement (1) ALONE is sufficient but statement (2) ALONE is not sufficient.

   (*b*) Statement (2) ALONE is sufficient but statement (1) ALONE is not sufficient.

   (*c*) BOTH statements TOGETHER are sufficient, but NEITHER statement ALONE is sufficient.

   (*d*) EACH statement ALONE is sufficient.

   (*e*) Statements (1) and (2) TOGETHER are not sufficient.

2. What is the slope of line 1?

   1. Line 1 passes through origin
   2. Line 1 is equidistant from the two points (1, 11) and (7, 7).

   (*a*) Statement (1) ALONE is sufficient but statement (2) ALONE is not sufficient.

   (*b*) Statement (2) ALONE is sufficient but statement (1) ALONE is not sufficient.

   (*c*) BOTH statements TOGETHER are sufficient, but NEITHER statement ALONE is sufficient.

   (*d*) EACH statement ALONE is sufficient.

   (*e*) Statements (1) and (2) TOGETHER are not sufficient.

3. What all quadrants in the xy-plane does line k pass through?

   1. Line k is defined by $3x + 4y = 8$
   2. Line k has a negative slope

   (*a*) Statement (1) ALONE is sufficient but statement (2) ALONE is not sufficient.

   (*b*) Statement (2) ALONE is sufficient but statement (1) ALONE is not sufficient.

   (*c*) BOTH statements TOGETHER are sufficient, but NEITHER statement ALONE is sufficient.

   (*d*) EACH statement ALONE is sufficient.

   (*e*) Statements (1) and (2) TOGETHER are not sufficient.

4. Does line k pass through the II quadrant in the xy-plane?

   1. Line k is defined by $3x + 4y = 8$
   2. Line k has a negative slope

   (*a*) Statement (1) ALONE is sufficient but statement (2) ALONE is not sufficient.

   (*b*) Statement (2) ALONE is sufficient but statement (1) ALONE is not sufficient.

   (*c*) BOTH statements TOGETHER are sufficient, but NEITHER statement ALONE is sufficient.

   (*d*) EACH statement ALONE is sufficient.

   (*e*) Statements (1) and (2) TOGETHER are not sufficient.

5. Does line k pass through (–14, 10)?

   1. Line k passes through (0, 5) and (7, 0)
   2. Line k parallel to line $y = \left(\frac{-5}{7}\right)x + 10$

   (*a*) Statement (1) ALONE is sufficient but statement (2) ALONE is not sufficient.

   (*b*) Statement (2) ALONE is sufficient but statement (1) ALONE is not sufficient.

   (*c*) BOTH statements TOGETHER are sufficient, but NEITHER statement ALONE is sufficient.

   (*d*) EACH statement ALONE is sufficient.

   (*e*) Statements (1) and (2) TOGETHER are not sufficient.

6. What is the x-intercept of line k?

1. Equation of line k is $y = 4x + 5$
2. y-intercept of line k is $(0, 5)$

(a) Statement (1) ALONE is sufficient but statement (2) ALONE is not sufficient.

(b) Statement (2) ALONE is sufficient but statement (1) ALONE is not sufficient.

(c) BOTH statements TOGETHER are sufficient, but NEITHER statement ALONE is sufficient.

(d) EACH statement ALONE is sufficient.

(e) Statements (1) and (2) TOGETHER are not sufficient.

7. Is point Q closer to the point (10, 3) than to the point (3, 10)?

1. Point Q lies on the line $y = x$.
2. Point Q lies on the line $y = -x$.

(a) Statement (1) ALONE is sufficient but statement (2) ALONE is not sufficient.

(b) Statement (2) ALONE is sufficient but statement (1) ALONE is not sufficient.

(c) BOTH statements TOGETHER are sufficient, but NEITHER statement ALONE is sufficient.

(d) EACH statement ALONE is sufficient.

(e) Statements (1) and (2) TOGETHER are not sufficient.

Answer Key

1. (b)	**3.** (a)	**5.** (a)	**7.** (a)
2. (c)	**4.** (d)	**6.** (a)	

Answer Explanations

1. (b) Considering statement (1) alone:

Just knowing the equation of one line doesn't help.

INSUFFICIENT

Eliminate AD

Considering statement (2) alone:

If the two lines do not intersect, then the two lines are parallel.

Hence the angle formed by them must be 0, SUFFICIENT

Eliminate CE.

The answer is (b).

2. (c) **Considering statement (1) alone:**

Just knowing one point on a line doesn't help.

INSUFFICIENT

Eliminate AD.

Considering statement (2) alone:

Line 1 passes through the midpoint (1, 11) and (7, 7)i.e (4, 9)

Just knowing one point on a line doesn't help.

INSUFFICIENT

Eliminate B.

Considering both the statements together:

Line I passes through (0, 0) and (4, 9)

Hence, the slope of the line is $\frac{9}{4}$

INSUFFICIENT

Eliminate E.

The answer is (c).

3. (a) **Considering statement (1) alone:**

If we know the equation of a line, then we can plot it and find the quadrants that it passes through.

SUFFICIENT

Eliminate BCE

Considering statement (2) alone:

If the slope is negative, then the line passes through quadrant II and IV for sure. But, it is not enough to determine whether it passes through any other quadrant.

SUFFICIENT

Eliminate D

The answer is (a).

4. (d) If we know the equation of a line, then we can plot it and find the quadrants that it passes through.

SUFFICIENT

Eliminate BCE

Considering statement (2) alone:

If the slope is negative, then the line passes through quadrant II and IV for sure.

SUFFICIENT

Eliminate A

The answer is (d).

5. (a) **Considering statement (1) alone:**

To find whether a line passes through three given points. find the slopes with each of them.

Slope of a line that passes through (0, 5) and (7, 0) = $-\frac{5}{7}$

As the two slopes are not same, the line does not pass through (–14, 10) Sufficient

Eliminate BCE

Considering statement (2) alone:

With this, we just know the slppe of line k. However, that is not helpful to find whether the line passes through (–14, 10) Insufficient.

Eliminate D.

The answer is (a).

6. (a) **Considering statement (1) alone:**

x-intercept means putting y = 0 in the equation.

Hence, x-intercept of line k is $\left(-\frac{5}{4},0\right)$

Sufficient

Elimiante BCE

Considering statement (2) alone:

Knowing the y-intercept does not help find the x-intercept.

Insufficient

Eliminate D

The answer is (a).

7. (a) **Considering statement 1 alone:**

Say the co-ordinates of Point Q on the line y = x is (a, a).

The distance from a point (x_1, y_1) from a point (x_2, y_2) is given by

$$\left|\sqrt{\left[(x_1-x_2)^2+(y_1-y_2)^2\right]}\right|,$$

we can find the distances from both the given points.

Distance of Point Q (a, a) from the point (10, 3)

$$=\left|\sqrt{\left[(10-a)^2+(3-a)^2\right]}\right|;$$

Similarly, the distance of Point Q (a, a) from the point (3, 10)

$$=\left|\sqrt{\left[(13-a)^2+(10-a)^2\right]}\right|.$$

Since both distances are the same, we can conclude that the two points (10, 3) and (3, 10) are equidistant from any point on the line y = x; Statement 1 alone is sufficient.

Hence, eliminate B/C/E.

Considering Statement 2 alone :

Say the co-ordinates of Point Q on the line y = –x is (a, –a).

Distance of Point Q (a, –a) from the point (10, 3)

$$=\left|\sqrt{\left[(10-a)^2+(3-a)^2\right]}\right|$$

$$=\left|\sqrt{100-20a+a^2+9+6a+a^2}\right|$$

$$=\left|\sqrt{[109-14a+2a]}\right|$$

Similarly, the distance of Point Q (a, a) from the point (3, 10)

$$=\left|\sqrt{\left[(13-a)^2+(10-a)^2\right]}\right|$$

$$=\left|\sqrt{9-6a+a^2+100+20a+a^2}\right|$$

$$=\left|\sqrt{109-14a+2a^2}\right|$$

If a = 0, we have

$$=\left|\sqrt{109-14a+2a^2}\right|$$

$$=\left|\sqrt{109+14a+2a^2}\right|,$$

else not. No unique answer.

Statement 2 alone is insufficient.

Hence, eliminate B.

The correct answer is Option (a.)

Chapter 5

Statistics

Statistics topic deals with the collection, analysis, interpretation, presentation, and organization of data. It involves using mathematical and computational tools to gather insights from data and to make informed decisions.

Mean, Median, Mode, Range

Mean

The mean is a measure of central tendency that represents the average value of a set of data. It is calculated by summing all the values in the dataset and dividing by the total number of values.

The formula for calculating the mean is :

$$\text{Mean} = \frac{(\text{sum of all values})}{(\text{number of values})}$$

Example, suppose you have a dataset of test scores : 75, 82, 91, 68, and 88. To calculate the mean, you would add up all the values and divide by the total number of values:

$$\text{Mean} = \frac{(75+80+91+68+88)}{5} \ \text{Mean} = \frac{404}{5} \ \text{Mean} = 80.8$$

Therefore, the mean test score for this dataset is 80.8.

Median

The median is a measure of central tendency that represents the middle value of a dataset.

To find the median, you first need to order the values in the dataset from lowest to highest (or highest to lowest). If the dataset has an odd number of values, the median is the middle value. If the dataset has an even number of values, the median is the average of the two middle values.

Example : Suppose you have a dataset of test scores: 75, 82, 91, 68, and 88. To find the median, you would first order the values from lowest to highest:

$$68, 75, 82, 88, 91$$

Since the dataset has an odd number of values, the median is the middle value, which is 82. Therefore, the median test score for this dataset is 82.

Now let's take an example where the dataset has an even number of values: 75, 82, 91, 68, 88, and 93. To find the median, you would first order the values:

$$68, 75, 82, 88, 91, 93$$

Since the dataset has an even number of values, the median is the average of the two middle values, which are 82 and 88. Therefore, the median test score for this dataset is $\frac{(82+88)}{2} = 85$.

Mode

The mode is a measure of central tendency that represents the most commonly occurring value in a dataset. The mode is the value that appears with the highest frequency in the dataset.

Example, suppose you have a dataset of test scores: 75, 82, 91, 68, 88, 82, 93, 82. The mode of this dataset is 82, because it appears three times and no other value appears more than once.

It's possible for a dataset to have multiple modes if there are two or more values that occur with the same highest frequency. This is called a bimodal or multimodal distribution.

Note that not all datasets have a mode, for example, if all the values in a dataset occur only once, then there is no mode. If two or more values have the same highest frequency, then the dataset is said to have multiple modes.

Range

The range is a measure of dispersion that represents the difference between the maximum and minimum values in a dataset. The range gives an idea of how spread out the values are in the dataset.

The formula for calculating the range is :

$$\text{Range} = \text{maximum value} - \text{minimum value}$$

Example, suppose you have a dataset of test scores: 75, 82, 91, 68, and 88. To calculate the range, first find the maximum and minimum values:

$$\text{Maximum value} = 91 \quad \text{Minimum value} = 68$$

Then subtract the minimum value from the maximum value:

$$\text{Range} = 91 - 68 \quad \text{Range} = 23$$

Therefore, the range of this dataset is 23.

The range can be affected by extreme values or outliers in the dataset.

Standard Deviation

The standard deviation is a measure of dispersion that represents how much the values in a dataset deviate from the mean. The standard deviation is a way of measuring the amount of variability or spread in the dataset.

The steps for calculating the standard deviation is:

1. Find the average (arithmetic mean) of the set.
2. Subtract the average of the set from each term in that set.
3. Square each result.
4. Take the average of those squares.
5. Calculate the positive square root of that average.

Example : suppose you have a dataset of test scores: 75, 82, 91, 68, and 88. To calculate the standard deviation, first find the mean:

$$\text{Mean} = \frac{(75 + 82 + 91 + 68 + 88)}{5} \quad \text{Mean} = \frac{404}{5} \quad \text{Mean} = 80.8$$

Next, calculate the deviation of each value from the mean, square each deviation, and sum the squared deviations:

$$(75 - 80.8)^2 + (82 - 80.8)^2 + (91 - 80.8)^2 + (68 - 80.8)^2 + (88 - 80.8)^2$$

$$= 24.64 + 1.44 + 103.04 + 155.84 + 6.76 = 291.72$$

Then divide the sum of squared deviations by the number of values and take the square root of the result:

$$\text{Standard deviation} = \text{square root of} \left(\frac{291.72}{5}\right)$$

Standard deviation = 7.64

Therefore, the standard deviation of this dataset is 7.64

Example : {1, 2, 3} and {101, 102, 103} have the same standard deviation, since they both have one term on the average and two terms exactly one unit away from the average.

Normal Distribution

The normal distribution is a common topic in the quantitative section of the GMAT. The test may include questions that require you to understand the properties of the normal distribution and use them to solve problems.

A normal distribution (also known as a Gaussian distribution) is a probability distribution that is characterized by a bell-shaped curve. The curve is symmetric around the mean and the spread of the distribution is determined by the standard deviation.

According to the standard deviation about 68% of the values in a normal distribution fall within one standard deviation of the mean, about 95% fall within two standard deviations, and about 99.7% fall within three standard deviations.

Normal Distribution

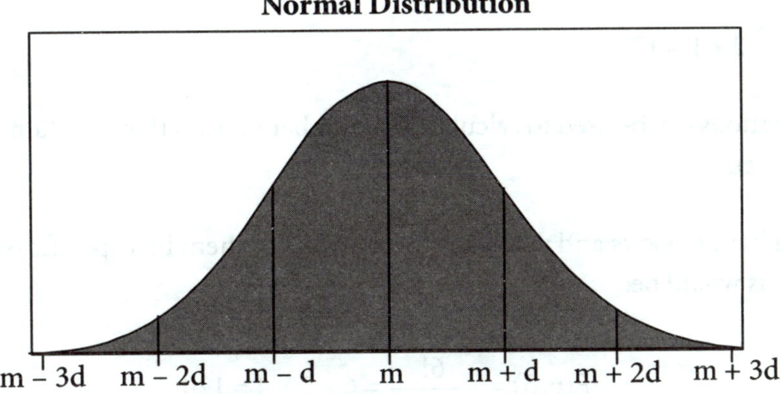

Such data are said to be approximately normally distributed and have the following properties.

- The mean, median, and mode are all nearly equal.
- The data are grouped fairly symmetrically about the mean.
- About two-thirds of the data are within 1 standard deviation of the mean.
- Almost all of the data are within 2 standard deviations of the mean.

Example : Suppose the heights of students in a class are normally distributed with a mean of 68 inches and a standard deviation of 3 inches. What percentage of students in the class are between 62 inches and 74 inches tall?

Solution : To find the percentage of students between 62 inches and 74 inches tall, we need to find the area under the curve between those two points.

Using a standard normal distribution table, we can find that the area under the curve between -2 and 2 is approximately 0.9545. Therefore, approximately 95.45% of students in the class are between 62 inches and 74 inches tall.

Permutation

Some GMAT questions ask you to count the number of possible ways to select a small subgroup from a larger group. If the selection is unordered, then it's a combinations question. But if the selection is ordered, it is a permutations question.

In permutation, order matters.

In permutations, A – B – C and B – A – C are not the same because the ordering is different, though each has the same number of each type of object: A, B, and C as in the base set.

The number of permutations of a set of n distinct objects taken r at a time is denoted by the symbol P(n, r) and can be calculated using the following formula:

$P(n, r) = \frac{n!}{(n-r)!}$, where n! (pronounced "n factorial") represents the product of all positive integers from 1 to n, inclusive.

Example : $5! = 5 \times 4 \times 3 \times 2 \times 1 = 120$.

The formula for permutations can be used to calculate the number of ways that a certain number of objects can be arranged in a specific order.

Example : Suppose you have 6 books and you want to arrange 3 of them in a specific order on a bookshelf. The number of ways to do this would be:

$$P(6,3) = \frac{6!}{(6-3)!} = 6 \times 5 \times 4 = 120$$

Therefore, there are 120 different ways to arrange 3 books out of 6 in a specific order.

Example, if we want to find the number of permutations of 4 objects taken 2 at a time, we have:

$$\frac{4!}{(4-2)!} = \frac{4!}{2!} = 12$$

This means that there are 12 different ways of arranging 2 objects out of a set of 4 objects.

Combination

Combination is a way of selecting a subset of objects from a larger set, where the order of selection does not matter.

Example : if we have a set of three objects {A, B, C}, we can select two objects in different ways:

AB

AC

BC

Note that the order of selection does not matter, so AB and BA are considered the same combination.

The number of combinations of r objects taken from a set of n objects is given by the formula:

$$\frac{b!}{(r!(n-r)!)},$$

where n is the total number of objects in the set, and r is the number of objects being selected in each combination. The exclamation mark represents the factorial operation.

Example, if we want to find the number of combinations of 4 objects taken 2 at a time, we have:

$$\frac{4!}{(2!(4-2)!)} = 6$$

This means that there are 6 different ways of selecting 2 objects out of a set of 4 objects.

In general, if we have n objects and we want to select r objects from them, we have:

$$\frac{n!}{(r!(n-r)!)} \text{ combinations}$$

Example, if we have a set of 5 objects and we want to select 3 objects from it, there are:

$$\frac{5!}{(3!(5-3)!)} = 10 \text{ combinations}$$

Example : Suppose we have a group of 10 people and we want to select a committee of 4 people from this group. How many different committees can we form?

We can use the formula for combinations:

$$\frac{n!}{(r!(n-r)!)},$$

where n is the total number of objects (people in this case) and r is the number of objects being selected (4 people in this case).

Substituting the values, we get :

$$\frac{10!}{(4!(10-4)!)} = 210$$

Probability

Probability is the measure of the likelihood that a particular event will occur. The probability of an event is always a number between 0 and 1, where 0 represents an impossible event and 1 represents a certain event.

The formula for probability is:

P(E) = number of favorable outcomes / total number of outcomes

where P(E) is the probability of event E.

Example : if we roll a fair six-sided die, the probability of getting a 4 is $\frac{1}{6}$, because there is only one favorable outcome (getting a 4) out of six possible outcomes (rolling any number from 1 to 6).

Here are some more examples of probability:

- **Coin toss :** Suppose we toss a fair coin. The probability of getting heads is 1/2, and the probability of getting tails is also 1/2.
- **Dice roll :** Suppose we roll a fair six-sided die. The probability of getting a specific number (e.g., 3) is 1/6, because there is only one favorable outcome out of six possible outcomes.
- **Card draw :** Suppose we draw a card from a standard deck of 52 playing cards. The probability of drawing a spade is 13/52, because there are 13 spades in the deck.

Probability can also be expressed as a percentage or a fraction.

Example : A probability of 0.5 is equivalent to a probability of 50% or a fraction of $\frac{1}{2}$.

The sum of the probabilities of all possible outcomes of an experiment must be equal to 1. This is known as the *law of total probability*.

Example : if we toss a coin, the probability of getting either heads or tails is $\frac{1}{2}+\frac{1}{2}=1$.

Probability is the likelihood that a desired outcome will occur.

Example : If you have 12 shirts in a drawer and 9 of them are white, the probability of picking a white shirt at random is $\frac{9}{12}=\frac{3}{4}$

For events E and F, we have the following rules:

- P(E or F, or both, occur) = P(E) + P(F)– P(both E and F occur), which is the inclusion-exclusion principle applied to probability.
- If E and F are mutually exclusive, then P (both E and F occur) = 0, and therefore, P (E or F, or both, occur) = P(E) + P(F).
- E and F are said to be independent if the occurrence of either event does not affect the occurrence of the other. If two events E and F are independent, then P(both E and F occur) = P(E)P(F).

Set Theory

Set theory is a branch of mathematics that deals with the study of sets, which are collections of objects or elements that share a common property. The objects are called the elements of the set. A set with a finite number of elements may be denoted by listing its elements within a pair of braces. The order in which the elements are listed does not matter.

Example : $\{-5, 0, 1\}$ is the same set as $\{0, 1, -5\}$; that is, $\{-5, 0, 1\} = \{0, 1, -5\}$.

The union of two sets A and B is the set of all elements that are in A or in B or in both.

The union is denoted by $A \cup B$.

Example : $\{3, 4\} \cup \{4, 5, 6\} = \{3, 4, 5, 6\}$

The intersection of two sets A and B is the set of all elements that are both in A and in B. The intersection is denoted by $A \cap B$.

Example : $\{3, 4\} \cap \{4, 5, 6\} = \{4\}$

When counting elements that are in overlapping sets, the total number will equal the number in one group plus the number in the other group minus the number common to both groups.

A Venn Diagram of the Intersection of Two Sets

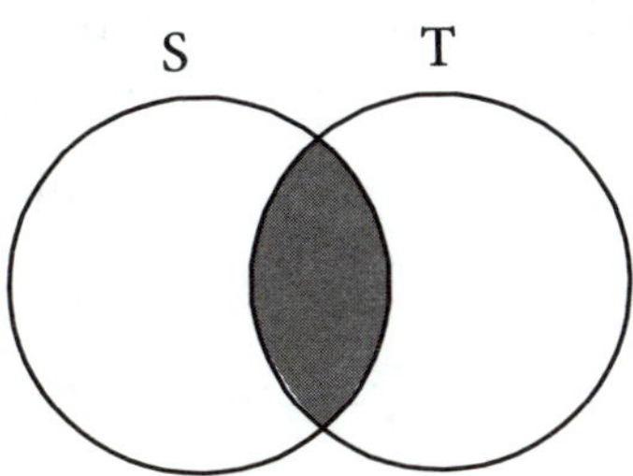

Example, if Set A = $\{1, 2, 6\}$ and Set B = $\{6, 10, 21\}$, then the union of sets A and B would be $\{1, 2, 6, 10, 21\}$ and the intersection would be $\{6\}$

Problem Solving

1. How many 3-digit passwords can be created?

(*a*) $^{9}C_3$

(*b*) $^{9}P_3$

(*c*) 3^9

(*d*) 9^3

(*e*) 10^3

2. Using each digit of the number 12334, how many 5-digit numbers can be formed?

(*a*) 5!

(*b*) $\frac{5!}{2!}$

(*c*) $\frac{^{5}C_5}{2!}$

(*d*) $\frac{^{5}P_5}{2!3!}$

(*e*) $\frac{^{5}C_5}{2!3!}$

3. In an examination, there are 2 sections, and four questions are to be answered. In the first section, there are 3 questions and two must be answered. In the second section, there are four questions and two must be answered. The first section is to be completed before the second section. In how many ways the test can be answered?

(*a*) 12

(*b*) 15

(*c*) 36

(*d*) 72

(*e*) 90

4. In how many ways can the letters of the word MOBILE be rearranged such that the vowels are together?

(*a*) $3! \times 3!$

(*b*) $\frac{6!}{2!}$

(*c*) $\frac{4! \times 3!}{2!}$

(*d*) $4! \times 3!$

(*e*) $\frac{3! \times 3!}{2!}$

5. In how many ways can be letters of the word COLOUR be rearranged such that the vowels are together?

(*a*) $\frac{7!}{2! \times 2!}$

(*b*) $\frac{4! \times 3!}{2! \times 2!}$

(*c*) $\frac{4! \times 3!}{2!}$

(*d*) $\frac{5!}{2! \times 2!}$

(*e*) $\frac{5! \times 3!}{2! \times 2!}$

6. If three couples are standing in a row, how many standing arrangements are possible such that couples are together?

(*a*) 6

(*b*) 12

(*c*) 24

(*d*) 48

(*e*) 96

7. In how many ways 6 people can be seated around a circular table?

(*a*) 6

(*b*) 24

(*c*) 120

(*d*) 720

(*e*) 5040

8. In how many ways three prizes can be distributed among three students such that no one gets more than one prize?

(*a*) 6

(*b*) 24

(*c*) 27

(*d*) 64

(*e*) 128

9. In how many ways three prizes can be distributed among three students such that a student may get any number of prizes?

(*a*) 6

(*b*) 24

(*c*) 27

(*d*) 64

(*e*) 128

10. How many three-digit numbers can be formed with distinct digits?

(*a*) 648

(*b*) 700

(*c*) 720

(*d*) 864

(*e*) 1000

11. In how many ways, a committee of 2 men and 2 women can be formed out of 5 men and 6 women?

(*a*) 6

(*b*) 10

(*c*) 25

(*d*) 128

(*e*) 150

12. In how many ways 5 identical red balls 4 identical balls can be arranged in a now such that no two blue balls are together?

(*a*) 6

(*b*) 10

(*c*) 25

(*d*) 128

(*e*) 150

13. In how many ways 5 men and 5 women can be seated around a circular table such that no two women are together?

(*a*) 24

(*b*) 120

(*c*) 576

(*d*) 2880

(*e*) 3080

14. There is a 10% chance that it won't snow all winter long. There is a 20% chance that schools will not be closed all winter long. What is the greatest possible probability that it will snow and schools will be closed during the winter?

(*a*) 55%

(*b*) 60%

(*c*) 70%

(*d*) 72%

(*e*) 80%

15. There are y different trvelers who each have a choice of vacationing at one of n different destinations. What is the probability that all y travelers will end up vacationing at the same destination?

(a) $\frac{1}{n!}$

(b) $\frac{n}{n!}$

(c) $\frac{1}{n^y}$

(d) $\frac{1}{n^{y-1}}$

(e) $\frac{n}{y^n}$

16. A small, experimental plane has three engines, one which is redundant. That is, as long as two of the engines are working, the plane will stay in the air. Over the course of a typical flight, there is a $\frac{1}{3}$ chance that engine one will fail. There is a 75% probability that engine two will work. The third engine works only half the time. What is the probability that the plane will crash in any given flight?

(a) $\frac{7}{12}$

(b) $\frac{1}{4}$

(c) $\frac{1}{2}$

(d) $\frac{7}{24}$

(e) $\frac{17}{24}$

17. Ms. Barton has four children. You are told correctly that she has at least two girls but you are not told which two of her four children are those girls. What is the probability that she also has two boys? (Assume that the probability of having a boy is the same as the probability of having a girl.)

(a) $\frac{1}{4}$

(b) $\frac{3}{8}$

(c) $\frac{5}{11}$

(d) $\frac{1}{2}$

(e) $\frac{6}{11}$

18. Laura has a deck of standard playing cards with 13 of the 52 cards designated as a "heart". If Laura shuffles the deck thoroughly and then deals 10 cards off the top of the deck, what is the probability that the 10th card dealt is a heart?

(a) $\frac{1}{4}$

(b) $\frac{1}{5}$

(c) $\frac{5}{26}$

(d) $\frac{12}{42}$

(e) $\frac{13}{42}$

19. A license plate in the country Kerrania consists of four digits followed by two letters. The letters A, B, and C are used only by government vehicles while the letters D through Z are used by non-government vehicles. Kerrania's intelligence agency has recently captured a message from the country Gonzalia indicating that an electronic transmitter has been installed in a Kerrania government vehicle with a license plate starting with 79. If it takes the police 10 minutes to inspect each vehicle, what is the probability that the police will find the transmitter within three hours?

(*a*) $\frac{18}{79}$

(*b*) $\frac{1}{6}$

(*c*) $\frac{1}{25}$

(*d*) $\frac{1}{50}$

(*e*) $\frac{1}{900}$

20. A grid of light bulbs measures x bulbs x bulbs, where $x > 2$. If 4 light bulbs are illuminated at random, what is the probability, in terms of x, that the 4 bulbs form a 2 bulb by 2 square?

(*a*) $\frac{1}{63}$

(*b*) $\frac{2}{63}$

(*c*) $\frac{3}{63}$

(*d*) $\frac{4}{63}$

(*e*) $\frac{5}{63}$

21. Baseball's World Series matches 2 teams against each other in a best-of-seven series. The first team to win four games wins the series and no subsequent games are played. If you have no special information about either of the teams, what is the probability that the World Series will consist of fewer than 7 games?

(*a*) 12.5%

(*b*) 25%

(*c*) 31.25%

(*d*) 68.75%

(*e*) 75%

22. How many diagonals does a polygon with 12 sides have?

(*a*) 54

(*b*) 66

(*c*) 108

(*d*) 132

(*e*) 144

23. There are 5 digit code numbers and each digits of these codes are composed of 0, 1, 2, 3, 4, and 5. The first digit doesn't use "0", and the code doesn't use the same number for different digits. How many such codes are possible?

(*a*) 120

(*b*) 240

(*c*) 360

(*d*) 500

(*e*) 600

24. If you list up 6 letters S, C, H, O, O, and L, how many cases are possible such that at least one letter is in between O and O?

(*a*) 120

(*b*) 180

(*c*) 200

(*d*) 240

(*e*) 280

25. If n is integer between 1 and 30, inclusive, what is the probability that n(n + 1) (n + 2) is divisible 6?

(*a*) 1

(*b*) $\frac{5}{6}$

(*c*) $\frac{4}{5}$

(*d*) $\frac{3}{4}$

(*e*) $\frac{2}{3}$

26. When n is between 1 and 100 inclusive, what is the probability that n(n + 1) is a multiple of 5?

(*a*) $\frac{1}{4}$

(*b*) $\frac{1}{2}$

(*c*) $\frac{3}{4}$

(*d*) $\frac{2}{5}$

(*e*) $\frac{2}{5}$

27. The code numbers consist of 4-digit and 2 digits are different and 2 digits are the same and none of them is zero, for example, 1122, 1212. How many such code numbers are possible?

(*a*) 196

(*b*) 216

(*c*) 236

(*d*) 256

(*e*) 316

28. The club contains 3 female members and 4 male members. If you randomly select 2 members from the club, what is the probability that at least one female will be included?

(*a*) $\frac{3}{4}$

(*b*) $\frac{2}{3}$

(*c*) $\frac{1}{2}$

(*d*) $\frac{5}{7}$

(*e*) $\frac{3}{7}$

29. There are 10 pairs of socks with each pair in different colors. If we select 2 from the 20 socks, what's the probability of selecting the same color socks?

(*a*) $\frac{1}{15}$

(*b*) $\frac{1}{16}$

(*c*) $\frac{1}{17}$

(*d*) $\frac{1}{18}$

(*e*) $\frac{1}{19}$

30. What is the difference between the mean and the median of Set C, a set of the first 100 positive integers?

(*a*) 0

(*b*) 25

(*c*) 50

(*d*) 75

(*e*) Cannot be determined

31. 3, 5, 7, 9

If another number N is added to the list above, which of the following could be the median of the new list of five numbers?

I. 5

II. 6

III. 7

(*a*) None of the above

(*b*) I only

(*c*) II only

(*d*) I and III only

(*e*) I, II and III

32. The "range" of a set of data is defined as the absolute difference between the least value and the greatest value in the set. Four positive integers have an averages (arithmetic mean) of 10. What tis the greatest possible range of the set?

(*a*) 40

(*b*) 36

(*c*) 32

(*d*) 25

(*e*) 10

33. The median of a set of 23 consecutive numbers is 25. What is the largest number in the set?

(*a*) 32

(*b*) 33

(*c*) 34

(*d*) 35

(*e*) 36

34. What is the average of $(x + 4)^2$ and $(x - 4)^2$?

(*a*) x^2

(*b*) $x^2 + 16$

(*c*) $x^2 + 32$

(*d*) $x^2 + 16x$

(*e*) $x^2 + 32x$

35. **Set A :** 4, 7, 9, 20

Set B : x, 4, 7, 9, 20

If the median of Set A is the same as Set B, then what is the value of x?

(*a*) 6

(*b*) 7

(*c*) 8

(*d*) 9

(*e*) 10

36. 4, x, 3, 9, y, 4

The arithmetic mean of the list of numbers above is 5. If x and y are integers and $x \neq y$, what is the median of the list?

(*a*) 2

(*b*) 3

(*c*) 4

(*d*) 5

(*e*) Cannot be determined

37. The average weight of a group of x people is 50 kilograms. If a person weighing 90 kilograms joins the group, the group average increases to 55 kilograms, what is the value of x?

(*a*) 11

(*b*) 10

(*c*) 9

(*d*) 8

(*e*) 7

38. There are ten people in a group. Out of them, 3 people weigh 50kg each, 3 people weigh 55 kg each, and the rest 4 weigh 45 kg each. What is the median weight of the group?

(*a*) 45

(*b*) 47

(*c*) 50

(*d*) 50.5

(*e*) 55

39. What is the difference between range and median of the numbers, x, x + 2, x + 3, x + 5, x + 10?

(*a*) –7

(*b*) –1

(*c*) x – 10

(*d*) x – 7

(*e*) x + 3

40. If the average of 21 consecutive integers is 152, what is the least of these integers?

(*a*) 139

(*b*) 140

(*c*) 141

(*d*) 142

(*e*) 143

41. The average score of seven students in an exam is 81. If score of one student is removed, the average score of the six students is 78. What is the score of the students which is removed.

(*a*) 98

(*b*) 99

(*c*) 100

(*d*) 101

(*e*) 102

42. In list A there are 10 numbers whose average is 70 and in list B there are 30 numbers whose average is 62. What is the average of these 40 numbers when both the lists are combined?

(*a*) 63

(*b*) 64

(*c*) 65

(*d*) 66

(*e*) 67

43. In list A there are 11 numbers whose median is 70 and in list B there are 9 numbers whose median is 62. What is the median of these 20 numbers when both the lists are combined?

(*a*) 62

(*b*) 64

(*c*) 68

(*d*) 70

(*e*) Cannot be determined

44. Set X = {1, 2, 3, 4, 5}

Set Y = {3, 3, 3, 3, 3}

Set Z = {0, 1, 5, 3, 4.5, 6}

Which set has the least standard deviation?

(*a*) Set X

(*b*) Set Y

(*c*) Set Z

(*d*) Set X and Set Y both

(*e*) Set Y and Set Z both

45. Which of the following sets has the smallest standard deviation?

(*a*) {–8, –8, –8, –8, -8}

(*b*) {–2, 0, 0, 0, 2}

(*c*) {1, 2, 3, 4, 5}

(*d*) {–1, –1, –1, –1, 0}

(*e*) {0, 1, 1, 1, 1}

46. If x and y are positive integers and the median of the numbers $3^{x-1}5^{y}$, $3^{x}5^{y-1}$, and $3^{x}5^{y}$, not in order, is 6,075, what is the value of xy?

(*a*) 8

(*b*) 9

(*c*) 10

(*d*) 12

(*e*) 15

47. Seven friends have a few candies with them. The numbers of candies with them are 21, 23, 45, 51, 66, 71, and 73.

They redistribute the candies among themselves such that each has at least one candy. The number of candies with them is distinct, and the median number of candies is maximum. What is the range of the number of candies with them?

(*a*) 86

(*b*) 87

(*c*) 88

(*d*) 89

(*e*) 90

48. If two numbers are selected randomly from Set A = {1, 2, 3, 4}, what is the probability that the sum of the numbers is even?

(*a*) $\frac{1}{3}$

(*b*) $\frac{1}{8}$

(*c*) $\frac{2}{3}$

(*d*) $\frac{1}{2}$

(*e*) $\frac{11}{16}$

49. There are five bulbs in a room, and each has its own switch. In how many ways can the room be illuminated if at least one bulb is on?

(*a*) 5

(*b*) 10

(*c*) 25

(*d*) 31

(*e*) 32

50. A committee requires four members. There are six members who are willing to be part of the committee: J, E, M, L, H, and P.E does not want to be in a committee with M, while P wants to be in the committee only if E is part of it. How many committees of four members can be formed?

(*a*) 3

(*b*) 5

(*c*) 6

(*d*) 7

(*e*) 8

51. Drake has 15 clients and wants to identify his clients with either a single character or a pair of two characters. What is the minimum number of characters needed to represent his clients of changing the order of characters does not produce a new pair?

(*a*) 3

(*b*) 4

(*c*) 5

(*d*) 6

(*e*) 7

52. If three single shoes are selected from a group of six pairs of different shoes, what is the probability that no two shoes will make a pair?

(*a*) $\frac{1}{1.320}$

(*b*) $\frac{1}{110}$

(*c*) $\frac{2}{33}$

(*d*) $\frac{13}{33}$

(*e*) $\frac{8}{11}$

53. If Set Q contains the numbers a, b, and c, which of the following set of numbers must have the same standard deviation as Set Q?

(*a*) (a + 1, b, c)

(*b*) (a, b + 1, c)

(*c*) (a, b, c + 1)

(*d*) [(a + bc), b (1 + c), c(b + 1)]

(*e*) (a – 1, b + 1, c)

54. The table below gives the number of victories the tennis player Roger has achieved against opponents. What are the minimum and maximum values of the sum of the median number of victories and the average number of victories for Roger?

Number of victories	Number of opponents
0	5
1	3
2	1
3	4
4	2

(*a*) 0 and 1

(*b*) 1 and 2

(*c*) 2 and 3

(*d*) 3 and 4

(*e*) 4 and 5

55. The mean of a set of eight integers is x. If all the integers in the set are multiplied by 3, then mean is still x. Which of the following statements holds true for the set?

I. x = 0

II. The largest integer in the set = negative of the smallest integer in the set.

III. The set contains both positive and negative integers.

(*a*) I only

(*b*) II only

(*c*) III only

(*d*) I and II only

(*e*) I, II and III

56. The average (arithmetic mean) as well as the median of nine distinct positive integers of a set is 30. If the terms of the set are such that their product is the greatest, what is the difference between the largest and the smallest terms of the set?

(*a*) 10

(*b*) 9

(*c*) 8

(*d*) 5

(*e*) 0

57. Of the 25 students in a class, 10 play football, and 8 play both cricket and football. If 10 students play none of these sports, how many students play cricket but not football?

(*a*) 3

(*b*) 4

(*c*) 5

(*d*) 6

(*e*) 13

Answer Key

1. (*e*)
2. (*b*)
3. (*d*)
4. (*d*)
5. (*c*)
6. (*c*)
7. (*c*)
8. (*a*)
9. (*c*)
10. (*a*)
11. (*e*)
12. (*e*)
13. (*d*)
14. (*e*)
15. (*d*)
16. (*d*)
17. (*e*)
18. (*a*)
19. (*d*)
20. (*b*)
21. (*d*)
22. (*b*)
23. (*e*)
24. (*d*)
25. (*a*)
26. (*d*)
27. (*b*)
28. (*d*)
29. (*e*)
30. (*a*)
31. (*e*)
32. (*b*)
33. (*e*)
34. (*b*)
35. (*c*)
36. (*c*)
37. (*e*)
38. (*c*)
39. (*d*)
40. (*d*)
41. (*b*)
42. (*b*)
43. (*e*)
44. (*b*)
45. (*a*)
46. (*d*)
47. (*d*)
48. (*d*)
49. (*d*)
50. (*b*)
51. (*c*)
52. (*e*)
53. (*d*)
54. (*c*)
55. (*a*)
56. (*c*)
57. (*c*)

Answer Explanations

1. (e) A password can be made using any of the digits from 0 to 9, so there are 10 choices.

A password could be 122 or 221, hence repetition on digits are allowed.

Using slot approach, password can be created with slots, ___ AND__ AND ___

First slot can be filled in 10 ways

Second slot can be filled in 10 ways

Third slot can be filled in 10 ways

Hence, by the fundamental principle of counting (If an event occurs in p different ways, and another event occurs in q different ways, then the total number of ways the events occur is $p \times q$ ways)

Total number of passwords

$$= 10 \times 10 \times 10 = 10^3.$$

The correct answer is option (e).

2. (b) There are 5 digits given to us 1, 2, 3, 4 out of which 3 coming 2 times

We know, 5 digits can be arranged in 5! Ways

Also, as digit 3 which is 2 times can rearrange within themselves in 2! Ways

Hence, the number of ways the digits can be arranged in $\frac{5!}{2!}$ Ways

The correct answer is option (b).

3. (d) In the first section, there are 3 questions and 2 mut be answered, as answering Q1 then Q2 is different from

Number of ways to answer the first section $= {}^3P_2$

Similarly in the second section, there are 4 questions and 2 must be answered, as answering Q1 and Q2 then Q3 is different from answering Q2, then Q1 then Q3. Hence, order matter, this is permutation question.

Number of ways to answer second section $= {}^4P_2$

Total number of ways of answering the test $= {}^3P_2 \times {}^4P^2 = 6 \times 12 = 72$

The correct answer is option (d).

4. (d) There are 6 different objects M O, B, I, L, E

Since vowels are together consider O, I, E to be one group.

Now, there are 4 object (M, B, L, group of vowels)

These 4 objects can be arranged in 4! ways

Also 3 distinct objects in the group of vowels can be arranged in 3! ways

Hence, by The fundamental principal of counting (If an event occurs in p different ways, and another event occurs in q different ways, then the total number of ways the events occur is $p \times q$ ways)

Therefore, total number of ways $= 4! \times 3!$

The correct answer is option (d).

5. (c) There are 6 objects C, O, L, O, U, R

Since vowels are objects (C, L, R, group of vowels), which can be arranged in 4! Ways Also 3 objects (O, O, U) in the group of vowels can be arranged in $\frac{3!}{2!}$ Ways (as O is coming 2 times)

Hence, by the fundamental principal of counting, total number of ways

$$= \frac{4! \times 3!}{2!}$$

The correct answer is option (c)

6. (c) Let's consider a couple as a group.

So there are three groups, we can arrange three groups of couples in 3! ways = 6 ways

Now, first group of couple can rearrange within themselves in 2! ways

Similarly, second group of couple can rearrange within themselves in 2! Ways

And first third of couple can rearrange within themselves in 2! Ways

Hence, total number of ways in which they can be standing in a row

$= 3! \times 2! \times 2! \times 2!$

$= 6 \times 2 \times 2 \times 2 = 48$ ways

The correct answer is option (d)

7. (c) The number of ways in which n people can be seated around a circular table is $(n - 1)!$ Ways Hence, number of ways 6 people can be seated around a circular table

$= (6 - 1) = 5! = 120$ ways

The correct answer is option (c).

8. (a) The first prize can be given to any of the 3 students, hence there are 3 ways to give first prize.

The second prize can be given to any of the remaining 2 students in 2 ways.

Similarly, third prize can be given to 1 student in 1 way.

Hence, total number of ways are $3 \times 2 \times 1 = 6$

The correct answer is option (a)

9. (c) First prize can be given to any one of the 3 students.

Second prize can be given to any one of the 3 students.

Similarly, third prize can be given to any of the 3 students.

Hence, number of ways in which prizes can be distributed

$= 3 \times 3 \times 3 = 27$

The correct answer is option (c)

10. (a) To fill the hundreds place there are 9 choices, except 0 (as the three-digit number cannot have 0 in the hundreds place)

To fill tens place there are 9 choice (as 0 can come but as repetition is not allowed 1 digit already used in the hundreds place cannot be counted)

To fill one's place there are 8 choices (as repetition is not allowed, 2 digits already used in the hundreds and tens place cannot be counted)

Total number of three-digit numbers

$= 9 \times 9 \times 8 = 648$

The correct answer is option (a)

11. (e) As the order does not matter in the questions, it is combination.

Number of ways in which 2 men can be selected out of 5 men is ${}^5C_2 = 10$

Number of ways in which 2 women can be selected out of 6 women is ${}^6C_2 = 15$

A committee is to be formed of 2 men AND 2 women

$= 10 \times 15 = 150$

The correct answer is option (e)

12. (e) 5 red balls can be arranged only in one way as they are identical.

_R_R_R_R_R_

There are 6 places available for arranging 4 balls. So, 4 can be arranged in 6 places in 6C4 ways = 15 ways

Hence, total number of ways in which 5 identical red balls 4 identical blue balls can be arranged = $1 \times 15 = 15$ ways

The correct answer is option (e)

13. **(d)** If there are n distinct objects they can be arranged around a circular in (n – 1)! Ways.

Hence, 5 men can be seated at a circular table such that there is a vacant seat between every pair of men in (5 – 1)! = 4! Ways.

Now 5 vacant seats can be occupied by 5 women in 5! Ways.

Hence the required number of seating arrangements

$$= 4! \times 5! = 24 \times 120 = 2880$$

The correct answer is option (d)

14. **(e)** These is a strong temptation to solve this problem by simply finding probability that it will snow (90%) and the probability that schools will be closed (80%) and multiplying these two probabilities. This approach would the incorrect answer (72%), choice (d).

However, it is only possible to multiply probabilities of separate events if you know that they are independent from each other. This fact is not provided in the problem. In fact, we would assume that school being closed and snow are, at least to some extent, dependent on each other. However, they are not entirely dependent on each other, it is possible for either one to happen without the other. Therefore, there is an unknown degree of dependence; hence there is a range of possible probabilities, depending on to what extent the events are dependent on each other.

Set up a matrix as sown below. Fill in the probability that schools will not be closed and the probability that there will be no snow.

	Schools closed	Schools not closed	Total
Snow			
No snow			10
Total		20	100

Then use subtraction to fill in the probability that schools will be closed and the probability that there will be snow.

	Schools closed	Schools not closed	Total
Snow			90
No snow			10
Total	80	20	100

To find the greatest possible probability that schools will be closed and it will snow, fill in the remaining cells with the largest possible number in the upper left cell.

	Schools closed	Schools not closed	Total
Snow	80	10	90
No snow	0	10	10
Total	80	20	100

The greatest possible probability that schools will be closed and it will snow is 80%.

The correct answer is (e).

15. **(d)** The easiest way to attack this problem is to pick some real, easy numbers as values for y and n. Let's assume there are 3 travelers (A, B, C) and 2 different destinations (1, 2).

We can chart out the possibilities as follows:

Destination 1	Destination 2
ABC	
AB	C
AC	B
BC	A
	ABC
C	AB
B	AC
A	BC

Thus there are 8 possibilities and in 2 of them all travelers end up at the same destination. Thus the probability is $\frac{2}{8}$ or $\frac{1}{4}$. By plugging in y = 3 and n = 2 into each answer choice, we see that only answer choice D yields a probability of $\frac{1}{4}$.

Alternatively, consider that each traveler can end up at any one of n destinations. Thus, for each traveler there are n possibilities. Therefore, for y travelers, there are n^y possible outcomes.

Additionally, the "winning" outcomes are those where all travelers end up at the same destination.

Since there are n destinations there are n "winning" outcomes.

Thus, the probability

$$= \frac{\text{winning outcomes}}{\text{total outcomes}} = \frac{n}{n^y} = \frac{1}{n^{y-1}}.$$

The answer is (d).

16. **(d)** There are four scenarios in which the plane will crash. Determine the probability of each of these scenarios individually:

Case one : Engine 1 fails, Engine 2 fails, Engine 3 works

$$= \frac{1}{3} \times \frac{1}{4} \times \frac{1}{2} = \frac{1}{24}$$

Case two : Engine 1 fails, Engine 2 works, Engine 3 fails

$$= \frac{1}{3} \times \frac{3}{4} \times \frac{1}{2} = \frac{3}{24}$$

Case three : Engine 1 works, Engine 2 fails, Engine 3 works

$$= \frac{2}{3} \times \frac{1}{4} \times \frac{1}{2} = \frac{2}{24}$$

Case four : Engine 1 fails, Engine 2 fails, Engine 3 fails

$$= \frac{1}{3} \times \frac{1}{4} \times \frac{1}{2} = \frac{1}{24}$$

To determine the probability that any one of these scenarios will occur, sum four probabilities:

$$\frac{1}{24} + \frac{3}{24} + \frac{2}{24} + \frac{1}{24} = \frac{7}{24}$$

The correct answer is (d).

17. **(e)** Since each of the 4 children can be either a boy or a girl, there are $2 \times 2 \times 2 \times 2 = 2 = 16$ possible ways that the children might be born, as listed below:

BBBB (all boys)

BBBG, BBGB, BGBB, GBBBM (3 boys, 1 girl)

BBGG, BGGB, BGBG, GGBB, GBBG, GBGB (2 boys, 2 girls)

GGGB, GGBG, GBGG, BGGG (3 girls, 1 boy)

GGGG (all girls)

Since we are told that there at least 2 girls, we an eliminate 5 possibilities - the one possibility in which all of the children are boys (the first row) and the four possibilities in which only one of the children is a girl (the second row).

That leaves 11 possibilities (the third, fourth, and fifth row) of which 6 are comprised of two boys and two girls (the third row). Thus, the probability that Ms. Barton also has 2 boys is $\frac{6}{11}$.

The correct answer is option (e).

18. **(a)** Although this maybe counter-intuitive at first, the probability that any card in the deck will be a heart before any cards are seen in $\frac{13}{52}$ or $\frac{1}{4}$.

One way to understand this is to solve the problem analytically for any card by building a probability "tree" and summing the probability of all of its "branches."

For example, let's find the probability that the 2nd card dealt from the deck is a heart. There are two mutually exclusive ways this can happen: (1) both the first and second cards are hearts or (2) only the second card is a heart.

Case 1 : Using the multiplication rule, the probability that the first card is a heart AND the second card is a heart is equal to the probability of picking a heart on the first card (or $\frac{13}{52}$, which is the number of hearts in a full deck divided by the number of cards) times the probability of picking a heart on the second card (or $\frac{12}{51}$, which is the number of hearts remaining in the deck divided by the number of cards remaining in the deck).

$$\frac{13}{52} \times \frac{12}{51} = \frac{12}{204}$$

Case 2 : Similarly, the probability that the first card is a non-heart AND the second card is a heart is equal to the probability that the first card is NOT a heart (or $\frac{39}{52}$) times the probability of subsequently picking a heart on the 2nd card (or $\frac{13}{51}$).

$$\frac{39}{52} \times \frac{13}{51} = \frac{39}{204}$$

Since these two cases are mutually exclusive, we can add them together to get the total probability f getting a heart as the second card:

$$\frac{12}{204} + \frac{29}{204} = \frac{51}{204} = \frac{1}{4}$$

We can do a similar analysis for any card in the deck, and although the probability tree gets more complicated as the card number gets higher, the total probability that the nth card dealt will be a heart will always end up simplifying to $\frac{1}{4}$.

The correct answer is (a).

19. (d) Since the first two digits of the license plate are known and there are 10 possibilities for each of the remaining two digits (each can be any digit from 0 to 9), the total number of combinations for digits on the license plate will equal $10 \times 10 = 100$.

Because there are only 3 letters that can be used for government license plates (A, B, or C), there are a total of nine two-letter combinations that could be on the license plate (3 possibilities for first letter × 3 possibilities for the second letter).

Given that we have 100 possible digit combinations and 9 possible letter combinations, the total number of vehicles to be inspected will equal $100 \times 9 = 900$.

Since it takes 10 minutes to inspect one vehicle, the police will have time to inspect 18 vehicles in three hours (3 hours = 180 minutes).

Thus, the probability of locating the transmitter within the allotted time is $\frac{18}{900} = \frac{1}{50}$.

The correct answer is (d).

20. (b) Trying to figure this problem out directly is time-consuming and risky. The safest and most efficient way to handle this is to assign a value to x, figure out the probability, and then plug that value into the answer choice until you find one choice that yields the correct probability.

Since x must be greater than 2, let's assign x a value of 3. This produces a 3-by-3 grid as follows (where each letter represents a bulb):

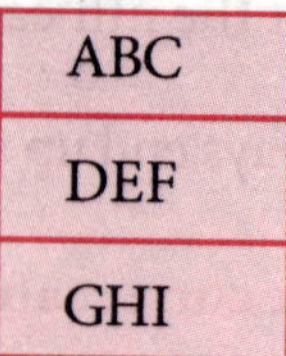

In order to determine the probability, we need to first figure out how many different groups of 4 bulbs could be illuminated. Since we have 9 bulbs, we can represent one way that exactly four bulbs could be illuminated as follows (each letter represents a bulb):

A	B	C	D	E	F	G	H	I
Yes	Yes	Yes	Yes	No	No	No	No	No

There are many other ways this could happen. Using the permutation formula, there are $\frac{9!}{(4!)(5!)} = 126$ different combinations of exactly four illuminated bulbs.

How many of these 126 groups of 4 form a 2-by-2 square? If you analyze the 3-by-3 grid above you'll see there are only 4 groups that form a 2-by-2 square (ABDE, BCEF, DEGH, & EFHI).

Thus the correct probability is $\frac{4}{126}$ or $\frac{2}{63}$.

If we plug in 3 for x in the answer choices, only choice (b) reduces to the same answer.

The correct answer is (b).

21. (d) In order to determine the probability that the World Series will last fewer than 7 games, we can first determine the probability that the World Series Will last exactly 7 games and then subtract this value from 1.

In order for the World Series to last exactly 7 games, the first 6 games of the series must results in 3 wins and 3 losses for each team.

Let's analyze one way this could happen :

Game 1	Game 2	Game 3	Game 4	Game 5	Game 6
T1 Wins	T1 Wins	T1 Wins	T1 Loses	T1 Loses	T1 Loses

There are many other ways this could happen. Using the permutation formula, there are $\frac{6!}{(3!)(3!)} = 20$ ways for the two teams to split the first 6 games (3 wins for each).

There are then 2 possible outcomes to break the tie in Game 7. Thus there are a total of $20 \times 2 = 40$ ways for the World Series at last the full 7 games.

The probability that any one of these 40 ways occurs can be calculated from the fact that the probability of a team winning a game equals the probability of a team losing a game $= \frac{1}{2}$.

Given that 7 distinct events must happen in any 7 game series, and that each of these events has a probability of $\frac{1}{2}$, the probability that any one particular 7 game series occurs is $\left(\frac{1}{2}\right)^7 = \frac{1}{128}$. Since there are 40 possible different 7 game series, the probability that the World Series will last exactly 7 games is:

$$40 \times \frac{1}{128} = \frac{40}{128} = .3125 = 31.25\%$$

Thus the probability that the World Series will last fewer than 7 games is 100% – 31.25% = 68.75%.

The correct answer is (d).

22. (b) The number of diagonals in any polygon is

$$\frac{n(n-3)}{2}$$

Here n = 12

$\Rightarrow$ The number of polygons

$$= \frac{12(12-3)}{2} = 12 \times \frac{9}{2} = 54$$

The answer is (a)

23. (e) $\Rightarrow$ Since you are forming 5 digit code numbers, from

0, 1, 2, 3, 4, 5

The first digit can't be a 0, so there are 5 ways, and for second digit, since you can't have the same number as the first digit, so there are also 5 ways (since you can have 0 here), and there are 4 ways for third digit. 3 ways for fourth digit, and 2 digit for the fifth digit, so you get (5) (5) (4) (3) (2) = 600.

The correct answer is option (e).

24. (d) The number of ways to list the letters S, C, H, O, O, L is $\frac{6!}{2!}$ since there are 6 letters and 2 letters (O, O) of them are the same so you divide it by 2!. In other words, when listing S, C, H, O, O, L, the number of ways that at least one letter is in between O and O is the total number of ways- the number of ways that O and O is next to each other. Thus, from $\frac{6!}{2!}$ (OO)SCHL, you need to subtract the case where OO is next to each other. Then, from $\frac{6!}{2!} - 5! = 360 = 120 = 240$.

The answer is (d).

25. **(a)** $\Rightarrow$ Probability $= \frac{\text{Want}}{\text{Total}}$. Then,

Since there is a total of 30 integers, you get Total $= {}_{30}C_1 = 30$.

Since the product of 3 consecutive integers always become the multiple of 6, so it is always divisible by 6 because the 3 consecutive integers always contain 3, and at least 1 is an even number. Then, you get Want $= {}_{30}C_1$ $= 30$. Thus, when N is a positive integer from 1 to 30, the probability that n(n + 1) (n + 2) is divisible by 6 becomes $\frac{30}{30} = 1$.

The answer is (a).

26. **(d)** In general, it is best to directly substitute for remainder questions. In other words, the multiple of 5 means that the remainder is 0 when divided by 5, so it becomes a remainder question. If you solve it by direct substitution.

n = 1, (1) (1) $\neq$ multiple of 5 ...... n = 96, (96) (97) $\neq$ multiple of 5

n = 2, (2) (3) $\neq$ multiple of 5 ...... n = 97, (97) (98) $\neq$ multiple of 5

n = 3, (3) (4) $\neq$ multiple of 5 ...... n = 98, (98) (99) $\neq$ multiple of 5

n = 4, (4) (5) = multiple of 5 ...... n = 99, (99) (100) = multiple of 5

n = 5, (5) (6) = multiple of 5 ...... n = 100, (100) (101) = multiple of 5

The correct answer is option (d).

27. **(b)** First, the number of possible ways of to list 1, 1, 2, 2 is $\frac{4!}{2!2!} = 6$, which are (1, 1, 2, 2), (1, 2, 1, 2), (2, 1, 1, 2), (2, 2, 1, 1), (2, 1, 2, 1), or (1, 2, 1, 2).

Then, from the total 4 digits, each 2 digits are the same, from the 9 numbers 1, 2, 3, 4, 5, , 7, 8, 9, the number of ways to select two numbers is ${}_9C_2\,\frac{(9)(8)}{2!} = 36$, and the since each of the code numbers can be in 6 ways as shown above, you get (6) (36) = 216.

The answer is (b).

28. **(d)** It is "at least" question, so from the 7 members, it is the probability of selecting at least 1 female member when randomly selecting 2 members. Thus, you get 1-the probability of not selecting at least one female member=1-the probability of not selecting both male members. Then, the probability of selecting two male members is from $\frac{\text{Want}}{\text{Total}}$, since you are selecting 2 out of 7, you get Total $= {}_7C_2 = \frac{(7)(6)}{2!} = 21$ and since it is the probability of selecting both males, you get Want $= {}_4C_2 = \frac{(4)(3)}{2!} = 6$. Thus, the probability of selecting at least 1 female member when randomly selecting 2 out of 7 members is

$$1 - \frac{6}{21} = 1 - \frac{2}{7} = \frac{5}{7}.$$

Therefore, (d) is the answer.

29. **(e)** Probability $= \frac{\text{Want}}{\text{Total}}$. Then since there are 20 socks in total, you get Total ${}_{20}C_2 = \frac{(20)(19)}{2!} = 190$, and since you need to select same colored.

socks, from the total 10 pairs, you must select 1 pair, and from the pair, you must select both socks, so you get Want = $({}_{10}C_1)\ ({}_2C_2)$ = (10) (1) = 10. The probability of selecting 2 same colored socks from 20 socks becomes

$$\frac{10}{190} = \frac{1}{19}.$$

The answer is (e).

30. **(a)** For a set of consecutive integers, the mean

$$= \text{median} = \frac{(1^{st}\text{ term} + \text{last term})}{2}$$

Hence, the difference between mean and the median is 0.

The answer is (a).

31. **(e)** Here, we need to take cases

If P < 5, then the new set would be

P, 3, 5, 7, 9 or 3, P, 5, 7, 9

Hence, the median would be 5.

If P = 6, then the new set would be 3, 5, 6, 7, 9

Hence, the median is 6.

If P > 7, then the new set would be

3, 5, 7, P, 9 or 3, 5, 7, 9, P

Hence, the median would be 7.

The answer is (e)

32. **(b)** $\text{Average} = \frac{\text{Sum}}{\text{Number of terms}}$

$$10 = \frac{\text{Sum}}{4}$$

$\Rightarrow$ Sum = 40

If the four numbers are A, B, C, and D, then A + B + C + D = 40

For the greatest range, A must be the smallest and D must be the greatest integer. Smallest positive integer is 1. So, let A, B, and C be 1 each.

Hence 1 + 1 + 1 + D = 40

3 + D = 40

$\Rightarrow$ D = 37

Hence, the range = 37 – 1 = 36

The answer is (b)

33. **(e)** In a set of 23 consecutive numbers, the 12th numbers is the median.

Hence, the 12th number is 25.

There are 11 numbers greater than 25.

Hence, the largest number in the set is 25 + 11 = 36

The answer is (e)

34. **(b)** $(x + 4)^2 = x^2 + 16 + 8x$

$(x - 4)^2 = x^2 + 16 - 8x$

$$\Rightarrow (x + 4)^2 + (x - 4)^2$$
$$= (x^2 + 16 + 8x) + (x^2 + 16 - 8x)$$
$$= 2(x^2 + 16)$$

$$\text{Average} = \frac{2(x^2 + 16)}{2} = x^2 + 16$$

The answer is (b)

35. **(c)** Median of Set A is $\frac{(7+9)}{2} = 8$

For the median of Set B to be 8, x must be 8

The answer is (c)

36. **(c)** $\frac{(4 + x + 3 + 9 + y + 4)}{6} = 5$

$(20 + x + y) = 30$

$x + y = 10$

As $x \neq y$, there are some possible sets (1, 9), (2, 8), (3, 7), and (4, 6)

If $x = 1$ and $y = 9$, then the set is 1, 3, 4, 4, 9, 9 – The median is 4

If $x = 2$ and $y = 8$, then the set is 2, 3, 4, 4, 8, 9 – The median is 4

If $x = 3$ and $y = 7$, then the set is 3, 3, 4, 4, 7, 9 – The median is 4

If $x = 4$ and $y = 6$, then the set is 3, 4, 4, 4, 6, 9 – The median is 4

Hence, the answer is (c)

37. (e) We know, Average = sum of readings/ number of readings

50 = sum of weight of x people /x

Sum of weight of x people = 5x

New average = 55

$$= \frac{(\text{sum of weight of x people} + 90)}{(x+1)}$$

$55(x + 1) = 50x + 90$

$55x + 55 = 50x + 90$

$5x = 35$

$x = 7$

The correct answer is option (e)

38. (c) Since there are 10 entries, the median weight of the group is the average of the 5th and 6th entries when the weights are arranged in order from least to greatest.

In order from least to greatest, the 5th and 6th entry are:

45, 45, 45, 45, 50, 50

Average of the 5th and 6th entry

$$= \frac{(50 + 50)}{2} = 50$$

The correct answer is option (c)

39. (d) $x, x + 2, x + 3, x + 5, x + 10$

median of the five numbers is the third number, $x + 3$

Range is the difference between greatest and smallest number

$$= x + 10 - x = 10$$

Median – Range $= x + 3 - 10 = x - 7$

The correct answer is option (d)

40. (d) Consecutive integers are in arithmetic progression where common difference between any two consecutive numbers is same.

In an AP, average = median = 152 is the middle term

Since there are 21 consecutive integers, the 11th number is the middle term.

Hence, the smallest integer must be 10 less than 152 = 142

The correct answer is option (d)

41. (b) Average score of seven students = 81

Then the sum of these seven students

$$= 7 \times 81 = 567.$$

Since, if one of score is removed, the average of the six-remaining score = 78,

Then the sum of these six scores

$$= 6 \times 81 = 567.$$

Since, if one of score is removed, the average of the six-remaining score = 78,

Then the sum of these six scores

$$= 6 \times 78 = 468.$$

Hence, removed score = 567 – 468 = 99

The correct answer is option (b)

42. **(b)** As average and number of readings in the two given lists is known, we can calculate their respective sums.

Sum of numbers of list A = $10 \times 70 = 700$

Sum of numbers of list B = $30 \times 62 = 1860$

Therefore, sum of 50 numbers

$$= 700 + 1860 = 2560$$

Hence, average of the 50 numbers

$$= \frac{2560}{40} = 64$$

The correct answer is option (b)

43. **(e)** Median of 11 numbers in list A is 70 means 6th reading is 70

Median of 9 numbers in list B is 62 means 5th reading is 62

When both the lists are combined, there are 20 readings, and median is the average of the 10th and 11th reading.

But, from the given information value of the 10th and 11th reading cannot be determined.

The correct answer is option (e)

44. **(b)** Standard deviation measures dispersion around the mean. The closer the readings, the lesser is the standard deviation. The more far away the readings, the greater is the standard deviation.

In set X, mean is 3 with two readings below and above the mean, hence there is deviation

In set Y, mean is 3 and all readings are same, hence there is no deviation around the mean.

In set Z, mean is 3 with two readings below and above the mean, hence there is deviation.

The correct answer is option (b)

45. **(a)** The computation of standard deviation (SD) is not within the scope of the GMAT; however, its analysis is.

Standard deviation is the measure of the spread of values within a set with respect to its mean. The farther the values are on either side of the mean, the greater the standard deviation and vie-versa.

The smallest possible value of SD is 0, and that's when all of the terms in a set are the same. We see that only the set {–8, –8, –8, –8, –8} has all the terms same; thus, its SD = 0, minimum.

Other sets will have SD > 0. We are not asked to choose a set that has the largest SD; had that been the question, the answer would have been option C: {1, 2, 3, 4, 5} because collectively, the spread of the terms in the set w.r.t is mean (=3) would be greater than that in any other set.

The correct answer is option (a).

46. **(d)** We have the first number, $3^{x-1}\,5^{y} = \frac{3^x 5^y}{3}$

And the second number, $3^{x}\,5^{y-1} = \frac{3^x 5^y}{5}$

Thus, the smallest of the three numbers is $\frac{3^x 5^y}{5}$ and the largest is $3^x 5^y$.

Thus, the three numbers, when arranged in ascending order are $\frac{3^x 5^y}{5}$, $\frac{3^x 5^y}{3}$ and $3^x 5^y$.

Thus, the median = the middle-most number $\frac{3^x 5^y}{3} = 3^{x-1} 5^y$

Thus, we have

$$3^{x-1}5^y = 6{,}075 = 3^5 5^2$$

$\Rightarrow$ $x - 1 = 5, \Rightarrow x = 6$ and y 2

$\Rightarrow$ $xy = 12$

The correct answer is option (d).

47. (d) Thus, total number of candies with the 7 friends

$$= 21 + 23 + 45 + 51 + 66 + 71 + 73 = 360$$

We need to maximize the median value.

The median of 7 terms $= \left(\frac{7+1}{2}\right)^{th}$ term

$$= 4^{th} \text{term}$$

Let's arrange the number of candies with the keep terms distinct, the terms following the median, i.e., 6th,6th, and 7th should be 1 greater, 2 greater, and 3 greater than the median, respectively.

We minimize the 1st, 2nd, 7th friends have x, (x + 1), (x + 2), and (x + 3) candies, where x is the median.

Thus, we have

$x + (x + 1) + (x + 2) + (x + 3) = 354 \Rightarrow x = 87$

Thus, the numbers of candies are 1, 2, 3, 87, 88, 89, and 90 (the median is maximized).

Thus, the range = 90 – 1 = 89

The correct answer is option (d).

48. (d) Set A contains one even number (2) and three odd numbers (1, 3, and 5).

The sum of two positive integers would be even if both are even or both are odd. Since there's only one even number, we cannot have two even numbers upon selection; thus we must focus on the selection of two odd numbers.

Number of ways of randomly selecting two odd numbers out of three odd numbers from Set A

$$= C_2^3 = C_1^3 = 3; \text{ not that } C_r^n = C_{n-r}^n.$$

Number of ways of randomly selecting two numbers out of four numbers from Set A

$$= C_2^4 = \frac{4.3}{1.2} = 6$$

Thus, the probability that the sum of the two selected numbers is even $\frac{3}{6} = \frac{1}{2}$.

The correct answer is option (d).

49. (d) Each bulb can either be on or off (2 ways). Since there are five bulbs, the number of possibilities are

$$2 \times 2 \times 2 \times 2 \times 2 = 2^5 = 32.$$

From all the above possibilities, we have to subtract the possibility of all the bulbs being switched off, i.e., when the room is not illuminated. Therefore, the answer is 32 – 1 = 31, number of ways the room can have at least one bulb on.

The correct answer is option (d).

50. (b) A committee can be formed either with without E.

Therefore, total number of committees

= Number of committees with E in the committee + Number of committees without E in the committee

Let us find the number of committees with E in the committee.

Since E does not want to be in the committee with M, we can exclude M. P can be in the committee as E is in the committee. Hence the other 3 committee members apart from E can be chosen from J, Luiz, H, and P.

Number of ways of selecting 3 people out of

$4 = {}^3C_4 = 4.$

Number of committees formed without E in the committee.

Paul would not want to be the part of the committee as E is not in the committee.

Hence, the number of ways of forming a 4-member committee out of (J, L, H, and M) is 1.

Total number of committees = 4 + 1 = 5.

The correct answer is option (b).

51. (c) Let x be the number of total characters. Then, as per the question,

No. of clients with single character = ${}^xC_1$;

No. of clients with two character = ${}^xC_2$;

As per the question,

$${}^xC_1 + {}^xC_2 \geq 15 \Rightarrow x + {}^xC_2 \geq 15$$

Instead of calculating the value of x, try plugging in 3, 4, 5... etc. for.

It may be time-consuming to solve this question by the traditional approach. The optimum approach is to plug-in the values from the options. But which option should you try first? If start plugging in from options (a), (b), (c) onwards then you may lose more time in case the answer is (d) or (e).

The best way to plug-in is to try option (b), and then (d). It is called (b)/(d) plug in approach for Problem Solving questions.

Under this approach, the values in the options must be arranged in ascending order from options (a) through (e).

Option (b): $x = 4 \Rightarrow 4 + \dfrac{4.3}{1.2} = 10 \geq 15;$

This is wrong, as 10 cannot be greater than 15. It means that x must be greater than 4. So let us try Option (d).

Option (d): $x = 6 \Rightarrow 6 + \dfrac{6.5}{1.2} = 21 \geq 15;$

This value qualifies, but we cannot conclude that x = 6 is the minimum possible value, so let's try Option (c).

Option (c): $x = 5 \Rightarrow 5 + \dfrac{5.4}{1.2} = 15 \geq 15;$

This qualifies and is the minimum possible value of x.

The correct answer is option (c).

52. (e) There are 6 pairs or 12 single shoes. Once we select the first shoe, then there is $\dfrac{10}{11}$ chance that the second shoe selected is NOT its pair. We took 10 shoes for the selection because the paired shoe must be excluded. Similarly, for the third one, there is $\dfrac{8}{10}$ chance that the third shoe is NOT a pair of the first two.

So, the probability that no two shoes will make a pair

$$= \left(\frac{10}{11}\right) \times \left(\frac{8}{10}\right) = \frac{8}{11}.$$

The correct answer is option (e).

53. (d) Adding or subtracting a constant from each element of a set has no effect on its standard deviation (SD).

For example, the SD of a set {10, 11, 13} is pay p, then the SD for the set {12, 13, 14} will also be p since a constant '2' is added to the original set to get the new set.

Say a = 1, b = 2, and c = 3. Do not calculate the SD now. Let us analyze the options by plugging in the values of a, b, and c. The values would be as follows.

(a) 2, 2, 3

(b) 1, 3, 3

(c) 1, 2, 4

(d) 7, 8, 9 – This is the correct answer as a constant '6' is added to a, b, and c, implying the same SD.

(e) 0, 2, 3

The correct answer is option (d).

54. (c) We write the number of victories against each player: 0, 0, 0, 0,0, 1, 1, 1, 2, 3, 3, 3, 3, 4, 4.

You must do this mentally. The median is the middle term = 1 victory per opponent

The average can be calculated as

$$\frac{\text{Total no. of victories}}{\text{Total no. of apponents}}$$

$$= \frac{0\times5+1\times3+2\times1+3\times4+4\times2}{15}$$

= 1.668 victories per opponent

The sum of the median and the average = 1 + 1.668 = 2.667 victories per opponent

Since 2.667 lies between 2 and 3, option (c) is the answer.

The correct answer is option (c).

55. (a) When all the numbers of a set are multiplied by a number, the mean also gets multiplied by the same number.

After the multiplication by 3, the mean remains same; it can happen only if mean = 0, hence the statement (I) is true.

Statement (II) is not necessary true as the set {–8, 1, 2, 3, 4, 5, 6, 8} does not satisfy the given condition. We can see that the largest number

= 8 = negative of the smallest number

= –(–8).

Statement (III) is also not necessary true because the set may contain all zeros.

The correct answer is option (a).

56. (c) Let the seven distinct positive integers be a, b, c, d, e, f, g, h and i, such that $a < b < c < d < e < f < g < h < i$.

Since the median is 30, we have:

$e = 30$ ...(i)

Since the mean is 30, we have

$$\frac{a+b+c+d+30+f+g+h+i}{9} = 30$$

$\Rightarrow$ $a+b+c+d+f+g+h+i$

$= 270 - 30 = 240$ ...(ii)

Since the value of e equal to 30 is fixed, and we need to maximize the product of the nine integers, we need to maximize the product of $(a \times b \times c \times d \times f \times g \times h \times i)$.

We know that, for a given value of the sum, the product is maximum if the numbers are equal. (For example, if p, q, r, and s are four numbers and $p + q + r + s = 8$, the maximum value of the product $(p \times q \times r \times s)$ occurs when $p = q = r = s\frac{8}{4} = 2$, and the value of

$(p \times q \times r \times s) = 2 \times 2 \times 2 \times 2 = 16.$

Proceeding using the above logic, we should have a

$$= b = c = d = f = h = i = \frac{240}{8} = 30$$

However, we need to keep the numbers distinct as well. Thus, we should assign such values for a, b, c, d, f, g, h, and i that their values are as close as possible to each other and at the same time, they remain distinct.

Thus, the nine distinct integers as close as possible to each other are: 26, 27, 28, 29, 30, 31, 32, 33, and 34.

The difference of the smallest and largest numbers = 34 – 26 = 8

The correct answer is option (c).

57. (c) Let the number of students who play cricket be X.

The total number of students = 25

We know that for two sets A and B, A or B

$$= A + B - A \,\&\, B.$$

25 = Number of students who play cricket + number of students who play football + number of students who play none – number of students who play both

$25 = X + 10 + 10 - 8$

$X = 25 - 12 = 13$

Therefore, people who play only cricket

= number of people who play cricket

– number of people who play both sports

$= 13 - 8 = 5.$

The correct answer is option (c).

Data Sufficiency

1. In an office, there are x employees, how many different committees of 5 employees can be formed?

   (I) If the office had x + 2 employees, then 126 different 5 employees committees can be formed.

   (II) If the office had x + 1 employees, then 56 different 3 employees committees can be formed.

   (*a*) Statement (I) ALONE is sufficient but statement (II) ALONE is not sufficient.

   (*b*) Statement (II) ALONE is sufficient but statement (I) ALONE is not sufficient.

   (*c*) BOTH statements TOGETHER are sufficient, but NEITHER statement ALONE is sufficient.

   (*d*) EACH statement ALONE is sufficient.

   (*e*) Statements (I) and (II) TOGETHER are not sufficient.

2. In how many ways k number of students can be selected from 20 students?

   (I) There are 1140 ways to select (k + 1) number of students out of 20 students.

   (II) There are 20 ways to select (k – 1) number of students out of 20 students.

   (*a*) Statement (I) ALONE is sufficient but statement (II) ALONE is not sufficient.

   (*b*) Statement (II) ALONE is sufficient but statement (I) ALONE is not sufficient.

   (*c*) BOTH statements TOGETHER are sufficient, but NEITHER statement ALONE is sufficient.

   (*d*) EACH statement ALONE is sufficient.

   (*e*) Statements (I) and (II) TOGETHER are not sufficient.

3. In the game of Funball, each batter can either hit a home run, hit a single, or strikeout, and the likelihood of each outcome is completely determined by the opposing pitcher. A Funball batter scores a point for their team by advancing sequentially through each of four "bases", according to the following rules: Home run: The batter and any players already on a base advance through all four bases.

   Single : The batter advances to first base, and any players already on a base advance one base each.

   Strikeout : No one advances any bases, and the batter loses his/her turn.

   If the batting team has a runner on first base, which pitcher (Roger or Greg) is more likely to allow a point before recording a strikeout?

   (I) Greg is twice as likely as Roger to allow a single, and four times as likely as Roger to record a strikeout.

   (II) Greg is twice as likely as Roger to allow a single, and one fourth as likely as Roger to allow a home run.

   (*a*) Statement (I) ALONE is sufficient but statement (II) ALONE is not sufficient.

   (*b*) Statement (II) ALONE is sufficient but statement (I) ALONE is not sufficient.

   (*c*) BOTH statements TOGETHER are sufficient, but NEITHER statement ALONE is sufficient.

   (*d*) EACH statement ALONE is sufficient.

   (*e*) Statements (I) and (II) TOGETHER are not sufficient.

4. Mike recently won a contest in which he will have the opportunity to shoot free throws in order to win \$10,000. In order to win the money Mike can either shoot 1 free throw and make it, or shoot 3 free throws and make at lest 2 of them. Mike occasionally makes shots and occasionally misses shots. He knows that his probability of making a single free throw is p, and that this probability doesn't change. Would Mike have a better chance of winning if he chose attempt 3 free throws?

(I) $p < 0.7$

(II) $p > 0.6$

(*a*) Statement (I) ALONE is sufficient but statement (II) ALONE is not sufficient.

(*b*) Statement (II) ALONE is sufficient but statement (I) ALONE is not sufficient.

(*c*) BOTH statements TOGETHER are sufficient, but NEITHER statement ALONE is sufficient.

(*d*) EACH statement ALONE is sufficient.

(*e*) Statements (I) and (II) TOGETHER are not sufficient.

5. There were r red cards and w white cards in bag. If these cards are to be displayed on a wall with 30 possible display boards, in how many ways can they arranged?

(I) $r + 2w = 15$

(II) $2r + 2w = 20$

(*a*) Statement (I) ALONE is sufficient but statement (II) ALONE is not sufficient.

(*b*) Statement (II) ALONE is sufficient but statement (I) ALONE is not sufficient.

(*c*) BOTH statements TOGETHER are sufficient, but NEITHER statement ALONE is sufficient.

(*d*) EACH statement ALONE is sufficient.

(*e*) Statements (I) and (II) TOGETHER are not sufficient.

6. What is the probability of getting 5 on the sixth roll of a dice?

(I) The dice is a regular fair dice with numbers from 1 to 6

(II) The first five rolls had 5 as the result

(*a*) Statement (I) ALONE is sufficient but statement (II) ALONE is not sufficient.

(*b*) Statement (II) ALONE is sufficient but statement (I) ALONE is not sufficient.

(*c*) BOTH statements TOGETHER are sufficient, but NEITHER statement ALONE is sufficient.

(*d*) EACH statement ALONE is sufficient.

(*e*) Statements (I) and (II) TOGETHER are not sufficient.

7. A box is filled with marbles of three colors – red, blue, and green. Is the probability of getting a red marble the same as probability of getting a green marble?

(I) There are a total of 11 marbles in the box.

(II) The number of blue marbles is more than the number of green marbles.

(*a*) Statement (I) ALONE is sufficient but statement (II) ALONE is not sufficient.

(*b*) Statement (II) ALONE is sufficient but statement (I) ALONE is not sufficient.

(*c*) BOTH statements TOGETHER are sufficient, but NEITHER statement ALONE is sufficient.

(*d*) EACH statement ALONE is sufficient.

(*e*) Statements (I) and (II) TOGETHER are not sufficient.

8. What is the probability that either event A or event B will occur but not both?

(I) Probability of event A happening is 0.3

(II) Probability of event B happening is 0.7

(a) Statement (I) ALONE is sufficient but statement (II) ALONE is not sufficient.

(b) Statement (II) ALONE is sufficient but statement (I) ALONE is not sufficient.

(c) BOTH statements TOGETHER are sufficient, but NEITHER statement ALONE is sufficient.

(d) EACH statement ALONE is sufficient.

(e) Statements (I) and (II) TOGETHER are not sufficient.

9. A box has Physics, Chemistry, and Math books. If a books is randomly selected, what is the probability that it is Math book?

(I) There are 6 Physics books and 4 Chemistry books.

(II) There are 3 times as many Math books as all the other books combined.

(a) Statement (I) ALONE is sufficient but statement (II) ALONE is not sufficient.

(b) Statement (II) ALONE is sufficient but statement (I) ALONE is not sufficient.

(c) BOTH statements TOGETHER are sufficient, but NEITHER statement ALONE is sufficient.

(d) EACH statement ALONE is sufficient.

(e) Statements (I) and (II) TOGETHER are not sufficient.

10. A box has Physics, Chemistry, and Math books. There are a total of 5 Math books. If two books are randomly selected, what is the probability that both will be Math books?

(I) The probability that the first book picked is Math is $\frac{1}{2}$

(II) If the first selected book is Math, then the probability of selecting the second book as Math book is $\frac{4}{9}$

(a) Statement (I) ALONE is sufficient but statement (II) ALONE is not sufficient.

(b) Statement (II) ALONE is sufficient but statement (I) ALONE is not sufficient.

(c) BOTH statements TOGETHER are sufficient, but NEITHER statement ALONE is sufficient.

(d) EACH statement ALONE is sufficient.

(e) Statements (I) and (II) TOGETHER are not sufficient.

11. Sam is a newbie football player. Is his probability of hitting the goal with a single free kick lower than the probability of hitting at least two goals with three free kicks?

(I) Probability of hitting a goal in any kick < 0.7

(II) Probability of hitting a goal in any kick > 0.6

(a) Statement (I) ALONE is sufficient but statement (II) ALONE is not sufficient.

(b) Statement (II) ALONE is sufficient but statement (I) ALONE is not sufficient.

(c) BOTH statements TOGETHER are sufficient, but NEITHER statement ALONE is sufficient.

(d) EACH statement ALONE is sufficient.

(e) Statements (I) and (II) TOGETHER are not sufficient.

12. A box has Physics, Chemistry, and Math books. If a book is randomly selected from the box, what is the probability that it will be Physics or Chemistry book?

(I) The probability that it will a Physics book is $\frac{1}{5}$

(II) The probability that it will be Math book is $\frac{1}{3}$

(*a*) Statement (I) ALONE is sufficient but statement (II) ALONE is not sufficient.

(*b*) Statement (II) ALONE is sufficient but statement (I) ALONE is not sufficient.

(*c*) BOTH statements TOGETHER are sufficient, but NEITHER statement ALONE is sufficient.

(*d*) EACH statement ALONE is sufficient.

(*e*) Statements (I) and (II) TOGETHER are not sufficient.

13. A stationary shop has an inventory of 1,345 different products - all of which it categorizes as "business," "personal," or both. What is the number of products characterized as "personal" only?

(I) 740 products are categorized as "business" only

(II) 520 products are categorized as both

(*a*) Statement (I) ALONE is sufficient but statement (II) ALONE is not sufficient.

(*b*) Statement (II) ALONE is sufficient but statement (I) ALONE is not sufficient.

(*c*) BOTH statements TOGETHER are sufficient, but NEITHER statement ALONE is sufficient.

(*d*) EACH statement ALONE is sufficient.

(*e*) Statements (I) and (II) TOGETHER are not sufficient.

14. If one fruit is randomly selected from a certain box that has only apples and oranges, what is the probability that an apple will be selected?

(I) The total number of fruits that has the box is 20

(II) $\frac{2}{5}$ of all the fruits in the box are the oranges.

(*a*) Statement (I) ALONE is sufficient but statement (II) ALONE is not sufficient.

(*b*) Statement (II) ALONE is sufficient but statement (I) ALONE is not sufficient.

(*c*) BOTH statements TOGETHER are sufficient, but NEITHER statement ALONE is sufficient.

(*d*) EACH statement ALONE is sufficient.

(*e*) Statements (I) and (II) TOGETHER are not sufficient.

15. If the probability of a tossed coin to be tail is not $\frac{1}{2}$, what is the probability of two tossed coins to be both tails?

(I) The probability of two tossed coins to be one head and the other to be tail is $\frac{4}{9}$

(II) The probability of two tossed coins to be both heads is $\frac{1}{9}$

(*a*) Statement (I) ALONE is sufficient but statement (II) ALONE is not sufficient.

(*b*) Statement (II) ALONE is sufficient but statement (I) ALONE is not sufficient.

(*c*) BOTH statements TOGETHER are sufficient, but NEITHER statement ALONE is sufficient.

(*d*) EACH statement ALONE is sufficient.

(*e*) Statements (I) and (II) TOGETHER are not sufficient.

16. In a school X, 40 percent of all the students are females and 50 percent of all the students have Physical major. In school X, what percent of all students are female students who have Physics major?

(I) In school X, 50 percent of the female students have Physics major.

(II) In school X, 30 percent of all students are male students who have Physics major.

(*a*) Statement (I) ALONE is sufficient but statement (II) ALONE is not sufficient.

(*b*) Statement (II) ALONE is sufficient but statement (I) ALONE is not sufficient.

(*c*) BOTH statements TOGETHER are sufficient, but NEITHER statement ALONE is sufficient.

(*d*) EACH statement ALONE is sufficient.

(*e*) Statements (I) and (II) TOGETHER are not sufficient.

17. Set X has only four numbers. Is the average of set X less than 4?

(I) Set X has a mode of 7 and a median of 4

(II) The smallest number in Set X is 0

(*a*) Statement (I) ALONE is sufficient but statement (II) ALONE is not sufficient.

(*b*) Statement (II) ALONE is sufficient but statement (I) ALONE is not sufficient.

(*c*) BOTH statements TOGETHER are sufficient, but NEITHER statement ALONE is sufficient.

(*d*) EACH statement ALONE is sufficient.

(*e*) Statements (I) and (II) TOGETHER are not sufficient.

18. What is the average of x, y, and z?

(I) $x + 2y + 3c = 10$

(II) $3x + 2y + c = 14$

(*a*) Statement (I) ALONE is sufficient but statement (II) ALONE is not sufficient.

(*b*) Statement (II) ALONE is sufficient but statement (I) ALONE is not sufficient.

(*c*) BOTH statements TOGETHER are sufficient, but NEITHER statement ALONE is sufficient.

(*d*) EACH statement ALONE is sufficient.

(*e*) Statements (I) and (II) TOGETHER are not sufficient.

19. Is the range of the given integers 5, 7, x, 6, y, and 9 greater than 5?

(I) $x = 3y$

(II) $x < 2y$

(*a*) Statement (I) ALONE is sufficient but statement (II) ALONE is not sufficient.

(*b*) Statement (II) ALONE is sufficient but statement (I) ALONE is not sufficient.

(*c*) BOTH statements TOGETHER are sufficient, but NEITHER statement ALONE is sufficient.

(*d*) EACH statement ALONE is sufficient.

(*e*) Statements (I) and (II) TOGETHER are not sufficient.

20. What is the median number of hours worked by employees on a particular day at company X, if the number of hours worked is an integer?

(I) 15 percent of employees worked 7 or fewer hours.

(II) 25 percent of the employees sat the company worked 9 or more hours

(*a*) Statement (I) ALONE is sufficient but statement (II) ALONE is not sufficient.

(*b*) Statement (II) ALONE is sufficient but statement (I) ALONE is not sufficient.

(*c*) BOTH statements TOGETHER are sufficient, but NEITHER statement ALONE is sufficient.

(*d*) EACH statement ALONE is sufficient.

(*e*) Statements (I) and (II) TOGETHER are not sufficient.

21. Set X consists of 3 distinct numbers, Is the median of the set equal to the arithmetic mean of set X?

(I) Difference between any two numbers is the same.

(II) Sum of the greatest and smallest is equal to twice the median.

(*a*) Statement (I) ALONE is sufficient but statement (II) ALONE is not sufficient.

(*b*) Statement (II) ALONE is sufficient but statement (I) ALONE is not sufficient.

(*c*) BOTH statements TOGETHER are sufficient, but NEITHER statement ALONE is sufficient.

(*d*) EACH statement ALONE is sufficient.

(*e*) Statements (I) and (II) TOGETHER are not sufficient.

22. Is Jack's average score of his last three tests not greater than 82?

(I) Jack's average score before the last three tests was 86.

(II) Jack's average score after the last three tests was 83.

(*a*) Statement (I) ALONE is sufficient but statement (II) ALONE is not sufficient.

(*b*) Statement (II) ALONE is sufficient but statement (I) ALONE is not sufficient.

(*c*) BOTH statements TOGETHER are sufficient, but NEITHER statement ALONE is sufficient.

(*d*) EACH statement ALONE is sufficient.

(*e*) Statements (I) and (II) TOGETHER are not sufficient.

23. The average (arithmetic mean) of Set L is what percent of the sum of its numbers?

(I) Set L consists of 10 numbers.

(II) The sum of the numbers in Set L is 90.

(*a*) Statement (I) ALONE is sufficient but statement (II) ALONE is not sufficient.

(*b*) Statement (II) ALONE is sufficient but statement (I) ALONE is not sufficient.

(*c*) BOTH statements TOGETHER are sufficient, but NEITHER statement ALONE is sufficient.

(*d*) EACH statement ALONE is sufficient.

(*e*) Statements (I) and (II) TOGETHER are not sufficient.

24. What is the median number of players per team in the Asian Cricket League?

(I) Sixty percent of the teams in the Asian Cricket League have 25 or more players in their teams.

(II) Sixty percent of the teams in the Asian Cricket League have 25 or fewer players in their teams.

(*a*) Statement (I) ALONE is sufficient but statement (II) ALONE is not sufficient.

(*b*) Statement (II) ALONE is sufficient but statement (I) ALONE is not sufficient.

(*c*) BOTH statements TOGETHER are sufficient, but NEITHER statement ALONE is sufficient.

(*d*) EACH statement ALONE is sufficient.

(*e*) Statements (I) and (II) TOGETHER are not sufficient.

25. Does set P have all of its terms smaller than 20?

(I) The smallest term in the set is 5.

(II) The range of set X is 15.

(*a*) Statement (I) ALONE is sufficient but statement (II) ALONE is not sufficient.

(*b*) Statement (II) ALONE is sufficient but statement (I) ALONE is not sufficient.

(*c*) BOTH statements TOGETHER are sufficient, but NEITHER statement ALONE is sufficient.

(*d*) EACH statement ALONE is sufficient.

(*e*) Statements (I) and (II) TOGETHER are not sufficient.

26. Is the median of set M greater than its arithmetic mean?

(I) The set consists of consecutive multiples of 5.

(II) Sum of the elements of the set is 30.

(a) Statement (I) ALONE is sufficient but statement (II) ALONE is not sufficient.

(b) Statement (II) ALONE is sufficient but statement (I) ALONE is not sufficient.

(c) BOTH statements TOGETHER are sufficient, but NEITHER statement ALONE is sufficient.

(d) EACH statement ALONE is sufficient.

(e) Statements (I) and (II) TOGETHER are not sufficient.

27. If p, q, r, s, t, u, and v are seven consecutive odd integers, what is the average (arithmetic mean) of the seven integers?

(I) $p + t = 38$

(II) $r + v = 46$

(a) Statement (I) ALONE is sufficient but statement (II) ALONE is not sufficient.

(b) Statement (II) ALONE is sufficient but statement (I) ALONE is not sufficient.

(c) BOTH statements TOGETHER are sufficient, but NEITHER statement ALONE is sufficient.

(d) EACH statement ALONE is sufficient.

(e) Statements (I) and (II) TOGETHER are not sufficient.

28. The average daily salary of a factory staff consisting of only engineers and supervisors is \$50. If each engineer and each supervisor receive their respective equal salaries, does the staff have a greater number of engineers than supervisors?

(I) The average daily salary of 40% of the engineers and 60% of the supervisors is \$45.

(II) The average daily salary of 60% of the engineers and 40% of the supervisors is \$55.

(a) Statement (I) ALONE is sufficient but statement (II) ALONE is not sufficient.

(b) Statement (II) ALONE is sufficient but statement (I) ALONE is not sufficient.

(c) BOTH statements TOGETHER are sufficient, but NEITHER statement ALONE is sufficient.

(d) EACH statement ALONE is sufficient.

(e) Statements (I) and (II) TOGETHER are not sufficient.

29. If a, b, c and d are distinct positive numbers, can be the average of the four numbers?

(I) The sum of c and d is 3b.

(II) The sum of a, b and c is 3b.

(a) Statement (I) ALONE is sufficient but statement (II) ALONE is not sufficient.

(b) Statement (II) ALONE is sufficient but statement (I) ALONE is not sufficient.

(c) BOTH statements TOGETHER are sufficient, but NEITHER statement ALONE is sufficient.

(d) EACH statement ALONE is sufficient.

(e) Statements (I) and (II) TOGETHER are not sufficient.

30. Does the group have at least 9 people?

(I) The average are of the group is less than 22 years.

(II) If 3 people with an average age of 44 years leave the group, the average age of the group decreases by half of its initial average.

(a) Statement (I) ALONE is sufficient but statement (II) ALONE is not sufficient.

(b) Statement (II) ALONE is sufficient but statement (I) ALONE is not sufficient.

(c) BOTH statements TOGETHER are sufficient, but NEITHER statement ALONE is sufficient.

(d) EACH statement ALONE is sufficient.

(e) Statements (I) and (II) TOGETHER are not sufficient.

31. What was the temperature on Friday?

(I) The average temperature for the consecutive four days, starting Monday was 40°C.

(II) The average temperature for the consecutive four days, starting Tuesday was 35°C.

(*a*) Statement (I) ALONE is sufficient but statement (II) ALONE is not sufficient.

(*b*) Statement (II) ALONE is sufficient but statement (I) ALONE is not sufficient.

(*c*) BOTH statements TOGETHER are sufficient, but NEITHER statement ALONE is sufficient.

(*d*) EACH statement ALONE is sufficient.

(*e*) Statements (I) and (II) TOGETHER are not sufficient.

32. Two varieties of tea, a pounds of one, priced at \$x per pounds and b pounds of the other, priced at \$(3x) per pounds are mixed. Is the average price of the mixture greater than $\$\left(\frac{3}{2}x\right)$ pounds?

(I) $a > 2b$

(II) $a = 3b$

(*a*) Statement (I) ALONE is sufficient but statement (II) ALONE is not sufficient.

(*b*) Statement (II) ALONE is sufficient but statement (I) ALONE is not sufficient.

(*c*) BOTH statements TOGETHER are sufficient, but NEITHER statement ALONE is sufficient.

(*d*) EACH statement ALONE is sufficient.

(*e*) Statements (I) and (II) TOGETHER are not sufficient.

33. A box contains only red and black balls. If two balls are randomly drawn from the box, what is the probability that both balls are black?

(I) The ratio of block to red balls is 2 : 3.

(II) There are 10 more red balls in the box that black balls.

(*a*) Statement (I) ALONE is sufficient but statement (II) ALONE is not sufficient.

(*b*) Statement (II) ALONE is sufficient but statement (I) ALONE is not sufficient.

(*c*) BOTH statements TOGETHER are sufficient, but NEITHER statement ALONE is sufficient.

(*d*) EACH statement ALONE is sufficient.

(*e*) Statements (I) and (II) TOGETHER are not sufficient.

34. The terms of a set are multiples of 3. Is the standard deviation of the set 0?

(I) Each term of the set is positive.

(II) All the terms of the set are equal.

(*a*) Statement (I) ALONE is sufficient but statement (II) ALONE is not sufficient.

(*b*) Statement (II) ALONE is sufficient but statement (I) ALONE is not sufficient.

(*c*) BOTH statements TOGETHER are sufficient, but NEITHER statement ALONE is sufficient.

(*d*) EACH statement ALONE is sufficient.

(*e*) Statements (I) and (II) TOGETHER are not sufficient.

35. Are the elements of Set smaller than 10?

(I) The smallest element in Set Q is 1.

(II) The range of Set is 10.

(*a*) Statement (I) ALONE is sufficient but statement (II) ALONE is not sufficient.

(*b*) Statement (II) ALONE is sufficient but statement (I) ALONE is not sufficient.

(*c*) BOTH statements TOGETHER are sufficient, but NEITHER statement ALONE is sufficient.

(*d*) EACH statement ALONE is sufficient.

(*e*) Statements (I) and (II) TOGETHER are not sufficient.

36. What is the arithmetic mean of Set Q ?

(I) Set Q is comprised of consecutive even integers.

(II) The range of Set Q is 10.

(*a*) Statement (I) ALONE is sufficient but statement (II) ALONE is not sufficient.

(*b*) Statement (II) ALONE is sufficient but statement (I) ALONE is not sufficient.

(*c*) BOTH statements TOGETHER are sufficient, but NEITHER statement ALONE is sufficient.

(*d*) EACH statement ALONE is sufficient.

(*e*) Statements (I) and (II) TOGETHER are not sufficient.

37. Each of the 40 students in class A is shorter than each of the 40 students in class B. Is the median height of the 80 students less than 160 centimeters?

(I) The shortest student in class A is 150 centimeters in height.

(II) The shortest student in class B is 160 centimeters in height.

(*a*) Statement (I) ALONE is sufficient but statement (II) ALONE is not sufficient.

(*b*) Statement (II) ALONE is sufficient but statement (I) ALONE is not sufficient.

(*c*) BOTH statements TOGETHER are sufficient, but NEITHER statement ALONE is sufficient.

(*d*) EACH statement ALONE is sufficient.

(*e*) Statements (I) and (II) TOGETHER are not sufficient.

38. An auditorium has 40 rows with 20 seats in each row. How many of the seats were occupied for a certain show?

(I) For the front 18 rows, on average (arithmetic mean), there were 5 unoccupied seats per row.

(II) For the back 22 rows, on average (arithmetic mean), there were 15 unoccupied seats per row.

(*a*) Statement (I) ALONE is sufficient but statement (II) ALONE is not sufficient.

(*b*) Statement (II) ALONE is sufficient but statement (I) ALONE is not sufficient.

(*c*) BOTH statements TOGETHER are sufficient, but NEITHER statement ALONE is sufficient.

(*d*) EACH statement ALONE is sufficient.

(*e*) Statements (I) and (II) TOGETHER are not sufficient.

39. Was the average (arithmetic mean) weight of the shipments sent to a certain destination greater than 500 grams?

(I) The total weight of the shipments sent to the destination was greater than 20,000 grams.

(II) Fewer than 40 shipments were shipped to the destination.

(*a*) Statement (I) ALONE is sufficient but statement (II) ALONE is not sufficient.

(*b*) Statement (II) ALONE is sufficient but statement (I) ALONE is not sufficient.

(*c*) BOTH statements TOGETHER are sufficient, but NEITHER statement ALONE is sufficient.

(*d*) EACH statement ALONE is sufficient.

(*e*) Statements (I) and (II) TOGETHER are not sufficient.

Answer Key

1. (*d*)
2. (*c*)
3. (*d*)
4. (*b*)
5. (*b*)
6. (*a*)
7. (*e*)
8. (*c*)
9. (*b*)
10. (*d*)
11. (*b*)
12. (*b*)
13. (*c*)
14. (*b*)
15. (*b*)
16. (*d*)
17. (*a*)
18. (*c*)
19. (*a*)
20. (*c*)
21. (*d*)
22. (*c*)
23. (*a*)
24. (*c*)
25. (*c*)
26. (*a*)
27. (*d*)
28. (*c*)
29. (*a*)
30. (*c*)
31. (*e*)
32. (*b*)
33. (*c*)
34. (*b*)
35. (*c*)
36. (*e*)
37. (*b*)
38. (*c*)
39. (*c*)

Answer Explanations

1. (d) **Considering statement (I) alone :**

Committee of 5 employees can be formed from (x + 2) employees in $^{(x+2)}C_5$

Hence, $^{(x+2)}C_5 = 126$.

On simplification this would give

$$\frac{(x+2)!}{5!\times(x-3)!}=126$$

$$\frac{(x+2)(x+1)\times(x-1)(x-2)}{5!}=126$$

$(x + 2)\ (x + 1) \times (x- 1)\ (x -2) = 5! \times 126$

Product of 5 consecutive numbers is $5! \times 126$

Now, here only one such of x is possible. We don't need to calculate (x = 7)

Sufficient Eliminate B/C/E.

Considering statement 2 alone :

Committee of 3 employees can be formed from (x + 1) employees in $^{(x+1)}C_3$

Hence, $^{(x+1)}C_3 = 56$.

Om simplification this would give

$$\frac{(x+1)!}{3!-(x-2)!}=56$$

$$\frac{(x+1)\times(x-1)}{3!}=56$$

Product of 3 consecutive numbers is $3! \times 56$

Now, here only one such of x is possible. We don't need to calculate (x = 7) Sufficient

The correct answer is option (d)

2. (c) Since $^nC_r = {}^nC_{(n-r)}$,

for example $^6C_2 = {}^6C_4$

Here n = 20 and we need to determine value of k

Considering statement 1 alone :

Value of $^{20}C_{(k+1)} = 1140$

From this information we will get two values of k + 1

k + 1 could be 3 or 17, hence k could be 2 or 16

Insufficient Eliminate A/D.

Considering statement 2 alone :

Value of $^{20}C_{(k-1)} = 20$

From the information we will get two values of k

k – 1 could be 1 or 19, hence k could be 2 or 20

Insufficient. Eliminate B.

Considering statement (I) and (II) together :

Only one value of k = 2 satisfies both the statements.

Sufficient

The correct answer is option (c)

3. (d) If Roger pitches, let H_R be the probability of a home run, S_R be the probability of a single, and K_R be the probability of a strikeout (all batters face these same probabilities, since the problem states that these probabilities are completely determined by the pitcher).

In Greg pitches, let H_G be the probability of a home run, S_G be the probability of a single, and K_G be the probability of a strikeout.

The following are the only three event sequences in which no points will score before a strikeout occurs:

1. The current batter strikes out. (K)
2. The current batter hits a single, and the next batter strikes out. (SK)

3. The current batter hits a single, the next batter hits a single, and the following batter strikes out. (SSK)

(Note that if three consecutive batters it singles, or if any batter hits a home run, then the batting team will score at least one point.)

If Roger pitches, the probability of any one of the three sequences mentioned above occurring is:

$$R = K_R + S_R K_R + S_R S_R K_R$$

I Greg pitches, the probability of any one of the three sequences occurring is:

$$G = K_G + S_G K_G + S_G S_G K_G$$

We need to be able to determine whether R or G is greater in order to solve the problem.

Statement (I) gives us the following :

$S_G = 2S_R$ and $K_G = 4K_R$ (Note: We also know that S_G, S_R, K_G, and K_R cannot be equal to 0).

We can substitute these equations in the probability expressions for G:

$$R = K_R + S_R K_R + S_R S_R K_R$$

$$G = K_G + S_G K_G + S_G S_G K_G$$

$$= 4K_R + (2S_R)(4K_R) + (2S_R)(2S_R)(4K_R)$$

$$= 4K_R + 8S_R K_R + 16S_R S_R K_R.$$

Since all of the unknowns are positive values, we can see from these equations that G will always be greater than R. This means that Greg is more likely than Roger to record a strikeout before allowing be point (which, in turn, means that Rorger is more likely than Greg to allow a point before recording a strikeout.) Therefore statement (I) is sufficient to solve the problem.

Statement (II) gives us the following :

$S_G = 2S_R$ and $H_G = \frac{H_R}{4}$ (Note: We also know that S_G, S_R, H_G, and H_R cannot be equal to 0).

Note that the probabilities G and R are expressed in terms of that S_G, S_R, K_G, and K_R. Whereas statement (I) tells us that and $S_G > S_R$ and $K_G > K_R$ (and therefore that $G > R$, solving the problem), statement (II) lacks information about the size of K_G relative to K_R. (Information about the size of H_G relative to H_R does not help us at all since neither of these variables are part of the probability expressions for G and R.)

As such, the information in statement (II) is insufficient, but statement (II) alone is not sufficient.

The correct answer is option (d).

4. (b) The question require us to determine whether Mike's odds of winning are better if he attempts 3 shots instead of 1. For that to be true, his odds of making 2 out of 3 must be better than his odds of making 1 out of 1.

There are two ways for Mike to at least 2 shots: Either he hits 2 and misses 1, or he hits all 3 :

Odds of hitting 2 and missing 1 $p \times p \times (1 - p)$	# of ways to hit 2 and miss 1 3(HHM, HMH, MHH)	**Total Probability** $3p^2(1 - p)$
Odds of hitting all 3 $p \times p \times p$	**# of ways to hit all 3** 1 (HHH)	p^3
Mike's probability of hitting at least 2 out of 3 free throws =		$3p^2(1 p) + p^3$

Now, we can rephrase the question as the following inequality :

Is $3p^2(1 - p) + p^3 < p$? (Are Mike's odds of hitting at least 2 of 3 greater than his odds of hitting 1 of 1?)

This can be simplified as follows :

$3p^2(1-p)+p^3>p$

$3p^2-3p^3+p^3<p$

$3p^2-2p^3>p$ (we can divide by p since p > 0)

$3p-2p^2>1$

$-2p^2+3p-1<0$

(divide by –2, flipping the inequality)

$p3-1.5p+.5<0$

$(p-5)(p-1)<0$

In order for this inequality to be true, p must be greater than. 5 but less than 1 (since this is the only way to ensure that the left side of the equation is negative). But we already know what p is less than 1 (since Mike occasionally misses some shots). Therefore, we need to know whether p is greater than .5. If it is, then the inequality will be true, which means that Mike will have a better chance of winning if he takes 3 shots.

Statement (I) tells us that p < .7. This does not help us to determine whether p > .5, so statement (I) is not sufficient.

Statement (2) tells us that p > .6. This means that p must be greater than .5. This is sufficient to answer the question.

The correct answer is (b).

5. (b) If he wants the same number on both the dice, then he can get any number on the first dice and the same number on the second dice.

Probability of getting any number of the first dice = $\frac{6}{6}$

Probability of getting the same number on the second dice $\frac{1}{6}$

Hence, the total probability

$$=\left(\frac{6}{6}\right)\times\left(\frac{1}{6}\right)=\frac{1}{6}$$

The answer is (b).

6. (a) **Considering statement (I) alone :**

As it is a regular dice, the chances of getting 5 on any roll of a dice is $\frac{1}{6}$

SUFFICIENT

Eliminate BCE

Considering statement (II) alone :

We don't known if the dice was fair.

INSUFFICIENT

The answer is (a)

7. (e) For the probability of getting a red marble be the same as probability of getting a green marble, the number of red marbles

Considering statement (I) alone :

No information about the number of marbles of each color.

INSUFFICIENT

Eliminate AD

Considering statement (II) alone :

Blue marbles > Green marbles

No information about the relation between number of red marbles and number of green marbles.

INSUFFICIENT

Eliminate B

Considering both the statements together:

No information about the relation between number of red marbles and number of green marbles.

INSUFFICIENT

The answer is (e)

8. (c) Probability (A or B) = P(A) + P(B) – (A and B)

Considering statement (I) alone :

No information about P(B)

INSUFFICIENT

Eliminate AD

Considering statement (II) alone :

No information about P(A)

INSUFFICIENT

Eliminate B

Considering both the statements togethe r:

$$\text{Probability (A or B)} = P(A) + P(B) - (A \& B)$$
$$= 0.3 + 0.7 - (0.3 \times 0.7)$$
$$= 1 - 0.21 = 0.79$$

INSUFFICIENT

The answer is (c)

9. (b) **Considering statement (I) alone :**

No information about number of math books.

INSUFFICIENT

Eliminate AD

Considering statement (II) alone :

Let the number of Physics and Chemistry books be x

$\Rightarrow$ The number of Math books is 3x

$\Rightarrow$ Hence, the total number of books is $x + 3x = 4x$

$$\text{Probability (Math book)} = \frac{3x}{4x} = \frac{3}{4}$$

SUFFICIENT

The answer is (b)

10. (d) **Considering statement (I) :**

Let the total number of books be x

P(math book) = Number of math books/ Total number of books

$$\text{P(math boo)} = \frac{5}{x}$$

Given that $\frac{5}{x} = \frac{1}{2}$

$\Rightarrow$ $x = 10$

Hence, Probability (Math and Math)

$$= \left(\frac{5}{10}\right) \times \left(\frac{4}{9}\right) = \frac{2}{9}$$

SUFFICIENT

Eliminate BCE

Considering statement (II) alone:

After a math book is selected, there are 4 more math books

P(Second book as a Math book)

$$= \left(\frac{4}{(x-1)}\right) = \frac{4}{9} \Rightarrow \frac{1}{(x-1)} = \frac{1}{9} \Rightarrow x = 10$$

SUFFICIENT

The answer is (d).

11. (b) If the probability of hitting a goal in one free kick is p, then

Probability of hitting at least two goals in three free kicks is $3C2 \times (p)(p)(! - p) + p^3$

$3(p^2)(1 - p) + p^3 = p^2(3 - 2p)$

Question : Is $p^2(3 - 2p) > p$?

Is $p(3 - 2p) > 1$?

Is $3p\ 2p^2 - 1 > 0$?

Is $2p^2 - 3p + 1 < 0$?

Is $\left(\frac{p-1}{2}\right)(p-1) < 0$?

Is $p > \frac{1}{2}$ or $p < 1$?

Is $\frac{1}{2} < p < 1$?

Considering statement (I) alone :

$p < 0.7$

If $p = 0.6$, then we get Yes

If $p = 0.4$, then we get No

INSUFFICIENT

Considering statement (II) alone :

If $p > 0.6$, then $p > 0.5$

SUFFICIENT

The answer is (b).

12. (b) Probability (Physics of Chemistry)

= 1 – Probability (Math)

Considering statement (I) alone :

Probability (Physics) $= \frac{1}{5}$

No information about Math or Chemistry

INSUFFICIENT

Eliminate AD

Considering statement (II) alone :

Probability (Math) $= \frac{1}{3}$

⇒ Probability (Physics or Chemistry = 1 – Probability (Math)

⇒ Probability (Physics or Chemistry $= 1 - \frac{1}{3}$

⇒ Probability (Physics or Chemistry $= \frac{2}{3}$

SUFFICIENT

The answer is (b)

13. (c) Business only + personal only + both = Total

Considering statement (I) alone :

Business only = 740

Still have two more variables.

INSUFFICIENT

Eliminate AD

Considering statement (II) alone :

Both = 520

Still have two more variables.

INSUFFICIENT

Eliminate B

Considering both the statement together :

740 + personal only + 520 = 1345

Personal only = 85

SUFFICIENT

The answer is (c).

14. (b) In the original condition, there are 2 variables (apples' number and oranges' number) and i n order to match the number of variables to the number of equations, there must be 2 equations. Since there is 1 for con 1 and 1 for con 2, C is most likely to be the answer. By solving and con 2 together, there are 20 fruits i n the box, but since $\frac{2}{5}$ are oranges, $20\left(\frac{2}{5}\right) = 8$ are oranges and 20 – 8 = 12 are apples. Then, the probability that an apple will be randomly selected becomes $\frac{^{12}C_1}{^{20}C_1} = \frac{12}{20} = \frac{3}{5}$, hence it is unique and sufficient.

The answer is (c).

15. (b) If you modify the original condition and the question, when assuming T

(probability of getting a tail) and H (probability of getting a head), you get T + H = 1, and T^2 = ? Then, there are 2 variables (T, H) and 1 equation (T + H = 1), and in order to match the number of variables to the number of equations, there must be 1 more equation. Since there is 1 for con 1 and 1 for con 2, (d) is most likely to be the answer.

For con 1, from $TH + HT = \frac{4}{9}$, if you substitute $H = 1 - T$, you get $T(1-T) + (1-T)T = \frac{4}{9}$, $T - T^2 + T - T^2 = \frac{4}{9}$, $2T - 2T^2 = \frac{4}{9}$, and if you divide both sides by 2, from $T - T^2 = \frac{2}{9}$, $9T^2 - 9T + 2 = 0$, you get $(3T-1)(3T-2) = 0$, $T = \frac{1}{3}, \frac{2}{3}$, hence it is not unique and not sufficient.

For con 2, from $H^2 = \frac{1}{9} = \left(\frac{1}{3}\right)^2$, $H = \frac{1}{3}$, $H + T = 1$, you get $\frac{1}{3} + T = 1$, in other words, $T = \frac{2}{3}$, hence it is unique and sufficient.

Therefore, the answer is (b).

16. (d) If you modify the original condition and the question, this is a "2 by 2" question that appears most frequently on current GMAT, as shown in the table below.

100%	Physics major (50%)	Not Physics major (50%)
Females (40%)	x%	(40 – x)%
Males (60%)	(50 – x)%	(x + 10)%

As shown above, there is 1 variable (x) and in order to match the number of variables to the number of equations, there must be 1 equation. Since there is 1 for con 1 and 1 for con 2, D is most likely to be the answer.

For con 1, from 40% (50% = 20% = x%, you get x = 20, hence it is unique and sufficient.

For con 2, from (50 – x)% = 30%, you get 50 – x = 3, x = 20, hence it is unique and sufficient.

The answer is also (d).

17. (a) **Considering statement (I) alone:**

Mode is the most repeated number in the set. Hence, there must be at lest 2 numbers equal to 7 in the list.

Also, the median would be the average of the two middle numbers.

As the median is smaller than the mode, the two 7s must be the last two numbers.

So, the list would be x, y, 7, 7.

For the median of the set to be 4, y must be 1.

To make the highest possible average, x must be as high as possible. The highest possible value of x must be 0.

Hence, the maximum possible average of the set is $\frac{(0+1+7+7)}{4} = 3.75$

SUFFICIENT

Eliminate BCE

Considering statement (II) alone:

No information about the other three numbers in the set.

INSUFFICIENT

The answer is (a).

18. (c) Considering statement (I) alone :

No way to find the value of $x + y + z$

INSUFFICIENT

Eliminate AD

Considering statement (II) alone :

Now way to find the value of $x + y + z$

INSUFFICIENT

Eliminate B

Considering the both the statements together:

Adding the two equations, $4x + 4y + 4z = 24$

$\Rightarrow \quad x + y + z = 6$

SUFFICIENT

The answer is (c).

19. (a) The range is the difference between the greatest and the smallest reading.

It is given that, the smallest known integer is 5, and the greatest known integer is 9. x and y are two unknown integers. The question "Is the Range greater than 5?"

Considering statement (I) alone :

From Statement (I) alone, we have $x = 3y$.

Condition 1 : If y is less than 5, lets say $y = 4$, then $x = 12$, range is greater than 6.

Condition 2 : If y is equal to 5, then $x = 15$, range is greater than 5.

Condition 3 : If y is greater than 5, lets say $y = 6$, then $x = 18$, range is greater than 5.

That means with any value of y, range of the integers is greater than 5.

Sufficient

Eliminate A/D.

Considering statement (II) alone :

From Statement (II) alone, we have that $x < 2y$

Condition 1 : If y is less than 5, lets say $y = 4$, then $x < 8$, let $x = 7$, range is not greater than 5.

Condition 2 : If y is equal to 5, then $x < 10$, let $x = 9$, range is not greater than 5.

Condition 3 : If y is greater than 5, lets say $y = 6$, then $x < 12$, let $x = 11$, range is greater than 5.

Insufficient

The answer is (a).

20. (c) Considering statement (I) alone :

We only know that 15 percent of employees worked 7 or fewer hours there is information about the rest 85 percent of the employees. Hence, the median cannot be determined. Insufficient.

Eliminate A/D.

Considering statement (I) alone :

We only know that 25 percent of employees worked 9 or more hours but there is information about rest 75 percent of the employees.

Hence, median cannot be determined, Insufficient.

Eliminate B.

Considering statement (I) & (II) together :

It is known that 15 percent of employees worked 7 of fewer hours and 25 percent of the employees at the company worked 9 or more hours, which means rest 60 percent (100% – 15% – 25%) of the employees must have worked for exactly 8 hours.

As median is the middle term when data is arranged in the ascending or descending order, hence median of the data is 8 hours.

Sufficient

The correct answer is option (c).

21. (d) Let three distinct numbers be a, b, and c such that $a < b < c$

Considering statement (I) alone :

If the difference between any two numbers is the same, means that the numbers are in arithmetic progression.

In an AP, median is equal to the average (arithmetic mean)

Sufficient

Eliminate B/C/E

Considering statement (II) alone :

Sum of the greatest and smallest is equal to twice the median

$c + a = 2b$

so, sum of the three numbers

$$= a + b + c = 3b$$

average of the numbers

$$= \frac{3b}{3} = b = \text{median}$$

Sufficient

The correct answer is option (d).

22. (c) Let the number of tests taken by Jack before the last three tests = x.

Considering statement (I) alone :

We have no information about the average score after taking the last three tests.

Insufficient Hence, eliminate A/D

Considering statement (II) alone :

We have no information about the average score before taking the last three tests.-

Insufficient

Hence, eliminate B.

Considering statement (I) and (II) together :

Total marks obtained by Jack before taking the last three tests = 86x.

Total marks obtained by Jack after taking the last three tests = 83 (x + 3)

Thus, the total marks scored by Jack in the last three tests

$$= 83(x + 3) - 86x = 249 - 3x$$

Since x (The number of tests taken) is a positive integer, we have $x \geq 1$, or $3x \geq 3$

$\Rightarrow \quad 249 - 3x \leq 246$

Thus, Jack scored at most 246 marks in his last 3 tests.

Thus, Jack's average score in his last 3 tests is at the most $\frac{246}{3} = 82$.

The answer is yes – Sufficient

The correct answer is option (c).

23. (a) Let the number of terms in Set L = n

Let the sum of the n numbers = S

Thus, average of the n numbers = $\frac{5}{n}$

Thus, the required percent value

$$\frac{\frac{5}{n}}{S} \times 100\% = \frac{100}{n}\%$$

Considering statement (I) alone :

$$n = 10$$

Thus, the required percent value

$$\frac{100}{10}\% = 10\% \text{ – Sufficient}$$

Hence, eliminate B/C/E.

Considering statement (II) alone:

The count of numbers in Set L is not known. The value of the sum is redundant.

Insufficient

Hence, eliminate (d).

24. (c) Considering Statement (I) alone:

When the number of players in each team is arranged in ascending order, the median number of players per team for the Asian Cricket League would be the average of the number of players in the team that is ranked 50% and the average of the number of players in the team that is ranked 51%.

Since we do not known the number of players in the teams ranked 50% and 51%, the statement is insufficient.

Hence, eliminate A/D.

Considering statement (II) alone :

With the same reasoning as above, this statement is also insufficient.

Hence, eliminate B.

Considering statement (I) and (II) together :

Followed both the statements, we can deduce that in the band of 40%-60%, where the teams ranked 50% & 51% lie, the average of the number of players per team would be EXACTLY 25, as shown in the image below.

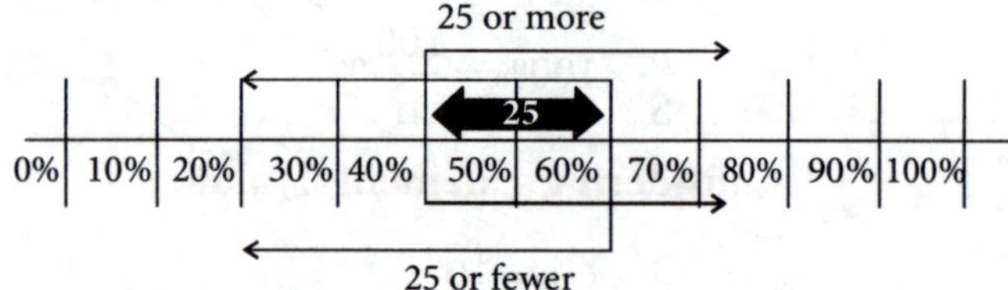

Thus, together, both the statements are sufficient and the median is 25 number of players.

The correct answer is option (c).

25. (c) Considering statement (I) alone:

We do not know anything about the remaining terms, so this statement alone is not sufficient.

Hence, eliminate A/D.

Considering statement (II) alone :

Range is 15.

Range = Max. value – Min. value

We do not know anything about the terms of the set, so this statement alone is not sufficient.

Hence, eliminate B.

Considering statements (I) and (II) together :

Smallest element = 5; Range = 15

Range = Max. value – Min. value

$\Rightarrow$ 5 = Largest term –5

$\Rightarrow$ Largest term = 20

Largest term = 20. The answer is no; a unique answer. Hence, statements (I) & (II) together are sufficient.

There is at least one term that is 20. Note that there may be more than one term that is exactly 20.

The correct answer is option (c).

26. (a) Considering Statement (I) alone :

It states that the set consists of consecutive multiples of 5.

Note that for any evenly spaced set, Arithmetic mean = Median

For example, for set: {5, 10, 15}: Mean = Median = 10; and

For set: {5, 10, 15, 20};

$$\text{Mean} = \text{Median} = \frac{10+15}{2} = 12.5$$

The answer is no, the median of set M is not greater than its arithmetic mean, a unique answer!

Therefore, statement (I) alone is sufficient.

Hence, eliminate B/C/E.

Considering statement (II) alone :

It states that the sum of the elements in the set is 30, but we don't have any information about the elements of the set. We cannot calculate either mean or median.

Therefore, statement (II) alone is insufficient.

Hence, eliminate D.

The correct answer is option (a).

27. (d) Since the numbers are consecutive and there are an odd number of integers, 7, the middlemost integer, s, would be the average (arithmetic mean) of the 7 integers. We have to find the value of s.

Thus, $q = p + 2; r = p + 4; s = p + 6; t = p + 8;$
$u = p + 10;$ & $v = p + 12$

Considering statement (I) alone :

$p + t = 38$

$\Rightarrow \quad p + p + 8 = 38$

$\Rightarrow \quad 2p = 30$

$\Rightarrow \quad p = 15$

$\Rightarrow \quad s = p + 6 = 15 + 6 = 21$, average. Sufficient.

Hence, eliminate B/C/E.

Considering statement (II) alone :

$r + v = 46$

$\Rightarrow \quad p + 4 + p + 12 = 46$

$\Rightarrow \quad 2p + 16 = 46$

$\Rightarrow \quad p = 30 \Rightarrow p = 15$

$\Rightarrow \quad s = p + 6 = 15 + 6 = 21$, average. Sufficient.

Hence, eliminate A.

The correct answer is option (d).

28. (c) **Considering statement (I) alone:**

The average salary of an engineer and the average salary of a supervisor are not known.

We only know that the average salary of all engineers and supervisors is \$50 and that of 40% of the engineers and 60% of the

supervisors is \$45.

Thus, we can only conclude that since the proportional share of engineers is reduced (40% against 60%) as compared to supervisors and as a result, the average salary gets reduced (\$45 against \$50), engineers' average salary must be greater than supervisors' average salary.

However, we cannot comment on the number of engineers and the number of supervisors. - Insufficient

Hence, eliminate A/D.

Considering statement (II) alone :

Statement 2 is like statement 1, following the same reasoning. - Insufficient

Hence, eliminate B.

Considering statements (I) and (II) together :

We see that…

For 100% engineers and 100% supervisors, the average salary is \$50.

For 40% engineers and 60% supervisors, the average salary is \$45, i.e., there is a decrease of \$5.

For 60% engineers and 40% supervisors, the average salary is \$55, i.e., there is an increase of \$5.

Thus, we see that when the percentage values of engineers and supervisors are interchanged, the increase and the decrease in the averages are of the same value.

Thus, the effect on the average is the same, only of different signs, implying that the number of engineers and the number of supervisors must be the same, with engineers having a higher salary than the supervisors.

The answer is no. – Sufficient

The correct answer is option (c).

29. **(a)** We need to determine whether b is the average of the four distinct (unequal) numbers a, b, c and d.

Say b is the average, then

$\Rightarrow b = \dfrac{a+b+c+d}{4}$

$\Rightarrow \quad 3b = a + c + d \quad$ ...(i)

Let's see each statement one by one.

Considering statement (I) alone :

The sum of c and d is 3b.

$\Rightarrow \quad c + d = 3b$

Thus, equation (i) would be valid only if a = 0.

However, it is not possible since a is a positive number.

Thus, was get specific answer that b cannot be the average of the four numbers a, b, c and d. The answer is No - Sufficient.

Hence, eliminate B/C/E.

Considering Statement (II) alone :

The sum of a, b, and c is 3b.

$\Rightarrow \quad a + b + c = 3b$

$\Rightarrow \quad a + = 2b$

Thus, equation (i) would be valid only if d = b.

However, it is not possible since the four numbers a, b, c and d are distinct.

Thus, again we get a specific answer than b cannot be the average of the four numbers a, b, c and d.

The answer is No. – Sufficient.

Hence, eliminate C/E.

The correct answer is option (a).

30. **(c)** Let the number of people in the group be n.

Let the average age of the members of the group be a.

Thus, the sum of the ages of the members in the group = na years.

We have to ascertain whether $n \geq 9$.

Let's see each statement one by one.

Considering statement (I) alone :

We only know that

Thus, nothing can be inferred about the number of people in the group. – Insufficient

Hence, eliminate A/D.

Considering Statement (II) alone :

If 3 people with an average age of 44 years leave the group, the number of members in the group decreases to (n – 3) and the total age decrease to $(na - 3 \times 44) = (na - 132)$ years.

Thus, the new average age of the members in the group

$= \left(\dfrac{na - 132}{n - 3}\right)$ years

Since the average age becomes half the initial value, we have

$\dfrac{na - 132}{n - 3} = \dfrac{a}{2}$

$\Rightarrow \quad 2na - 264 = na - 3a$

$\Rightarrow \quad a(n + 3) = 264 \quad$ ...(ii)

Since the value of a is not known, the number of people originally in the group maybe 9, less than 9 or greater than 9. – Insufficient

Hence, eliminate B.

Statements (I) and (II) together :

From (i): $a < 22$

Substituting the above in (ii):

$$n + 3 > \frac{264}{22} \Rightarrow n + 3 > 11$$

$$\Rightarrow n > 8 \Rightarrow m \geq 9$$

Thus, the answer to the question is Yes. - Sufficient

The correct answer is option (c).

31. **(e)** We have to find out the temperature on Friday.

Considering Statement (I) alone:

Let the temperatures on Monday, Tuesday, Wednesday, Thursday, and Friday be denoted by m, t, w, r and f, respectively.

Since the average temperature of consecutive four days, starting Monday was 40°C, we have $\frac{m + t + w + r}{4} = 40$

$$\Rightarrow \quad m + t + w + r = 160 \qquad ...(i)$$

Since there is no information about f, its value cannot be determined. – Insufficient

Hence, eliminate A/D.

Considering Statement (II) alone :

Since the average of consecutive four days, starting Tuesday was 35°, we have

$$\frac{t + w + r + f}{4} = 35$$

$$\Rightarrow \quad t + w + r + f = 140 \qquad ...(ii)$$

The value of f cannot be determined from (ii) alone. – Insufficient

Hence, eliminate B.

Considering statement (I) and (II) together :

Subtracting (ii) from (i) :

$$m - f = 20 \qquad ...(iii)$$

The value of f cannot be determined the above equation. – Insufficient

The correct answer is (e).

32. **(b)** The average price of the mixture formed by mixing the two varieties of tea, a pounds of one, priced at \$x per pounds and b pounds of the other, priced at \$(3x) per pounds is

$$= \$\left(\frac{ax + 3bx}{a + b}\right) = \$x\left(\frac{a + 3b}{a + b}\right) \quad ...(i)$$

Considering Statement (I) alone :

We have $a > 2b$

We have to ensure whether

$$x\left(\frac{a + 3b}{a + b}\right) > \frac{3}{2}x$$

$$\Rightarrow \left(\frac{a + 3b}{a + b}\right) > \frac{3}{2}$$

(Cancelling x from both sides)

$$\Rightarrow \quad 2a + 6b = 3a + 3b$$

$$\Rightarrow \quad 3b > a$$

Case 1 : For $a = 3$ & $b = 1$, $a > 2b$, but $3b = a$, So, answer is No.

Case 2 : For $a = 5$ & $b = 2$, $a > 2b$, and $3b > a$, answer is Yes.

Thus, the answer cannot be uniquely determined. - Insufficient

Hence, eliminate A/D

Considering Statement (II) alone :

We have $a = 3b$

The average price, from (i)

$$= \$\left(\frac{3bx + 3bx}{3b + b}\right) = \$\left(\frac{3x}{2}\right);$$

replacing a by 3b

Thus, the above price is $\$\left(\frac{3}{2}x\right)$, not greater than $\$\left(\frac{3}{2}x\right)$.

The answer to the question is 'No'. - Sufficient

Hence, eliminate C/E.

The correct answer is option (b).

33. (c) **Considering Statement (I) alone :**

Ratio of black (B) to red (R) balls = 2 : 3

Case 1: Let B = 2, R = 4;

Probability of drawing the first black ball

$$= \frac{\text{No. of black balls}}{\text{Total no. of balls}} = \frac{2}{5},$$

Probability of drawing the second black ball

$$= \frac{\text{No. of remaining black balls}}{\text{Total no. of remaining balls}} = \frac{1}{4}$$

Therefore, the required probability $= \left(\frac{2}{5}\right) \times \left(\frac{1}{4}\right) = \frac{1}{10}$

Case 2 : Let B = 4, R = 6;

Probability of drawing the first black ball

$$= \frac{\text{No. of black balls}}{\text{Total no. of balls}} = \frac{4}{10} = \frac{2}{5},$$

Probability of drawing the second black ball $\frac{3}{9} = \frac{1}{3}$

Therefore, the required probability $= \left(\frac{2}{5}\right) \times \left(\frac{1}{3}\right) = \frac{2}{15}$

The two answers are different - no unique solution - Insufficient.

Hence, eliminate A/D.

Considering Statement (II) alone :

This statement implies that R = B + 10. Different values of B, we get different values of R, and hence different probabilities. - no unique solution - Insufficient.

Hence, eliminate B.

Considering Statements (I) and (II) together :

If we combine the two statements.

Let B = 2k and R = 3k

R = B + 10

$\Rightarrow$ 3k = 2k + 10, k = 10, B = 20 and R = 30

Therefore, the probability of drawing two black balls $= \left(\frac{20}{30}\right) \times \left(\frac{19}{29}\right)$; there is no need to calculate the answer as it is finite and unique. Hence, both the statements together are sufficient.

The correct answer is option (c).

34. (b) **Considering Statement (I) alone :**

A set may be like {3, 3, 3} or {9, 9, 9}; in either case, the standard deviation (SD) would be 0 since there is no deviation among the terms. The answer is Yes.

If the set is like {3, 6, 9}, the SD would not be equal to 0 since there are deviations among the terms. The answer is No.

No unique answer; hence, this statement alone is not sufficient.

Hence, eliminate A/D.

Considering Statement (II) alone :

This statement implies that the set consists of only one number with its multiple occurrences.

These sets may be like {3, 3, 3}; {9, 9, 9, 9}; or {12, 12}. In each case, there is no deviation among the terms, therefore SD = 0; answer is Yes.

A unique answer; hence, Statement (II) alone is sufficient.

Hence, eliminate C/E.

The correct answer is option (b).

35. (c) **Considering Statement (I) alone :**

The smallest element is 1. We do not know anything about the remaining elements. The largest element may or may not be smaller than 10.

Hence this statement alone is not sufficient.

Hence, eliminate A/D.

Considering Statement (II) alone :

The Range is 10.

We know that Range (10) Largest element Smallest element

But we do not know anything about the values of the elements. The largest element may or may not be smaller than 10.

Hence this statement alone is not sufficient.

Hence, eliminate B.

Considering statements (I) and (II) together:

Smallest element 1

Range Largest element Smallest element

$\Rightarrow$ Largest element 11. The answer is No; a unique answer.

Hence, statements (I) and (II) together are sufficient.

The correct answer is option (c).

36. (e) **Considering Statement (I) alone :**

Statement 1 is insufficient, as there can be an infinite number of sets that comprise elements of consecutive even integers, thereby have different values of mean.

Hence, eliminate A/D.

Considering Statement (II) alone :

Again, statement 2 is insufficient, as there can be an infinite number of sets that comprise elements that have the range = 10, thereby have different values of mean.

Hence, eliminate B.

Considering statements (I) and (II) together :

Even considering both statements, multiple sets are possible. Set Q could be {2, 4, 6, 8, 10, 12} or {12, 14, 16, 18, 20, 22}. Each set has a different mean with the same Range value = 10. Thus, even both statements are insufficient.

The correct answer is option (e).

37. (b) We are given that each of the 40 students in class A is shorter than each of the 40 students in class B.

(Height of the tallest student in class A) (Height of the shortest student in class B)

You must not assume that the heights of all the 40 students in class A are the same; they could all be of different heights, the same height, or a few of them could be of the same height. The same is true for the students in class B.

We are asked to determine whether the median height of the 80 students is less than 160 centimeters.

We know that to find the median of a dataset, the terms of the dataset must be arranged in either ascending or descending order.

Let's assume that all the 80 students are arranged as per the ascending order of their height. All 40 students of class A would be on the left, arranged as per their increasing heights, and all 40 students of class B would be on the right, arranged as per their increasing heights. Thus, in this ordered arrangement of the 80 students, the tallest student in class A (40th student in order) would be immediately to the left of the shortest student in class B (the 41st in order).

You must know that

(Median value of a dataset) = (Value of the middlemost term)

When the number of terms in the dataset is even, the median is equal to the average of the values of the two middlemost terms.

Thus, (the median height of 80 students)

(Average of the height of the 40th student and the height of the 41st student in the ordered arrangement)

We know that the 41st student is the 1st student of class B.

So, to get the median height of the 80 students, we must know the height of the tallest student in class A and the shortest student in class B.

Note: In the above analysis, we arranged the students into the two groups in ascending order of their heights. If you chose to arrange them in descending order of heights instead, that is fine too. The analysis remains the same.

Considering Statement (I) alone :

The height of the shortest student in class A 150 centimeters

This information is of no use to us as we want the height of the 40th and 41st students to calculate the median height. - Insufficient

Hence, eliminate A/D.

Considering Statement (II) alone :

(Height of the shortest student in class B)

= (Height of the 41st student in ascending order of height)

= 160 centimeters

Though we do not know the height of the 40th student, we can make a deduction about the median. The question does not ask the value of the median; it asks whether the median height of the 80 students is less than 160 centimeters. This is a "Yes/No" type of question.

Since the height of the 41st student = 160 centimeters, and since we're given that even the tallest student in class A is shorter than the shortest student in class B, we can write:

(The height of the 40th student) < 160 centimeters

Say, the height of the 40th student = 159.99 centimeters

Thus, median. The answer is yes. – Sufficient

The correct answer is option (b).

38. **(c)** Total number of seats = $40 \times 20 = 800$

Thus, the number of occupied seats

= Total number of seats

– Number of unoccupied seats

Considering Statement (I) alone :

The total number of unoccupied seats in the front 18 rows

$= 18 \times 5 = 90$

However, the total number of unoccupied seats in the back rows (40 – 18 = 22) is not known – Insufficient

Hence, eliminate A/D.

Considering Statement (II) alone :

The total number of unoccupied seats in the back 22 rows

$= 22 \times 15 = 330$

However, the total number of unoccupied seats in the front rows is not known. – Insufficient

Hence, eliminate B.

Considering Statements (I) and (II) together:

The total number of unoccupied seats in the auditorium

$= 90 + 330 = 420$

The total number of occupied seats in the auditorium

$= 800 - 420 = 380$ – Sufficient

The correct answer is option (c).

39. (c) Average weight of the shipments

$$= \frac{\text{Total weight of the shipments}}{\text{Number of shipments}}$$

Considering Statement (I) alone :

The number of shipments is not known. - Insufficient

Hence, eliminate A/D.

Considering Statement (II) alone :

The total weight of the shipments is not known. - Insufficient

Hence, eliminate B.

Considering Statements (I) and (II) together :

Total weight of the shipments is greater than 20,000 grams.

Number of shipments is less than 40.

Let us work with the total weight as 20,000 (least value) and the number of shipments as 39 (greater value):

Average weight of the shipments

$$= \frac{20{,}000}{39} > \left[\frac{20{,}000}{40} = 500\right]$$

When the total weight is greater than 20,000 and the number of shipments is fewer than 39, the average weight would rather increase.

Thus, the average weight of shipments is greater than 500 grams. - Sufficient

The correct answer is option (c).

Chapter 6

Data Sufficiency Practice Questions Set - 1

Multiple Choice Questions

1. The average score in a class of four students is 100. If none of them scored less than 0, how many students scored greater than 90?

   I. The two top scorers each scored 155.

   II. The median score for the class is 90.

   (a) Statement (I) ALONE is sufficient but statement (II) ALONE is not sufficient.

   (b) Statement (II) ALONE is sufficient but statement (I) ALONE is not sufficient.

   (c) BOTH statements TOGETHER are sufficient, but NEITHER statement ALONE is sufficient.

   (d) EACH statement ALONE is sufficient.

   (e) Statements (I) and (II) TOGETHER are not sufficient.

2. In a co-ordinate plane, if the triangle AXB is right-angled at Point X, what is the value of the x-coordinate of Point X?

   I. The coordinates of the points A and B are (4, 5) and (6, 3), respectively.

   II. The area of the triangle AXB is 2.

   (a) Statement (I) ALONE is sufficient but statement (II) ALONE is not sufficient.

   (b) Statement (II) ALONE is sufficient but statement (I) ALONE is not sufficient.

   (c) BOTH statements TOGETHER are sufficient, but NEITHER statement ALONE is sufficient.

   (d) EACH statement ALONE is sufficient.

   (e) Statements (I) and (II) TOGETHER are not sufficient.

3. A merchant purchased three products, P, Q, and R, for \$50,000. Did he pay more than \$20,000 for R?

   I. The sum the merchant paid for P and Q combined was 3 times the sum he paid for P.

   II. The merchant paid more for R than for Q.

   (a) Statement (I) ALONE is sufficient but statement (II) ALONE is not sufficient.

   (b) Statement (II) ALONE is sufficient but statement (I) ALONE is not sufficient.

   (c) BOTH statements TOGETHER are sufficient, but NEITHER statement ALONE is sufficient.

   (d) EACH statement ALONE is sufficient.

   (e) Statements (I) and (II) TOGETHER are not sufficient.

4. If x is a prime number, is $(15x^3 + 30x^2 + 6x + 9)$ divisible by x^2?

   I. $4 < x^2 < 30$

   II. $x^2 - 10x + 21 = 0$

   (a) Statement (I) ALONE is sufficient but statement (II) ALONE is not sufficient.

   (b) Statement (II) ALONE is sufficient but statement (I) ALONE is not sufficient.

   (c) BOTH statements TOGETHER are sufficient, but NEITHER statement ALONE is sufficient.

   (d) EACH statement ALONE is sufficient.

   (e) Statements (I) and (II) TOGETHER are not sufficient.

5. If ab is a two-digit number, where a and b are its tens and units digits, respectively, is the number ab divisible by 21?

   I. The sum of the digits is 7.

   II. The product of the digits is 6.

(*a*) Statement (I) ALONE is sufficient but statement (II) ALONE is not sufficient.

(*b*) Statement (II) ALONE is sufficient but statement (I) ALONE is not sufficient.

(*c*) BOTH statements TOGETHER are sufficient, but NEITHER statement ALONE is sufficient.

(*d*) EACH statement ALONE is sufficient.

(*e*) Statements (I) and (II) TOGETHER are not sufficient.

6. Is x = 4 ?

I. $\sqrt{5x^2 - 64} = x$

II. $\sqrt{x^2 + 5} = x + 2$

(*a*) Statement (I) ALONE is sufficient but statement (II) ALONE is not sufficient.

(*b*) Statement (II) ALONE is sufficient but statement (I) ALONE is not sufficient.

(*c*) BOTH statements TOGETHER are sufficient, but NEITHER statement ALONE is sufficient.

(*d*) EACH statement ALONE is sufficient.

(*e*) Statements (I) and (II) TOGETHER are not sufficient.

7. What is the standard deviation of 1, 2, 3, k, 5, 6 and 7 ?

I. Standard deviation of 2, 3, 4, (k + 1), 6, 7 and 8 is 2.

II. Standard deviation of 0, 1, 2, (k – 1), 4, 5, and 6 is 2.

(*a*) Statement (I) ALONE is sufficient but statement (II) ALONE is not sufficient.

(*b*) Statement (II) ALONE is sufficient but statement (I) ALONE is not sufficient.

(*c*) BOTH statements TOGETHER are sufficient, but NEITHER statement ALONE is sufficient.

(*d*) EACH statement ALONE is sufficient.

(*e*) Statements (I) and (II) TOGETHER are not sufficient.

8. What is the value of $(a^2 - b^2)$?

I. a – b = 0

II. a + b = 0

(*a*) Statement (I) ALONE is sufficient but statement (II) ALONE is not sufficient.

(*b*) Statement (II) ALONE is sufficient but statement (I) ALONE is not sufficient.

(*c*) BOTH statements TOGETHER are sufficient, but NEITHER statement ALONE is sufficient.

(*d*) EACH statement ALONE is sufficient.

(*e*) Statements (I) and (II) TOGETHER are not sufficient.

9. If x and y are distinct single-digit positive integers, what is the value of x ?

I. The sum of *x* and *y* is 8.

II. Both *x* and *y* are multiples of 2.

(*a*) Statement (I) ALONE is sufficient but statement (II) ALONE is not sufficient.

(*b*) Statement (II) ALONE is sufficient but statement (I) ALONE is not sufficient.

(*c*) BOTH statements TOGETHER are sufficient, but NEITHER statement ALONE is sufficient.

(*d*) EACH statement ALONE is sufficient.

(*e*) Statements (I) and (II) TOGETHER are not sufficient.

10. The population of a country increased by X% after the first year and by Y% after the second year. What is the percentage increase in population after 2 years?

I. XY = 50

II. 100X + 100Y + XY = 2, 150

(*a*) Statement (I) ALONE is sufficient but statement (II) ALONE is not sufficient.

(*b*) Statement (II) ALONE is sufficient but statement (I) ALONE is not sufficient.

(*c*) BOTH statements TOGETHER are sufficient, but NEITHER statement ALONE is sufficient.

(*d*) EACH statement ALONE is sufficient.

(*e*) Statements (I) and (II) TOGETHER are not sufficient.

11. A case has at least one white, one pink, and one black marble and no marbles of any other color. If one marble is drawn randomly from the case, is the probability that the marble is white the same as the probability that the marble is black but NOT the same as the probability that the marble is pink?

I. The case contains 5 marbles.

II. The case contains more pink marbles than black marbles.

(*a*) Statement (I) ALONE is sufficient but statement (II) ALONE is not sufficient.

(*b*) Statement (II) ALONE is sufficient but statement (I) ALONE is not sufficient.

(*c*) BOTH statements TOGETHER are sufficient, but NEITHER statement ALONE is sufficient.

(*d*) EACH statement ALONE is sufficient.

(*e*) Statements (I) and (II) TOGETHER are not sufficient.

12. If Amy and Betty together can complete a project in 50 days, is Amy the most efficient of Amy, Betty, and Cherry?

I. Betty and Cherry, together, can complete the same project between 30 to 40 days.

II. Cherry alone can complete the same project in 60 days.

(*a*) Statement (I) ALONE is sufficient but statement (II) ALONE is not sufficient.

(*b*) Statement (II) ALONE is sufficient but statement (I) ALONE is not sufficient.

(*c*) BOTH statements TOGETHER are sufficient, but NEITHER statement ALONE is sufficient.

(*d*) EACH statement ALONE is sufficient.

(*e*) Statements (I) and (II) TOGETHER are not sufficient.

13. Steve rows a certain distance upstream (rowing against the stream) in Boat B in 6 hours. How long would it take him to row the same distance upstream if he used Boat C that runs twice as fast as Boat B?

I. It takes Steve 4 hours to cover the same distance downstream (rowing with the stream) using the slower of the two boats.

II. Rowing upstream, Steve covers 12 miles distance.

(*a*) Statement (I) ALONE is sufficient but statement (II) ALONE is not sufficient.

(*b*) Statement (II) ALONE is sufficient but statement (I) ALONE is not sufficient.

(*c*) BOTH statements TOGETHER are sufficient, but NEITHER statement ALONE is sufficient.

(*d*) EACH statement ALONE is sufficient.

(*e*) Statements (I) and (II) TOGETHER are not sufficient.

Answer Key

1. (*a*)
2. (*e*)
3. (*c*)
4. (*c*)
5. (*d*)
6. (*d*)
7. (*d*)
8. (*d*)
9. (*e*)
10. (*b*)
11. (*e*)
12. (*a*)
13. (*a*)

Answer Explanations

1. (a) **Considering Statement I alone :**

Since there are four students, the total score of the four students $= 4 \times 100 = 400$.

Let A, B, C, D be the four students' scores. This statement implies that $C + D = 155 \times 2 = 310 \Rightarrow A + B = 90$. Therefore, given that no student scored less than 0, we can conclude that neither A nor B scored greater than 90. The answer is that two students scored greater than 90.

This statement alone is sufficient.

Hence, eliminate (b)/(c)/(e).

Considering Statement II alone :

Given that that median = 90.

Again, since there are four students, the total score of the four students

$$= 4 \times 100 = 400.$$

Let's take a couple of cases.

Case1: Say the three scores are 90, each; thus, the fourth score $400 - 3 \times 90 = 130$.

Median $= \frac{90 + 90}{2} = 90$. The answer is that only one student scored greater than 90.

Case 2: Say the three scores are 80, 80, 100, and 140; Media n $= \frac{80 + 100}{2} = 90$ and the total score = 400. The answer is that two students scored greater than 90.

No unique answer.

This statement alone is insufficient.

Hence, eliminate (d).

The correct answer is option (a).

2. (e) Let the coordinates of Point X be (m, n).

We need to determine the value of m.

Considering Statement I alone :

It can be seen in the diagram below that there are two possible positions of Point X (X and X') so that triangle AXB is right-angled at Point X.

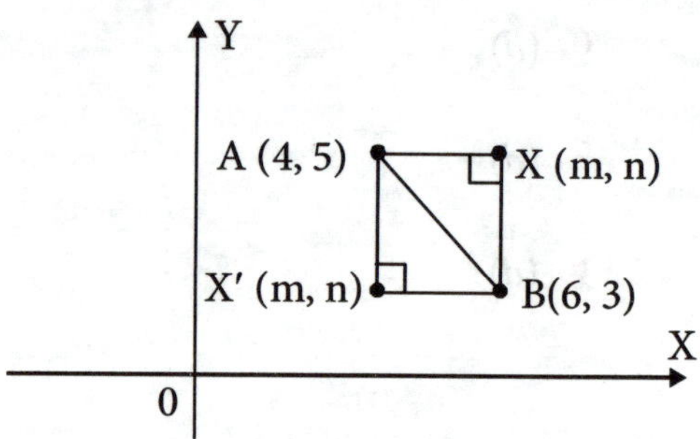

The x-coordinate of X is the same as that of B and the Y coordinate of X is the same as that of A.

Thus, the coordinates of X are (6, 5)

$\Rightarrow \quad m = 6$

The X coordinate of X' is the same as that of A and the Y coordinate of X' is the same as that of B.

Thus, the coordinates of X' are (4, 3)

$\Rightarrow \quad m = 4$

Thus, there is no unique value of m. – Insufficient

Hence, eliminate (a)/(d).

Considering Statement II alone :

We only know that the area of triangle AXB is 2.

We cannot determine the coordinates of X. – Insufficient

Hence, eliminate (b).

Considering statements I and II together :

As in Statement I, for the position X OR X', the area of triangle AXB

$$= \frac{1}{2}(AX)(XB) = \frac{1}{2} \times 2 \times 2 = 2$$

Thus, the coordinates of X are not unique.

Thus, there is no unique value of m. – Insufficient

The correct answer is option (e).

3. (c) We are given that the amount spent on buying P, Q, and R is $50,000.

Say the amounts spent on buying P, Q, and R are x, y, and z, respectively.

$\Rightarrow x + y + z = 50{,}000$ ... (1)

We have to determine whether $z > 20{,}000$.

Considering Statement I alone:

We are given that the sum the merchant paid for P and Q combined was 3 times the sum he paid for P.

$\Rightarrow x + y = 3x$

$y = 2x$ ... (2)

Substituting equation (2) in equation (1):

$\Rightarrow x + 2x + z = 50{,}000 \Rightarrow 3x + z = 50{,}000$. We have an unknown x. So, we cannot determine whether $z > 20{,}000$. Insufficient!

Hence, eliminate (a)/(d).

Considering Statement II alone:

We are given that the merchant paid more for R than for Q.

$\Rightarrow z > y$ ... (3)

With the help of equation (1): $x + y + z = 50{,}000$ and inequality (2): $z > y$, we cannot determine whether $z > 20{,}000$. Insufficient!

Hence, eliminate (b).

Considering statements I and II together:

Let's put down the two equations (1) and (2) and the inequality (3).

$x + y + z = 50{,}000$ ... (1)

$y = 2x$ ... (2)

$z > y$ ... (3)

Since the inequality (3) has only z and y variables, let's eliminate variable x from equation (1) and (2).

From equation (2), we have $x = \frac{y}{2}$. By plugging in the value x in equation (1), we get

$$\frac{y}{2} + y + z = 50{,}000$$

$y + 2y + 2z = 100{,}000$

$3y + 2z = 100{,}000$ ... (4)

$$y = \frac{100{,}000 - 2z}{3} \quad \text{... (5)}$$

Substituting (5) in (3):

$$z = \frac{100{,}000 - 2z}{3}$$

$5z > 100{,}000$

$z > 20{,}000$

So, the answer is 'Yes'. The two statements together are sufficient!

Alternate approach :

Alternate way of solving further after equation (4): $3y + 2z = 100{,}000$

Let's assume that $y = z = n$, and analyze what their values are.

Thus, from equation (4), $3n + 2n = 100{,}000$ $\Rightarrow 5n = 100{,}000 \Rightarrow n = 20{,}000$

Thus, $y = z = 20{,}000$;

However, this goes against the fact (Statement II) given in inequality (3): $z > y$.

Thus, $y < 20{,}000$ & $z > 20{,}000$. The answer is Yes. Sufficient!

The correct answer is option (c).

4. **(c)** Since the first two terms of the expression $(15x^3 + 30x^2 + 6x + 9)$ are divisible by $x^2\left[\frac{15x^3 + 30x^2 + 6x + 9}{x^2} = (15x + 30) + \frac{6x + 9}{x^2}\right]$, the question becomes whether $(6x + 9)$ is divisible by x^2.

Considering statement I alone :

Since x is a prime number and $4 < x^2 < 30$, the set of x would be {3, 5}.

Case 1: If $x = 3$, we see that $(6x + 9)$ is divisible by x^2.

$6x + 9 = 6 \times 3 + 9 = 27$ is divisible by $x^2 = 3^2 = 9$. The answer is YES.

Case 2: If $x = 5$, we see that $(6x + 9)$ is not divisible by x^2.

$6x + 9 = 6 \times 5 + 9 = 39$ is not divisible by $x^2 = 5^2 = 25$. The answer is NO.

No unique answer!

Statement I alone is not sufficient. Hence, eliminate (a)/(d).

Considering statement II alone :

Upon solving $x^2 - 10x + 21 = 0$, we get $x = 3$ or 7. We already know that for $x = 3$, the expression $(6x + 9)$ is divisible by x^2 and the answer is YES. However, for $x = 7$, $(6x + 9)$ is not divisible by x^2

$\Rightarrow (6x + 9 = 6 \times 7 + 9) = 51$, not divisible by $x^2 = 7^2 = 49$. So the answer is NO. Again no unique answer!

Statement II alone is also not sufficient. Hence, eliminate (b).

Considering Statement I and II together :

The only common value of x between statements (1) and (2) is 3, and for $x = 3$, we know that the expression is divisible, hence the answer is yes; a unique answer.

The correct answer is option (c).

5. **(d)** A two-digit number is divisible by 21 only if it is divisible by both 3 and 7.

Let's see each statement one by one.

Considering Statement I alone :

Since the sum of digits is 7, we have the following cases:

a	b	ab
1	6	16
2	5	25
3	4	34
4	3	43
5	2	52
6	1	61
7	0	70

Thus, the possible numbers are 16, 25, 34, 43, 52, 61, and 70; none of these are divisible by 21.

Hence, Statement I is sufficient to answer the question, the answer is No – (a) unique answer. Sufficient

Hence, eliminate (b)/(c)/(e).

Considering Statement II alone :

Since the product of the digits is 6, we have the following cases:

a	b	ab
1	6	16
2	3	23
3	2	32
6	1	61

Thus, the possible numbers are 16, 23, 32 and 61; none of these are divisible by 21.

Hence, Statement II is also sufficient to answer the question, the answer being No – (a) unique answer.

Hence, eliminate (a).

The correct answer is option (d).

6. (d) **Considering Statement I alone :**

We have $\sqrt{5x^2 - 64} = x$

Squaring both sides

$(5x^2 - 64) = x^2$

$\Rightarrow 4x^2 = 64$

$\Rightarrow x^2 = 16$

$\Rightarrow x = 4 \text{ or } -4$

Seeing two values of x, you may hurriedly conclude that you cannot get the unique value of x; thus, Statement I is insufficient. However, the left-hand side of the equation: $\sqrt{5x^2 - 64}$ is a square root, which is always non-negative.

Thus, $x \neq -4$.

Thus, we obtain only one value of $x = 4$.

Thus, Statement I is sufficient to answer the question and the answer is Yes.

Hence, eliminate (b)/(c)/(e).

Considering Statement II alone :

We have $\sqrt{x^2 + 20} = x + 2$

Squaring both sides

$x^2 + 20 = (x + 2)^2$

$\Rightarrow x^2 + 20 = x^2 + 4x + 4$

$\Rightarrow x = 4$

Thus, we obtain only one value of $x = 4$.

Thus, Statement II is also sufficient to answer the question and the answer is Yes.

Hence, eliminate (a).

The correct answer is option (d).

7. (d) The standard deviation (SD) of a data set is a measure of the deviations of the numbers in the set w.r.t. their average (arithmetic mean). The more deviated (more distant) the numbers are from the mean, the greater their standard deviation, and vice-versa.

Standard deviation doesn't get affected on addition or subtraction of a constant to each term in a given set.

Let's analyze each statement one by one.

Considering Statement I alone :

Note that if each number of a set is decreased by a constant, the standard deviation of the resultant set does not change.

We are given that the standard deviation of 2, 3, 4, (k + 1), 6, 7 and 8 is 2.

This implies that the standard deviation of (2 – 1),(3 – 1),(4 – 1), (k + 1 – 1), (6 – 1), (7 – 1) and (8 – 1) is also 2.

⇒ The standard deviation of 1, 2, 3, k, 5, 6 and 7 is 2. Sufficient.

Hence, eliminate (b)/(c)/(e).

Considering Statement II alone :

Note that if each number of a set is increased by a constant, the standard deviation of the resultant set does not change.

We are given that the standard deviation of 0, 1, 2, (k – 1), 4, 5, and 6 is 2.

This implies that the standard deviation of (0 + 1),(1 + 1),(2 + 1), (k – 1 + 1), (4 + 1), (5 + 1) and (6 + 1) is also 2.

⇒ The standard deviation of 1, 2, 3, k, 5, 6 and 7 is 2. Sufficient.

Hence, eliminate (a).

The correct answer is option (d).

8. (d) We know that $a^2 - b^2 = (a - b)(a + b)$.

Considering Statement I alone :

Substituting a – b = 0 in the given equation:

$a^2 - b^2 = (a - b)(a + b) = 0 \times (a + b) = 0$; a unique answer. Sufficient.

Hence, eliminate (b)/(c)/(e).

Considering Statement II alone :

Substituting a + b = 0 in the given equation:

$a^2 - b^2 = (a - b)(a + b) = 0 \times (a - b) = 0$; a unique answer. Sufficient.

Hence, eliminate (a).

The correct answer is option (d).

9. (e) **Considering Statement I alone :**

Multiple combinations are possible for x and y: (1, 7), (2, 6), (3, 5), etc. Therefore, Statement I alone is insufficient.

Hence, eliminate (a)/(d).

Considering Statement II alone :

Again, multiple values are possible for x and y: 2, 4, 6, and 8. Therefore, Statement II alone is insufficient.

Hence, eliminate (b).

Considering statements I and II together :

Both statements together lead to only one combination for x and y: (2, 6). x and y each cannot be 4 since they are distinct. Moreover, even with only one possible combination for x and y, we cannot fix which of the two values 2 and 6 is the value of x. No unique answer. Insufficient.

The correct answer is option (e).

10. (b) Let the population at start of the first year $= P_0$;

So, the population after first year

$$= P_1 = P_o\left(1+\frac{X}{100}\right)$$

$$= P_o + P_o x.\left(\text{Assuming } x = \frac{X}{100}\right);$$

So, the population after 2 years

$$= P_2 = P_1\left(1+\frac{Y}{100}\right)$$

$$= P_1 + P_1 y.\left(\text{Assuming } Y = \frac{X}{100}\right);$$

$= P_o + P_o x + P_o y + P_o xy$; by replacing the value of $P_1 = P_o + P_o x$;

Percentage increase in population

$$= \left[\frac{(P_o + P_o x + P_o y + P_o xy)}{P_o}\right] \times 100\%$$

$$= \frac{(P_o x + P_o y + P_o xy)}{P_o} \times 100\%$$

$= (x + y + xy) \times 100\%$;

taking P_0 common from numerator and denominator and then cancelling it.

So, Percentage increase in population

$= 100(x + y + xy)\%$;

Therefore, we need to find the value of $(x + y + xy)$.

Considering Statement I alone :

Since XY = 50, we get $xy = \frac{50}{10,000}$. But we don't have values for x and y. This statement is not sufficient.

Hence, eliminate (a)/(d).

Considering Statement II alone :

We know that 100X + 100Y + XY = 2,150. Substituting the values of x and y, we get 10,000x +10,000y +10,000xy = 2,150 $\Rightarrow x + y + xy = 0.215$. Therefore, required percentage =100 (x + y + xy)% = 100 × 0.215% = 21.5%.

This statement is sufficient.

Hence, eliminate (c)/(e).

The correct answer is option (b).

11. (e) We are given that the case has marbles of three different colors–white, pink, and black, and the number of marbles of each color is at least one in count. Thus, the minimum number of marbles in the case = 3.

Let's understand what the question asks.

Say, the probability of drawing a white marble = p(w); the probability of drawing a black marble = p(b); and the probability of drawing a pink marble = p(p).

The question asks: Is $p(w) = p(b) \neq p(p)$?

So, the question boils down to:

"Does the case have white marbles equal to black marbles but NOT equal to pink marbles?"

Considering Statement I alone :

The case contains 5 marbles.

Let's distribute the 5 marbles in three colors such that we have at least one marble of each color.

Case 1 : White: 1 marble; Black: 1 marble; Pink: 3 marbles

We have white marbles equal to black marbles, and NOT equal to pink marbles; the answer is yes.

Case 2 : White: 2 marbles; Black: 1 marble; Pink: 2 marbles

We have white marbles NOT equal to black marbles, but equal to pink marbles; the answer is no.

No unique answer. Insufficient.

Note : Other cases are possible too, but we need not consider them all because, from just two cases, we deduced that Statement I is not sufficient to get a unique answer.

Hence, eliminate (a)/(d).

Considering Statement II alone :

Only with this information, we can deduce that the probability that the marble is pink is NOT equal to the probability that the marble is black; however, we have no clue about the count of white marbles; the count of white marbles may or may not be equal to the count of black marbles. Insufficient.

Hence, eliminate (b).

Considering statements I and II together :

Both the cases discussed in Statement I are applicable here too.

So, this does not add any value. – Insufficient

The correct answer is option (e).

12. (a) We know that Amy and Betty together can complete a project in 50 days ... (i)

Considering Statement I alone :

Betty and Cherry, together, can complete the same project between 30 to 40 days ... (ii)

Thus, from (i) and (ii), we see that if Amy is replaced by Cherry, the time required for the project decreases (30 to 40 days from 50 days).

Thus, the efficiency of Cherry must be greater than that of Amy.

Thus, the efficiency of Amy cannot be the greatest among Amy, Betty and Cherry. – Sufficient

Hence, eliminate (b)/(c)/(e).

Considering Statement II alone :

We only know that the time taken by Cherry to complete the project is 60 days.

Since the individual times taken by Amy and Betty are not known, the efficiency of Amy cannot be compared with that of Betty or Cherry. – Insufficient

Hence, eliminate (d).

The correct answer is option (a).

13. (a) Let the distance Steve covers be d miles.

Given that he uses Boat C that is twice as fast as Boat B, the slower boat is Boat B.

Let the speed of the slower boat (Boat B) in still water be b miles per hour.

Let the speed of the stream be r miles per hour.

Thus, speed while rowing upstream = (b – r) miles per hour.

Thus, time taken to cover d miles upstream $=\left(\frac{d}{b-r}\right)$ hours.

Thus, we have

$$\frac{d}{b-r}=6 \quad \text{... (i)}$$

If Steve uses Boat C that is twice as fast as Boat B, the speed of Boat C in still water = 2b miles per hour.

Thus, upstream speed = (2b – r) miles per hour.

Thus, time taken to cover d miles upstream $=\left(\frac{d}{2b-r}\right)$ hours.

Thus, we need to determine the value of $\left(\frac{d}{2b-r}\right)$.

Considering Statement I alone :

Speed while going downstream using the slower boat = (b + r) miles per hour

Thus, time taken to cover d miles downstream $=\left(\frac{d}{b+r}\right)$ hours

Thus, we have

$$\frac{d}{b+r}=4 \quad \text{... (ii)}$$

Dividing (i) by (ii):

$$\frac{b+r}{b-r}=\frac{6}{4} \Rightarrow 4b+4r=6b-6r \Rightarrow b=5r$$

Thus, from (ii):

$$\frac{d}{5r+r}=4 \Rightarrow d=24r$$

Thus, we have

$$\frac{d}{2b-r}=\frac{24r}{10r-r}=\frac{8}{3} \text{ hours – Sufficient}$$

Hence, eliminate (b)/(c)/(e).

Considering Statement II alone :

Only knowing the actual value of the distance does not help to establish a relation between b and r. – Insufficient

Hence, eliminate (d).

The correct answer is option (a).

Chapter 7

Data Sufficiency Practice Questions Set - 2

Multiple Choice Questions

1. What is the value of the positive integer x ?

I. The number of trailing zeros in x! is 2.

II. The number of trailing zeros in (x + 1)! is 3.

(a) Statement (I) ALONE is sufficient but statement (II) ALONE is not sufficient.

(b) Statement (II) ALONE is sufficient but statement (I) ALONE is not sufficient.

(c) BOTH statements TOGETHER are sufficient, but NEITHER statement ALONE is sufficient.

(d) EACH statement ALONE is sufficient.

(e) Statements (I) and (II) TOGETHER are not sufficient.

2. Is $|x| < \frac{1}{4}$?

I. $x = \frac{1}{4+y^2}$

II. y is a non-positive integer.

(a) Statement (I) ALONE is sufficient but statement (II) ALONE is not sufficient.

(b) Statement (II) ALONE is sufficient but statement (I) ALONE is not sufficient.

(c) BOTH statements TOGETHER are sufficient, but NEITHER statement ALONE is sufficient.

(d) EACH statement ALONE is sufficient.

(e) Statements (I) and (II) TOGETHER are not sufficient.

3. If the symbol ⊗ represents one of the following operations: addition, subtraction, multiplication, or division, what is the value of $3 \otimes 5$?

I. $6 \otimes 8 < 1$

II. $4 \otimes 3 > 1$

(a) Statement (I) ALONE is sufficient but statement (II) ALONE is not sufficient.

(b) Statement (II) ALONE is sufficient but statement (I) ALONE is not sufficient.

(c) BOTH statements TOGETHER are sufficient, but NEITHER statement ALONE is sufficient.

(d) EACH statement ALONE is sufficient.

(e) Statements (I) and (II) TOGETHER are not sufficient.

4. If $a^2 - 4a = 0$, and $b \neq 0$, is $\frac{a}{b} = 0$?

I. $b^2 - 16 = 0$

II. $a^2 + 8a = 0$

(a) Statement (I) ALONE is sufficient but statement (II) ALONE is not sufficient.

(b) Statement (II) ALONE is sufficient but statement (I) ALONE is not sufficient.

(c) BOTH statements TOGETHER are sufficient, but NEITHER statement ALONE is sufficient.

(d) EACH statement ALONE is sufficient.

(e) Statements (I) and (II) TOGETHER are not sufficient.

5. What is the value of y, if x = 2 ?

I. $|x| = |y|$

II. $y^2 = 4$

(a) Statement (I) ALONE is sufficient but statement (II) ALONE is not sufficient.

(b) Statement (II) ALONE is sufficient but statement (I) ALONE is not sufficient.

(c) BOTH statements TOGETHER are sufficient, but NEITHER statement ALONE is sufficient.

(*d*) EACH statement ALONE is sufficient.

(*e*) Statements (I) and (II) TOGETHER are not sufficient.

6. Is xyz = 10 ?

I. $z = \frac{1}{\sqrt{x}} - \left(\frac{y^2 + 2xy}{\sqrt{x}} + \frac{x^2}{\sqrt{x}}\right)\left(\frac{1}{(x+y^2)}\right)$

II. x = z

(*a*) Statement (I) ALONE is sufficient but statement (II) ALONE is not sufficient.

(*b*) Statement (II) ALONE is sufficient but statement (I) ALONE is not sufficient.

(*c*) BOTH statements TOGETHER are sufficient, but NEITHER statement ALONE is sufficient.

(*d*) EACH statement ALONE is sufficient.

(*e*) Statements (I) and (II) TOGETHER are not sufficient.

7. In a certain office, a manager distributed a few food coupons and a few gas coupons to the employees such that each employee got an equal number of food coupons and an equal number of gas coupons. How many employees are there in the office?

I. The manager distributed 200 food coupons and 60 gas coupons.

II. The total number of coupons received by each employee was less than 20.

(*a*) Statement (I) ALONE is sufficient but statement (II) ALONE is not sufficient.

(*b*) Statement (II) ALONE is sufficient but statement (I) ALONE is not sufficient.

(*c*) BOTH statements TOGETHER are sufficient, but NEITHER statement ALONE is sufficient.

(*d*) EACH statement ALONE is sufficient.

(*e*) Statements (I) and (II) TOGETHER are not sufficient.

8. A carpenter distributed nuts, bolts, and screws among the apprentices in his class, such that each apprentice got an equal number of nuts, an equal number of bolts, and an equal number of screws. How many apprentices were in the class?

I. Each apprentice got nuts, bolts, and screws in the ratio 3 : 4 : 5, respectively.

II. The carpenter distributed a total of 27 nuts, 36 bolts, and 45 screws.

(*a*) Statement (I) ALONE is sufficient but statement (II) ALONE is not sufficient.

(*b*) Statement (II) ALONE is sufficient but statement (I) ALONE is not sufficient.

(*c*) BOTH statements TOGETHER are sufficient, but NEITHER statement ALONE is sufficient.

(*d*) EACH statement ALONE is sufficient.

(*e*) Statements (I) and (II) TOGETHER are not sufficient.

9. Did Andrew eat a greater number of toffees than Ricky?

I. Thrice the number of toffees that Andrew ate was greater than 6 less than thrice the number of toffees that Ricky ate.

II. Twice the number of toffees that Andrew ate was greater than 4 less than twice the number of toffees that Ricky ate.

(*a*) Statement (I) ALONE is sufficient but statement (II) ALONE is not sufficient.

(*b*) Statement (II) ALONE is sufficient but statement (I) ALONE is not sufficient.

(*c*) BOTH statements TOGETHER are sufficient, but NEITHER statement ALONE is sufficient.

(*d*) EACH statement ALONE is sufficient.

(*e*) Statements (I) and (II) TOGETHER are not sufficient.

10. While going to the office, Edward drove his car at an average speed of 50 kilometers per hour. While returning home, he drove at a slower speed. What was Edward's average speed for the entire journey?

I. While returning home and taking the same route, Edward drove at a constant speed of 45 kilometers per hour.

II. It takes Edward 1 hour to drive to the office.

(*a*) Statement (I) ALONE is sufficient but statement (II) ALONE is not sufficient.

(*b*) Statement (II) ALONE is sufficient but statement (I) ALONE is not sufficient.

(*c*) BOTH statements TOGETHER are sufficient, but NEITHER statement ALONE is sufficient.

(*d*) EACH statement ALONE is sufficient.

(*e*) Statements (I) and (II) TOGETHER are not sufficient.

11. If $z = xy$, is $z = 1$?

I. $x(y - x) = 0$

II. $y(x - y) = 0$

(*a*) Statement (I) ALONE is sufficient but statement (II) ALONE is not sufficient.

(*b*) Statement (II) ALONE is sufficient but statement (I) ALONE is not sufficient.

(*c*) BOTH statements TOGETHER are sufficient, but NEITHER statement ALONE is sufficient.

(*d*) EACH statement ALONE is sufficient.

(*e*) Statements (I) and (II) TOGETHER are not sufficient.

12. Is abc an odd integer?

I. ab is an odd integer.

II. bc is an odd integer.

(*a*) Statement (I) ALONE is sufficient but statement (II) ALONE is not sufficient.

(*b*) Statement (II) ALONE is sufficient but statement (I) ALONE is not sufficient.

(*c*) BOTH statements TOGETHER are sufficient, but NEITHER statement ALONE is sufficient.

(*d*) EACH statement ALONE is sufficient.

(*e*) Statements (I) and (II) TOGETHER are not sufficient.

Answer Key

1. (c)
2. (e)
3. (c)
4. (b)
5. (e)
6. (a)
7. (c)
8. (e)
9. (e)
10. (a)
11. (e)
12. (c)

Answer Explanations

1. (c) This question deals with the number of trailing 0s in $x! = 1 \times 2 \times 3 \times 4 \times 5 \times 7 \times 6 \ldots x$

Let's discuss how a 0 comes up upon multiplying positive integers.

A trailing 0 comes up when 2 is multiplied by 5. Since $5 > 2$, it's sufficient to count the number of 5s in x! to get the number of trailing 0s.

Examples :

- $7! = 1 \times 2 \times 3 \times 4 \times 5 \times 6 \times 7 = 5040$; since 7! has only one 5, it would have only one trailing 0.
- $12! = 1 \times 2 \times 3 \times 4 \times 5 \times 6 \times 7 \times 8 \times 9 \times 10 \times 11 \times 12 = 479001600$; since 12! has two 5s (one in 5 and one in 10), it would have two trailing 0s.

Let's analyze each statement one by one.

Considering statement I alone :

The number of trailing zeros in x! is 2.

The minimum value of x such that the number of trailing zeros in x! is 2 is 10.

At x! = 10!, we already saw that we have two 5s (one in 5 and one in 10).

One more 5, we would get when x! = 15!. Thus, when x = 10 to 14, we have two trailing 0s in x! We do not have a unique value of x. Insufficient

Hence, eliminate A/D.

Considering statement II alone :

The number of trailing zeros in (x + 1)! is 3.

The minimum value of x such that the number of trailing zeros in (x + 1)! is 3 is 14.

At (x + 1)! = 15!, we already saw that we have three 5s (one in 5, one in 10 and one from 15).

One more 5, we would get when (x + 1)!=20! Thus, when x = 14 to 19, we have three trailing 0s in (x + 1)!. We do not have a unique value of x. Insufficient.

Hence, eliminate (b).

Considering statements I and II together :

Only one value of x is common in both the statements, i.e., 14; thus, both the statements together gives us a unique value of x = 14. Sufficient

The correct answer is option (c).

2. (e) We have to ascertain whether $|x| < \frac{1}{4}$.

The minimum value of $|x|$ is 0, thus, we have to determine whether $0 \leq |x| < \frac{1}{4}$.

Let's take each statement one by one.

Considering statement I alone :

$$x = \frac{1}{4+y^2}$$

Though the value of y is not given, we must not dismiss statement I only because of this reason.

Observe that the minimum value of y^2 is 0 since y^2 is a non-negative number. Whether y is positive or negative, y^2 is positive.

Note that as the value of y^2 increases, the value of $\frac{1}{4+y^2}$ decreases. As y^2 approaches infinity, $\frac{1}{4+y^2}$ approaches 0.

Conversely, as the value of y^2 decreases, the value of $\frac{1}{4+y^2}$ increases. As y^2 approaches 0, $\frac{1}{4+y^2}$ approaches $\frac{1}{4}$.

This implies that $0 \le \frac{1}{4+y^2} \le \frac{1}{4}$.

Case 1 : If $0 \le \frac{1}{4+y^2} < \frac{1}{4}$, the answer is Yes.

Case 2 : If $\frac{1}{4+y^2} = \frac{1}{4}$, the answer is No.

Note that at y = 0, we have $x = \frac{1}{4+y^2} = \frac{1}{4+0^2} = \frac{1}{4} \not< \frac{1}{4}$.

No unique answer. Insufficient.

Hence, eliminate (a)/(d).

Considering statement II alone :

y is a non-positive integer.

We do not have any information on the relationship of y with x.

No unique answer. Insufficient.

Hence, eliminate (b).

Considering statements I and II together :

Both the cases discussed in statement I are applicable here too.

Case 1 : At y = 0 (a non-positive integer), we have $x = \frac{1}{4+y^2} = \frac{1}{4+0^2} = \frac{1}{4} \not< \frac{1}{4}$, the answer is No, $|x| \not< \frac{1}{4}$.

Case 2 : At y = –1 (a non-positive integer), we have

$$x = \frac{1}{4+y^2} = \frac{1}{4+(-1)^2} = \frac{1}{4+1} = \frac{1}{5} < \frac{1}{4},$$

the answer is Yes, $|x| < \frac{1}{4}$.

No unique answer. Insufficient.

The correct answer is option (e).

3. (c) We have to determine the value of $3 \otimes 5$. To get this, we must know which arithmetic operation the symbol $\otimes$ represents. Since there can be four different values of $3 \otimes 5$.

- $3 \otimes 5 = 3 + 5 = 8$
- $3 \otimes 5 = 3 - 5 = -2$
- $3 \otimes 5 = 3 \times 5 = 15$
- $3 \otimes 5 = 3 \div 5 = 0.6$

Question rephrased : What operation does the symbol $\otimes$ represent?

Let's analyze each statement one by one.

Considering statement I alone : $6 \otimes 8 < 1$

- Assuming that $\otimes$ is addition, then $6 \otimes 8 < 1 \Rightarrow 6 + 8 (= 14) \not< 1$. Not correct
- Assuming that $\otimes$ is subtraction, then $6 \otimes 8 < 1 \Rightarrow 6 - 8 (= -2) < 1$. Correct
- Assuming that $\otimes$ is multiplication, then $6 \otimes 8 < 1 \Rightarrow 6 \times 8 (= 48) \not< 1$. Not correct
- Assuming that $\otimes$ is division, then $6 \otimes 8 < 1 \Rightarrow 6 \div 8 (= 0.75) < 1$. Correct

$\otimes$ can be either subtraction or division. No unique answer. Insufficient.

Hence, eliminate (a)/(d).

Considering Statement II alone: $4 \otimes 3 > 1$

- Assuming that $\otimes$ is addition, then $4 \otimes 3 > 1 \Rightarrow 4 + 3 (= 7) > 1$. Correct
- Assuming that $\otimes$ is subtraction, then $4 \otimes 3 > 1 \Rightarrow 4 - 3 (= 1) \not> 1$. Not correct
- Assuming that $\otimes$ is multiplication, then $4 \otimes 3 > 1 \Rightarrow 4 \times 3 (= 12) > 1$. Correct
- Assuming that $\otimes$ is division, then $4 \otimes 3 > 1 \Rightarrow 4 \div 3 (= 1.33) > 1$. Correct

$\otimes$ can be addition, multiplication or division. No unique answer. Insufficient.

Hence, eliminate (b).

Considering statements I and II together:

Statement 1 concludes that $\otimes$ can be either subtraction or division, while statement II concludes that $\otimes$ can be addition, multiplication or division. Only one operation is common in both the statements, i.e., division. Thus, $\otimes$ is subtraction. Sufficient.

There is no need to calculate the value of $3 \otimes 5$ since we know which arithmetic operation the symbol $\otimes$ represents.

For the sake of completeness:

$3 \otimes 5 = 3 \div 5 = 0.6$

The correct answer is option (c).

4. (b) We know that $a^2 - 4a = 0$. we have to determine whether $\frac{a}{b} = 0$.

$\Rightarrow a(a - 4) = 0$

$\Rightarrow a = 0$ or 4

Let's see each statement one by one.

Considering statement I alone:

$b^2 - 16 = 0$

$\Rightarrow b = \pm 4$

Case 1: If $a = 0$ then $\frac{a}{b} = \frac{0}{+4} = 0$

Case 2: If $a = 4$ then $\frac{a}{b} = \frac{4}{+4} = \pm 1$

No unique answer. Insufficient.

Hence, eliminate (a)/(d).

Moreover, since $\frac{a}{b} = 0$ is possible only when $a = 0$ and statement I doesn't give us any information about a.

Considering statement II alone:

$a^2 + 8a = 0$

$\Rightarrow a(a + 8) = 0$

$\Rightarrow a = 0$ or -8

Since from the question $(a^2 - 4a = 0)$, we know that $a = 0$ or 4, we can conclude that $a = 0$. We can ignore the values 4 and -8.

At $a = 0$, we have $\frac{a}{b} = \frac{0}{b} = 0$. There is no need to know the value of b.

Unique answer. Sufficient.

Hence, eliminate (c)/(e).

The correct answer is option (b).

5. (e) **Considering statement I alone:**

$|x| = |y| = 2 \Rightarrow y = 2$ or -2. No unique value of y. This statement is insufficient.

Hence, eliminate (a)/(d).

Considering statement II alone:

$y^2 = 4 \Rightarrow y = 2$ or -2. No unique value of y. This statement is insufficient.

Hence, eliminate (b).

Considering statement I and II together :

Since y = 2 or −2 is common in both statements, both statements together are insufficient.

The correct answer is option (e).

6. (a) **Considering statement I alone :**

We can simplify the given equation as shown below:

$$z=\frac{1}{\sqrt{x}}-\left(\frac{y^2+2xy}{\sqrt{x}}+\frac{x^2}{\sqrt{x}}\right)\left(\frac{1}{(x+y)^2}\right)$$

$$z=\frac{1}{\sqrt{x}}-\left(\frac{y^2+2xy+x^2}{\sqrt{x}}\right)\left(\frac{1}{(x+y)^2}\right)$$

$$z=\frac{1}{\sqrt{x}}-\left(\frac{(x+y)^2}{\sqrt{x}}\right)\left(\frac{1}{(x+y)^2}\right)$$

$$z=\frac{1}{\sqrt{x}}-\left(\frac{(x+y)^2}{(x+y)^2\sqrt{x}}\right)$$

$$z=\frac{1}{\sqrt{x}}-\frac{1}{\sqrt{x}}$$

$$z=0$$

Thus, $xyz = xy \times 0 = 0$. Sufficient

Hence, eliminate (b)/(c)/(e).

Considering statement II alone :

x = z gives us no idea whether any of x, y or z is 0. Hence, we cannot conclude that xyz is 0.

Thus, this statement is not sufficient.

Hence, eliminate (d).

The correct answer is option (a).

7. (c) Given: Each employee gets an equal number of food coupons and an equal number of gas coupons

Do not assume : Number of food coupons = Number of gas coupons

To find out : The number of employees in the office

Considering statement I alone:

We know that each employee received an equal number of food coupons and an equal number of gas coupons.

Thus, the GCD of the number of food coupons and the number of gas coupons is the largest possible number of employees in the office.

- $200 = 2^3 \times 5^2$
- $60 = 2^2 \times 3 \times 5$

The terms common to both $= 2^2 \times 5 = 20$

⇒ GCD of 200 and 60 = 20

Thus, the number of employees could be any number that is a factor of 20 (1, 2, 4, 5, 10, and 20):

- **Case #1**

  Number of employees = 20 (Maximum possible number of employees):

  Number of food coupons received by each employee $= \frac{200}{20} = 10$

  Number of gas coupons received by each employee $= \frac{60}{20} = 3$

- **Case #2**

  Number of employees = 10

  Number of food coupons received by each employee $= \frac{200}{10} = 20$

Number of gas coupons received by each employee $= \frac{60}{10} = 6$

- **Case #3**

Number of employees = 5

Number of food coupons received by each employee $= \frac{200}{5} = 40$

Number of gas coupons received by each employee $= \frac{60}{5} = 12$

There are three more possible cases for the number of employees, i.e., 4 or 2 or 1. Of these, the possibility of the number of employees being 1 can be rejected because the question mentions employees, in plural.

So, the number of employees can be 20, 10, 5, 4, or 2.

Thus, there is no unique answer. – Insufficient

Hence, eliminate (a)/(d).

Considering statement II alone :

There is no information about the number of food coupons and the number of gas coupons distributed. – Insufficient

Hence, eliminate (b).

Considering statements I and II together :

Combining both statements, we find that since the total number of coupons received by each employee is less than 20, the only possible case is case #1, where:

- The number of employees = 20.
- Total number of coupons received by each employee $= 10 + 3 = 13 < 20$.

The total number of coupons received by each employee in other cases is more than 20.

Therefore, we've arrived at a unique answer, the number of employees is 20. Sufficient

The correct answer is option (c).

8. (e) We are given that a carpenter gave an equal number of nuts, an equal number of bolts, and an equal number of screws to each apprentice.

You must NOT assume:

(Number of nuts per apprentice)

= (Numbers of bolts per apprentice)

= (Number of screws per apprentice)

The number of nuts that an apprentice—say apprentice A—got may be different from the number of bolts and from the number of screws he got; however, each apprentice got as many nuts as apprentice A got (and likewise, as many bolts and screws as apprentice A got).

Let the total number of apprentices in the class be n, and each apprentice got x number of nuts, y number of bolts, and z number of screws.

We have to find out n.

Considering statement I alone :

Each apprentice got nuts, bolts, and screws in the ratio 3 : 4 : 5, respectively.

Thus, we have,

$x : y : z = 3 : 4 : 5$

$\Rightarrow x = 3k, y = 4k, z = 5k$, where k is a constant of proportionality.

However, we have no information on n. -- Insufficient!

Hence, eliminate (a)/(d).

Considering statement II alone :

We know that the carpenter distributed a total of 27 nuts, 36 bolts, and 45 screws.

Thus, $nx = 27, ny = 36, nz = 45$

We have no information about x, y, z.

Hence, we cannot determine the value of n. – Insufficient

Hence, eliminate (b).

Considering statements I and II together :

Substituting the values of x, or y, or z from statement I in the information from statement II, we have

$nx = 27 = 3k$

$n = \frac{9}{k}$

Since k is unknown, we cannot determine n.

The valid values of k can be 1, 3, and 9, which render the values of n = 9, 3, and 1. (k cannot be greater than 9 because n, the number of apprentices, cannot be a fraction. And k cannot be a fraction, for example, $\frac{1}{2}$ etc., because we know that $x = 3k$, $y = 4k$, & $z = 5k$. Since x, y, & z denote the number of items, they cannot be fractions. For x, y, & z to have integer values, k must be an integer.)

No unique value of n. – Insufficient

The correct answer is option (e).

9. (e) We have to find out whether Andrew ate a greater number of toffees than Ricky.

Say Andrew ate x number of toffees, while Ricky ate y number of toffees.

So, we need to determine whether $x > y$.

Considering statement I alone :

We are given that thrice the number of toffees that Andrew ate was greater than 6 less than thrice the number of toffees that Ricky ate.

$\Rightarrow 3x > 3y - 6$

$\Rightarrow x > y - 2$

We cannot determine whether $x > y$, since x is greater than a quantity y, which itself is decreased by 2.

Let us take an example.

Say $y = 12$, thus $x > 12 - 2 \Rightarrow x > 10$.

If $x = 11$, then $x \not> y$ and the answer is No.

However, if $x = 13$, then $x > y$ and the answer is Yes. No unique answer. Insufficient!

Hence, eliminate (a)/(d).

Considering statement II alone :

We are given that twice the number of toffees that Andrew ate in the test was greater than 4 less than twice the number of toffees that Ricky ate.

$\Rightarrow 2x > 2y - 4$

$\Rightarrow x > y - 2$

This inequality is the same that we had in statement I. Insufficient!

Hence, eliminate (b).

Considering statements I and II together :

Since each statement gives the same inequality, even combining both statements cannot answer the question! Insufficient.

The correct answer is option (e).

10. (a) The average speed of any travel can be calculated by Total Distance Traveled divided by Total Time Taken.

Let's see each statement one by one.

Considering statement I alone:

The statement gives us the speed of his return journey.

Say the distance between the home and the office is 900 kms. The assumed value of the distance, 900 km, is a convenient number so that it is divisible by both 50 and 45. You can assume any value, say 450 (LCM of 50 and 45). The time taken between home and the office

would be $\frac{900}{50}$ = 18 hrs. Similarly, the time

taken between office to home would be

$\frac{900}{45}$ = 20 hrs. So, the total time taken for

the entire journey would be equal to 18 + 20 = 38 hrs.

Now we know the total time distance traveled = 900 + 900 = 1,800 kms, so the average speed would be $\frac{1,800}{38}$ kmph.

There is no need to calculate the value, as in a DS question, if we are sure of the unique answer, there is no need to get the value.

Statement I is sufficient.

Hence, eliminate (b)/(c)/(e).

Considering statement II alone:

From this information, we know that the distance is 50 kms. However, the statement does not tell us anything about the speed of the return journey and is, therefore, insufficient.

Hence, eliminate (d).

The correct answer is option (a).

11. (e) Since $z = xy$, we are supposed to find out the value xy.

Considering statement I alone:

$x(y - x) = 0$ implies that either $x = 0$ or $x = y$. If $x = 0$, we have $z = xy = 0 \times y = 0$: the answer is no; however, if $x = y = 1$, $z = xy = 1$: the answer is yes. No unique answer. statement I alone is not sufficient.

Hence, eliminate (a)/(d).

Considering statement II alone:

Same as statement I, we have $y(x - y) = 0$ implies that either $y = 0$ or $x = y$. If $y = 0$, we have $z = xy = x \times 0 = 0$: the answer is no; however, if= $y = 1$, $z = xy = 1$: the answer is yes. No unique answer. statement II alone is not sufficient.

Hence, eliminate (b).

Considering statements I and II together:

Even after combining both statements, we cannot get the unique value of xy.

The correct answer is option (e).

12. (c) Remember that

- Even × Even = Even;
- Even × Odd = Even;
- Odd × Odd = Odd

The products of any two integers would be Odd, only if both the integers are Odd. Similarly, the products of any two integers would be Even if even only one of the two integers is Even; we need not look for the nature of the other integer.

Considering statement I alone:

Statement I states that ab is an odd integer. It means that a and b are odd integers. But we don't have any information regarding c; if c = odd, abc = odd; however, if c = even, abc = even. No unique answer, therefore, statement I alone is insufficient.

Hence, eliminate (a)/(d).

Considering statement II alone :

Statement I states that bc is an odd integer. It means that b and c are odd integers. But we don't have any information regarding a; if a = odd, abc = odd; however, if a = even, abc = even. No unique answer, therefore, statement I alone is insufficient.

Hence, eliminate (b).

Considering statements I and II together :

Both statements together confirm that a, b and c are odd integers, therefore abc must be an odd integer.

The correct answer is option (c).

Chapter 8

Problem Solving Practice Set 1

Multiple Choice Questions

1. If the standard deviation of Set Y = {1, 3, 5, 7} is S, which of the following set(s) have a standard deviation less than S.

   U = {12, 14, 16, 18}

   V = {– 6, – 8, –10, –12}

   W = {2, 4, 6, 8}

   (*a*) Set U

   (*b*) Set V

   (*c*) Set W

   (*d*) Set U and V

   (*e*) None of the sets

2. Which of the following could be the range of a set consisting of odd integers?

   (*a*) –10

   (*b*) 3

   (*c*) 5

   (*d*) 6

   (*e*) 49

3. Two friends, Jack and Jill start walking towards each other's home at a speed of 3 kilometers per hour. The distance between their homes is 36 kilometers. Simultaneously, Francis leaves Jack's home on his bicycle at a speed of 6 kilometers per hour towards Jill's home. When Francis meets Jill, he turns around and starts moving towards Jack. When he meets Jack, he turns around and starts moving towards Jill. He keeps repeating this until Jack and Jill meet and stop at the same point where they all meet. What is the total distance (in kilometers) covered by Francis?

   (*a*) 25

   (*b*) 36

   (*c*) 37.5

   (*d*) 45

   (*e*) 60

4. David and Jack have 12 oranges, each. They toss a coin 6 times; for every head, David receives an orange from Jack, and for every tail, Jack receives an orange from David. After the coin was tossed 6 times, what is the probability that David has more than 12, but fewer than 18 oranges?

   (*a*) $\frac{5}{6}$

   (*b*) $\frac{21}{64}$

   (*c*) $\frac{21}{32}$

   (*d*) $\frac{1}{64}$

   (*e*) $\frac{15}{64}$

5. If $xy = 16$, what is the value of $y(x + x^2 y)$?

   (*a*) 180

   (*b*) 200

   (*c*) 224

   (*d*) 272

   (*e*) Cannot be determined

6. The terms of a series $x_1, x_2, x_3 \ldots x_n$ has the following relation with one other.

   $x_n = x_{n-1} + s$; where s is a constant.

   What is the 5th term of the series if the 4th term is 16 and 7th term is 31 ?

   (*a*) 5

   (*b*) 18

   (*c*) 21

   (*d*) 25

   (*e*) 30

7. How many real roots does the equation $\sqrt{(a^2+3)+(a^2+4)} = 2$ have?

(a) None

(b) One

(c) Two

(d) Three

(e) Four

8. Which of the following expressions has the largest value?

(a) 9^{50}

(b) 8^{100}

(c) 3^{300}

(d) 7^{200}

(e) 5^{250}

9. How many 2-digit numbers are divisible by 5 ?

(a) 10

(b) 17

(c) 18

(d) 19

(e) 20

10. If a, b and c are positive integers, how many ordered sets (a, b, c) are possible such that $a + b + c = 7$?

(a) 6

(b) 8

(c) 9

(d) 10

(e) 15

11. If $4m + n = 20$, and $|n| \leq 20$

How many ordered pairs (m, n) exist if m and n are integers?

(a) Ten

(b) Eleven

(c) Twenty

(d) Twenty-one

(e) Forty-one

12. If $x^3 + y^6 > 0$, which of the following must be true?

(a) $x > 0$

(b) $y > 0$

(c) $x^3 < 0$

(e) $(x + y^2)$ and $(x^2 + y^4 - xy^2)$ are either both positive or both negative

(e) 60

13. What percent of 19 is 30 percent of 361 ?

(a) 19

(b) 30

(c) 57

(d) 551

(e) 570

14. How many distinct quadrilaterals can be formed using seven distinct points in a plane if no three of them are in a straight line?

(a) 5

(b) 10

(c) 31

(d) 35

(e) 60

Answer Key

1. (*e*)
2. (*d*)
3. (*b*)
4. (*b*)
5. (*d*)
6. (*c*)
7. (*a*)
8. (*e*)
9. (*c*)
10. (*e*)
11. (*b*)
12. (*d*)
13. (*e*)
14. (*d*)

Answer Explanations

1. (e) Adding or subtracting a constant term from all the elements of a set does not change its standard deviation (SD). We see that all the sets: U, V, and W can be obtained by adding or subtracting a constant from the given Set Y, hence all sets have equal standard deviations (SD). The correct answer is option (e).

Remember, if you multiply each element of a set by a constant 'n', then the changed SD would be n times the SD. Say, each element of the set is multiplied by 4, then the revised SD would be 4 times the SD = 4 × SD.

Similarly, if you divide each element of the set by a constant n, then the revised SD would be $\frac{1}{n}$ times the SD.

The correct answer is option (e).

2. (d) Range of a set = Maximum value − Minimum value = a nonnegative value

Since the set consists of only odd integers, the range is even as both the maximum, and the minimum values are odd. Odd − odd = even. Therefore, in the case of odd integers, the range should be even.

Since range cannot be negative, option (a), −10 is ruled out.

The only nonnegative even number among the given options is 6. Hence, Option (c) can be the range of a given set.

The correct answer is option (d).

3. b) **Concept of Relative speed**

1. If two objects are moving in the same direction at a speed of x and y kilometers per hour, their relative speed is $|x - y|$ kilometers per hour.

2. If two objects are moving in the opposite direction at a speed of x and y kilometers per hour, their relative speed is (x + y) kilometers per hour.

Thus, the relative speed of Jack and Jill = 3 + 3 = 6 kilometers per hour since they are moving in opposite directions.

We know that both Jack and Jill met after covering 36 kilometers, hence the total time spent = $\frac{36}{3+3}$ = 6 hours. Thus, Francis has been riding his bicycle for 6 hours at a speed of 6 kilometers per hour. Therefore, Francis rode his bicycle for 6 × 6 = 36 kilometers

The correct answer is option (b).

4. (b) Since David must have more than 12 oranges, it means that he must win at least 4 times out of 6 times; also, since he must have less than 18 oranges, it means he must not win all 6 times. So, he should win 4 or 5 times.

Since he can win 4 or 5 times in any order, the number of ways, he can win

$$= {}^6_4C + {}^6_5C = {}^6_2C + {}^6_1C$$

$$= \left(\frac{6 \times 5}{1 \times 2}\right) + 6 = 15 + 6 = 21$$

ways; ${}^n_rC = {}^n_{n-r}C$

Probability of winning 4 times and losing 2 times in a particular trial

$$= \left(\frac{1}{2}\right)^5 \times \frac{1}{2} = \left(\frac{1}{2}\right)^6 = \frac{1}{64}$$

probability of getting 'Head' = probability of getting 'Tail' = $\frac{1}{2}$.

Similarly, the probability of winning 5 times and losing once in a particular trial

$$= \left(\frac{1}{2}\right)^5 \times \frac{1}{2} = \left(\frac{1}{2}\right)^6 = \frac{1}{64}$$

Since the probability of winning 4 times or 5 times in a particular trial is equal, the probability of winning 4 times or 5 times

$$= 21 \times \left(\frac{1}{64}\right) = \frac{21}{64}$$

The correct answer is option (b).

5. (d) Simplify the expression $y(x + x^2 y)$.

$$= xy + x^2 y^2$$
$$= xy + (xy)^2$$
$$= 16 + 16^2$$
$$= 16 + 256$$
$$= 272$$

The correct answer is option (d).

6. (c) We know that $x_4 = 16$ and $x_7 = 31$.

$x_5 = x_4 + s = 16 + s$

$x_6 = x_5 + s$

and $x_7 = x_6 + s = x_5 + 2s = x_4 + 3s = 16 + 3s$

Hence, $16 + 3s = 31 \Rightarrow s = 5$.

Thus, $x_5 = 16 + s = 21$

7. (a) For the equation

$$\sqrt{(a^2+3)} + \sqrt{(a^2+4)} = 2,$$

the minimum value for $a^2 = 0$ since a^2 is always non-negative.

Substituting $a = 0$ in the equation $\sqrt{(a^2+3)} + \sqrt{(a^2+4)} = 2$, we get

$$\sqrt{(0+3)} + \sqrt{(0+4)} = \sqrt{(3)} + \sqrt{(4)}$$

$$= \sqrt{(3)} + 2$$

$$= 1.73 + 2 = 3.73,$$

the minimum value of the left-hand side, which, however is greater than the right-hand side: 2; however, this is not possible. Hence, no real value can satisfy the equation. Thus, the equation does not have any real roots.

The correct answer is option (a).

8. (e) We convert each number given in the options to a form such that they have the same exponent. The number with the largest base would be the largest.

(*a*) 9^{50} = Let's keep the exponent 50.

(*b*) $8^{100} = (8^2)^{50} = 64^{50}$

(*c*) $3^{300} = (3^6)v = 729^{50}$

(*d*) $7^{200} = (7^4)^{50} = 2{,}401^{50}$

(e) $5^{250} = (5^5)^{50} = 3{,}125^{50}$

So, we can very easily see that the base of the number 5^{250}: 3,125 is the largest, so 5^{250} is the largest among all.

The correct answer is option (e).

9. (c) The first 2-digit number divisible by 5 is 10.

The last 2-digit number divisible by 5 is 95.

Difference between the two numbers = 85.

The multiples of 5 will come at an interval of 5.

Hence, number of such intervals

$$= \frac{85}{5} = 17.$$

Since the number of intervals is 17, the number of such terms will be one more, i.e., $17 + 1 = 18$.

Alternate approach :

The first 2-digit number divisible by 5 is 10

$= 5 \times 2$

The last 2-digit number divisible by 5 is 95

$= 5 \times 19$

Thus, the number of such multiples is 5×2, $5 \times 3 \ldots 5 \times 18$, 5×19, i.e., counting from 2 to 19 = (19 – 2) + 1 = 18 numbers

The correct answer is option (c).

10. **(e)** The number 7 can be represented as a sum of three positive integers in 4 ways:

(*a*) $1+1+5=7$. It will have $\frac{3!}{2!} = 3$ ordered pairs.

(*b*) $1+2+4=7$. It will have $3! = 6$ ordered pairs.

(*c*) $1+3+3=7$. It will have $\frac{3!}{2!} = 3$ ordered pairs.

(*d*) $2+2+3=7$. It will have $\frac{3!}{2!} = 3$ ordered pairs.

Hence, the total number of possible sets

$= 3 + 6 + 3 + 3 = 15.$

The correct answer is option (e).

11. **(b)** Given that $|n| \leq 20$, the integer values of n range from –20 to +20. inclusive.

The set of n is (– 20, – 19, – 18, ...0, 1, 2, ...18, 19, 20). We see that there are 41 integer values.

Now let us see how many integer values m can have.

$$4m + n = 20$$

$$\Rightarrow \quad m = \frac{20 - n}{4};$$

$$\Rightarrow \quad m = 5 - \frac{n}{4}$$

We see that for m to be an integer, $\frac{n}{4}$ must be an integer; this follows that n must be a multiple of 4.

Out of the 41 possible values of n above, only 11 values are multiple of '4;' note 0 is also multiple of 4. The set of eligible values of n is (– 20, – 16, – 12, – 8, – 4, 0, 4, 8, 12, 16, 20).

Therefore, there are only 11 ordered (m, n) pairs possible.

The correct answer is option (b).

12. **(d)** We are given that $x^3 + y^6 > 0$.

Let us discuss each option one by one. Since this is a Must Be True question, our focus will be to find exceptions to the conditions presented in these options. If we can find even one case in which the condition presented in an option is not fulfilled and yet the given expression is positive, then we can reject that option.

(*a*) **$x > 0$:**

If x is positive, then indeed $(x^3 + y^6)$ is positive.

Let's evaluate whether it is possible that if x is NOT positive, but $(x^3 + y^6)$ is positive?

x is NOT positive when either $x = 0$ or $x < 0$.

Case 1 : If $x = 0$, then $x^3 + y^6 = 0 + y^6 = y^6$ is still a positive number. Thus, x need not be positive.

Case 2 : $x < 0$. Say $x = -1$, $y^6 = 8$. For these values, the given expression will be positive.

Thus, we see that for the given expression to be positive, x need not be positive.

(*b*) **$y > 0$:**

Since the exponent of y is 6, an even integer, y^6 must be positive, irrespective of the nature of y: positive or negative. We need not be interested in the nature of y.

For example : $2^6 = (-2)^6 = 32$.

(*c*) **$x3 < 0$:**

Even $x^3 = 0$ or a positive value of x can make $x^3 + y^6 > 0$; this is possible if y^6 is a large value.

Thus, x^3 need not be negative.

(*d*) $(x + y^2)$ and $(x^2 + y^4 - xy^2)$ are either both positive or both negative:

This one is little tricky. At first glance, the expressions $(x + y^2)$ and $(x^2 + y^4 - xy^2)$ seem unrelated to the given expression $(x^3 + y^6)$. However, the phrase 'either both positive or both negative' gives us an idea.

What happens when two numbers are either both positive, or both negative? Then, there product is positive.

So, from this phrase, we get the idea to multiply $(x + y^2)$ and $(x^2 + y^4 - xy^2)$.

$(x + y^2)(x^2 + y^4 - xy^2)$

$= x^3 + xy^4 - x^2y^2 + x^2y^2 + y^6 - xy^4$

$= x^3 + y^6$

Thus, we see that the product of $(x + y^2)$ and $(x^2 + y^4 - xy^2)$ is $(x^3 + y^6)$.

Since we are given that $(x^3 + y^6) > 0$, it follows that $(x + y^2)$ and $(x^2 + y^4 - xy^2)$ must have the same sign: they must either both be positive, or both be negative.

So, option (d) does indeed represent a Must Be True condition.

(*e*) **$|x3| < y6$:**

We can easily think of a case where $|x^3|$ is greater than y^6 and still the given expression is positive.

Say x = 2 and y = 1, then $|2^3| > 1^6$ and $(x^3 + y^6) > 0$. Thus, for $(x^3 + y^6)$ to be positive, it is not necessary that $|x^3| < y^6$.

The correct answer is option (d).

13. **(e)** Say x% of 19 is 30% of 361.

x% of 19 = 30% of 361

x% × 19 = 30% × 361

$$\frac{x}{100} \times 19 = \frac{30}{100} \times 19^2$$

x = 570; after cancellation

The correct answer is option (e).

14. **(d)** Instinctively, one is tempted to count the number of possible quadrilaterals out of 7 distinct points. However, this method is time-consuming and error prone. A better way of solving this problem would be to use Combination.

Here, we just need to identify the number of ways of selecting 4 points out of 7 (which is the same as combinations). Using the Combination formula, this can be written as

$$^7C_4 = \left[\frac{7.6.5.4}{1.2.3.4}\right] = 35.$$

Alternatively, memorize the following important properties.

On a plane, if there are n points, of those, no three points are collinear, then

1. The number of straight lines that can be formed by joining them is ${}^{n}C_2$.
2. The number of triangles that can be formed by joining them is ${}^{n}C_3$.
3. The number of polygons with k sides that can be formed by joining them is ${}^{n}C_k$.

On a plane, if there are n points, of those, m points are collinear, then

1. The number of straight lines that can be formed by joining them is ${}^{n}C_2 - {}^{m}C_2 + 1$.
2. The number of triangles that can be formed by joining them is ${}^{n}C_3 - {}^{m}C_3$.
3. The number of polygons with k sides that can be formed by joining them is ${}^{n}C_k - {}^{m}C_k$.

The correct answer is option (d).

Chapter 9

Problem Solving Practice Set 2

Multiple Choice Questions

1. If $(4x - 1)^2 = 81$, which of the following is one of the possible values of x ?

(a) –2

(b) – 1

(c) 1

(d) $\frac{3}{2}$

(e) $\frac{7}{2}$

2. David bought 18 items from a hardware store. The items were of three kinds: nails, hooks, and screws. These items cost 1 cent, 2 cents, and 3 cents per piece, respectively. The total sum that David paid was 32 cents. If David bought twice as many nails as screws, how many hooks did he buy?

(a) 4

(b) 6

(c) 7

(d) 8

(e) 10

3. If the function f(z) is a sum of unique prime factors of z, what is the value of f(f(250))?

(a) 3

(b) 6

(c) 8

(d) 7

(e) 17

4. David took 10 examinations. If range of his scores is zero, what is the standard deviation of his scores?

(a) 0

(b) 0.1

(c) 1

(d) 10

(e) Cannot be determined

5. If X is more than Y by 110%, and Z is less than X by 10%, then Z is what percent of Y ?

(a) 53

(b) 89

(c) 189

(d) 210

(e) 213

6. If A : B : C : D = 2 : 3 : 4 : 5, what is the value of $\frac{A}{B}:\frac{B}{C}:\frac{C}{D}:\frac{D}{A}$?

(a) 5 : 4 : 3 : 2

(b) 40 : 45 : 48 : 150

(c) 20 : 15 : 48 : 120

(d) 3 : 4 : 5 : 2

(e) 8 : 5 : 12 : 10

7. A 20-liter blend of orange juice and water contains juice and water in a ratio of 3 : 2. Ten liters of the blend are removed and refilled with orange juice, and this process is repeated once more. At the end of the two removals and refills, what is the ratio of orange juice to water in the resulting blend?

(a) 2 : 1

(b) 3 : 2

(c) 4 : 1

(d) 5 : 1

(e) 9 : 1

8. The probability that a tourist at the market buys a pack of chips is $\frac{1}{4}$. If four tourists come to the market today, what is the probability that exactly two of them will buy packs of chips?

(a) $\frac{1}{16}$

(b) $\frac{9}{256}$

(c) $\frac{27}{128}$

(d) $\frac{3}{128}$

(e) $\frac{1}{128}$

9. What is the units digit in $2^{18} \times 7^{12} \times 5^{56}$?

(a) 0

(b) 1

(c) 4

(d) 5

(e) 7

10. Which of the following numbers is a perfect number? A perfect number is one whose sum of factors other than itself is equal to the number itself.

(a) 12

(b) 2

(c) 28

(d) 48

(e) 60

11. If $\sqrt{12+(a-3)^2} = 4$, what could be the value of a?

(a) –5

(b) 1

(c) 3

(d) 9

(e) 19

12. If a right triangle has base a and height b such that $a^2 + b^2 - 4a = 0$; where a and b are integers, which of the following is the set of three corresponding sides of the triangle?

(a) (2, 3, 4)

(b) (2, 2, 2.82)

(c) (3, 3, 4.2)

(d) (2, 2.75, 3)

(e) (2, 4, 5)

13. Two guards are patrolling a 5-kilometer long road, starting to walk simultaneously, at their respective constant speeds, from the opposite ends of the road. When they reach either end, they turn over. The speeds of the guards are 3 kilometers/hour and 2 kilometers/hour. What total distance, in kilometers, would they have covered when they crossed each other the second time?

(a) 6

(b) 10

(c) 12

(d) 15

(e) 30

Answer Key

1. (*a*)
2. (*b*)
3. (*d*)
4. (*a*)
5. (*c*)
6. (*b*)
7. (*e*)
8. (*c*)
9. (*a*)
10. (*c*)
11. (*b*)
12. (*b*)
13. (*d*)

Answer Explanations

1. (a) We have $(4x - 1)^2 = 81$

$(4x - 1)^2 = 9^2$

$(4x - 1)^2 = \pm 9$

$4x - 1 = 9$ or -9

$\Rightarrow x = \frac{5}{2}$ or -2

The correct answer is option (a).

2. (b) Let S be the number of screws, N the number of nails, and H the number of hooks bought by David.

We have $N + 2H + 3S = 32$

$\Rightarrow$ Given $N + H + S = 18$;

and $N = 2S$

$\Rightarrow 3S + H = 18$ ---(1)

$\Rightarrow N + 2H + 3S = 32$

$\Rightarrow 5S + 2H = 32$ ---(2)

Solving the above two equations, we get H = 6.

The correct answer is option (b).

3. (d) The factors of 250 $= 2 \times 5 \times 5 \times 5$

Unique prime factors of 250 = 2 and 5

Sum of unique prime factors = 2 + 5 = 7 = f(250);

Note that the sum of the unique prime factors of 250 is not 2 + 5 + 5 + 5 = 17, since 2 and 5 are the only two unique prime factors.

Thus, f(f(250)) = f(7)

Similarly, unique prime factors of 7 = 7

Sum of unique prime factors = 7

$\Rightarrow$ f(f(250)) = f(7) = 7

The correct answer is option (d).

4. (a) Range refers to the difference between the maximum and minimum values of a set.

Range = Maximum value – Minimum value

The range of David's scores is zero implies that the scores in all the examinations are same–no question of maximum or minimum values.

Standard deviation of a data set comes into picture when there is a variation in data set or there is at least one different value from the others. However, in this case, the standard deviation must be zero for there is no variation at all.

The correct answer is option (a).

5. (c) Say Y = 100, then X = (100 + 110)% of 100

= 210% of 100 = 210

Note that X is not more by 10%; it is more by 110%.

Given : Z = X – 10% of X = 100% of X – 10% of X = 90% of 210 = 189; Z = 189.

Say Z is p% of Y, then $p = \frac{Z}{Y} \times 100\%$

$\Rightarrow p = \frac{189}{100} \times 100\% - 189\%$

The correct answer is option (c).

6. (b) We are given that A : B : C : D = 2 : 3 : 4 : 5, and we have to find out the value of

$\frac{A}{B}:\frac{B}{C}:\frac{C}{D}:\frac{D}{A}$

Assume that A = 2x; B = 3x; C = 4x; and D = 5x and plug-in these values in

$\frac{A}{B}:\frac{B}{A}:\frac{C}{D}:\frac{D}{A}$

So, $\frac{A}{B}:\frac{B}{C}:\frac{C}{D}:\frac{D}{A}=\frac{2x}{3x}:\frac{3x}{4x}:\frac{4x}{5x}:\frac{5x}{2x}$

$=\frac{2}{3}:\frac{3}{4}:\frac{4}{5}:\frac{5}{2}$.

Taking LCM of the denominators (3, 4, 5 and 2) = 60

Thus, $\frac{A}{B}:\frac{B}{C}:\frac{C}{D}:\frac{D}{A}=\frac{2}{3}:\frac{3}{4}:\frac{4}{5}:\frac{5}{2}$

$=\frac{40}{60}:\frac{45}{60}:\frac{64}{60}:\frac{150}{60}$

= 40 : 45 : 48 : 150.

The correct answer is option (b).

7. (e) As per the given ratio of 3 : 2, the initial 20-liter blend contains 12 liters of juice and 8 liters of water. Each time, 10 liters of mixture are removed and refilled with juice, or we can say that each time, 50% of the mixture is removed and refilled with only juice. This means that each time, 50% of the juice and 50% of the water are removed.

After the first removal of 10 liters, the remaining mixture will have 6 liters of juice (12 – 50% of 12) and 4 liters of water (8 – 50% of 8). Adding 10 liters of juice will give us a mixture of 16 liters of juice (6 + 10) and 4 liters of water.

Removing 10 liters of this mixture gives us a mixture with 8 liters of juice (16 – 50% of 16) and 2 liters of water (4 – 50% of 4). Adding 10 liters of juice will give us a mixture of 18 liters of juice (8+10) and 2 liters of water. The ratio of juice to water is 18 : 2 or 9 : 1.

The correct answer is option (e).

8. (c) Probability of a tourist to buy a pack of chips $\frac{1}{4}$;

Hence, the probability of a tourist not to buy a pack of chips $= 1-\frac{1}{4}=\frac{3}{4}$;

Probability of two tourists to buy chips and two tourists not to buy chips

$-\left(\frac{1}{4}\times\frac{1}{4}\right)\times\left(\frac{3}{4}\times\frac{3}{4}\right)=\frac{9}{256}$;

Number of ways two tourists, who buy chips, can be chosen is ${}^4_2C$ ways

Hence, the probability that exactly two tourists will buy a pack of chips

$={}^4_2C\times\left(\frac{9}{256}\right)$

$=\left(\frac{4.3}{1.2}\right)\times\left(\frac{9}{256}\right)=\frac{27}{128}$

The correct answer is option (c).

9. (a) Product of one 2 and one 5 makes 10. We see that $2\times5=10$ appears in the expression $2^{18}\times7^{12}\times5^{56}$, hence the units digit of $2^{18}\times7^{12}\times{}^{556}$ will be 0. The other number 7 doesn't make a difference at the units' place.

The correct answer is option (a).

10. **(c)** The best approach is to apply the trial-and-error method.

Option (a) : 12 ⇒ Factors, other than 12 = {1, 2, 3, 4, 6},

Sum of factors = 1 + 2 + 3 + 4 + 6 = 16 ≠ 12 (Number).

This is not the answer.

Option (b) : 20 ⇒ Factors, other than 20 = {1, 2, 4, 5, 10},

Sum of factors = 1 + 2 + 4 + 5 + 10 = 22 ≠ 20 (Number).

This is not the answer.

Option (c) : 28 ⇒ Factors, other than 28 = {1, 2, 4, 7, 14},

Sum of factors = 1 + 2 + 4 + 7 + 14 = 28 = 28 (Number).

This is the answer.

For your ready reference, a few perfect numbers are 6, 28, & 496.

The correct answer is option (c).

11. **(b)** We are given that $\sqrt{12+(a-3)^2} = 4$.

Taking the square of both sides, we get, $12+(a-3)^2=16$

$$\Rightarrow \quad (a-3)^2 = 16 - 12 = 4$$

$$\Rightarrow \quad (a-3)^2 = 4;$$

Taking the square root of both sides, we get either

$$a - 3 = \pm 2 \Rightarrow a = 5 \text{ or } 1.$$

Note this is a "could be" type of a question, not a must be true type of question.

The correct answer is option (b).

12. **(b)** We know that for a right triangle, the base and the height are always smaller than the hypotenuse. So a and b must be smaller than the third side.

So, if the two smaller integer values satisfy the equation $a^2 + b^2 - 4a = 0$, and the third side matches the third side or hypotenuse, we will consider it the correct answer.

Now have a look at $a^2 + b^2 - 4a = 0$ or $4a - a^2 = b^2$. Since b is a positive integer, and looking at the options, we find that the minimum value of any side is 2, thus, the minimum value of b^2 is 2^2 or 4; thus, $4a - a^2$ ^{3} 4. Rearranging the inequality, we get

$$a^2 - 4a + 4 \leq 0$$

$$\Rightarrow \quad (a-2)^2 \; 0$$

$$\Rightarrow \quad 1 \leq a \leq 2$$

since a is a positive integer; thus, a can be 1 or 2.

Quickly scanning the options, we find option (a), (c) and (d) cannot be the answers as for options (a) and (e), the popular Pythagorean triplet (2, 3, 5) is refuted; for option D, the two smaller sides are not positive integers (one of them is 2.75), and for option (c), both the smaller sides cannot be 3 since at least one side must be less than 3 ($a \leq 2$).

Plugging the values from option B satisfy the equation. Let's check.

$$a^2 + b^2 - 4a = 0$$

$$\Rightarrow \quad 2^2 + 2^2 - 4 \times 2 = 0$$

$$\Rightarrow \quad 0 = 0.$$

Let's calculate the hypotenuse.

$$c^2 = a^2 + b^2$$

$$\Rightarrow \quad c^2 = 2^2 + 2^2 = 8$$

$$\Rightarrow \quad c = 2\sqrt{2}$$

$$= 2 \times 1.414 = 2.82.$$

The correct answer is option (b).

13. **(d)** Guard A with the speed of 3 kilometers/hr and guard B with the speed of 2 kilometers/hr will cross each other for the first time when A covered 3 kilometers and B covered 2 kilometers, i.e., in 1 hour.

Then guard A will move onwards, cover 2 kilometers, turn over, and cover 1 kilometer in the next 1 hour, while guard B will cover 2 kilometers at the same time.

Now in the 3rd hour, guard A will cover 3 kilometers, and B will cover 1 kilometer, turn over, and cover 1 more kilometer. The guard B will cross guard A at the end of the 3rd hour.

So, the total distance covered by both

= distance covered by guard A + distance covered by guard B

$$= (3 + 2 + 1 + 3) + (2 + 2 + 1 + 1)$$

= 15 kilometers

The correct answer is option (d).

Data Insight

Chapter 1

Multi Source Reasoning

PASSAGE-1

Software Company Government Response

A bill before Parliament would require all of government to use only open-source software, i.e., software that is nonproprietary, based on code the user is allowed to redistribute and alter in any way. The bill appears to assume that open-source software is free. However, research has shown that the purchase cost of open source software is about 8% of the total cost associated with the use of the software, and that the cost of utilization–the sum of all non-purchase costs including installation, maintenance, administration, and downtime–is much higher than it is in the case of proprietary software.

The bill would require government to undergo an intensive program of software migration, at considerable immediate cost and risk. And because multiple versions of open-source software exist, the bill's measures are likely to increase compatibility problems between the information-technology systems of government agencies, as well as between government systems and private-sector systems.

Software Company Government Response

We are aware that open-source software is not always offered free of charge. And although savings are indeed mentioned in the bill, its primary aim is to protect citizen's free access to information. Because the bill requires that encoding of data not be tied to a single software provider, it is able to guarantee this free access.

The bill would indeed require government to begin an intensive process of software migration that would not otherwise be undertaken. However, the high cost of software migration in general is an argument in favor of the bill. The longer a particular information technology system is used, the more expensive migration to a different system becomes. Because open-source software allows the encoding of data in standard and adaptable formats, software migration becomes much easier and less expensive once open-source software is installed. And of course, migration from proprietary to open-source software would entail no greater cost than would migration between two different proprietary software systems.

For each of the following statements, select Undermines if it would, if true, undermine the arguments made in one or the other of the two passages. Otherwise, select Does not undermine.

Undermines	Does not undermine	
		Migration from proprietary software to open-source software would be significantly more expensive for the government thant would migration from proprietary software to other proprietary software.
		The measures included in the bill will, if complied with, ensure compatibility among software systems used by all the various relevant stakeholders.
		As a software package is used for a longer period of time, it becomes less expensive to migrate from that package to another.

PASSAGE 2

T1

The Sterling Plant utilizes a assembly line setup comprising of three conveyor belts. Furthermore, there are three inspection stations, each positioned at the end of a conveyor belt. In the tenth year of operation (Y10), the plant employed a total of 15 workers directly involved in the assembly line, with three workers assigned to man the inspection stations, one per station. During Y10, the assembly line at Sterling Plant produced 250,000 units, resulting in a profit of $15,000,000.

T2

For Year 11 (Y11), the Sterling Plant assembly line was modernized as follows:

Conveyor-belt speeds were increased by a fixed percentage.

The assembly line's administrative unit was restructured to maximize efficiency.

Each inspection post was automated, and the 3workers who formerly staffed the posts were laid off and were not replaced.

There were no other personnel changes on the assembly line for Y11.

T3

Year 10 > Year 11 > Table

Sterling Plant Assembly Line Modemization, Y11

Element of modermization project	Resulting increase in output for Y11, as % of Y10 output	Resulting increase in profit for Y11, as % of Y10 profit	Total cost of implement
Inspection-post automation	2%	5%	$100,000
Conveyor-belt speed increase	3%	4%	$45,000
Administrative unit restructuring	—	1%	$15,000
Total	5%	10%	$160,000

1. Which one of the following statements is supported by the information provided about the assembly line and the assembly-line modernization plan at the Sterling Plant?

A. On the assembly line, conveyor-beit speed is directly proportional to total annual output of assembled units.

B. Administrative unit restructuring accounted for the greatest increase in the dollar amount of profit from Y10 to Y11.

C. Conveyor-belt speed increase accounted for the greatest increase in the dollar amount of profit from Y10 to Y11.

D. Conveyor-belt speed increase accounted for the greatest increase in annual output of assembled units from Y10 to Y11.

E. Inspection-post automation accounted for the greatest increase in annual output of assembled units from Y10 to Y11.

2. For a given production year, let Q denote the total output, in assembled units, from the Sterling Plant assembly line, and let N denote the number of workers employed directly on the line. For each of the following statements about the quotient Q/N, select Yes if it is true based on the information provided. Otherwise, select No.

Yes	No	
		Q/N was less than 10,000 for Y10.
		Q/N was unchanged from Y10 to Y11.
		Q/N remained below 30,000 in Yi0 and Y11.

PASSAGE 3

T1: Discussion

Star Research is in the process of relocating to a new office space, which is laid out according to the provided Floor Plan. The office space consists of eight individual offices (numbered 111, 112, 114, 115, 116, 117, 120, and 121) and four cubicles (numbered 119A through 119D). Each employee will be assigned a single workspace, either an office or a cubicle, and there will be no more than one employee per office or cubicle. It should be noted that supervisors will not be assigned to work in cubicles. In cases where an employee has an immediate supervisor, the employee's workspace, whether an office or cubicle, must be located adjacent to their supervisor's office.

T2 : Table

The table lists the ten employees at Star Research and shows each employee's immediate supervisor, if any. The supervisors are also employees, so each supervisor's name appears in both columns.

Employee	Supervisor
Saina	Claire
Regal	Stuart
Stuart	
Joey	Lara
Lara	
Amold	Jerad
Emma	Claire
Jerad	
Mary	Jerad
Claire	Lara

T3 : Floor Plan

Discussion | **Table** | **Floor Plan**

The floor plan shows the office space that Star Research will occupy, in the northeast corner of one floor of a building. Two offices are adjacent to each other if and only if they are separated by a common wall. A different definition of adjacent applies to cubicles : cubicles 119A and 119B are adjacent only to office 121, while 119C and 119D are adjacent only to office 120.

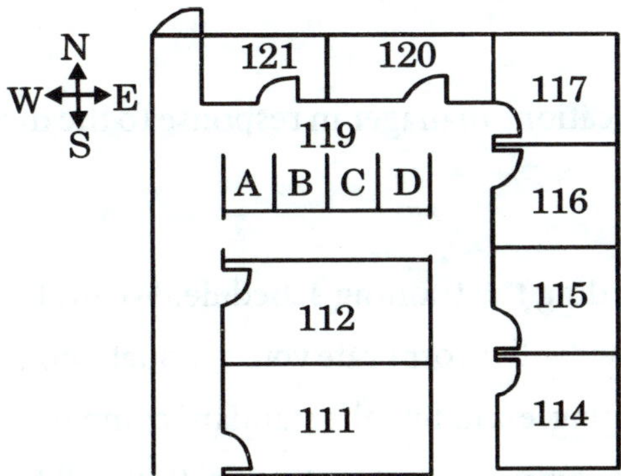

Based on the information and workspace assignment rules provided, how many employees are there, each of whom could be assigned to office 112?

A. 1 B. 2 C. 3 D. 4 E. 5

For each of the following situations, select Yes if, based on the information and workspace assignment rules provided, it would PREVENT some employees from being assigned workspace using the current rules. Otherwise, select No.

Yes	No	
○	○	Mary, Joey and Saina need offices because the projects they work on require the highest levels of security.
○	○	Two additional employees are hired and will be supervised by Jerad.
○	○	Regal resigns his position at Star Research.

PASSAGE 4

T1

E-mail from the director of the training department to the technical publications manager

September 12, 8:03 A.M.

We are in the process of finalizing the schedule for the training session of new clients for our EXM software, which is planned to take place on November 1st. As of now, we have received 23 reservations, and we anticipate that the class will reach its maximum capacity of 35 students, which is the capacity of our training room. The training manuals are currently being produced and will be available for content review on September 15th. Assuming a two-week turnaround for the developer's review, we expect to have a three-week timeframe for your department to handle the necessary formatting, inclusion of standard company information, and printing of the manuals. It would be helpful if you could provide us with a specific delivery date for 35 manuals before October 21st. Please note that we will require an additional week to 10 days to allow our trainers enough time to prepare their computer-based exercises.

T2

E-mail from the technical publications manager in response to the director of the training department

September 12, 9:12 A.M.

Thank you for the update regarding the training schedule. We understand the importance of meeting the heavy schedule in October, and we will incorporate your manual into our calendar accordingly. To provide an estimate, the manual we are creating, excluding the standard company information, is expected to be a certain number of pages. The standard company information section will be fixed at 3 pages. Please note that our department will be charged on a per-page basis, along with the fixed costs of collating and preparation, which are currently $2.00 per manual. Additionally, if the manual includes color graphics, an extra cost of $0.50 per page will be incurred, in addition to the standard rate of $0.25 per page for black and white text. If the total number of pages in the manual is less than 100, we should be able to deliver it by your deadline.

T3

E-mail from the director of the training department in response to the technical publications manager

September 12, 9:46 A.M.

The manual for this three-day training will exceed 100 pages and may run as long as 115 pages, with 5 pages of color graphics. I will know the exact number once the review is completed on October 1.

1. If the information contained in all three e-mails is correct, the total cost of the requested manuals will be closest to __________.

A. $1,060

B. $1,080

C. $1,100

D. $1,120

E. $1,190

2. **Consider each of the following statements. Does the information in the three sources support the inference as stated?**

Yes	No	
		The director of the training department believes that the software training class will be filled to capacity.
		The director of the training department expects that printing of the training manual will exceed the department's printing budget.
		The technical publications department will most likely be able to deliver 35 copies of the training manual by October 21st.

PASSAGE 5

Tab 1 : Memo

Following is a memo between Riley Green, head of the Admissions office for Syrandon College for 20 years, and Vice President Larry Show, who was brought in to Syrandon after short administrative tenures at two state universities.

To : Larry Shaw, Vice President; Syrandon College

From : Riley Green, Head of Admissions; Syrandon College

I have some concerning news to share. After analyzing the data, it appears that our in-state undergraduate admissions have declined by 25% since 2010. It's worth noting that many of our in-state freshmen are legacies, meaning they have family members who attended Sarandon before them. On the other hand, out-of-state undergraduate admissions tend to consist of transfer students who come to Sarandon. Our strongest connections and relationships are with our in-state undergraduate students, and a majority of our alumni were once in-state undergraduates themselves. Unfortunately, this decrease in the percentage of in-state admissions may have a noticeable impact on future alumni sponsorship, which is crucial for our small private college. We heavily rely on our alumni to fund special projects that are not covered by tuition.

Given this situation, I highly recommend implementing a more aggressive recruiting program. The goal is to hopefully compensate for the decline in in-state admissions and achieve higher numbers of in-state graduates next year. I have attached a graphic that provides a visual breakdown of our admissions for 2011, which might help illustrate the situation more clearly.

Tab 2 : Graph

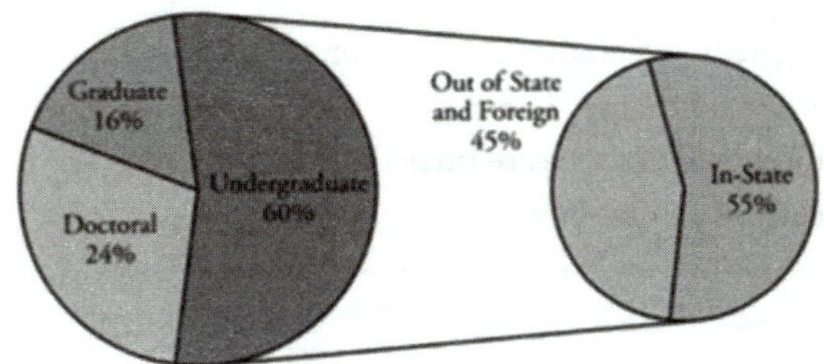

Tab 3 : Response

The below is an excerpt of Vice President response.

To : Riley Green, Head of Admissions; Syrandon College

From : Larry Shaw, Vice President; Syrandon College

While there has been a decline in the percentage of in-state graduate students this year, it is important to note that our overall student population is not significantly different from last year. We do not have an excess of empty spaces at the moment. Based on my experience at other educational institutions, when there is a decrease in a specific student demographic, other demographics tend to fill those vacancies. This is particularly true for international students. To provide an example, at Western State University, we were forced to reject 50% of qualified foreign applicants due to limited capacity. These are students who would be eager to enroll in a reputable institution like Sarandon.

Therefore, considering the situation, there is potential for us to attract a greater number of foreign students who can contribute to our student body. It may be beneficial to explore opportunities to enhance our recruitment efforts and attract qualified international applicants who are seeking admission to a respected institution like Sarandon.

1. **For 2011, if foreign students comprise exactly 1/8 of the number of out-of-state undergraduates, indicate which could be the number of in-state undergraduates.**

Yes	No	Statements
		200
		330
		1320

2. **Indicate which statements could properly be inferred based on the text and the graph. Select Yes if the statement can be inferred. Otherwise, select No.**

Yes	No	Statements
		In-state undergraduates comprise the largest proportion of all the admitted students for 2011.
		The in-state undergraduate admissions were 25% higher in 2010 than in 2011.
		Some foreign students were turned away from Western State for reasons other than academic suitability.

3. Which of the following is an assumption underlying Vice President Shaw assertion in the excerpt of her response to Relay Green?

A. The number of admitted students has not increased since last year.

B. Foreign students are just as likely to attend a private college as a state university.

C. Universities in the United States offer courses that would otherwise not be available to foreign students.

D. The number of foreign students attending Syrandon is steadily rising.

E. The amount of financial support offered by the alumni will remain constant.

PASSAGE 6

The features of five mobile communication devices are compared in the table. Each feature is rated from 0 to 5, with greater ratings indicating greater quality. A device (P) is said to be ratings-dominant over another device (Q) if P matches or exceeds the ratings of Q for every single feature in the table but Q does not match all of the ratings of P.

Feature Quality Ratings

	Device				
Feature	**X1**	**X2**	**XS**	**XL**	**XZ**
A	5	0	1	0	0
B	2	0	2	5	1
C	0	3	3	4	2
D	0	3	5	0	2
E	0	0	4	4	0
F	0	0	0	0	1
G	0	0	0	3	0
H	0	2	2	1	0

For each of the following devices, select Yes if the device is ratings-dominant over any of the other devices in the table. Otherwise, select No.

Yes	No	
		Device X1
		Device XS
		Device XZ

PASSAGE 7

FINANCES

Stephen University offers seven spring break destinations for tourists. The provided table presents information such as the price of plane tickets, discounted prices (if applicable), the spring break operator, rates for waterfront beach houses in the block area, and the lowest rate available for a waterfront beach house. It's important to note that the rates for beach houses are listed per night and per group, and each group will require four nights of lodging. All plane ticket prices are also per group, accommodating up to six passengers, as each beach house has six beds. If waterfront options are not available, the lowest rate for a beach house outside of the waterfront is $70.

ARTICLE

The waterfront beach houses are arranged in three rows. The spring break company has allocated a block of beach houses, specifically the first row along the waterfront, for its clients. These beach houses in the block area have higher rates compared to the normal waterfront beach houses.

Although many spring breakers prefer staying in beach houses along the waterfront, they often adopt alternative strategies to avoid the additional cost of reserving a house in the block area. Some attendees opt for reserving beach houses outside the waterfront area, following the ROWFA strategy. Others choose to reserve beach houses outside the allocated block, known as the ROB strategy, and instead secure beach houses in row 2 or row 3 along the waterfront.

Spring break operators have effectively reduced the frequency of these alternative strategies by increasing the plane ticket price by a fixed amount. However, they offer an equivalent discount on the plane ticket price to spring breakers who book beach houses within the front waterfront block. Research has demonstrated that if this plane ticket discount is equal to at least half of the potential savings associated with a spring breaker's chosen cost-saving strategy, they are significantly more likely to reserve a beach house within the first row of the waterfront block.

Destination	Ticket Price	Discounted Ticket Price	Tour Guide	Block Rate	Lowest Rate for Waterfront
Miami	$210	$150	Contiki	$100	$70
Hawaii	$525	$450	World Springs	$140	$115
Jamaica	$220	$200	Spring Breakers	$160	$135
Cancun	$480	$350	Cancuna Breakers	$150	$120
Daytona	$200	$170	Spring Bling	$135	$100
Bahamas	$240	$210	Sun Fun	$115	$90
Puerto Rico	$425	$400	Beach Burn	$200	$150

1. **Jill and her friends are planning a 5-day/4-night spring break trip to Cancun. Their group has 10 people and they want to stay in the first block of the waterfront area. What is the total cost for Jill and her friends traveling from Stephen University?**

A. $500

B. $950

C. $1000

D. $1900

E. $5000

2. **For each of the following destinations, select Yes if a spring break traveler group would spend more money by employing the ROB strategy -- paying the lowest possible waterfront beach house rate in the waterfront area and paying the nondiscounted plane ticket price -- than by reserving a beach house in the first row of the waterfront block. Otherwise, select No.**

Yes	No	Statements
		Cancun
		Jamaica
		Miami

Assume that all beach houses at the waterfront are available for the 4 days indicated and all beach houses in the city are available at their lowest rates during these 4 days.

3. **Which one of the following destinations is most likely to have spring break travelers favoring the ROB strategy over the ROWFA strategy?**

A. Hawaii

B. Jamaica

C. Daytona

D. Miami

E. Bahamas

Assume that spring break operators receive a reimbursement from the waterfront beach housing organization (which owns the waterfront beach houses) for 25% of the front row block rate for each unoccupied beach house in the front row block of the waterfront area.

4. **For each of the following spring break operators, select Yes if the spring break operator would lose beach house revenue if a room in the block is vacant because a traveler group employed the ROB strategy. Otherwise, select No.**

Yes	No	Statements
		Contiki
		WorldSprings
		SunFun

5. **Select Yes if the percentage discount on the plane ticket (compared to the original price) exceeds the percentage discount for reserving the lowest rate beach house in the waterfront area (compared to the block rate in the waterfront area). Otherwise, select No.**

Yes	No	Statements
		Miami
		Hawaii
		Cancun

6. **For each of the following spring break destinations, select Yes if a spring break traveler going for the 4-night package would spend less money by employing the ROWFA strategy -- paying the lowest possible beach house rate outside the waterfront area and paying the non-discounted plane ticket price -- than by reserving a front row beach house in the block. Otherwise, select No.**

Yes	No	Statements
		Cancun
		Daytona
		Puerto Rico

7. Many individuals stand to benefit financially from spring breakers coming out for their vacations. For each of the following individuals, choose Gain if the individual would likely earn more money if beach houses in the front row block are vacant because of attendees using ROWFA strategies. Otherwise select No Gain.

Yes........	No........	Statements
		Rap artist hired to throw a concert alongside the waterfront beach houses.
		Morning breakfast delivery by a delivery waitress at the beach house whose earnings are primarily from gratuities.
		Taxi cab driver bringing guests from outside of the waterfront area to the waterfront area where vacationers tend to hangout.

Assume that for the four nights that spring break travelers stay, beach houses outside the waterfront area are available at their lowest rate.

8. For the following cities, select Yes if spring break traveler groups would be more likely to reserve a beach house in the front row of the waterfront block than getting a beach house outside the waterfront area. Otherwise, select No.

Yes	No	Statements
		Miami
		Jamaica
		Cancun

PASSAGE 8

Promotions

Quantity (packs)	Diapers	Toys	Baby Food
20–49	5% off	10% off	None
50+	10% off	10% off	20% off

Product

Product	Package	Price
HuggyD's Diapers	6 diapers per pack	$ 15
Barney's Action Toys	2 toys per pack	$ 20
Mighty Avenger Toys	3 toys per pack	$ 12
Baby Food	5 cans per pack	$ 25

Babycare

BabyCare, a daycare center catering to babies aged 0-5, is in the process of purchasing supplies for the month. In February, BabyCare will be responsible for taking care of 30 babies, operating 5 days a week for the duration of 4 weeks. Each day, each baby will require two diaper changes and consume 3 cans of baby food. Additionally, every baby will be provided with one toy. It's worth noting that the daycare center regularly refreshes the toys in the playpens, introducing new toys every 2 weeks and disposing of the old ones.

1. Assess the following statements as either True or False based on the information provided.

True.......	False.......	Statements
		The cost of supplying baby food for the month for BabyCare is more than $7,500.
		The pre-discount cost of getting all Mighty Avenger Toys for the month is cheaper than getting all Barney's Action Toys for the month.
		BabyCare can supply enough toys for the month with a budget of less than $220.

2. Baby Care is placing this month's order for 400 cans of baby food. How much will BabyCare have to pay for the 400 cans of baby food?

A. $1,500

B. $1,600

C. $2,000

D. $5,000

E. $10,000

While BabyCare is currently accomodating 30 babies per month, it is contemplating improving its quality of service or increasing the number of babies it cares for in order to increase profit. Currently, management is trying to determine whether to run its business at a 20-baby maximum or at a 50-baby maximum.

3. Which of the following pieces of information would increase the total cost per baby of running a 50-baby maximum day care center versus a 20-baby maximum day care center. Assume the business runs at full capacity and it is not eligible for any bulk discounts for the month of February.

Yes	No	Statements
		At a 20-baby maximum, each baby gets his own toy; at a 50-baby maximum each baby must share his toy with one other baby.
		At a 20-baby maximum, BabyCare plans to allot 1 baby food package per baby per day and supply 1 diaper package per baby per week.
		At a 20-baby maximum, BabyCare will supply 1 package of diapers each week to the babies but no toys. At a 50-baby maximum, the babies' parents will have to supply their own diapers; BabyCare will not supply diapers. BabyCare will, however, supply a Barney's Action toy package to each baby each week.

PASSAGE 9

Stainless Steel

Stainless steels are iron and carbon alloys that also include a minimum of 10.5% chromium and various other alloying elements, such as molybdenum, manganese, and nickel. These steels are identified with three-digit SAE numbers typically ranging from the 200s to the 600s, sometimes followed by a single letter. The three primary categories of stainless steel are explained below, and tables following the descriptions list seven specific varieties within each category.

Ferritic steels consist of 12.5%-17% chromium, less than 0.1% carbon, and up to 1% nickel. They exhibit magnetic properties and can be strengthened through cold working but are not suitable for heat treatment. Ferritic steels find application in automotive exhaust systems, agricultural equipment, and high-temperature environments like furnaces and boilers.

Austenitic steels contain 16%-26% chromium, up to 0.8% carbon, and 6%-15% nickel. They are nonmagnetic and cannot be heat treated. Austenitic steels are the most commonly used stainless steels worldwide, finding application in food-processing equipment, piping systems, and kitchen utensils.

Martensitic steels consist of 10.5%-17% chromium, up to 1.2% carbon, and not more than 0.4% nickel. They are magnetic and can undergo heat treatment. Martensitic steels are frequently employed in the manufacturing of knives, cutting tools, and dental and surgical equipment.

Partial Composition of Various Stainless Steels

SAE number	Chromium %	Carbon %	Nickel %
304	18.0-20.0	0.08	8.0-10.5
309S	22.0-24.0	0.08	12.0-15.0
316	16.0-18.0	0.08	10.0-14.0
321	17.0-19.0	0.08	9.0-12.0
409	10.5-11.75	0.08	0.50
410	11.5-13.5	0.15	0.75
430	16.0-18.0	0.20	0.75

Select Physical Properties of Various Stainless Steels

SAE number	Density (Kg/M^3)	Rockwell hardness	Heat treatable	Magnetic
304	7,900	90	No	No
309S	7,950	85	No	No
316	8,000	95	No	No
321	7,900	95	No	No
409	7,800	75	No	Yes
410	7,850	80	Yes	Yes
430	7,800	89	No	Yes

1. Consider each of the following statements. Indicate Yes if the given information supports the statement. Otherwise, indicate No.

Yes	No	
		All of the listed stainless steels with a carbon content of 0.08% are Austenitic.
		A stainless steel among those listed with a Rockwell hardness of at least 85 must be either Austenitic or Ferritic.
		Of the steels listed, the average density of Austenitic steels is greater than the average density of Ferritic steels.

2. Based on the information in the passage and tables, the stainless steel with the highest ratio of carbon to nickel has which of the following hardness ratings?

A. 80

B. 85

C. 89

D. 90

E. 95

PASSAGE 10

Table 1: Expectancy Value model

Marketers propose that consumers' purchase decisions are influenced by their perception of value. This perception is often shaped by conducting a cost-benefit analysis, where adding more features or reducing the price can manipulate the perception of value. This concept is known as the expectancy-value model. Let's consider an example to understand this better.

Steve is in the market to buy a laptop and has narrowed down his options to four different laptop brands (A, B, C, D). He is interested in evaluating these brands based on five attributes: Processor Performance (PP),

Graphics Capability (GC), Size & Weight (SW), Battery Life (BL), and Marked Price (MP). Steve assigns different priorities to these attributes, with 30% weightage given to Processor Performance, 10% to Graphics Capability, and equal importance to Size & Weight, Battery Life, and Price. To assess the offerings of each brand, Steve calculates a value called Composite Attribute Value, which represents the weighted average of how well each brand performs in relation to his priorities.

Brands	**Attributes**				
	Processor Performance (PP)	Graphic Capability (GC)	Size & Weight (SW)	Battery Life (BL)	Marked Price (MP)
A	8	6	4	4	8
B	6	9	6	4	6
C	5	4	9	7	4
D	7	8	4	6	7

Table 2 : Customer Cost and Benefit

Cost Heads ($)	**A**	**B**	**C**	**D**
Marked Price (MP)	120	100	80	75
Acquisition Cost	17	20	20	15
Usage Cost	3	8	11	15
Maintenance Cost	2	2	3	4
Ownership Cost	3	4	4	5
Disposal Cost	5	5	9	8
Customer Cost	**150**	**139**	**127**	**122**

Customer Value is the difference between Customer Benefit and Customer Cost, where Customer Benefit is calculated by multiplying Customer cost with Customer Composite Attribute Value and dividing the product by 5.

1. Consider each of the information given in tabs. Does the information in three tabs support the inference as stated below?

Yes	**No**	
		Composite Attribute Value for Steve is greatest for brand A
		Steve purchase brand A based on customer value
		Brand C scores lowest both in terms of customer value and Customer benefit

2. Let X denote Customer Value, Y denote Customer Cost, and let Z denote Composite Attribute Value. Which of the following algebraic expressions represents relationship among X, Y & Z?

A. $X = \frac{Y(Z-5)}{5}$ B. $X = \frac{4}{5 * Y * Z}$ C. $X = \frac{Y(5-Z)}{5}$

D. $X = \frac{Y}{5(5-Z)}$ E. $X = \frac{YZ-5Z}{5}$

3. If Steve will decide buying laptop based on Customer Value, which of the possible strategies should company C implement so that it becomes Jack's preferred choice?

Yes	No	
		Reduce the marked price to $60
		Add a faster processor to increases its Processor Performance rating to 9
		Improve its graphics capability to the highest possible ranking

PASSAGE 11

Table 1 : Flow Chart

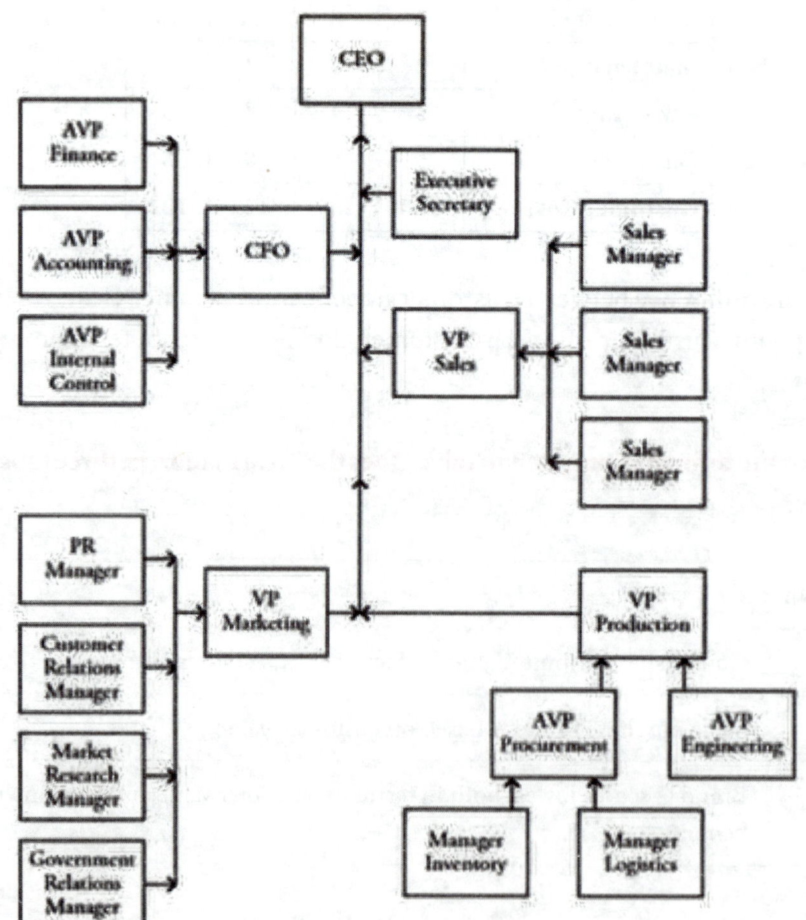

Tab 2: Memo

Please find attached the organizational chart for Articulus Partners in Spring 2010. In response to recent growth in the past few quarters, the company has made some structural changes by introducing two new VP-level positions: AVP Accounting and AVP Procurement. Additionally, a Chief Financial Officer (CFO) has been added to the organization. As per the revised hierarchy, the CFO will report directly to the CEO. The AVP of Accounting will report directly to the CFO, while the AVP of Procurement will report to the VP of Production.

In terms of salary levels within the organization, all employees reporting directly to the CEO are classified as salary level A. Subsequent reporting levels are classified as salary level B, and employees below the B-level employees are classified as salary level C.

1. Based on the flow chart and the text in the Memo tab, indicate whether each of the following statements is true or false.

True	False	
		Sales managers are B-level employees.
		The new AVP of Procurement is a C-level employee.
		The AVP of Engineering is under the new AVP of Procurement.

2. Based on the flow chart and the text in the Memo tab, indicate whether each of the following statements is true or false.

True	False	
		The ratio of B-level employees to C-level employees is 6:1.
		The ratio of B-level employees to A-level employees is 5:1.
		Each A-level employee has at least 3 employees below him or her.

3. If employees at each level of the organizational chart earn close to 1.2 times what employees one level below earn, then the CEO earns approximately how many times what the AVP of Accounting earns?

A. 1.2

B. 1.4

C. 2.2

D. 2.4

E. 3.2

PASSAGE 12

TAB 1: Price List

Chocolate Cost :	$3.58/lb	Dark Chocolate
	$3.24/lb	Milk Chocolate
	$2.94/lb	White Chocolate/Vanilla
	$3.78/lb	Specialty Colors
		Colors Available Include :
		Pink, Light Green, Dark Green, Yellow, Orange
		Purple, Light Blue, Dark Blue and Red
	$5.85/lb	Sugar-Free Chocolates
		Flavors Available Include :
		Dark Chocolate, Vanilla, and Milk Chocolate
	$2.95/lb	Coconut Shavings
	$5.20/lb	Caramel
	$1.40/oz	High-Quality Flavorings for Chocolate

TAB 2: Email Order

Hi Candy Man,

I would like to make a request to order chocolate mints for a retirement celebration scheduled on April 14th. We will need 6 pounds of small mints, preferably in the midsize range. It would be appreciated if the presentation of the mints includes at least three colors, with a preference for including blue and green, as they are the primary colors in our company logo. The shape of the mints is not a significant factor as long as they maintain a professional appearance. Basic round mints or flower-shaped mints would both be acceptable options.

Thanks,

Betsy Carver

Tab 3 : Invoice

Invoice :# 200515 — Customer : Betsay Carver, Bandercom Inc.

Order: April 1, 2015 — Delivery Date : April 14, 2015

Order # 1

	2 pounds white mint discs	$7.89	$15.78
	2 pounds blue floral mints	$8.99	$17.98
	2 pounds green leaf mints	$8.99	$17.98
Delivery Charge (not taxed)		$10.00	
	Subtotal	$61.74	
	Tax (7.85%)	$4.06	
	Total	**$65.80**	

Consider each of the following statements. Does the information in the three sources support the inference as stated?

Yes	No	
		The average price per pound of the mints including tax and delivery is $10.29.
		Sugar-free chocolates cost about 80% more, on average, than regular varieties of chocolate.
		The Candy Man charged $0.75 per pound for delivery services.

PASSAGE 13

The following emails came from Public Relations Division of a large non-profit organization

EMAIL 1

Hello Diana!

We are currently in the process of selecting a caterer for our upcoming gala event. There are two caterers that we are considering: DoxySource and BrightRight. While DoxySource has provided satisfactory service in the past, we anticipate that our First Annual Sponsors Gala will be our largest event to date. BrightRight is reputed for their expertise in planning and executing large-scale events. However, before making a decision to switch from a trusted contractor, I would like to gather more information. Additionally, I want to explore how to justify any potential additional costs if we choose BrightRight and exceed our budget. It is important to note that we can only engage the services of one provider.

To assist with the evaluation, I would like to request a comparison of the costs of services and rentals for both BrightRight and DoxySource. Specifically, we require information on tables, audio equipment, food services, and the availability of a punch fountain or fountains (with the possibility of a dessert fountain as well). Our allocated budget for the event is $6,000.00, and we anticipate a maximum attendance of 400 people.

Thanks!

Arren Smith

Gala Coordinator

Email 2

Hello Arren

I've broken out the data in the following chart :

	Doxy Source		Bright Right	
	Description	**Price**	**Description**	**Price**
AUDIO	200 Watt P.A. System (up to 40 people)	$65.00	Party Sound System	$650.00
	500 Watt P.A. System (up to 120 people)	$90.00	Marquee Sound System	$850.00
CATERING	Choice of appetizers (shrimp or spring roll)	$2.00 per piece	The Classic Western BBO	$14.00 per person
	Choice of entrée (chicken or beef w/rice)	$6.25 per piece	The Greek Feast	$17.50 per person
	Choice of dessert (cupcakes or lemon bars)	$3.40 per piece	The Far East Extravaganza	$19.50 per person
TABLES	Trestle Table (seats 8)	$15.50 each	Classroom (seats 8)	$20.00 each
	Circular Table (seats 7)	$17.00 each	Bistro/Hightop (seats 6)	$22.00 each
FOUNTAINS	Chocolate Fountain (supplies not included)	$105.00	Chocolate Fountain (supplies included)	$500.00
	Punch Fountain (7 gallons, provided, serves approx. 70)	$47.00	Punch Fountain, waterfall tier (40 gallons, provided)	$350.00

Bright Right provides more upscale and comprehensive packages, albeit at a higher cost, offering options like "The Greek Feast" for the entire gala. Choosing DoxySource, on the other hand, may be more cost-effective and flexible, but it requires more hands-on involvement from our side.

The most significant price difference lies in the audio systems. BrightRight, accustomed to hosting large-scale events, offers complex setups that include lighting, sound effects, and high-definition audio reproduction. In contrast, DoxySource offers two standard public address systems. While I'm uncertain if the Gala necessitates the flashy features of a high-end sound system, the projected attendance exceeds the recommended capacity for DoxySource's P.A. systems. However, we should note that due to electrical limitations, we can only accommodate one P.A. system at the gala.

Diana Ross

Administrative Assistant, Public Relations

1. **If the maximum number of guests attend the gala, determine if each of the statements is true or false based on the information in the two emails.**

True	False	Values
		If the coordinator uses DoxySource and orders one appetizer, one entrée, and one dessert per person, then the least amount that can be spent on tables to seat all guests is approximately 16.6% of the cost of food.
		If the large punch fountain from BrightRight is sufficient for 400 guests, then using smaller fountains from DoxySource to serve the same number of guests would cost at least 20% less per gallon.
		If BrightRight is used, the project will go over its present budget by at least 15%.

2. Suppose the Gala Coordinator uses DoxySource for the maximum number of guests. If she wants to use at least one of each type of table, what is the least possible cost for the tables?

A. $775.00

B. $787.00

C. $792.00

D. $873.21

E. $971.43

3. Based on the information in the messages between the Gala Coordinator and the Administrative Assistant, select Yes if the statement can be inferred. Otherwise, select No.

Yes	No	Values
		The Gala Coordinator is willing to ask for a budgetary increase, if necessary.
		According to the Administrative Assistant, audio costs are not the only determining factor in choosing one event planning service over another.
		Fountains are an optional element of the gala.

PASSAGE 14

TAB 1: Residents Association

Statement by Medical Residency Association president :

Medical residents play a crucial role in delivering medical care to the community, providing round-the-clock coverage and support to both physicians and nursing staff as they strive to obtain their medical licenses. Residents handle various tasks performed by licensed physicians, including patient intake, ordering tests and labs, making diagnoses, and administering treatments, including surgeries. However, residents often face significant challenges and unfair treatment within hospitals.

Residents are frequently subjected to exploitative practices, such as being assigned to 24-hour shifts and experiencing undermining or mistreatment from senior doctors, sometimes in the presence of patients. Additionally, they are compensated well below minimum wage, receiving a fixed salary based on the assumption that they only work one-third of the hours during their assigned shifts. Technically, they are considered to be "on call" during these shifts, although they are required to be present on the hospital grounds at all times and end up working far more hours than the assumed amount. In the past month alone, each resident has averaged 17.5 active working hours during a 24-hour shift, with only 3.5 hours of sleep at a time. Such working conditions pose significant risks to both patients and residents, leading to serious errors that have been caught by senior staff at the last minute.

It is crucial to address these unsafe working conditions to ensure the well-being of both patients and medical residents.

TAB 2 : Hospital Board

Response to Medical Residency Association president by Hospital Board Spokesperson :

We firmly believe that medical residents are essential members of the medical care delivery team within our network of hospitals. It is important to recognize that medical residencies are a vital part of the process for individuals to become licensed physicians. Until residents complete their residency, they cannot reasonably be considered fully licensed physicians. Residencies operate in a similar manner to traditional apprenticeships, providing hands-on training under the supervision and guidance of experienced mentors.

Contrary to the misconception, residents are not expected to work for the entire 24-hour duration of their shifts or even close to that. The purpose of assigning them 24-hour shifts is to ensure their presence on-site when beneficial learning opportunities arise. It is up to each resident to decide their level of involvement in routine activities that could be adequately managed by nursing or medical staff. The entire residency system is structured to provide both training and oversight. Whenever a resident is called upon to make a diagnosis or perform a minor procedure, there is always an experienced physician present to verify the diagnosis, take over the procedure if necessary, or rectify any potential errors.

The residency program is designed to strike a balance between training and supervision, ensuring the highest standard of patient care while providing residents with valuable learning experiences under the guidance of experienced physicians.

1. For each of the following statements, select Yes if it can be inferred that the Medical Residency Association president and the Hospital Board spokesperson both agree with the statement. Otherwise, select No.

Yes	No	
		The degree to which medical residents' errors pose a danger of lasting patient harm.
		Whether it is possible for medical residents to work more than 8 hours during a 24-hour shift.
		The degree to which a resident is as qualified as a licensed physician.

2. For each of the following statements, select Yes if, based on the information provided, both the Residency Association and the Hospital Board would likely accept that the statement is true. Otherwise, select No to indicate that it cannot be inferred that both individuals would likely accept the statement as true.

Yes	No	
		Medical residents should not be allowed to work for more than 8 hours during a 24-hour shift.
		A hospital should ensure that medical resident errors are minimized or prevented entirely.
		Medical residents should not be undermined or treated poorly by licensed physicians when patients are present.

3. **If residents are paid $105 per 24-hour shift, what is the difference, rounded to the nearest hundredth of a dollar, between the hourly wage based upon the assumed number of hours worked per 24-hour shift and the hourly wage based upon the actual average number of hours worked per 24-hour shift?**

A. $6.00

B. $6.49

C. $6.79

D. $7.00

E. $7.13

PASSAGE 15

TAB 1 : Chieftain

Among the three phones we evaluated, the Chieftain stands out with its significantly faster processor and superior search interface. This phone is particularly well-suited for individuals who intend to download and utilize a wide range of applications. However, it's worth noting that the baseline phone's internal memory may fill up rapidly. As a result, we strongly advise against purchasing this phone without also acquiring an additional memory card.

Display	3.50 inches diagonal
CPU speed	1.5 gigahertz
Camera	Back : 8 megapixel; Front : none
Memory	0.5 gigabytes
Average critical rating	4.3 of 5 stars
Average customer rating	3.8 of 5 stars
Price	$450.00
Price with 2-year contract	$150.00

TAB 2 : Estrella

If visual quality is a top priority, the Estrella LS is the ideal phone to consider. It features a generously-sized screen that not only stands out as the largest among the three phones reviewed but also excels at displaying vibrant and true-to-life colors. This makes it perfect for photography enthusiasts and web browsing. However, it is important to note that the Estrella's overall performance is hindered by its unusually slow processor. As a result, it may struggle to run high-definition games that would otherwise showcase its exceptional display capabilities.

Display	4.00 inches diagonal
CPU speed	0.9 gigahertz
Camera	Back : 10 megapixel; Front : 1.5 megapixel
Memory	2.0 gigabytes
Average critical rating	3.9 of 5 stars
Average customer rating	4.0 of 5 stars
Price	$500.00
Price with 2-year contract	$150.00

TAB 3 : Radical

Contrary to its name, Cortana's latest phone model, the Radical, does not bring anything particularly new to the table. In fact, it closely resembles a previous model with minimal changes. As a result, the Radical falls into the middle range among the three phones reviewed and fails to stand out in any significant manner, except for its weight, as it happens to be the heaviest among them. However, the Radical still performs adequately across all aspects. While it may not excel in any specific area, it is also free from any major drawbacks. Therefore, for customers who prioritize affordability, the Radical can serve as a suitable option without any notable shortcomings.

Display	3.75 inches diagonal
CPU speed	1.1 gigahertz
Camera	Back : 8 megapixel; Front : 1.5 megapixel
Memory	1.5 gigabytes
Average critical rating	3.7 of 5 stars
Average customer rating	4.1 of 5 stars
Price	$250.00
Price with 2-year contract	$0.00

1. For each of the following statements, indicate yes if the statement can be reasonably inferred from the tabbed reviews. Otherwise, indicate no.

Yes	No	
		The phone with the largest discount (in dollars) for purchasing a contract has the most memory.
		No front camera has more than 25 percent of the resolution, measured in megapixels, of a back camera.
		The reviewers considered factors other than those in the tables when writing their reviews.

2. For each of the following statements, select would help explain if the statement would, if true, help explain some of the information in the tabbed reviews. Otherwise select would not help explain.

Would help explain	Would not help explain	
		The Chieftain was more heavily advertised than the other two phones.
		Critics, unlike customers, don't pay for the products they review and are therefore less likely to let low prices influence their reviews of budget electronics.
		Using lighter parts to make a phone significantly increases manufacturing costs.

3. **If the phone with the smallest screen has received 40 critical ratings, how many additional 5-star critical ratings must it receive to improve its average critical rating to 4.5?**

   A. 4

   B. 8

   C. 12

   D. 16

   E. 20

PASSAGE 16

TAB 1 : Special Education

Pandora County boasts one of the largest school districts in its state, but it also faces the challenge of having one of the highest proportions of students with special needs across the nation.

In Pandora County, many students receive accommodations known as "504s," which are named after section 504 of the Rehabilitation Act of 1973. These accommodations are provided to students with physical disabilities, as well as those with cognitive or learning impairments that do not significantly hinder their ability to learn in a standard classroom setting. Students with 504s follow the same curriculum and grading standards as their peers but are offered various forms of assistance, such as text readers for those with visual impairments or preferential seating for students with attention-deficit disorders.

For students who have learning, cognitive, or emotional impairments that significantly impact their ability to learn, Individualized Education Plans (IEPs) are developed. These IEPs involve tailored curricula and grading standards. Whenever feasible, Pandora County strives for inclusive IEPs, where students receive accommodations within a regular classroom environment. However, students with the most severe needs are "mainstreamed," participating in select subjects within general education classes while spending the majority of their day in separate special-needs classrooms.

TAB 2 : Budget

In Pandora County, the expenses directly related to providing accommodations are covered by a county-wide fund. However, the individual schools within Pandora County bear the responsibility of managing the administrative costs associated with designing, certifying, and monitoring the 504s and IEPs of their students. Each school in Pandora County's budget includes provisions for administering an unlimited number of 504s. Additionally, they allocate resources for the administration of 12 inclusive IEPs and 4 mainstreamed IEPs for every 100 students enrolled.

TAB 3 : Employees

There are no educational requirements to work as an assistant to a student on a 504 plan in the Pandora County School District. Many assistants to students with mobility restrictions do not have high school diplomas.

All aides who provide assistance to students with must have college degrees. Additionally, these aides must complete a special six-month certification, unless they majored in education.

Pandora County teachers must have a master's degree. Teachers are occasionally allowed to begin working for the district while still enrolled in their master's programs, but this exception does not apply to teachers of children with special needs; these teachers must complete additional education and observation requirements after earning their degrees but before teaching.

1. **For each of the following scenarios, select Yes if the administrative costs of the accommodation described are within the school's budget, on the basis of the given information. Otherwise, select No.**

Yes	No	
		A 250-student middle school requires 32 sign-language interpreters for students with hearing impairments.
		A 1,000-student high school has 120 students who receive an exemption from the oral presentations that are normally part of final grading.
		A 500-student school has 30 students who spend most of the day in a special-needs classroom.

2. **For each of the following scenarios, select Possible if the described scenario is possible in the Pandora County School District, on the basis of the given information. Otherwise, select Not possible.**

Possible	Not Possible	
		A school with $50,000 remaining in its budget orders $100,000 of textbooks in Braille to meet the needs of its students with visual impairments.
		A student's need for alternative homework assignments requires the school to seek additional funding, as the certification of the student's accommodation would exceed the school's budget.
		A student with a severe learning disability spends most of the school day learning from a teacher with only a bachelor's degree.

3. **Suppose in an Pandora County school with a total student population of 316, there are 12 students with IEPs who are mainstreamed. Based on the information provided, select the answer that must be true about this group of 12 students.**

A. At least some of these students spend all of their class time in special needs classes.

B. The school's budget does not cover the administration of the IEP of at least one of these students.

C. Some of these students are taught the same curriculum and graded by the same standards as are students without IEPs.

D. All of the aides who assist these students have completed a special six month certification.

E. These students spend a minority of their time, if any, in general education classes.

Answer Explanations

PASSAGE 1

Solution

All the statements Undermine the point put forth

Explanation :

Undermines	Does not undermine	Statement
✓		Migration from proprietary software to open-source software would be significantly more expensive for the government than would migration from proprietary software to other proprietary software
	✓	The measures included in the bill will, if compiled with, ensure compatibility among software systems used by all the carious relevant stakeholders
✓		As a software package is used for a longer period of time, it becomes less expensive to migrate from that package to other

Statement 1 : Migration from proprietary software to open-source software would be significantly more expensive for the government than would migration from proprietary software to other proprietary software.

Undermines the government's argument. The government argues that the bill would make software migration easier and less expensive in the long run. However, if statement 1 is true, then the opposite would be the case. Migration from proprietary software to open-source software would be significantly more expensive than migration from proprietary software to other proprietary software, which would make the bill more expensive in the long run.

Statement 2 : The measures included in the bill will, if complied with, ensure compatibility among software systems used by all the various relevant stakeholders.

Does not undermine either argument. The company's argument is that the bill would increase compatibility problems, while the government's argument is that the bill would decrease compatibility problems. Statement 2 does not address either of these arguments directly, so it does not undermine either one.

Statement 3 : As a software package is used for a longer period of time, it becomes less expensive to migrate from that package to another.

Undermines the company's argument. The company argues that the cost of open-source software is much higher than the cost of proprietary software, and that this would make migration to open-source software more expensive. However, if statement 3 is true, then the opposite would be the case. As software packages are used for longer periods of time, they become more complex and interconnected, which would make migration from them more difficult and expensive.

PASSAGE 2

Solution

1. D. Conveyor-belt speed increase accounted for the greatest increase in annual output of assembled units from Y10 to Y11.

2.

Yes	No	Statement
	✓	Q/N was less than 10,000 for Y10.
	✓	Q/N was unchanged from Y10 to Y11.
✓		Q/N remained below 30,000 in Yi0 and Y11.

Explanation

1. As given in the first tab-

   Yr 10 : Output = 250,000 and Profit = 15,000,000

   For Yr 11- check third tab to find the changes in output and profit after Automation

   1. Inspection Post Automation- Increased output by 2% and Profit by 5% i.e Output = 255,000 and Profit = 15,750,000
   2. Conveyor Belt speed increase -Increased output by 3% and Profit by 4% i.e Output = 257500 & Profit = 15,600,000
   3. Administrative cost- Increased profit by 1% i.e Profit = 15,150,000

   Now lets check each given choices

   A. On the assembly line, conveyor-belt speed is directly proportional to total annual output of assembled units.

   - We do not know what was the speed of conveyor belt, we only know output. So Eliminate

   B. Administrative unit restructuring accounted for the greatest increase in the dollar amount of profit from Y10 to Y11.

   - As cal above , administrative unit restructuring is not the greatest increase in dollar amt of profit. It is lowest among all three elements. So Eliminate

   C. Conveyor-belt speed increase accounted for the greatest increase in the dollar amount of profit from Y10 to Y11.

   - Clearly no , conveyor belt speed accounted less than automation so eliminate.

   D. Conveyor-belt speed increase accounted for the greatest increase in annual output of assembled units from Y10 to Y11.

   - CORRECT-- Yes as can been seen from cal done above . Conveyor belt increase accounted for greatest increase in output.

E. Inspection-post automation accounted for the greatest increase in annual output of assembled units from Y10 to Y11.

- No it is incorrect based on cal above. So Eliminate.

2. Part 1: No.

output in year 10 was 250,000 (Q) and the number of direct line workers (N) was 15.

250,000/15 = 16,666.67 which is > than 10,000 and therefore not less than 10,000

Part 2: No.

Q/N in year 10 is 16,666,67 as calculated in part 1.

If we know N decreased, and we know Q increased, then we know the number increased overall. When the numerator increases the number as a whole increases, when the denominator decreases the whole number increases. This means between the two years, Q/N did NOT remain unchanged.

Part 3: Yes.

Q/N is 16,666.67 from part 1, which is less than 30,000

Now we need to check year 11.

In year 11, they laid off 3 people, meaning they now only have 12 workers (N).

Between year 10 and 11, output increased by 5%, so output went from 250,000 ⇒ 262,500

(1.05)(250,000) = 262,500

Q/N = 262,500/12 = 21,875, which is also less than 30,000.

PASSAGE 3

Solution

1. 2

2.

Yes	No	Statement
✓		Mary, Joey, and Saina need offices because the projects they work on require the highest levels of security
✓		Two additional employees are hired and will be supervised by Jerad
	✓	Regal resigns his position at Star Research

Explanation

1. The question asks for which people only have a single relationship. Lets go through the table one by one:

   1. Saina - If Saina is in 112, Ciaran can only be in 111 which leaves no place for Emma or Lara. Not qualified.
   2. Regal - If Regal is in 112, Stuard can be in 111. No other conditions need to be satisfied. Qualified.
   3. Stuard - Same reason as 2. Qualified.

4. Joey - If Joey is in 112, Lara can only be in 111 which leaves no place for Ciaran. Not qualified.
5. Lara - Same reason as 1. Not qualified.
6. Arnold - If Arnold is in 112, Jerad can only be in 111 which leaves no place for Mary. Not qualified.
7. Emma - Same reason as 1. Not qualified.
8. Jerad - Same reason as 6. Not qualified.
9. Mary - Same reason as 6. Not qualified.
10. Ciaran - Same reason as 1. Not qualified.

So, only Stuard and Regal are qualified

PASSAGE 4

Solution

1. E. $1,190

2.

Yes	No	
✓		The director of the training department believes that the software training class will be filled to capacity.
	✓	The director of the training department expects that printing of the training manual will exceed the department's printing budget.
	✓	The technical publications department will most likely be able to deliver 35 copies of the training manual by October 21st.

Explanation

1. Costs of collating and preparation, which is currently $2.00/manual

   total cost will be 2×35 : $70

   printing cost will be for 118 pages of which 110 pages are b/w , 5 pages are color and 3 pages are of company information

   Color graphics charges are $.75/page

   normal b&w $.25/page

   total charge per manual : $(.75 \times 5) + (113 \times .25) = \$32$

   total for manual 35 ; $35 \times \$32$; $1120

   net cost will be $70+$1120 ; $1190

2. The director of the training department believes that the software training class will be filled to capacity.

   Yes, the director expects class to be filled to 35 which is the the capacity training room

   The director of the training department expects that printing of the training manual will exceed the department's printing budget.

NO there is no information about budget of department

The technical publications department will most likely be able to deliver 35 copies of the training manual by October 21st.

NO since manual is more than 100 pages so it will not be possible to meet deadline

PASSAGE 5

Solution

1.

Yes	No	Statements
	✓	200
	✓	330
✓		1320

2.

Yes	No	Statements
✓		In-state undergraduates comprise the largest proportion of all the admitted students for 2011.
	✓	The in-state undergraduate admissions were 25% higher in 2010 than in 2011.
✓		Some foreign students were turned away from Western State for reasons other than academic suitability.

3. B. Foreign students are just as likely to attend a private college as a state university

Explanation

1. This question asks you to indicate which answers could be the number of in-state undergraduates, so you need to reference the graph on Tab 2. If foreign students comprise exactly 1/8 of the number of out-of-state undergraduates, then the number of in-state undergraduates would have to be a value that yields an integer value for the number of foreign students. In-state undergraduates are 55% of 60% of the total, or (.55)(.6) = (.33) of the total. Plug In the Answers to discover which values will work.

   If 200 is the number of in-state undergraduates, which comprise 33% of the total, then you can calculate the total number of admitted students:

   (0.33) (total) = 200 so total = 200/0.33 = 606.06

   Since this value does not return an integer for number of students, this answer is incorrect. So the answer for 200 is No.

PASSAGE 6

Solution

1.

Yes	No	Statements
	✓	Device X1
✓		Device XS
	✓	Device XS

Explanation

RO1

- To be ratings-dominant over one of the other devices, Device X1 must match or exceed all the ratings of the other device in every other category. In other words, it could not have a lower rating than the other device in any category. By sorting the table on X1, it is clear that Device X1 has a zero rating for every feature except A and B, and no other device has zero ratings in all those categories. Thus, Device X1 cannot be ratings-dominant over any of the other devices in the table.

The correct answer is No.

RO2

Sorting the table by XS shows that every rating for Device XS matches or exceeds the rating for Device X2. Moreover, the ratings for Features A, B, D, and E for Device XS exceed those of Device X2. Therefore, Device XS is ratings-dominant over Device X2.

The correct answer is Yes.

RO3

Sorting the table by XZ shows that Device XZ's ratings for both Features C and D exceed those of Device X1, but of no other device. However, Device X1 has higher ratings than Device XZ for Features A and B. Thus, Device XZ cannot be ratings-dominant over any of the other devices.

The correct answer is No.

PASSAGE 7

Solution

1. A. $500

2.

Yes	No	Statements
✓		Cancun
	✓	Jamaica
	✓	Miami

3. A. Haweli

4.

Yes	No	Statements
✓		Contiki
	✓	World Springs
	✓	Sun Fun

5.

Yes	No	Statements
	✓	Miami
	✓	Hawaii
✓		Cancun

6.

Yes	No	Statements
✓		Cancun
✓		Daytona
✓		Puerta Rico

7.

Yes	No	Statements
✓		Rap artist hired to throw a concert alongside the waterfront beach houses
✓		Morning breakfast delivery by a delivery waitress at the beach house whose earnings are primarily from gratuities
	✓	Taxi cab driver bringing guests from outside of the waterfront area to the waterfront area where vacationers tend to hangout

8.

Yes	No	Statements
✓		Miami
	✓	Jamaica
	✓	Cancun

Explanation

1. D,since the total flight price would be 350×2(since there are 10 people so two groups would be formed)+ $150 \times 4 \times 2$ (2 groups and 4 nights=1900

2. (a) Yes, In Cancun without ROB the price of 1 group for 1 night would be $350+150 \times 4$ (4 days) $= 950$

   While with ROB : $120 \times 4 + 480 = 960$

   (b) No, In Jamaica without ROB the price of 1 group for 1 night would be $200 + 160 \times 4 = 840$

   While with ROB : $220 + 135 \times 4 = 760$

   (c) No, In Miami without ROB the price of 1 group for 1 night would be $100 \times 4 + 150 = 550$

   While with ROB : $210 + 4 \times 70 = 490$

3. D, I think the answer should be Miami since the lowest cost for beach house is 70$ and outside is also 70$ so a person would prefer ROB

4. (a) In Contiki loss would be there since occupying 2nd row house will cost 70 while for the first row room which is not occupied the owner will get a discount of 25% so final price to him would be $100\text{-}100 \times .25 = 75$,so a loss of 5$ is there

   (b) In Worldsprings no loss would be there since occupying 2nd row house will cost 115 while for the first row room which is not occupied the owner will get a discount of 25% so final price to him would be $140\text{-}140 \times .25 = 105$, so no loss is there

   (c) In Sunfun no loss would be there since occupying 2nd row house will cost 90 while for the first row room which is not occupied the owner will get a discount of 25% so final price to him would be $115\text{-}115 \times .25 = 86.25$,so no loss is there

5. (a) No, In Miami the % discount on plane is (210 – 150)/210 = 28.57

   while discount on room in 1st block vs other rows = 100 –70/100 = 30

   (b) No,In Hawai the % discount on plane is (525 – 450)/525 = 14

   while discount on room in 1st block vs other rows = 140 – 115/140 = 17.8

   (c) Yes,In Cancun the % discount on plane is (480 – 350)/480 = 27

   while discount on room in 1st block vs other rows = 150 – 120/150 = 20

6. (a) Yes, In Cancun Total for 4 nights with RoWFA=480+70 × 4=760

   while occupying first block = 350 + 150 × 4 = 950

   (b) Yes, In Daytona Total for 4 nights with RoWFA = 200 + 70 × 4 = 480

   while occupying first block = 170 + 135 × 4 = 710

   (c) Yes, In Puerto Rico Total for 4 nights with RoWFA = 425 + 70 × 4 = 705

   while occupying first block = 400 + 200 × 4 = 1200

7. Here only cab driver will not suffer since he is bringing people from outside to inside the beach area in waterfront and if people are not staying inside then the rapper and waiter will not get a chance to perform or serve anyone and thus will have lossess

8. So here in this question only people in Miami they will try to book house in first block beacuse the price difference is lowest among the three choices given in the question as the difference between inside and outside is lowest for Miami = 100-70=30$,so the likelihood is also high here that people will book houses inside the first row here

PASSAGE 8

Solution

1.

False	True	Statements
✓		The cost of supplying baby food for the month for Baby Care is more than $7,500
	✓	The pre-discount cost of getting all Mighty Avenger Toys for the month is cheaper than getting all Barney's Action Toys for the month.
	✓	Baby Care can supply enough toys for the month with a budget of less than $220.

2. B. $1600

3.

Yes	No	Statements
	✓	At a 20-baby maximum, each baby gets his own toy; at a 50-baby maximum each baby must share his toy with one other baby.
	✓	At a 20-baby maximum, Baby Care plans to allot 1 baby food package per baby per day and supply 1 diaper package per baby per week.
✓		At a 20-baby maximum, Baby Care will supply 1 package of diapers each week to the babies but no toys. At a 50-baby maximum, the babies' parents will have to supply their own diapers; Baby Care will not supply diapers. Baby Care will, however, supply a Barney's Action toy package to each baby each week.

Explanation

1. (a) False, since the baby food requires:

   $30 \times 3 = 90$ cans ,now for 20 days it is

   $90 \times 20 = 1800$ cans, now each can is of 5\$, so total amount is $1800 \times 5 = 9000$, but on 50 + cans it is giving 20% off so final price would be $9000 \times .8 = 7200$, which is less than 7500

   (b) True, For babies each baby requires $30 \times 1 = 30$ toys and each one requires $30 \times 2 = 60$ toys,since after 2 weeks new toys are required, so for Barneys toys price per toy is 10\$, so total is 600,while for Mighty avenger per toy price is 4\$, so total is 240, hence mighty is cheaper than Barneys

   (c) True,yes after discount we can Mighty avenger toys with a budget < 220\$

2. B, So here for 400 cans the per can amount is 5\$,so total is $400 \times 5 = 2000$\$, now with a 20% discount final price is $2000 \times .8 = 1600$\$

3. (a) If sharing of toys is there then problem for 50 baby vs 20 baby wouldn't be there.

   (b) In this case the cost wouldn't increase.

   (c) If diapers are not supplied at 50 baby then the cost would increase and it will not be offset by giving toys

PASSAGE 9

Solution

1.

Yes	No	
	✓	All of the listed stainless steels with a carbon content of 0.08% are Austenitic.
✓		A stainless steel among those listed with a Rockwell hardness of at least 85 must be either Austenitic or Ferritic.
✓		Of the steels listed, the average density of Austenitic steels is greater than the average density of Ferritic steels.

2. C. 89

Explanation

1. Consider each of the following statements. Indicate Yes if the given information supports the statement. Otherwise, indicate No.

All of the listed stainless steels with a carbon content of 0.08% are Austenitic.

The text in Tab 1 indicates that Austenitic steels contain 16%-26% chromium, not more than 0.8% carbon, and 6%-15% nickel. These steels are also neither magnetic nor heat treatable. The question restricts itself to steels that are 0.08% carbon, so find those steels in Tab 2. They are SAE 304 through SAE 409. Of these, all have allowable chromium percentages, but SAE 409 has only 0.5% nickel. Therefore, it is not Austenitic. Alternatively, you could check Tab 3 for the magnetic and heattreatable characteristics. Here, you'll see that SAE 409 is magnetic and therefore not Austenitic.

The answer is No.

A stainless steel among those listed with a Rockwell hardness of at least 85 must be either Austenitic or Ferritic.

Because this specifies a hardness of 85 or above, begin by examining the table in Tab 3; all of the SAE 300-series steels and SAE 430 have a hardness of 85 or higher. Next, return to the text in Tab 1 to determine what constitutes Ferritic steel: it is magnetic but not heat treatable. You've already determined from the previous question that an Austenitic steel is neither. Put another way, any steel in the table that is not heat treatable is either Austenitic or Ferritic. According to the table in Tab 3, none of the SAE 300-series steels is heat treatable and neither is SAE 430, so

The answer is Yes.

Of the steels listed, the average density of Austenitic steels is greater than the average density of Ferritic steels.

From the first two questions in this set, you've determined from the information in the text and the table in Tab 3 that all of the SAE 300-series steels are Austenitic. You've also determined that SAE 409 and SAE 430 are Ferritic. A glance at Tab 3 will confirm that SAE 410, being both magnetic and heat treatable, is neither Austenitic nor Ferritic. Rather than doing complex calculations, notice that the two Ferritic steels, SAE 409 and SAE 430, each have a density of 7,800, while all of the Austenitic steels are above 7,850. Thus, you can conclude that the Austenitic steels have a higher average density, so

The answer is Yes.

2. Based on the information in the passage and tables, the stainless steel with the highest ratio of carbon to nickel has which of the following hardness ratings?

Because this question asks for a ratio of carbon to nickel, think of carbon as the numerator of a fraction and nickel as the denominator. The highest ratio will be the fraction with the largest numerator relative to the denominator. Therefore, you can quickly eliminate all of the SAE 300-series steels, since their denominators are many times greater than any of the SAE 400-series steels while their numerators are less than or equal to those of the 400 series. Now use estimation to compare SAE 409 to SAE 410: 0.08 over 0.50 is less than 0.15 over 0.75, since 0.15 is nearly twice 0.08 but 0.75 is considerably less than twice 0.50. What about SAE 430? Since it has a bigger numerator than SAE 410 but the same denominator, it must have the highest ratio. Now find its hardness rating in the table in Tab 3: 89.

Therefore, (C) is correct.

PASSAGE 10

Solution

1.

Yes	No	
	✓	Composite Attribute Value for Steve is greatest for brand A
✓		Steve purchase brand A based on customer value
✓		Brand C scores lowest both in terms of customer value and Customer benefit

2. A. $X = \frac{Y(Z-5)}{5}$

3.

Yes	No	
	✓	Reduce the marked price to $60
✓		Add a faster processor to increases its Processor Performance rating to 9
✓		Improve its graphics capability to the highest possible ranking

PASSAGE 11

Solution

1.

True	False	
✓		Sales managers are B-level employees.
	✓	The new AVP of Procurement is a C-level employee.
	✓	The AVP of Engineering is under the new AVP of Procurement.

2.

True	False	
✓		The ratio of B-level employees to C- level employees is 6:1
	✓	The ratio of B-level employees to A-level employees is 5:1
	✓	Each A-level employee has at least 3 employees below him or her

3. B. 1.4

PASSAGE 12

Solution

1.

Yes	No	
	✓	The average price per pound of the mints including tax and delivery is $10.29.
✓		Sugar-free chocolates cost about 80% more, on average, than regular varieties of chocolate.
	✓	The Candy Man charged $0.75 per pound for delivery services.

Explanation

A. The average price per pound of the mints including tax and delivery is \$10.29.

We just divide the final bill by 6 since that includes the (sum of 6 pounds) + (tax) + (delivery)

Hence, $65.8 / 6 = 10.96$ which is not 10.29

B. Sugar-free chocolates cost about 80% more, on average, than regular varieties of chocolate.

Here we average price of regular varieties (dark, milk and white)

We get $(3.58+3.24+2.94)/3 = 3.25$

Now increase 3.25 by 80% to see if it costs similar to Sugar free (which is 5.85)

Hence, $3.25 \times 1.8 = 5.85$ (Hence YES)

C. The Candy Man charged \$0.75 per pound for delivery services.

Delivery was 10\$ for 6 pounds hence it was more than 1\$ for a pound and NOT 0.75\$.

Hence NO

PASSAGE 13

Solution

1.

True	False	Values
✓		If the coordinator uses DoxySource and orders one appetizer, one entrée, and one dessert per person, then the least amount that can be spent on tables to seat all guests is approximately 16.6% of the cost of food.
✓		If the large punch fountain from BrightRight is sufficient for 400 guests, then using smaller fountains from DoxySource to serve the same number of guests would cost at least 20% less per gallon.
✓		If BrightRight is used, the project will go over its present budget by at least 15%.

2. C. \$ 792.00

3.

Yes	No	Values
✓		The Gala Coordinator is willing to ask for a budgetary increase, if necessary.
✓		According to the Administrative Assistant, audio costs are not the only determining factor in choosing one event planning service over another.
	✓	Fountains are an optional element of the gala.

Explanation

1. (a) True, since 16.67% of food is = $.1667 \times 11.65 = 1.93$ and cost of tables = $(1/8) \times 15.50$ (Per the least priced plan)

   (b) True, since the per gallon cost for Bright right is $350/40 = 8.75$ while for DoxySource it is $(47 \times (400/70))/40$ gallons $= 7$ which is at least 20% less than Bright right's value.

   (c) True, since if we choose Bright right with the least possible options it is providing the budget will go up by more than 15% (budget will be more than 6900)

2. Total cost is $17 \times 1 + 50 \times 15.50 = 792$

3. (a) Yes,since they are preferring Bright right for which more budget is required

   (b) Yes,since food also plays an important role here

   (c) No,it is required

PASSAGE 14

Solution

1.

Yes	No	
	✓	The degree to which medical residents' errors pose a danger of lasting patient harm.
✓		Whether it is possible for medical residents to work more than 8 hours during a 24-hour shift.
	✓	The degree to which a resident is as qualified as a licensed physician.

2.

Yes	No	
	✓	Medical residents should not be allowed to work for more than 8 hours during a 24-hour shift.
✓		A hospital should ensure that medical resident errors are minimized or prevented entirely.
	✓	Medical residents should not be undermined or treated poorly by licensed physicians when patients are present.

3. E. $7.13

Explanation

1. **Statement 1: No.** In the last sentence of the Residency Association statement, the president says:

   "Such working conditions are dangerous for both patients and residents; some serious mistakes have already been made and were caught only at the last minute by senior staff."

   The residency president, then, believes that the situation is dangerous and that there is at least the possibility of serious consequences from mistakes made by residents.

In the last sentence of the Hospital Board statement, the spokesperson says

"...there is always an experienced physician on hand to verify the diagnosis, take over the procedure, or otherwise correct any potential errors [made by residents]."

The spokesperson, then, believes that there is an oversight system in place that will correct any potential errors-in other words, that there is no danger of lasting harm due to a resident's mistake. Thus, the spokesperson and the president disagree.

Statement 2: Yes. The Residency Association president explicitly states that residents have averaged 17.5 hours during the past month, so the president does believe that residents are working more than 8 hours during a 24-hour shift. The Hospital Board spokesperson says that residents are not expected to work 24 hours in a 24-hour shift, nor anywhere close to that but also that if a resident chooses to participate in many routine activities that can ably be handled by the nursing or medical staff, that is the resident's choice. In other words, the spokesperson is acknowledging that it is possible for a resident to work more than 8 hours in a shift-if he or she chooses to do so. The two parties, then, both agree that it is possible for residents to work longer than 8 hours during a 24-hour shift.

Statement 3: No. The Hospital Board spokesperson states clearly that until someone has finished the residency, he or she is not, and cannot reasonably be considered, a licensed physician. The spokesperson, then, believes that residents are not as qualified as licensed physicians.

The Residency Association president states that residents are responsible for all of the licensed physician tasks, including intake, the ordering of tests and labs, diagnosis and treatment, including surgery (emphasis added). This could be taken as evidence that the residency president believes residents are as qualified as licensed physicians. Alternatively, it may be interpreted as not providing any opinion as to whether residents are as qualified. Either way, this is not the same as the spokesperson's opinion that residents are not as qualified as licensed physicians.

2. **Statement 1: No.** The Residency Association president indicates that the residents are assumed to work 1/3 of the 24-hour shift, or 8 hours, but the president does not claim that residents should not work more than that amount. They claim only that they work too much. It can be inferred that they think they should work less than 17.5 hours, but it is unclear what they think of an 8-hour cutoff. Likewise, the Hospital Board never indicates a specific time beyond which residents should not be able to work.

   Statement 2: Yes. As part of their argument, the residents complain that their working conditions are dangerous and that, as a result, serious mistakes have been made. It can be inferred, then, that the residents believe that the hospital is responsible for setting reasonable working hours in order to minimize or prevent errors made by residents (among other goals). The Hospital Board indicates that

   "...when a resident is called upon to make a diagnosis or perform a minor procedure, there is always an experienced physician on hand to verify the diagnosis, take over the procedure, or otherwise correct any potential errors."

   The board, then, also believes that the hospital is responsible for minimizing or preventing errors made by medical residents.

Statement 3: No. The residents state that they are taken advantage of terribly and complain that they are undermined or treated poorly by senior doctors-sometimes when patients are present. The residents, then, agree with this statement.

You might surmise that any ethical hospital board also would not want doctors to treat medical residents poorly when patients are present (or at any time!), but the Hospital Board's statement never addresses this aspect of the resident's complaint. Therefore, nothing can be inferred regarding the board's position on this issue.

3. According to the first tab, the association president states that residents are assumed to work one-third of the hours in our assigned shifts. If the shift is 24 hours long, then, a resident is assumed to work for one-third of that time, or 8 hours. In that case, the hourly wage would be \$105 / 8 hours = \$13.125. Rounded to the hundredths digit, this is \$13.13.

   The resident indicates that the average time worked over the past month was actually 17.5 hours in a 24-hour shift. The hourly wage in this case would be \$105 / 17.5 hours = \$6.00.

   The difference between the two is \$13.13 – \$6.00 = \$7.13.

   The correct answer is (E).

PASSAGE 15

Solution

1.

Yes	No	
✓		The phone with the largest discount (in dollars) for purchasing a contract has the most memory.
✓		No front camera has more than 25 percent of the resolution, measured in megapixels, of a back camera.
✓		The reviewers considered factors other than those in the tables when writing their reviews.

2.

Would help explain	Would not help explain	
	✓	The Chieftain was more heavily advertised than the other two phones.
✓		Critics, unlike customers, don't pay for the products they review and are therefore less likely to let low prices influence their reviews of budget electronics.
✓		Using lighter parts to make a phone significantly increases manufacturing costs.

3. D. 16

PASSAGE 16

1.

Yes	No	
✓		A 250-student middle school requires 32 sign-language interpreters for students with hearing impairments.
✓		A 1,000-student high school has 120 students who receive an exemption from the oral presentations that are normally part of final grading.
	✓	A 500-student school has 30 students who spend most of the day in a special-needs classroom.

2.

Possible	Not Possible	
✓		A school with $50,000 remaining in its budget orders $100,000 of textbooks in Braille to meet the needs of its students with visual impairments.
✓		A student's need for alternative homework assignments requires the school to seek additional funding, as the certification of the student's accommodation would exceed the school's budget.
	✓	A student with a severe learning disability spends most of the school day learning from a teacher with only a bachelor's degree.

3. E. These students spend a minority of their time, if any, in general education classes

Chapter 2

Table Analysis

PASSAGE 1

The table below shows the number of deaths (in thousands) due to car accidents and the total number of deaths due to all causes (in thousands) in Country Y over a period of 6 years.

Year	Total deaths	Deaths due to car accidents
2000	20	0.9
2001	22	1.12
2002	24.2	1.55
2003	26.62	2.02
2004	29.28	1.91
2005	32.21	2.42

1. Assuming that the trend of deaths have been consistent since 1990, what would be the estimate number of deaths in country Y in the year 1998

(A) 19800

(B) 19605

(C) 18180

(D) 16530

(E) 16200

2. During which two consecutive years did Country Y witness the greatest percentage change in the ratio of deaths caused by car accidents to the total number of deaths?

(A) 2000 - 2001

(B) 2001 - 2002

(C) 2002 - 2003

(D) 2003 - 2004

(E) 2004 - 2005

3. If the percentage of deaths caused by natural disasters in the year 2000 is equivalent to the percentage of deaths caused by car accidents in the year 2001 in Country Y, what is the approximate number of deaths resulting from natural disasters in 2000?

(A) 495

(B) 990

(C) 1020

(D) 1230

(E) 1410

4. If the number of deaths caused by heart disease doubles every year from 2001 to 2004, and the number of deaths attributed to heart disease in 2000 was 10,000, what would be the estimated number of deaths due to heart disease in 2004?

(A) 625

(B) 2,000

(C) 40,000

(D) 160,000

(E) It cannot be determined from the information given

PASSAGE 2

This table displays data on coffee sold by a Guatemalan producer in 2015.

VARIETY	SALES, National Share (%)	SALES, National Rank	EXPORTS, National Share (%)	EXPORTS, National Rank
Coarse ground	18	4	7	5
Dark roast	31	1	60	1
Espresso roast	12	4	87	1
Fine ground	20	5	15	4
French roast	53	2	49	2
Light roast	21	2	32	2
Medium ground	36	1	58	1
Medium roast	71	1	58	1
Whole bean	50	3	22	4

For each of the following statements, select Yes if the statement can be shown to be true based on information in the table. Otherwise, select No.

Yes	No	
		This producer is responsible for a majority of the nation's exports of French roast coffee.
		This producer exports more fine-ground than coarse-ground coffee.
		The top two exporters of light-roast coffee combined export a majority of the nation's light-roast coffee.

PASSAGE 3

Coastline region	State	Country	Number of hurricanes	Percent change in population, 1960–2008
Gulf of Mexico	Florida	Monroe County	15	50.8
Gulf of Mexico	Louisiana	Lafourche Parish	14	67.2
Atlantic	North Carolina	Carteret County	14	104.3
Atlantic	North Carolina	Dare County	13	465.9
Atlantic	North Carolina	Hyde County	13	10.1
Gulf of Mexico	Louisiana	Jefferson Parish	12	108.9
Atlantic	Florida	Palm Beach County	12	454.7
Atlantic	Florida	Miami-Dade County	11	156.5
Gulf of Mexico	Louisiana	St. Bernard Parish	11	17.2
Gulf of Mexico	Louisiana	Cameron Parish	11	4.8
Gulf of Mexico	Louisiana	Terrebonne Parish	11	78.7

The table provides information on the 11 coastal counties in the United States that experienced the highest number of hurricanes between 1960 and 2008. Additionally, it includes the percentage change in population for each county during the same time period. Positive percentages indicate population growth.

Consider the following statements. For each statement, evaluate whether that statement is True or False, according to the information in the table.

True	False	
		The median number of hurricanes in the Florida counties was higher than the median number of hurricanes in each of the other states' counties.
		The counties listed in the table that experienced the three greatest percent changes in population during the period are all part of the coastline region whose listed counties had the greater range in number of hurricanes during the same period.
		The Gulf of Mexico coastline region experienced fewer hurricanes per county listed in the table, on average, than did the Atlantic coastline region.

PASSAGE 4

Course	Certification			
	A	B	C	D
1	*	*	*	*
2	*	*		
3			*	
4		*		
5	*		*	
6		*		*
7	*			*
8			*	
9	*			

There are four technical certifications available (Certifications A, B, C, and D), each with its own set of required courses selected from Courses 1 through 9. To obtain a certification, candidates must complete all the courses specified for that particular certification. Notably, if a course is already completed for one certification, it does not need to be retaken for other certifications that also include it. The table displays the specific courses needed for each certification. For instance, Certification A mandates the completion of Courses 1, 2, 5, 7, and 9.

Meredith, who has not yet taken any of the courses, intends to acquire all four certifications. She has devised a strategic plan: she will initially focus on taking exclusively the courses required for the certification that has the fewest number of courses. Subsequently, she will proceed to the certification that requires the least number of additional courses compared to what she has already completed. Meredith will continue this approach until she has successfully completed all the required courses for all four certifications.

For each of the following statements about these certifications, select Yes if the statement is accurate based on the information provided. Otherwise, select No.

Yes	No	
		Meredith will receive Certification A first.
		Meredith will receive Certification B second.
		Meredith will receive Certification C third.

PASSAGE 5

Country	# of Pan-Global Games (Judge)	Average Score (Judge)	Highest Score given	Lowest Score Given	# of Pan-Global Games (Competitor)	Average Score (Competitor)
Albania	1	6.7	9.2	5.4	1	8.6
Estonia	2	8.4	9	6.9	3	7.7
Finland	3	6.2	8.9	4.2	2	8.5
Germany	3	8.2	9.4	7.6	2	8.3
Japan	1	7.3	9.7	6.4	3	8.8
Norway	2	7.9	8.4	5.2	4	6.5
Russia	5	6.8	9.6	5.4	3	7
South Korea	3	7.9	9.3	6.3	2	8.3
United States	4	8.1	9.2	7.1	2	7.1

The provided table presents information regarding a group of judges participating in the 2012 Pan-Global Games. It includes details such as the country represented by each judge, the number of previous Pan-Global Games they had participated in as a judge, their average score given as a judge, the highest score given, the lowest score given, the number of Pan-Global Games they had participated in as a competitor, and their average score received as a competitor. The scores are rated on a scale of 1 to 10, with increments of one-tenth of a point.

Consider each of the following statements about the Pan-Global Games judge's scores. For each statement indicate whether the statement is supported based on the information provided in the table.

Yes	No	
		On average, the lowest score given for judges who had judged in 3 Pan-Global Games was higher than that for judges who had competed in 3 Pan-Global Games.
		The judge with the greatest absolute difference between the highest score given and lowest score given also had the greatest percent difference between the lowest score given and highest score given.
		The average (arithmetic mean) number of Pan-Global Games that judges participated in as judges was higher than the average number of Pan-Global Games that judges participated in as competitors.
		The probability that a given judge competed in more Pan-Global Games than she judged is the same as the probability that a judge gave a higher average score as a judge than she received as a competitor.

PASSAGE 6

A research bureau conducted a survey among the residents of Catalonia to gather information about their attendance at entertainment and cultural events in the year 2015. The provided chart presents the percentages of citizens in different age groups who spent money to attend specific cultural events during that year.

Age	Galleries or museums	Sporting Events	Performing Arts Events	Movies or films
0 - 25	70	75	64	82
25 - 34	65	68	67	85
35 – 44	64	62	68	83
45 - 54	58	55	45	88
55 – 64	62	57	56	78
65 and older	68	45	64	62

1. **For each of the following statements, choose "would help explain" if it would, if true, help explain the information given in the chart. Otherwise, choose "would not help explain".**

Would help explain	Would not help explain	Statement
		Per capita spending on the performing arts is the highest among communities that invest heavily in the arts and that best advertise the performing arts.
		Most major sporting events take place in urban areas, where the average age of residents is significantly lower than that of rural or suburban areas.
		A greater percentage of towns contain at least one movie theater than contain at least one performing arts venue.

2. **Which of the following can be reasonably inferred from the information provided in the table?**

Can be reasonably inferred	Cannot be reasonably inferred	
		In Catalonia, per capita spending on sporting events tends to decrease as individuals age.
		The average age of Catalonia citizens who attended performing arts events in 2015 was under the age of 45.
		At least 45% of Catalonia citizens under the age of 25 attended both a sporting event and a gallery or museum in 2015.

PASSAGE 7

The table summarizes information in several categories about the 9 stores in a small grocery chain. The table also includes chain-wide averages where appropriate.

Store	Self-check express lanes	Self-check unlimited lanes	Pharmacy	Fuel	Restaurant	Average Customer Age
A	8	4	Yes	No	No	34.5
B	8	6	No	No	No	28.4
C	6	4	Yes	No	Yes	32
D	8	0	Yes	No	No	50.5
E	12	4	Yes	Yes	No	42.5
F	8	6	No	No	Yes	34.6
G	8	0	No	Yes	No	38.8
H	4	8	Yes	No	Yes	29.9
I	0	0	Yes	Yes	Yes	56.7
Averages	6.89	3.56	–	–	–	38.73

For each of the following statements, select True if the statement can be verified to be true based on the information provided. Otherwise, select False.

True	False	Statements
		In each store whose average customer age falls between 34 and 36, the number of self-check express lanes is above average.
		There is a negative correlation between the number of self-check unlimited lanes and the average customer age.
		Stores in this table that have fewer self-check express lanes than the chain-wide average are less likely to have restaurants than stores that have more self-check express lanes than the chain-wide average.

PASSAGE 8

Serial #	Weight, Ounces	Radius, inches	Shape	Magnetic?
K01	4.2	0.94	Cylinder	No
K02	2.3	0.16	Cone	Yes
K03	4.1	0.32	Sphere	Yes
K04	6.2	0.71	Cylinder	Yes
K05	4.3	0.76	Cylinder	No
K06	5.5	0.54	Cylinder	No
K07	4.4	0.84	Cone	Yes
K08	4.7	0.37	Sphere	No
K09	1	0.42	Sphere	No
K10	2.7	0.63	Cylinder	No
K11	6.3	0.67	Cone	No
K12	1.1	0.76	Sphere	No

Students measured a group of metallic solids of various alloys and represented their findings in the table above. In addition to weight and radius, information about shape and magnetism is depicted.

True	False	Statements
		The median weight is closer to the greatest weight than to the least weight.
		Ranking from greatest to least values, K05 has a higher rank according to weight than it does according to radius.
		The ratio of magnetic cones to magnetic spheres is equal to the percentage of solids that are either heavier than 5 ounces or magnetic.

PASSAGE 9

Country	Coastal	Water Polo	Rugby	Rowing	Cricket
Australia	Yes	25	23	26	26
China	No	18	56	18	8
France	No	13	48	14	25
India	No	9	21	5	65
New Zealand	Yes	44	8	35	13
South Africa	Yes	17	20	18	45
Spain	No	7	65	10	18

The table shows percentage of youngsters who train for specific sport in select few countries.

For each of the following statements select Would help explain if it would, if true, help explain some of the information in the table. Otherwise, select Would not help explain.

Would help explain	Would not help explain	Statements
		The proportion of the population of New Zealand that lives close to the ocean is larger than that of South Africa. Note that each youngster plays only one sport.
		Relative to other sports in South Africa, professional cricket players earn more money than any other professional sport players do.
		People in coastal countries have a greater interest in water sports than those in inland countries

PASSAGE 10

Manager	Employee satisfaction rating (%)	Yearly sales (thousands of dollars)	Percent change in sales over previous year	Underground parking	Free shipping	Size of sales force
L. Jenkins	32.3	58.4	5.3	no	no	5
P. Parsons	44.4	92	−7.8	yes	yes	11
A. Yangzhou	65.7	105.2	−1.2	no	yes	10
D. Xin	55.7	85.1	10.8	yes	yes	15
M. Stover	18	116.9	15.5	no	yes	12
Z. Szymes	50.1	64.7	4.8	no	no	8
T. Emerald	64.2	77.4	0.3	yes	no	11
O. McDonough	75.5	79.6	31.2	no	yes	8
K. Eriksson	46.9	58.9	−20.0	no	no	13
B. Stripley	48.7	101.7	-9.4	yes	yes	16

A small furniture store chain conducted performance reviews of its 10 branch managers. The managers' performance in several metrics over the last year has been compiled in the table. The table also lists some relevant features of each manager's branch.

For each of the following statements, select True if the statement can be verified to be true based on the given information. Otherwise, select False.

True	False	
		A majority of the managers who oversaw an increase in sales over the previous year have an employee satisfaction rating higher than the median.
		There is a positive correlation between the size of a branch's sales force and that branch's change in year-over-year sales.
		The branch that had the highest sales in the previous year has underground parking.

PASSAGE 11

The following table displays the recorded maximum and minimum temperatures, as well as humidity levels, observed over a span of 5 days in two coastal regions located in western India.

Date	Region	Maximum Temperature	Minimum Temperature	Humidity (%)
6/1/2012	Colaba	35.5	28.4	63
6/1/2012	Santacruz	34.5	28.6	60
6/2/2012	Colaba	35.5	28.6	68
6/2/2012	Santacruz	34.2	28.8	61
6/3/2012	Colaba	34.6	29	61
6/3/2012	Santacruz	35.2	28.2	70
6/4/2012	Colaba	34.6	29	61
6/4/2012	Santacruz	34.6	28	69
6/5/2012	Colaba	35.6	29	74
6/5/2012	Santacruz	34.3	27.9	66

For each of the following statements, select 'Yes' if statement is true based solely on the information provided in the table; otherwise select 'No'.

Yes	No	Statements
		If range is taken into consideration, then humidity in Sanatcruz is more consistent than humidity in Colaba.
		Median of temperature difference between maximum and minimum temperature in Santacruz is more than that in Colaba.
		Mean maximum temperature of 1st June is lower than that of 2nd & 4th June.

PASSAGE 12

The table contains data on 11 subway systems from around the world. For each subway system, the city and continent in which it is located is provided, along with the total number of lines and stations it contains. The length, measured in kilometers, of the average line in each system is also provided.

City	Continent	Lines	Average Line Length (km)	Stations
Buenos Aires, Argentina	South America	6	8.98	86
Toronto, Canada	North America	4	17.73	75
Santiago, Chile	South America	6	19.62	118
Beijing, China	Asia	20	28.6	306
Paris, France	Europe	16	13.74	302
Mexico City, Mexico	North America	12	16.76	163
Madrid, Spain	Europe	13	22.54	301
London, England	Europe	11	36.55	270
Chicago, USA	North America	8	20.75	145
New York, USA	North America	25	14.08	424
Singapore	Asia	5	39.84	119

Yes	No	
		The average (arithmetic mean) number of stations in the European subway systems is more than double the average (arithmetic mean) number of stations in the South American subway systems.
		The number of lines in the New York subway system exceeds the median number of lines by more than 13.
		The London subway system has the greatest total length as measured by kilometers of lines.

PASSAGE 13

Following table shows the percentage of population visiting Selected Cultural Institutions in one year

Country/political union	Public Library	Zoo/ Aquarium	Natural History Museum	Science/ technology museum
Russia	15	8	5	2
Brazil	25	28	7	4
European Union	35	27	20	18
South Korea	35	37	30	10
China	41	51	13	19
Japan	48	45	20	12
US	65	48	27	26

For each of the following statements select Would help explain if it would, if true, help explain some of the information in the table. Otherwise select Would not help explain.

Would help explain	Would not help explain	Statements
		The proportion of the population of Brazil that lives within close proximity to at least one museum is larger than that of Russia.
		Of the countries/political unions in the table, Russia has the fewest natural history museums per capita.
		Of the countries/political unions in the table, the three that spend the most money to promote their natural history museums are also those in which science is most highly valued.

PASSAGE 14

The table displays the performance scores of five computer models (Models V through Z) across three different tests (Tests A, B, and C). When sorted by a specific test, the models are arranged in ascending order based on their performance on that particular test, with the highest scores appearing at the top

Model	Test		
	A	B	C
X	10068	87	68
W	9675	104	82
Y	8369	121	103
Z	7667	130	93
V	6970	119	87

Sorted by Test B :

Model	Test		
	A	B	C
X	10068	87	68
W	9675	104	82
V	6970	119	87
Y	8369	121	103
Z	7667	130	93

Sorted by Test C :

Model	Test		
	A	B	C
X	10068	87	68
W	9675	104	82
V	6970	119	87
Z	7667	130	93
Y	8369	121	103

For each of the following performance tests, select Greater scores are better if greater numerical scores on that performance test indicate better performance. Otherwise, select Greater scores are worse.

Greater scores are better	Greater scores are worse	
		Test A
		Test B
		Test C

PASSAGE 15

Interstate Number	Length (Miles)	States Served	Westernmost State Served	Eastemmost State Served
1-10	2460	8	California	Florida
1-20	1539	6	Texas	South Carolina
1-40	2554	8	California	North Carolina
1-70	2153	10	Utah	Maryland
1-80	2900	11	California	New Jersey
1-90	3021	13	Washington	Massachusetts
1-94	1585	7	Montana	Michigan

The provided table presents data on the seven longest east-to-west Primary Interstate Highways in the United States. Along with the length of each Interstate in miles, the table includes the number of states that the Interstate serves and the western and eastern endpoints of the respective Interstate.

Consider each of the following statements about the Interstates. For each statement indicate whether the statement is true or false, based on the information provided in the table.

True	False	
		The ratio of the number of states served by the interstate with median length to the number of states served by the shortest interstate is equal to 4 to 3.
		The ratio of the length of the Interstate that serves the fewest states to the length of the Interstate that serves the most states is approximately 1 to 5.
		The Interstate with the median Interstate Number has a number of states served equal to the mode of the number of states served.

Answer Explanations

PASSAGE 1

1. D. 16530

For this question we need to know what is the % age is going on year over year.

From 32 to 29 to 26.6 to 24 to 22 to 20 it is approx. 10% each year.

The question required us to calculate the approximate total deaths in 1998

Let number of deaths in 1998 be x

$X \times 1.1 \times 1.1 = 20000$

$X = 16528.92$ which is approximately equal to 16530

The nearest answer is D

2. B. 2001 - 2002

percentage change in the ratio of number of deaths due to car accidents to total number of deaths year to year is equal to:

Year 2000 $\Rightarrow \frac{0.9}{20} \times 100 = 4.5\%$

Year 2001 $\Rightarrow \frac{1.12}{22} \times 100 = 5.09\%$

Year 2002 $\Rightarrow \frac{1.55}{24.2} \times 100 = 6.41\%$

Year 2003 $\Rightarrow \frac{2.02}{26.62} \times 100 = 7.59\%$

Year 2004 $\Rightarrow \frac{1.91}{29.28} \times 100 = 6.52\%$

Year 2005 $\Rightarrow \frac{2.42}{32.21} \times 100 = 7.51\%$

The question is the biggest difference between two years:

5,09 % (2001) to 6,41 % (2002) is the biggest difference of 1,32 %. So from 2001 to 2002 is the biggest difference in %, hence "B".

3. C. 1020

The percentage of deaths due to natural disasters in 2000 is the same as the percentage of deaths due to car accidents in 2001 = 5.09%

Approximately how many people died in 2000 due to natural disasters = 5.09/100 × 20 × 1000 = 1018

The nearest is C

4. E. It cannot be determined from the information given

We dont know the % difference of the numbers from 2000 to 2001, it can be everything. Wihtout the % or total 2001 number it cannot be determined from the information given.

PASSAGE 2

True	False	
✓		The median number of hurricanes in the Florida counties was higher than the median number of hurricanes in each of the other states' counties.
✓		The counties listed in the table that experienced the three greatest percent changes in population during the period are all part of the coastline region whose listed counties had the greater range in number of hurricanes during the same period.
	✓	The Gulf of Mexico coastline region experienced fewer hurricanes per county listed in the table, on average, than did the Atlantic coastline region.

(a) **No.** From the table we can clearly see that this exporter is only responsible for 49% of the nation's exports of French Roast Coffee. The majority needs to be more than 50%.

(b) **No.** There is no information in the table that would lead us to this conclusion. The table only shows the percentage of national share of exports, not the actual export quantities.

(c) **Yes.** The given producer is responsible for 32% of the nation's exports for light-roast coffee and is ranked in the 2nd place for exports in this category. Therefore, the producer who exports the most light-roast coffee will be greater than 32%. Therefore the top two exporters combined export a majority of the nation's light roast coffee.

PASSAGE 3

True	False	
✓		The median number of hurricanes in the Florida counties was higher than the median number of hurricanes in each of the other states' counties.
✓		The counties listed in the table that experienced the three greatest percent changes in population during the period are all part of the coastline region whose listed counties had the greater range in number of hurricanes during the same period.
	✓	The Gulf of Mexico coastline region experienced fewer hurricanes per county listed in the table, on average, than did the Atlantic coastline region.

(a) The median number of hurricanes in the Florida counties was higher than the median number of hurricanes in each of the other states' counties.

No. of hurricanes in Florida counties - 11,12,15

Median ⇒ 12

No. of hurricanes in Louisiana counties - 11,11,11,12,14

Median ⇒ 11

No. of hurricanes in North Carolina counties - 13,13,14

Median ⇒ 14

Clearly, the median number of hurricanes in the Florida counties was NOT higher than the median number of hurricanes in each of the other states' counties.

False

(b) The counties listed in the table that experienced the three greatest percent changes in population during the period are all part of the coastline region whose listed counties had the greater range in number of hurricanes during the same period.

Counties that experienced the three greatest percent changes in population during the period - Dare County, Palm Beach County, Miami-Dade County. All these 3 counties belong to the Atlantic coastline region.

Basically, the question stem is whether counties belonging to the Atlantic coastline had a greater range in the number of hurricanes than counties belonging to the Gulf of Mexico coastline?

Coastline region and its Range

Atlantic ⇒ 14 – 11 = 3

Gulf of Mexico ⇒ 15 – 11 = 4

False

(c) The Gulf of Mexico coastline region experienced fewer hurricanes per county listed in the table, on average, than did the Atlantic coastline region.

Total number of hurricanes experienced by the Gulf of Mexico coastline region – 73

The average number of hurricanes per county - 74/6 ⇒ 12.3

Total number of hurricanes experienced by the Atlantic coastline region – 63

The average number of hurricanes per county - 63/5 ⇒ 12.5

True

PASSAGE 4

Yes	No	
	✓	Marina will receive Certification A first.
✓		Marina will receive Certification B second.
	✓	Marina will receive Certification C third.

Sequence for Courses (based on the recommended sequence in the Stimulus)

D (Courses 1,6,7) → least number of courses

B (Courses 2,4) → least number of additional courses

A (Courses 5,9) → least number of additional courses

A (Courses 3,8) → least number of additional courses

Based on the above sequence, we get the answers as

Q.1. Marina will receive Certification A first. → NO

Q.2. Marina will receive Certification B second. → YES

Q.3. Marina will receive Certification C third. → NO

PASSAGE 5

Yes	No	
	✓	On average, the lowest score given for judges who had judged in 3 Pan-Global Games was higher than that for judges who had competed in 3 Pan-Global Games.
✓		The judge with the greatest absolute difference between the highest score given and lowest score given also had the greatest percent difference between the lowest score given and highest score given.
✓		The average (arithmetic mean) number of Pan-Global Games that judges participated in as judges was higher than the average number of Pan-Global Games that judges participated in as competitors.
✓		The probability that a given judge competed in more Pan-Global Games than she judged is the same as the probability that a judge gave a higher average score as a judge than she received as a competitor.

(1) No,since the lowest score given for judges who had judged in 3 Pan-Global Games (6.03) was lower than that for judges who had competed in 3 Pan-Global Games(7).

(2) Yes,Finland has the highest difference between the highest score and lowest score given (4.7) and even the % is greatest since here only the numerator(difference between the two values is greater than the denominator,when taking the lowest given as denominator

(3) Yes since the Avg for participation as a judge is 24/9 while as a competitor is 22/9

(4) Yes, since the probability that a given judge competed in more Pan-Global Games than she judged is= 3/9 and the probability that a judge gave a higher average score as a judge than she received as a competitor is 3/9, so both are same

PASSAGE 6

1.

Would help explain	Would not help explain	Statement
	✓	Per capita spending on the performing arts is the highest among communities that invest heavily in the arts and that best advertise the performing arts.
✓		Most major sporting events take place in urban areas, where the average age of residents is significantly lower than that of rural or suburban areas.
✓		A greater percentage of towns contain at least one movie theater than contain at least one performing arts venue.

2.

Can be reasonably inferred	Cannot be reasonably inferred	
	✓	In Federland, per capita spending on sporting events tends to decrease as individuals age.
	✓	The average age of Federland citizens who attended performing arts events in 2015 was under the age of 45.
✓		At least 45% of Federland citizens under the age of 25 attended both a sporting event and a gallery or museum in 2015.

PASSAGE 7

True	False	Statements
✓		In each store whose average customer age falls between 34 and 36, the number of self-check express lanes is above average.
✓		There is a negative correlation between the number of self-check unlimited lanes and the average customer age.
	✓	Stores in this table that have fewer self-check express lanes than the chain-wide average are less likely to have restaurants than stores that have more self-check express lanes than the chain-wide average.

The last row in the "Self-check express lanes" column indicates that the average number of self-check express lanes per store is 6.89. The only two stores with average customer ages between 34 and 36 are Store A and Store F, each of which has 8 self-check express lanes-more than the average number, 6.89. So in each store with an average customer age between 34 and 36, the number of self-check express lanes is above average.

The correct answer is True.

Sorting the table by the "Average customer age" column, we see that stores with higher average customer ages generally tend to have fewer self-check unlimited lanes. Thus, the table shows a negative correlation between average customer age and the number of self-check unlimited lanes.

The correct answer is True.

Sorting the table by the "Self-check express lanes" column, we see that all three stores with less than the average number of self-check express lanes have restaurants, whereas only one store of the six with more than the average number of self-check express lanes has a restaurant. Thus, stores with fewer self-check express lanes than average are more likely to have restaurants than are stores with more self-check express lanes than average, not less likely.

The correct answer is False.

PASSAGE 9

Would help explain	Would not help explain	Statements
✓		The proportion of the population of New Zealand that lives close to the ocean is larger than that of South Africa. Note that each youngster plays only one sport.
✓		Relative to other sports in South Africa, professional cricket players earn more money than any other professional sport players do.
	✓	People in coastal countries have a greater interest in water sports than those in inland countries.

45% plays cricket in South Africa which is greater than any other sports in SA so would help explain.

Australia is a coastal country but still, it has an almost equal proportion of sports interest while there is a different story for New Zealand so would not help explain

PASSAGE 10

True	False	
✓		A majority of the managers who oversaw an increase in sales over the previous year have an employee satisfaction rating higher than the median.
	✓	There is a positive correlation between the size of a branch's sales force and that branch's change in year-over-year sales.
✓		The branch that had the highest sales in the previous year has underground parking.

(a) Median of satisfactory rate should be 49-ish. Percent change over previous year - those with increases consists of 6 different managers. Majority would mean 4 out of 6. Turns out 4 out of 6 have satisfactory rate > 49. Answer True.

(b) No positive correlation as a decrease in year-over-year sales happens consistently even though sales force size increased. Answer False.

(c) Branch that had highest sales in previous year should be the ones around 100+ but yet with a -ve percent change in sales from the previous year, which means they dropped but still have the highest yearly sales (and the highest yearly sales is 100-ish). Stripley had a sales of 112.2 from the previous year which is the highest - it has underground parking. Answer True.

PASSAGE 11

Yes	No	Statements
✓		If range is taken into consideration, then humidity in Sanatcruz is more consistent than humidity in Colaba.
	✓	Median of temperature difference between maximum and minimum temperature in Santacruz is more than that in Colaba.
	✓	Mean maximum temperature of 1st June is lower than that of 2nd & 4th June.

First statement : If range is taken into consideration, then humidity in Sanatcruz is more consistent than humidity in Colaba.

My answer is (YES)

Range of humidity in Sanatcruz: 10

Range of humidity in Colaba: 13

Second statement : Median of temperature difference between maximum and minimum temperature in Santacruz is more than that in Colaba.

My answer is (NO)

temperature difference between maximum and minimum temperature in Santacruz: 5.9 5.4 7 6.6 6.4

Median: 6.4

temperature difference between maximum and minimum temperature in Colaba: 7.1 6.9 5.6 5.6 6.6

Median: 6.6

6.4 < 6.6

Third statement : Mean maximum temperature of 1st June is lower than that of 2nd & 4th June.

My answer is (NO)

Mean maximum temperature of 1st June: 35

Mean maximum temperature of 2nd June: 34.85 < 35

No need to check 4th June

PASSAGE 12

Yes	No	Statements
✓		The average (arithmetic mean) number of stations in the European subway systems is more than double the average (arithmetic mean) number of stations in the South American subway systems.
✓		The number of lines in the New York subway system exceeds the median number of lines by more than 13.
	✓	The London subway system has the greatest total length as measured by kilometers of lines.

(a) The arithmetic mean of the number of stations in the European subway systems

$= \text{(Paris, France)} + \text{(Madrid, Spain)} + \text{(London, England)}$

$= (302 + 301 + 270) = \frac{873}{3} = 291$

The arithmetic mean of the number of stations in the South American subway systems

$= \text{(Buenos Aires, Argentina)} + \text{(Santiago, Chile)}$

$= \frac{(118 + 86)}{2}$

Double this number is $= (118 + 86) = 204$

$291 > 204 \rightarrow$ YES

(b) Order the data by the Number of lines for this question. Then

The number of lines in the New York subway system = 25

The median number of lines = That of London = 11

$25 - 11 = 14 > 13 \rightarrow$ YES

(c) For this, keep the following formulae in mind

Average Line Length = (Total Line Length) / (Total Number of lines)

Then order the data by the Number of lines. Then

For London $\rightarrow 11 \times 36.55 = 402.05$

Examine the data. We can clearly see that for China, $20 \times 28.6 = 572$.

$572 > 402$. So Wrong $\rightarrow$ NO

PASSAGE 13

Would help explain	Would not help explain	Statements
✓		The proportion of the population of Brazil that lives within close proximity to at least one museum is larger than that of Russia.
✓		Of the countries/political unions in the table, Russia has the fewest natural history museums per capita.
	✓	Of the countries/political unions in the table, the three that spend the most money to promote their natural history museums are also those in which science is most highly valued.

RO1: Evaluate

If this statement is to be explanatory, it would likely be because, on average, people living closer to museums are also more likely to visit museums. Sorting on Natural history museum shows that, for the two museum categories (natural history and science/technology), a greater percentage of Brazil's population than of Russia's visits in a single year. Therefore, if, on average, Brazil's population lives closer than Russia's to museums, it could help explain information in the table.

The correct answer is Would help explain.

RO2: Evaluate

If this statement is to be explanatory, it would likely be because, among the countries/political unions listed in the table, the lowest average number of institutions per capita is associated with the lowest proportion of the population visiting such institutions. Sorting the table by Natural history museum shows that, among the countries/political unions shown, Russia has the smallest proportion of its population visiting natural history museums in a single year.

The correct answer is Would help explain.

RO3: Evaluate

If this statement is to be explanatory, it would likely be because the countries/political unions in which people are most likely to visit natural history museums are also those in which people are most likely to visit science/ technology museums. However, sorting the table by Natural history museum and Science/technology museum shows that the country/political union with the fifth highest proportion of the population visiting natural history museums (China) has the second highest proportion visiting science/technology museums, a proportion that is higher than that of the countries/political unions with the first (US), third (European Union), and fourth (Japan) highest proportions in the natural history category.

The correct answer is would not help explain.

PASSAGE 14

Greater scores are better	Greater scores are worse	
✓		Test A
	✓	Test B
	✓	Test C

The scores when sorted by score A is seen to be in descending order, that is, the greater scores are better

The scores when sorted by score B is seen to be in ascending order, that is, the greater scores are worse

The scores when sorted by score C is seen to be in ascending order, that is, the greater scores are worse

PASSAGE 15

True	False	
✓		The ratio of the number of states served by the interstate with median length to the number of states served by the shortest interstate is equal to 4 to 3.
	✓	The ratio of the length of the Interstate that serves the fewest states to the length of the Interstate that serves the most states is approximately 1 to 5.
	✓	The Interstate with the median Interstate Number has a number of states served equal to the mode of the number of states served.

The ratio of the number of states served by the interstate with median length to the number of states served by the shortest interstate is equal to 4 to 3......True

IS with median length (ISML) is I-10. Number of states served = 8

IS with shortest length (ISSL) is I-20. Number of states served = 6

$$\frac{\text{ISML}}{\text{ISSL}} = \frac{8}{6} = \frac{4}{3}$$

The ratio of the length of the Interstate that serves the fewest states to the length of the Interstate that serves the most states is approximately 1 to 5......False

IS serving fewest states is I-20 (serves 6 states). Length (ISFL) = 1539

IS serving most states is I-90 (serves 13 states). Length (ISML) = 3021

$$\frac{\text{ISFL}}{\text{ISML}} = \frac{1539}{3021}$$ Is approximately equal to ½

The Interstate with the median Interstate Number has a number of states served equal to the mode of the number of states served......False

IS with median IS number is I-70. Number of states it serves = 10

Mode of the number of states served = 8

Chapter 3

Graphic Interpretation

PASSAGE 1

The figure below shows the growth of global deinopid museum collections from 1800 through 2019, by decade, a period in which no such collections were decommissioned.

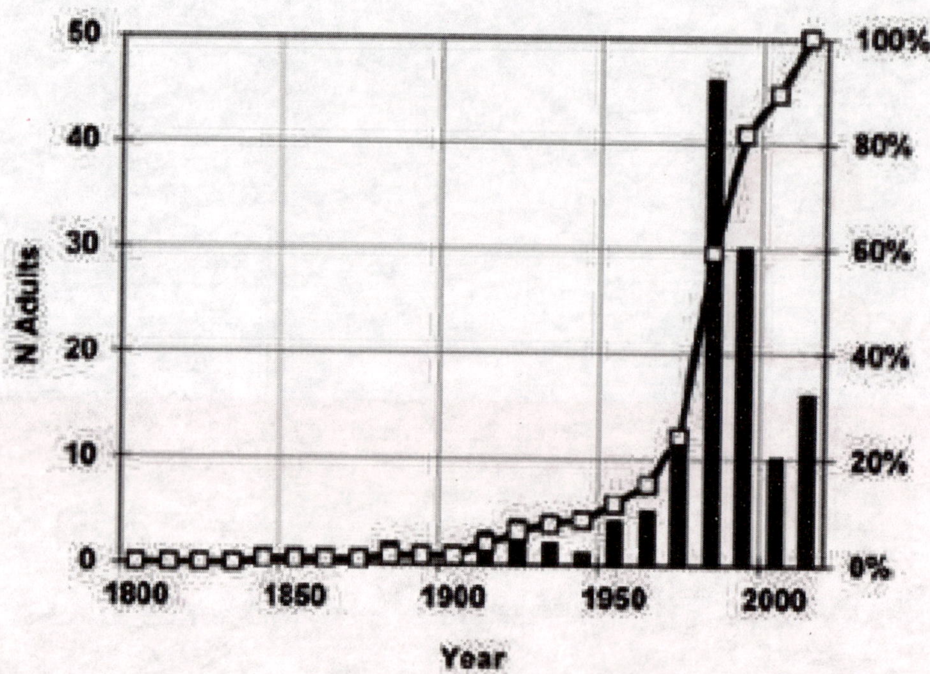

1. According to the figure, the total number of current deinopid museum collections is approximately ___________.

A. 100

B. 105

C. 120

D. 135

E. 150

2. According to the figure, in the 1980s the number of global deinopid museum collections grew by approximately_____________percent.

A. 30

B. 45

C. 50

D. 55

E. 60

PASSAGE 2

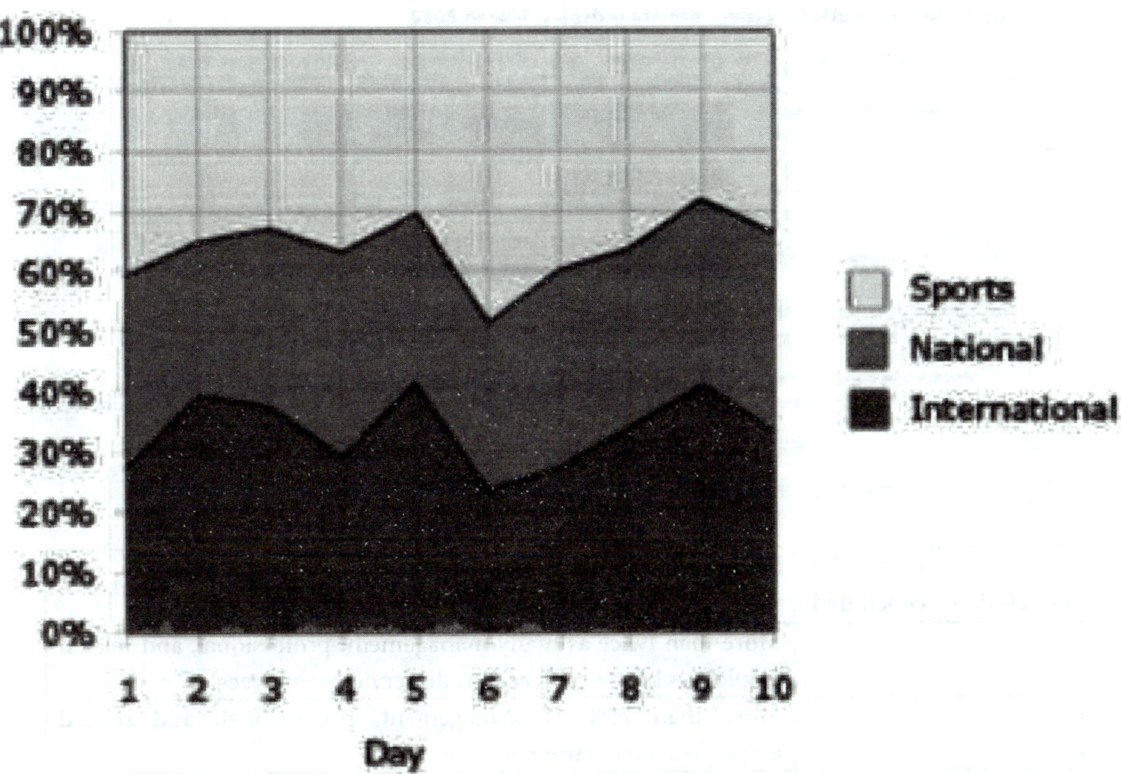

The graph is a stacked line graph that displays the proportion of visits to the three main news web pages of the Star news network. The x-axis represents the 10-day period during which the data was collected, while the y-axis represents the percentage of visits. The study did not differentiate between multiple visits by the same user on the same day or different days; it simply recorded the number of times the three websites were loaded

1. The news page whose percentage of hits was the most consistent over the 10 days measured was____________.

A. the international page

B. the national page

C. the sports page

2. If the total number of visits to Star doubled from Day 6 to Day 9, then the number of visits to the sports page____________ over the same period.

A. increased

B. remained constant

C. decreased

PASSAGE 3

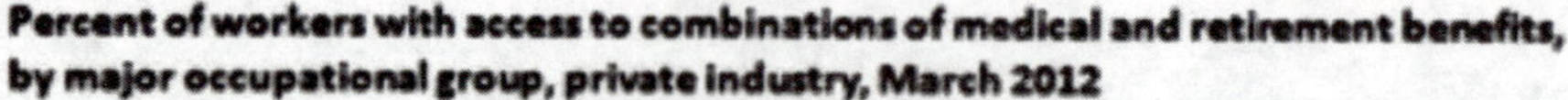

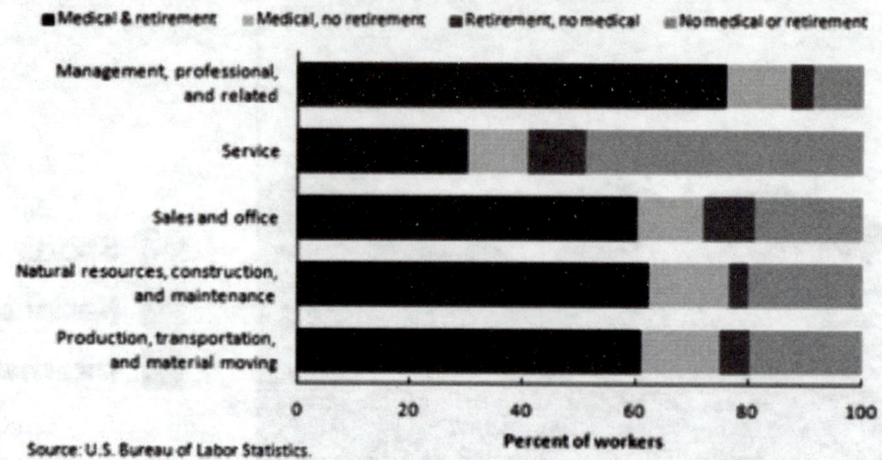

Can be concluded	Cannot be concluded	Statement
		More than twice as many management, professional, and related employees have health care as do service employees.
		More than 75% of management, professional, and related employees have retirement benefits.
		A higher percentage of natural resources, construction, and maintenance workers than of production, transportation, and material moving workers have some sort of retirement benefits.

PASSAGE 4

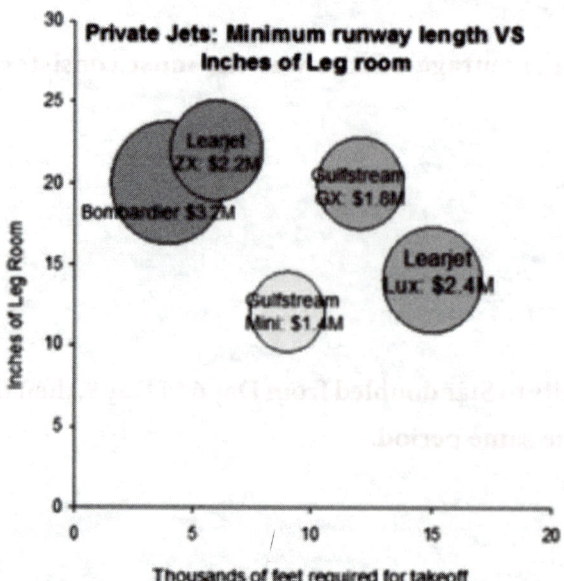

1. **The business jet that offers the best value per inch of leg room is the____________.**

   A. Bombardier

   B. Learjet ZX

   C. Gulfstream Mini

   D. Gulfstream GX

   E. Learjet Lux

2. **The owner of a Learjet Lux would have to pay____________more dollars per foot required for takeoff on a Bombardier?**

   A. 460$

   B. 450$

   C. 640$

   D. 720$

PASSAGE 5

The graph illustrates how voters' initial stance on working-time reduction affects the likelihood of their final decision aligning with their initial preference. For each political party represented in the graph, less than 10% of their supporters initially opposed the idea of reducing working hours.

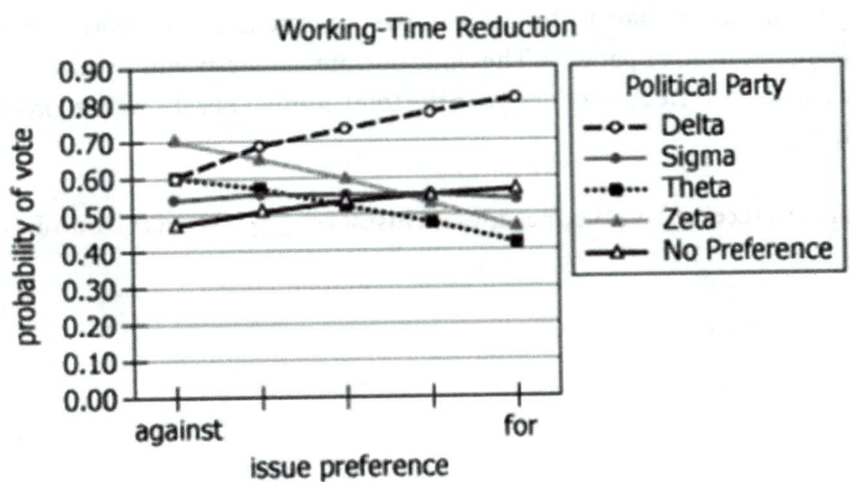

1. **Members of the____________party are most apt to vote according to their previously stated preference regarding the issue of working-time reduction.**

   A. Sigma

   B. Theta

   C. Delta

   D. Zeta

2. Members of the______________party are most apt to vote against the issue of working-time reduction if their previously stated preference regarding the issue of working-time reduction was also against.

A. Sigma

B. Theta

C. Delta

D. Zeta

PASSAGE 6

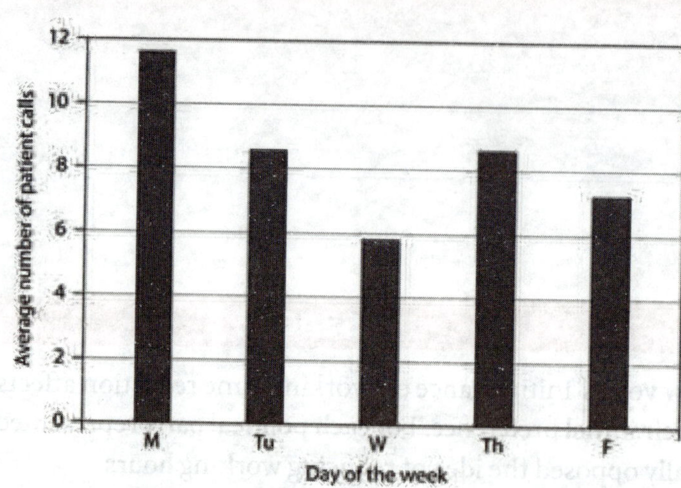

The given graph presents a bar chart featuring five bars, representing the average quantity of hourly calls received by a medical clinic from its patients. The clinic operates and responds to calls on weekdays, specifically Monday through Friday. Over the span of one year, the total number of calls was recorded and an average was calculated for each day.

1. The number of calls received on Wednesdays is closest to _______% of the number of calls received on Mondays.

A. 6

B. 12

C. 50

D. 60

E. 200

2. The relationship between number of calls received and time since the beginning of the week is best described as __________.

A. not meaningful

B. negative

C. positive

3. **Based on the information shown in the graph, if the clinic wishes to reduce the cost of maintaining its office staff while minimizing disruptions in service to its patients, it should cut down on the number of staff assigned to answer phone calls on __________.**

A. Mondays

B. Tuesdays

C. Wednesdays

D. Thursdays

E. Fridays

PASSAGE 7

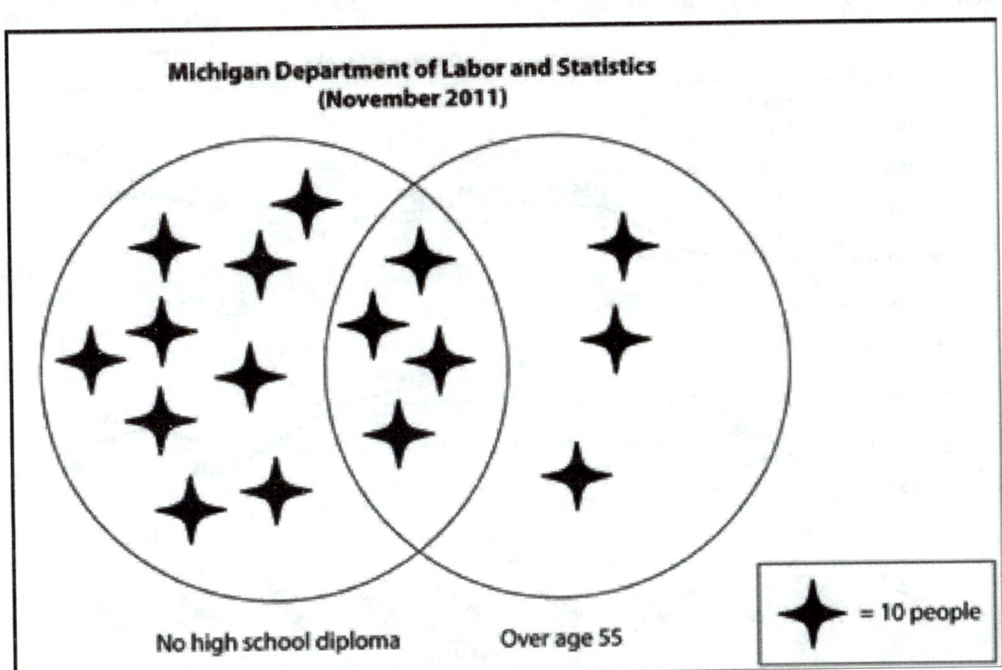

In a survey conducted with a sample of 1,000 individuals filing for unemployment, participants were asked to disclose details regarding their age and educational background. The Venn diagram above illustrates the survey findings, where each symbol represents a group of 10 individuals within the sample.

1. **Out of the entire sample, the probability that a randomly chosen person over age 55 has no high school diploma is __________.**

A. 1 out of 4

B. 3 out of 4

C. 4 out of 7

D. 7 out of 16

2. Out of the entire sample, the probability that a randomly chosen person with no high school diploma is over the age of 55 is________.

A. 1 out of 4

B. 4 out of 9

C. 4 out of 13

D. 9 out of 16

PASSAGE 8

The given graph depicts the stock price trends over a period of 10 days for two competing shoe companies listed on the NASDAQ. The data represents the stock prices recorded between January 10th and January 20th in the year 2015. The upper line represents the stock prices for NKE, while the lower line represents the stock prices for AG.

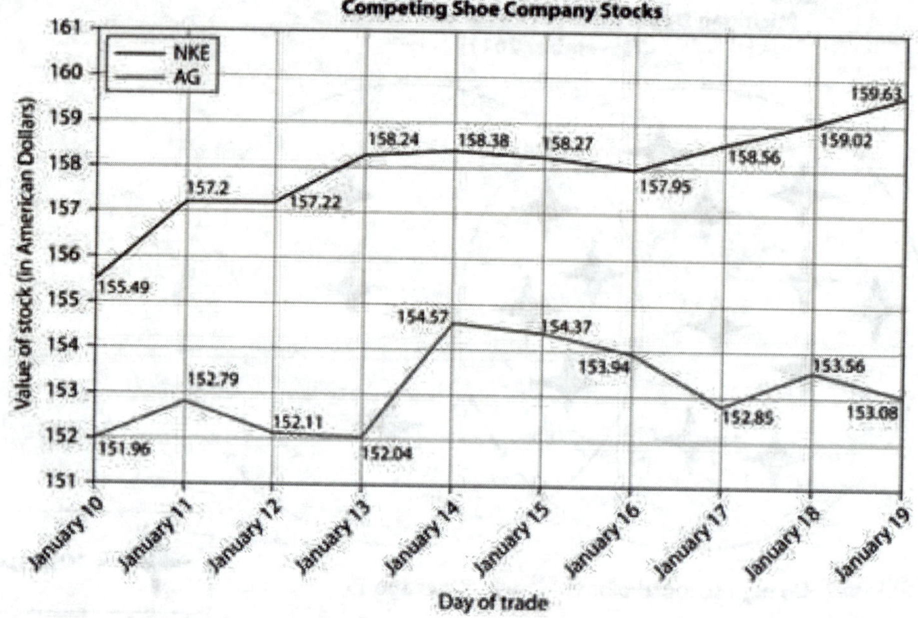

1. The percent change in the value of NKE stock over the entire ten days is about ________ the percent change in the value of AG stock over that same period.

A. equal to

B. 2 times

C. 4 times

2. For the span between January 13th and January 16th, the average (arithmetic mean) value of AG stock falls approximately between ________ dollars.

A. 151 and 153

B. 153 and 155

C. 157 and 159

PASSAGE 9

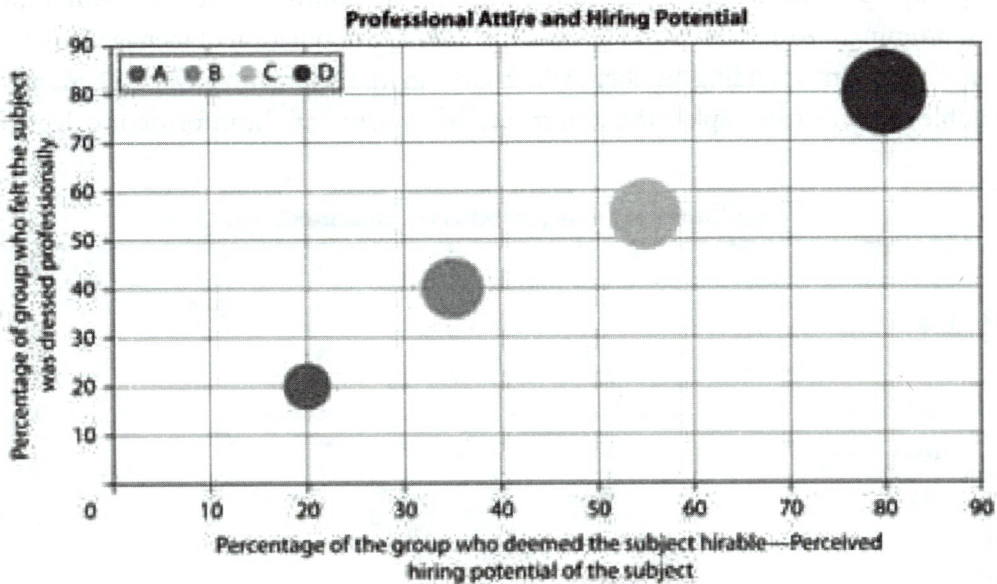

The provided graph illustrates the outcomes of a survey conducted among four distinct focus groups labeled A, B, C, and D. Each group was presented with a different image of the same man dressed in attire suitable for a professional job interview. The images varied in terms of the number of professional indicators, such as a tie, formal shoes, a briefcase, and other factors, with each subsequent image containing more professional markers than the previous one. Following the viewing of the image, focus group members were asked two questions: "Did you perceive the candidate as dressed professionally?" and "How likely is the candidate to be hired for the position?"

The positioning of each circle on the graph represents the perceived level of professionalism associated with the outfit in a particular photo, based on the percentage of focus group members who considered the attire as professional. The relative size of the circle indicates the extent to which focus group members indicated that the candidate would be hired for the job.

1. **The relationship between the percentage of the group who felt the subject was dressed professionally and the percentage of the group who believed the subject would be hired is ______.**

   A. negative

   B. zero

   C. positive

2. **The percentage of people in group B who felt the candidate was dressed professionally is closest to ______ times the percentage of people in group A who felt the candidate was dressed professionally.**

   A. 1.5

   B. 2

   C. 2.5

PASSAGE 10

The provided graph presents a scatter plot containing 35 data points, where each point represents the teen birth rate in a prominent American city. The data includes the population of teenage females, aged 15 to 19, measured against the corresponding number of births within that population over a 12-month period. Choose the most suitable response to complete the statements below based on the information depicted in the graph.

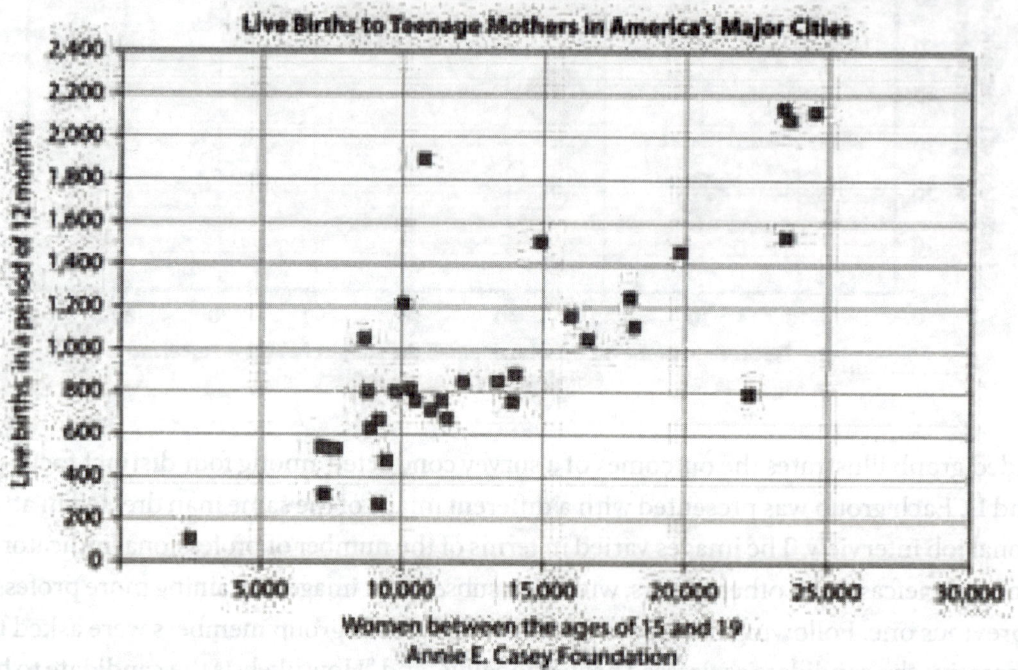

1. **The city with the largest population of 15- to 19-year-old women had about ______ percent as many births in that age group as the city with the smallest population.**

   A. 5

   B. 10

   C. 21

   D. 210

   E. 2,100

2. **The relationship between the number of women between 15 and 19 and the number of births within that population is ______.**

   A. negative

   B. zero

   C. positive

PASSAGE 11

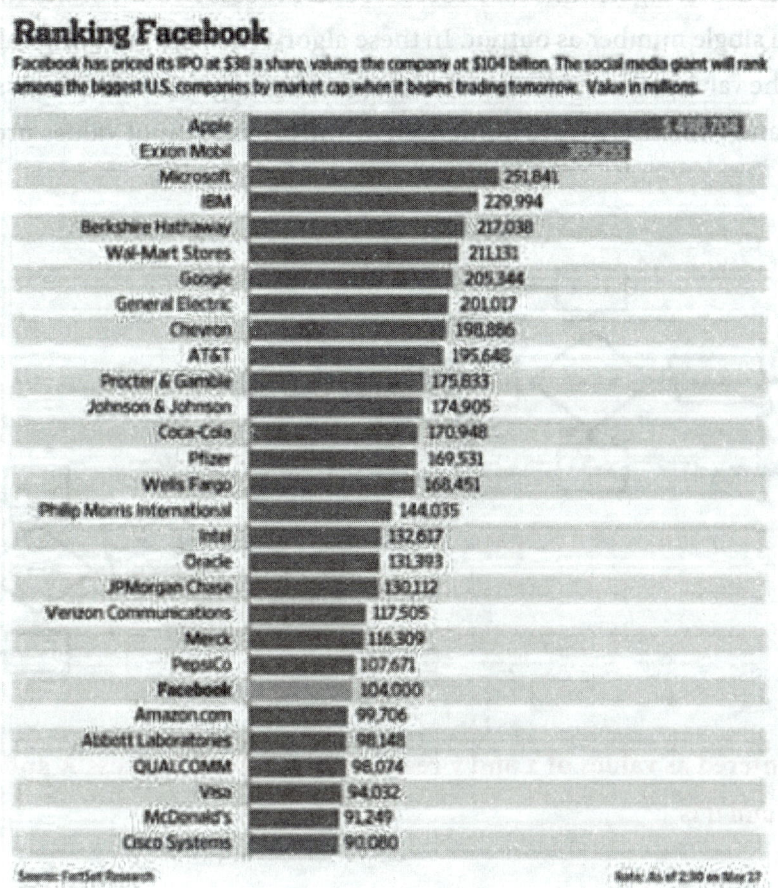

The graph shows the market capitalization value in millions of dollars for the largest companies in the market as of May 17, 2012. Facebook, priced at $38 for the IPO, is bolded and rankings in at $104 B market cap value.

1. **Facebook's stock would have to increase to roughly________________per share in order for Facebook's market capitalization value to reach the value of Apple's market cap.**

   A. 145$

   B. 183$

   C. 200$

2. **Of the 29 companies listed, the top 10 make up________________the remaining 19 companies combined.**

   A. More than

   B. The same

   C. Less than

PASSAGE 12

The given flowcharts depict algorithms for Process A and Process B, both of which require two integers as input and produce a single number as output. In these algorithms, the resulting values of variables p and q are determined by the values of variables x and y after undergoing a specific process. It is important to note that the values of x and y themselves are influenced by the original input values provided to the respective process.

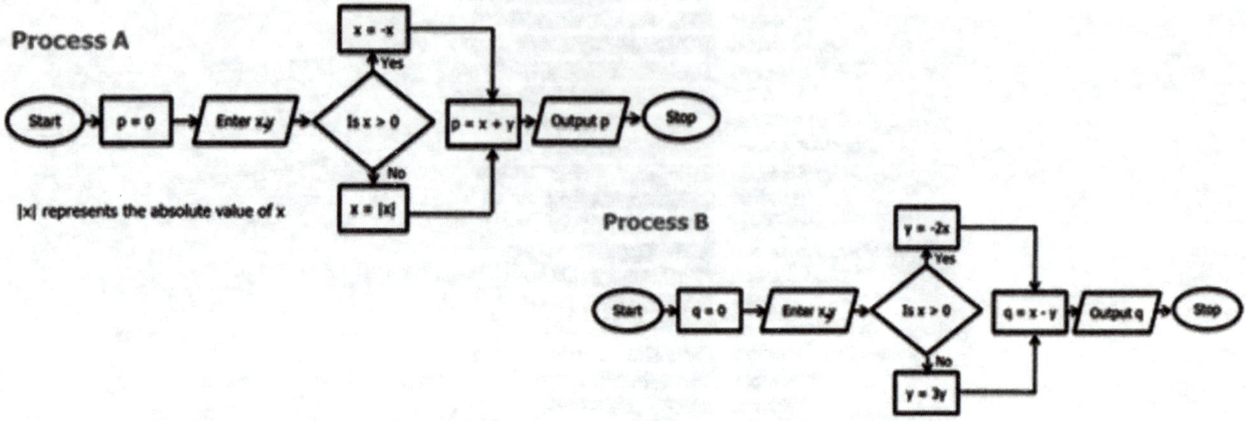

1. **If -2 and 1 are entered as values of x and y respectively in both Process A and Process B., the sum of output values p and q is ____________**

   A. –8

   B. –2

   C. 2

   D. 4

2. **If 2 and -3 are entered as values of x and y respectively in both Process A and Process B the value of |p-q| is ____________**

   A. 1

   B. 2

   C. 11

   D. 12

PASSAGE 13

Performance of a blue-chip company over 6 years has been represented in the chart below. Each circle indicates ratio of Revenue to Profit (value mentioned in the circle). The horizontal axis shows profits.

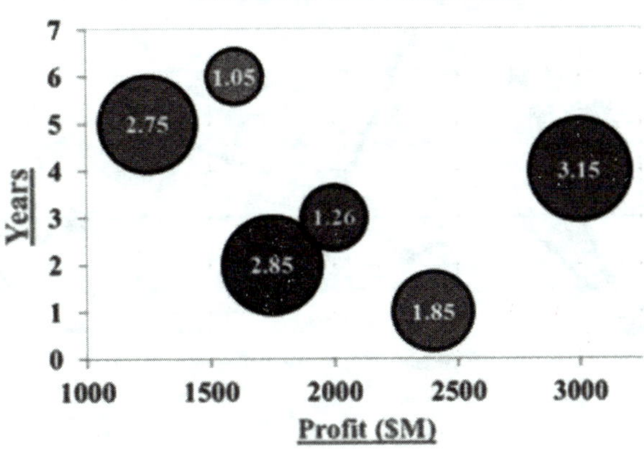

1. **The highest profit comparative to revenue was in the year __________.**

   A. 1

   B. 3

   C. 4

   D. 5

   E. 6

2. **Profit to expense ratio is least in the year ___________.**

   A. 1

   B. 2

   C. 3

   D. 4

   E. 6

3. **$ ___________ M was the least expense incurred in the 6 year period.**

   A. 60

   B. 80

   C. 520

   D. 800

   E. 1250

PASSAGE 14

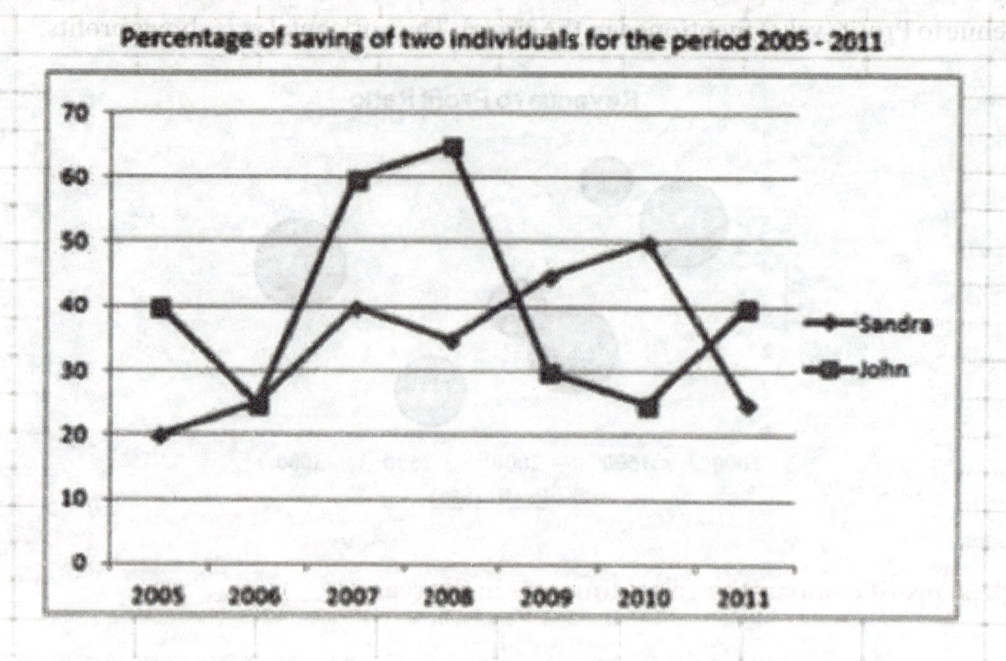

The figure above plots the percent of their incomes that John and Sandra each saved each year from 2005 to 2011.

1. If Sandra spent a total of $26000 in 2008, how much money did she save in 2008?

A. $4000

B. $14000

C. $18000

2. The incomes of Sandra and John in 2007 were in the ratio 4:5. What was the ratio of their expenses?

A. 4:5

B. 5:4

C. 6:5

3. If Sandra and John each saved $18000 in 2009, what was the difference in their incomes in that year?

A. $2700

B. $15000

C. $20000

PASSAGE 15

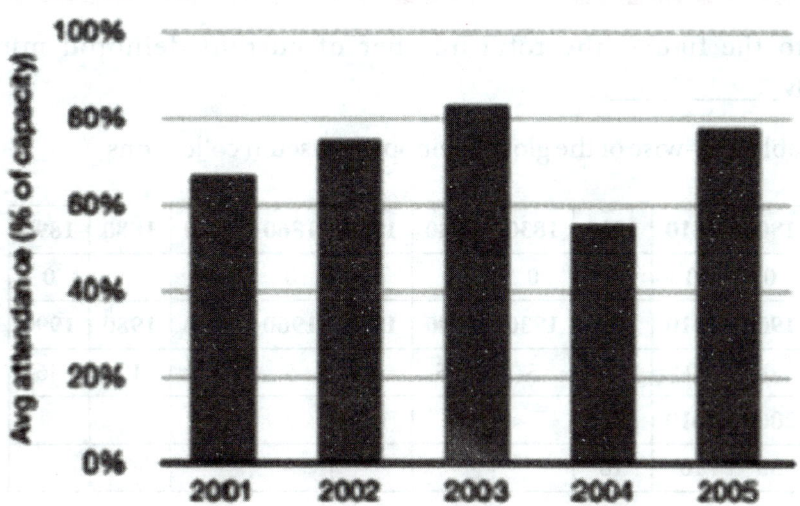

The attached chart graphs the average attendance per game for a certain sports franchise for 5 seasons, represented as percentage of stadium capacity. The stadium's capacity was increased from 60,000 seats to 90,000 seats before the 2004 season.

1. The franchise's highest average attendance occurred in ___________.

A. 2002

B. 2003

C. 2004

D. 2005

2. The highest total attendance for a season (the sum of individual game attendances) occurred in ___________.

A. 2002

B. 2003

C. 2004

D. It cannot be determined

3. From 2003 to 2004, the average attendance per game ___________.

A. Increased by more than 5%

B. Decreased by more than 5%

C. Stayed approximately the same

Answer Explanations

PASSAGE 1

1. According to the figure, the total number of current deinopid museum collections is approximately____________.

First make a table year-wise of the global deinopid museum collections

1800	1810	1820	1830	1840	1850	1860	1870	1880	1890
0	0	0	0	1	0	0	0	1	0
1900	**1910**	**1920**	**1930**	**1940**	**1950**	**1960**	**1970**	**1980**	**1990**
0	0	2	3	2.5	1	5	6	12	46
2000	**2010**	**2019**							
30	10	16							

Now Calculate for each year = 0 + 0 + 0 + 0 + 1 + 0 + 0 + 0 + 1 + 0 + 0 + 0 + 2 + 3 + 2.5 + 1 + 5 + 6 + 12 + 46 + 3 = +10 + 16 = 135.5 = D

Answer: D

2. According to the figure, in the 1980s the number of global deinopid museum collections grew by approximately____________percent.

To answer the second question add the global deinopid museum collections till the year 1970 and then compare it with the year 1980.

Global deinopid museum collections till the year 1970 = 21.5

Global deinopid museum collections till the year 1980 = 21.5 + 12 = 33.5

Percent change = 1221.5 = 55.81 = 1221.5 = 55.81% (33.5 – 21.5 = 12)(33.5 – 21.5 = 12)

Answer: D

PASSAGE 2

1. It is worth noting that the percentage of visits to a specific page on any given day is the size of the corresponding shade for that day. We observe that the size of "National" is more or less consistent (Decreases in "Sports" generally correspond to similar decreases in "International". Same for increases).

Answer: B

2. Percentages corresponding to "Sports" for the two days:

Day 6 : slightly less than 50%

Day 10 : slightly greater than 30%

30% of a quantity twice as large as another quantity is clearly larger than 50% of the smaller quantity.

Answer : A

PASSAGE 3

Can be concluded	Cannot be concluded	Statement
		More than twice as many management, professional, and related employees have health care as do service employees.
		More than 75% of management, professional, and related employees have retirement benefits.
		A higher percentage of natural resources, construction, and maintenance workers than of production, transportation, and material moving workers have some sort of retirement benefits.

More than twice as many management, professional, and related employees have health care as do service employees.....

Cannot Be Concluded

Almost 88%, of Management, Professional & Related employees have health care benefits, but only 42-43% of Service employees have those benefits. We can conclude that the %age of MP&R is twice that of Service employees, but since there are no details on the number of employees in each segment, this statement cannot be concluded.

More than 75% of management, professional, and related employees have retirement benefits.....

Can Be concluded

Employees in MP&R who have Medical & Retirement benefits are almost 78%, and those with Retirement and no Medical are almost 3-4%. Total MP&R with Retirement Benefits ~ 81%-82%. So, this statement can be concluded.

A higher percentage of natural resources, construction, and maintenance workers than of production, transportation, and material moving workers have some sort of retirement benefits.....

Cannot Be Concluded

%age of Natural Resource, Construction, and Maintenance workers with some sort of retirement benefits:

Medical & Retirement ~ 62%

Retirement & No Medical ~ 3%%

Total = 65%

%age of Production, Transportation, and Material moving workers with some sort of retirement benefits:

Medical & Retirement ~ 61%

Retirement & No Medical ~ 7%%

Total = 68%

PASSAGE 4

1. Gulfstream Mini = 1.4/12.5 = 0.112.

   Similarly for others :

   Learjet Lux = 0.184.

   Gulfstream GX-0.9.

   Learjet ZX-0.11

   Bombardier = 0.16.

   Hence Gulfstream GX

   Answer: D

2. Lear jet Lux = 2.4/15 = 0.16

   Bombardier = 3.2/4 = 0.8

   Difference in both = 0.8-0.16 = .64

   Now convert millioons and thousands of feet you get 640

   Answer: C

PASSAGE 5

1. **Members of the____________party are most apt to vote according to their previously stated preference regarding the issue of working-time reduction.**

   What's asked is which teams previously stated reference/actual preference is the highest, => which party voted for in the previously stated reference and in the actual preference.

   ⇒ the probability for such team would be highest.

   Thus, we can infer from the graph, that the probability is maximum for Delta party (~ 0.8).

   Answer C.

2. **Members of the______________party are most apt to vote against the issue of working-time reduction if their previously stated preference regarding the issue of working-time reduction was also against.**

   The party which would be most apt to vote against, would be which has a higher probability in against and a lesser one in for.

   From the graph,we can infer that the in case of against the Zeta has the highest probability which goes from 0.70 to 0.45, => Zeta's party members are most apt to vote against if their previous vote was also against.

   Answer D.

PASSAGE 6

1. Average Calls (Wednesday) / Average Calls (Monday) = 5.75 / 11.5 = 0.5 = 50%

   Answer C

2. No clear pattern (whether increasing / decreasing) over the week is deduced from the Graph

   Not Meaningful

   Answer A

3. Since the average number of calls (on Wednesdays) is the minimum, the clinic should cut the number of staff on Wednesdays

   Wednesdays

   Answer C

PASSAGE 7

For the given sample of 1000,

No High School Diploma; < 55 years = 90 ....(1)

No High School Diploma; > 55 years = 40 ....(2)

High School Diploma; > 55 years = 30 ....(3)

thus, High School Diploma; < 55 years = 1000– (90 + 40 + 30) = 840 ....(4)

Total sample = 1000

---

1. Persons over age 55 = 70

   $>$ 55 years; No High School Diploma = 40

   Probability = 40/70 = 4/7

   Answer C

2. Persons No High School Diploma = 130 (ie, 90+40)

   No High School Diploma; > 55 years; = 40

   Probability = 40/130 = 4/13

   Answer C

PASSAGE 8

1. NKE stock → 155.49 to 159.63

   (% change) = (159.63 - 155.49) / 155.49

   = 4.14 / 155.49

   = 2.7 (approx)

AG stock → 151.96 to 153.08

(% change) = (153.08 - 151.96) /151.96

= 1.12 / 151.96

= 0.7 (approx)

Thus, the answer = 2.7 / 0,.7 = 4 times (approx)

Answer C

2. For the AG stock, stock prices for Jan 13 to Jan 16 = 152.04 , 154.57 , 154.37, 153.94

   Hence, the mean = (152.04 + 154.57 + 154.37 + 153.94) / 4 = 153.73 (value between 153 and 155)

   Answer B

PASSAGE 9

1. % of the group who felt the subject was dressed professionally → The position of each circle on the graph.

   Degree to which focus group members indicated that the candidate would be hired for the job → The relative size of the circle.

   For any particular group, say A/B/C/D,

   As the % of the group who felt the subject was dressed professionally (indicated by the position shift to the right on the Y-axis of the graph) ie, increases, so does the Degree to which focus group members indicated that the candidate would be hired for the job (indicated by the relative size of the circle) increases.

   Answer C

2. For the group B, the Graph shows % (Hired Professionally) = 40%

   For the group A, the Graph shows % (Hired Professionally) = 20%

   Answer B

PASSAGE 10

1. Using the Scatter Plot,

   City with the smallest population (ie, 2500) ... No of Births = 100

   City with the largest population (ie, 24000) ... No of Births = 2100

   So, the 21 times (ie, 2100%)

   Answer E

2. Using the Scatter Plot, it can be seen that number of women (increases to the right along X-axis), number of child births (increases to the top along Y-axis).

   Thus, the Graph has a Positive slope.

   Answer C

PASSAGE 11

1. Apple's market cap is ~ \$499B. Therefore, Apple's market cap is 498/104~500/100 = 5 times bigger than Facebook's. Hence, Facebook's share price would have to increase 5 times to match Apple's. \$38 × 5 = \$190. \$183 is closer to \$190 than \$200, thus \$183 is the answer.

   Answer B

2. The top 10 ~ (\$499+\$385+\$252+\$230+\$217+\$211+\$205+\$201+\$199+\$196)B = \$2.595T.

   The remaining 19 ~ (\$176 + \$175 + \$171 + \$170 + \$168 + \$144 + \$133 + \$131 + \$130 + \$118 + \$116 + \$108 + \$104 + \$100 + \$98 + \$98 + \$98 + \$94 + \$91 + \$91)B = \$2.514T. Hence top 10 make up more than remaining 19.

   Answer A

PASSAGE 12

1. In process A and B value entered is $x = -2$ and $y = 1$

   For process A $x = -2$, $X < 0$ then $x = |X|$ so value of x is changed to 2

   Value of P = $X + Y = 2 + 1 = 3$

   For process B $x = -2$, $X < 0$ then $y = 3y$ so value of y is changed to 3

   Value of Q = $x - y = -2-3 = -5$

   The sum of values of p and q is $-5 + 3 = -2$

   Answer B

2. In process A and B value entered is $x = 2$ and $y = -3$

   For process A- $x = 2$, $x > 0$ so value of x is converted to $-x$, so value of $x = -2$

   Value of $p = x + y = -3-2 = -5$

   For process B $x = 2$, $X > 0$ then $y = -2x$ so value of y is changed to -4

   Value of Q = $x - y = 2 + 4 = 6$

   value of $|p - q| = |-5 -6| = |-11| = 11$

   Answer C

PASSAGE 13

1. E
2. D
3. B

PASSAGE 14

1. From Graph, In 2008, Sandra saved 35% of income. Let her income be x.

   So she spent $= x - 0.35x = 0.65x$ which is given as 26000

   $\Rightarrow 0.65x = 26000$

   $x = 40000$

   So Sandra saved $0.35x = 0.35*40000 = 14000$

   Answer B.

2. Given : The incomes of Sandra and John in 2007 were in the ratio 4:5.

   Lets assume the income of Sandra as 4x and of John as 5x.

   From graph, In 2007, Sandra saved 40% of her income. So her expense was 60% of her income. Lets call it Es

   Es = 60% × sandra's income $= 0.6 \times 4x = 2.4x$

   From graph, In 2007, John saved 60% of her income. So his expense was 40% of his income. Lets call it Ej

   Es = 40% × john's income $= 0.4 \times 5x = 2x$

   Ratio of Sandra's Expenditure/ John's Expenditure is $\Rightarrow 2.4x/2x = 1.2 \Rightarrow 6/5$

   Answer C.

3. Given : Each saved 18000 in 2009.

   From graph, In 2009, Sandra saved 45% of her income. let her income be x

   $45\% \times x = 18000$

   $\Rightarrow x = 40000$

   From graph, In 2009, John saved 45% of her income. let his income be y

   $30\% \times y = 18000$

   $\Rightarrow y = 60000$

   difference in income is $y - x = 60000 - 40000 = 20000$

   Answer C.

PASSAGE 15

1. We got to compare highest average attendance (in absolute numbers)

   Now for years before 2004 and after 2003 we can compare directly via avg percent attendance as the base (total capacity) is same. Hence, we need to compare between 2003 and 2005

   for 2003: Avg attendance = ~82%

Avg attendance in absolute numbers: $0.82 \times 60000 = \sim 49000$

for 2005: Avg attendance = ~78%

Avg attendance in absolute numbers: $0.78 \times 90000 = \sim 72000$

Answer D

2. To calculate the total absolute attendance we will need the total number of games played in the season. Without this information we cannot compute the total attendance for a season.

   Although we can compare the total attendance among different years based on avg attendance:

   from 2002

   Answer D

3. %Increase in attendance = (Attendance in 2004-Attendance in 2003)/Attendance in 2003

   Attendance in 2003 = %Attendance × capacity

   $= (0.58 \times 90000 - 0.82 \times 60000)/0.82 \times 60000 \sim 6\%$

   Answer A

Chapter 4

Two Part Analysis

PASSAGE 1

Steve is contemplating expanding his current rectangular garden, and he has two choices to consider. In the first option, he plans to extend the length of the existing garden by 5 meters while keeping the width the same. This expansion would result in an enlarged garden with an area twice that of the original garden. Alternatively, Steve could choose the second option, which involves increasing the width of the existing garden by 2 meters without altering the length. This adjustment would yield an enlarged garden with an area 1.5 times greater than that of the original garden.

From the Dimensions column in the following table, identify a length and a width, in meters, for Steve's existing garden that are consistent with Steve's two options. Make only two selections, one in for each column.

Length (m)	Width (m)	Dimensions
		3
		4
		5
		6
		7
		8

PASSAGE 2

At XYZ Inc., an employee will receive a verbal warning if they have accumulated 3 unexcused absences within a 365-day period. If the number of unexcused absences reaches 4, the employee will receive a written reprimand. The company defines the severity of an absence based on the duration of the missed work. Missing between 10 minutes and 2 hours counts as one-third of an absence, missing between 2 and 4 hours counts as half an absence, and missing more than 4 hours counts as a full absence. However, employees have the option to make up for up to 1 hour of an unexcused absence by staying late on the same day.

From the table provided, choose one description of an employee who met the criteria for a verbal warning, and select another employee who qualified for a written reprimand. Please make two selections, one from each column of the table.

Verbal warning	Written reprimand	Statements
		Absent all day on 5 Aprili 2010, 8 June 2010, 17 April 2011, and 14 June 2011
		Absent 4.5 hours but stayed 1 hour late on May 13 May 2010; absent all day on 2 June 2010, 1 May 2011, and 21 July 2011
		Absent 4.5 hours on 19 March 2010; stayed 1 hour late on 20 March 2010; absent all day on 8 and 9 February 2011; arrived 40 minutes late on 17 April 2011
		Absent 3.5 hours on 13 September 2010; absent 1 hour on 15 September 2010; absent 6 hours on 16 September 2010; absent 2.5 hours on 18 September 2010; absent 1 hour on 19 September 2010
		Absent 3 hours on 7 July 2010; absent 2.5 hours on 13 September 2010; absent all day on 31 January 2011 and 4 July 2011; absent 5 hours on 12 March 2011

PASSAGE 3

The events A and B are independent, and the probability that event A occurs is 0.4.

In the table below, choose the two numbers that are consistent with the information that is given. In the first column, select the row that shows the probability that at least one of the events A and B occurs, and in the second column, select the row that shows the probability that event B occurs.

Probability that at least one of the events A and B occurs	Probability that event B occurs	
		0.10
		0.25
		0.50
		0.55
		0.60
		0.80

PASSAGE 4

It is recommended that computer users employ distinct passwords for each of their online accounts to enhance security. These passwords should be strong, making them difficult for hackers to decipher. However, remembering multiple strong passwords can be challenging, particularly for users with numerous online accounts.

Fortunately, there are software solutions available at little or no cost that can securely store and encrypt passwords. Users only need to remember a single password to access all their stored passwords. By installing such software on a computer and entering the necessary information, users can comply with the recommendations of security experts. Some versions of this software can even be copied to portable devices like USB drives, enabling users to access their passwords from any compatible computer. For users with multiple accounts who would otherwise struggle to use different strong passwords for each account, following the advice of security experts may require making certain sacrifices in order to achieve significant gains in security.

Indicate by appropriate selections in the first and second column which of the items in the third column would describe a sacrifice for this user and which would be a gain. Make only two selections, one in each column.

Sacrifice	Gain	
		Money
		Computing Speed
		Security
		Number of online account
		Time

PASSAGE 5

Professor A : It is proposed that the aid industry should narrow its focus and allocate resources primarily towards primary schools located in the most impoverished regions. Additionally, there should be an emphasis on providing essential healthcare items like medicines and mosquito nets. Furthermore, attention should be given to a select number of significant agricultural initiatives.

Professor B : There is a belief that a substantial portion of education efforts has not yielded the desired outcomes. In cases where a village or town lacks adequate schooling, it is argued that providing infrastructure like roads might be more beneficial than solely focusing on hiring teachers. The rationale behind this perspective is that when local farmers are able to transport their produce to the market efficiently, their increased income can be utilized to support schools financially and ensure their long-term success.

Suppose that the professors' statements express their genuine opinions. Select statements (1) and (2) as follows : Professor A would likely disagree with (1) and Professor B would take (2) to present logical support for (1). Select only two statements, one per column.

(1)	(2)	Statements
		A. The aid industry should focus less on the areas of health and agriculture than it now does.
		B. The aid industry should focus more on primary education than it now does.
		C. The aid industry should focus its spending less on primary education than it now does.
		D. Projects in health and agriculture are more likely to be successful if they are not paid for by the aid industry.
		E. Projects in education are more likely to be successful if they are paid for by the aid industry.
		F. Projects in education are more likely to be successful if they are paid for by local people.

PASSAGE 6

Given the Eurostar's role as a high-speed train system, it offers rapid, efficient, and environmentally friendly transportation throughout Europe. When operating at a constant speed of T kilometers per hour (T km/hr), the Eurostar generates fuel emissions of CO_2 at a rate of E kilograms per kilometer (E kg/km) under typical travel conditions.

Choose the expression that represents the amount of CO_2 fuel emissions produced by the Eurostar during a one-hour journey at a constant speed, T, under normal travel conditions. Also, select the expression that represents the quantity of CO_2 emitted by the Eurostar while traveling at a constant speed, T, for a distance of 200 kilometers. Please make two selections, one from each column.

CO_2 emitted in 1 hour	CO_2 emitted in 200 kilometer	Expression
		200 E
		$\frac{E}{200}$
		ET
		$\frac{T}{200}$
		$\frac{T}{E}$

PASSAGE 7

The following excerpt is from a fictitious article in a journal of psychiatric medicine about a fictitious mental health condition called diaemotiopluralism.

For psychiatrists studying the behavior of those suffering from diaemotiopluralism, there is critical significance in observing the subject both when alone and when interacting with his or her peers. Such observations allow researchers to study not only the normal or "base" state of the affected person, including the effect that being alone has on an individual, but also the effects of diaemotiopluralism on social interactions, position in social order, and ability to participate in constructive workplace relationships. Individuals who suffer from diaemotiopluralism are often susceptible to overstimulation, particularly in situations involving high levels of interpersonal contact.

Moreover, there are varying degrees of diaemotiopluralism, with different social situations affecting individuals in unique ways. It is interesting to observe not only the actual symptoms of the disorder but also the coping mechanisms that the individual develops in an attempt to compensate for, overcome, or manage his or her condition.

From the table provided, determine the scenario that would pose the greatest challenge for an individual with diaemotiopluralism, as defined above. Additionally, identify the scenario that a person experiencing diaemotiopluralism would find the least challenging to handle.

Most Difficult	Least Difficult	Scenarios
		Working in an office
		Riding alone in a car
		Having lunch at home with a spouse
		Watching television with a friend
		Sleeping

PASSAGE 8

The gardener is in the process of planning the layout for a garden, which consists of two rectangular beds named A and B. Each bed will accommodate a total of 5 different types of shrubs or flowers. The gardener has a choice of 6 types of annual flowers, 4 types of perennial flowers, and 7 types of shrubs to select from for each bed. Bed A must include precisely 1 type of shrub and exactly 2 types of annual flowers. On the other hand, Bed B is required to have precisely 2 types of shrubs and at least 1 type of annual flower. It should be noted that no flower or shrub will be utilized more than once in each bed.

Identify the number of possible combinations of shrubs and flowers for bed A and the number of possible combinations of shrubs and flowers for bed B. Make only two selections, one in each column.

Bed A	Bed B	
		520
		630
		756
		1,028
		2,242
		2,436

PASSAGE 9

An employee of a certain company is creating the smallest possible cubic box into which a spherical piece of art will be placed for an exhibit. The longest distance around the piece of art is ? (2/4 meters).

Select the approximate value, in meters, of the sphere's diameter d and select the desired value, in meters squared, of the area A of the box's interior base. Make only two selections, one in each column.

d	A	
		0.56
		0.62
		0.68
		0.75
		0.79
		0.83

PASSAGE 10

The arboretum has the intention of establishing three new groves, each consisting of four trees. Specifically, each grove should comprise two distinct conifer trees and two different flowering trees. It is a requirement that at least one of the groves includes both a hemlock and a crabapple tree. Additionally, it is stipulated that no two groves can contain more than one tree of the same type, and it is prohibited to plant the same type of tree in all three groves.

Grove 1

- hemlock (conifer)
- spruce (conifer)
- magnolia (flowering)

Grove 2

- crabapple (flowering)
- dogwood (flowering)
- larch (conifer)

Grove 3

- cherry (flowering)
- crape myrtle (flowering)
- hemlock (conifer)

Select a tree that must be added to one of the groves. Then select a tree that cannot be added to any grove. Make only two selections, one for each column.

Must be added to one of the groves	Cannot be added to any grove	
		Cedar (conifer)
		Hemlock (conifer)
		Crabapple (flowering)
		Cypress (conifer)
		Fir (conifer)
		Pine (conifer)

PASSAGE 11

Samantha is considering two different phone plans. Plan A has a monthly fee of $15 and a per-minute rate of $0.1. Plan B has a monthly fee of $30 and a per-minute rate of $0.02. Samantha estimates that she will use 500 minutes per month. Based on this information, select for Average cost for the average monthly cost Samantha will pay for Plan A, and select for Amount saved the average amount Samantha will save per month by choosing Plan B over Plan A. Make only two selections, one in each column.

Average cost	Amount saved	
		$25.00
		$35.00
		$45.00
		$55.00
		$65.00

PASSAGE 12

A grocery store provides a discount program where customers can enjoy discounts on specific items. The program offers a 15% discount on all dairy products and a 10% discount on all fruits and vegetables. During the previous month, a customer made purchases amounting to $120 for dairy products and $80 for fruits and vegetables. In addition, the customer bought $50 worth of other items that were not eligible for any discounts.

In the table below select the total amount paid by the customer for all purchases including discounts, and the total amount paid by the customer for all purchases, without any discounts. Make only one selection in each column.

Total amount with discount	Total amount without discount	
		$200
		$219
		$224
		$245
		$250
		$304

PASSAGE 13

A committee of k members was formed from the n members of a certain company's board of directors. Each member of the committee sent exactly one email summarizing his or her perspective on the committee's findings to each board member who was not a member of the committee, and to no one else. The total number of these email summaries sent was 35.

Select values for k and for n that are jointly consistent with the given information. Make only two selections, one in each column.

k	n	
		4
		5
		7
		10
		12

PASSAGE 14

...esses a piece of land that is bounded by two roads intersecting at a right angle, forming a right ... the roads has a length of 2 kilometers (km), while the length of the other road is b km. The ...he boundary measures c km, and the area enclosed by the land is represented by A km^2.

In the table, select the value that is closest to c and the value that is closest to A so that the values are jointly consistent with the given information. Make only two selections, one in each column.

C	A	
		2.0
		2.8
		4.0
		5.7
		8.0

PASSAGE 15

A group of friends wants to order a pizza for a dinner party. To accommodate everyone's preferences, one-half of the pizza must contain at least 1 but no more than 3 kinds of meat and at least 2 but no more than 5 kinds of vegetable; the other half of the pizza must contain at least 2 but no more than 4 kinds of meat and at least 3 but no more than 6 kinds of vegetable. Below is the menu of options for both meats and vegetables.

Meats:

- Bacon
- Ham
- Pepperoni
- Sausage

Vegetables:

- Artichokes
- Mushrooms
- Olives
- Onions
- Peppers
- Spinach
- Tomatoes

Select a combination of ingredients that the friends could order for Each half of the pizza and a combination of ingredients that they can order for Neither half of the pizza. Make only two selections, one in each column.

Each half	Neither half	
		Bacon, artichokes, mushrooms, pepperoni, olives and sausage.
		Artichokes, mushrooms, pepperoni, peppers, spinach, and tomatoes.
		Artichokes, ham, olives, onions, peppers, sausage, spinach, and tomatoes.
		Artichokes, mushrooms, olives, onions, peppers, sausage, and spinach.
		Artichokes, ham, mushrooms, olives, onions, pepperoni, and tomatoes.

Answer Explanations

PASSAGE 1

Length (m)	Width (m)	Dimensions
		3
	✓	4
✓		5
		6
		7
		8

RO1

For any rectangle, the area is equal to the length (L) times the width (W). In Steve's garden, a length 5 m longer would yield an area twice as large. In other words, (L + 5)W = 2LW. Distributing the W gives LW + 5W = 2LW, and subtracting LW from both sides gives 5W = LW.

We are also told that a width 2 m longer would yield an area 1.5 times as large. In other words, L(W + 2) = 1.5LW. Distributing the L gives LW + 2L = 1.5LW, and subtracting 1.5LW from both sides gives 2L = 0.5LW. Multiplying both sides of the equation by 2 gives 4L = LW.

Thus, 5W = LW and 4L = LW, so 5W = 4L. Dividing both sides of the equation by 5 gives W=4/5L. The following table shows what the width of Steve's garden would be for each of several possible lengths:

L	$\frac{4}{5}$L
3	2.4
4	3.2
5	4
6	4.8
7	5.6
8	6.4

The only value for the width that is one of the possible options is 4. The corresponding length is 5.

The correct answer is 5.

RO2

The table provided in the analysis of RO1 shows that if the length is 5, the corresponding width is 4.

The correct answer is 4.

PASSAGE 2

Verbal warning	Written reprimand	Statements
		Absent all day on 5 Aprili 2010, 8 June 2010, 17 April 2011, and 14 June 2011
		Absent 4.5 hours but stayed 1 hour late on May 13 May 2010; absent all day on 2 June 2010, 1 May 2011, and 21 July 2011
✓		Absent 4.5 hours on 19 March 2010; stayed 1 hour late on 20 March 2010; absent all day on 8 and 9 February 2011; arrived 40 minutes late on 17 April 2011
		Absent 3.5 hours on 13 September 2010; absent 1 hour on 15 September 2010; absent 6 hours on 16 September 2010; absent 2.5 hours on 18 September 2010; absent 1 hour on 19 September 2010
	✓	Absent 3 hours on 7 July 2010; absent 2.5 hours on 13 September 2010; absent all day on 31 January 2011 and 4 July 2011; absent 5 hours on 12 March 2011

Verbal warning: Absent 4.5 hours on 19 March 2010; stayed 1 hour late on 20 March 2010; absent all day on 8, 9, and 10 of February 2011; arrived 40 minutes late on 17 April 2011

So here the employee would have only 3.5 absence here since March 2010 - March 2011 will be the one year period considered, so verbal warning would be there

Written reprimand: Absent 3 hours on 7 July 2010(.5 absence); absent 2.5 hours on 13 September 2010 (.5 absence); absent all day on 31 January 2011 and 4 July 2011(2 absenced); absent 5 hours on 12 March 2011 (1 absence)

PASSAGE 3

Probability that at least one of the events A and B occurs	Probability that event B occurs	
		0.10
	✓	0.25
		0.50
✓		0.55
		0.60
		0.80

We're asked to find the probability that event B occurs, such that one of the answer choices reflects the probability of either A or B occurring-in other words, any outcome other than neither A nor B occurring.

Since the only outcome we want to exclude is neither A nor B occurring (see stimulus explanation, above), we can create an equation by subtracting that one undesired outcome from the total of 1:

Probability that at least one of A and B occurs $= 1 - [0.6(1 - b)]$

$$= 1 - (0.6 - 0.6b)$$

$$= 1 - 0.6 + 0.6b$$

$$= 0.4 + 0.6b$$

(Note that there are two other ways to set this equation up. We could add the three desired outcomes together to yield $0.4b + 0.4(1 - b) + 0.6b$. Alternately, we could add the probabilities of A and B, then subtract the double-counted outcome of both occurring, yielding $0.4 + b - 0.4b$. On Test Day, go with whichever approach feels most straightforward-all of these approaches simplify to $0.4 + 0.6b$.)

Now let's consider the possible values given in the answer choice list. Thinking about the situation logically, we can determine that the probability that B occurs must be less than the probability that at least one of A or B occurs. We will therefore begin by plugging in the smaller values from our list for the variable b in the equation we set up above. If one of these values for b results in a probability for "at least one of the events A or B" that matches one of the given choices, we know we have found the correct answer.

If b were equal to 0.1, then the probability that at least one of A and B occurs would equal 0.46, which is not an answer choice. This strongly suggests that 0.25 is the probability that B occurs, since it is the only other small answer choice. A larger probability might be possible, since the probability of at least one of A and B might be as high as 0.8, but plugging in $b = 0.25$ is a reasonable next step.

We'll substitute $b = 0.25$ into our equation and see whether it produces one of the other answer choices. If it does, that pair will be correct. If it doesn't, we'll try a different value for b. Plugging $b = 0.25$ into our equation yields:

$$\begin{aligned} \text{Probability that at least one of A and B occurs} &= 0.4 + 0.6(0.25) \\ &= 0.4 + 0.15 \\ &= 0.55 \end{aligned}$$

This possible value matches one of the answer choices, so we have found the values that satisfy the conditions. Now, as always with Two-Part Analysis questions, we must be careful to select the correct answer choices in the appropriate columns; it would be a shame to do all the math correctly but lose the points for this question by mixing up the columns.

The correct response for the "probability that at least one of the events A and B occurs" is 0.55; the correct response for the "probability that event B occurs" is 0.25.

PASSAGE 4

Sacrifice	Gain	
		Money
		Computing Speed
	✓	Security
		Number of online account
✓		Time

In the second paragraph, the word "fortunately" suggests that the expert is recommending the special software as a way to solve the problems described in the first paragraph. The expert says the software is available at no cost, so no money need be sacrificed to use it. And the passage does not say or suggest anywhere that using the software would require sacrificing computing speed, security, or the user's number of online accounts. However, the passage does say it would take time to install the software and enter all the required information.

Thus, by recommending the software, the expert is effectively suggesting that users sacrifice some time in order to set it up.

The correct answer is Time.

The passage does not say or suggest anywhere that using the software would cause users to gain money, computing speed, or online accounts, nor that it would save them time. But the software does make it much easier for users to use a different strong password on every account even if they would not do so otherwise. The first paragraph says that this practice improves security. Thus, the expert is recommending the software as a way for users who would not otherwise use a different strong password on every account to gain security.

The correct answer is Security.

PASSAGE 5

(1)	(2)	Statements
		A. The aid industry should focus less on the areas of health and agriculture than it now does.
		B. The aid industry should focus more on primary education than it now does.
✓		C. The aid industry should focus its spending less on primary education than it now does.
		D. Projects in health and agriculture are more likely to be successful if they are not paid for by the aid industry.
	✓	E. Projects in education are more likely to be successful if they are paid for by the aid industry.
		F. Projects in education are more likely to be successful if they are paid for by local people.

The wording of the question suggests that the correctness of an answer for one of the response opportunities will depend on the correctness of the answer to the other. We are to find a statement such that the information indicates Professor A would likely disagree with the first statement and Professor B would take the second statement to present evidence against the first.

The only statement that the dialogue strongly suggests Professor A would disagree with is the third option. For example, if the relative distribution of spending by the aid industry between primary schools in the poorest areas, medicines and other basic supplies for health care such as mosquito nets, and the few key agricultural initiatives is maintained, while spending in other areas is drastically reduced, then the aid industry will thereby focus its spending more on primary education than it now does.

The correct answer is The aid industry should focus its spending less on primary education than it now does.

Given the answer above, the question requires identification of the statement that Professor B would take to be evidence for the statement that the aid industry should focus its spending less on primary education than it now does. The claims attributed to Professor B, in the context of the dialogue with Professor A, strongly suggest that she would take such evidence to be provided by the sixth option.

The correct answer is Projects in education are more likely to be successful if they are paid for by local people.

PASSAGE 6

CO_2 emitted in 1 hour	CO_2 emitted in 200 kilometer	Expression
	✓	200 E
		$\frac{E}{200}$
✓		ET
		$\frac{T}{200}$
		$\frac{T}{E}$

The total amount of CO_2 emitted equals the number of kilograms per kilometer times the number of kilometers. At a rate of T km/hr, the Eurostar travels T km in 1 hour, so the CO_2 emitted in that hour is E (the number of kilograms per kilometer) times T.

The total CO_2 emitted in 200 kilometers equals E (the number of kilograms per kilometer) times the number of kilometers, 200.

Answer:

CO_2 emitted in 1 hour: ET

CO_2 emitted in 200 kilometer: 200E

PASSAGE 7

Most Difficult	Least Difficult	Scenarios
✓		Working in an office
		Riding alone in a car
		Having lunch at home with a spouse
		Watching television with a friend
	✓	Sleeping

The correct answers are working in an office as most difficult to manage, and sleeping as least difficult to manage.

We know from the information given in the journal article that those with diaemotiopluralism have a problem with overstimulation from social interactions. Working in an office is the scenario in which there is likely to be the most social interaction to stimulate an individual. When sleeping, stimulation from outside sources would most likely not be an issue.

Answer:

Most Difficult: Working in an office

Least Difficult: Sleeping

PASSAGE 8

Bed A	Bed B	
		520
✓		630
		756
		1,028
		2,242
	✓	2,436

Bed A

For Bed A, we're told that the gardener must include exactly 1 type of shrub and exactly 2 types of annual flower. The problem also specifies that bed A must contain a total of 5 different types of shrubs or flowers, so bed A must also contain 2 types of perennial flower.

To choose 1 shrub from 7 possibilities, we calculate 7!/(1!6!) = 7. When choosing only 1, there is always the same number of possibilities as there is of items (7 possibilities, so 7 choices). To choose 2 annual flowers from 6 possibilities, we calculate 6!/(2!4!) = 15. To choose 2 perennial flowers from 4 possibilities, we calculate 4!/(2!2!) = 6. There are 7 possibilities for a shrub, 15 possibilities for the annual flowers, and 6 possibilities for the perennial flowers. In total, there are 7×15×6 = **630 possibilities for bed A.**

Bed B

For Bed B, we're told that the gardener must include exactly 2 types of shrub and at least 1 type of annual flower. This bed must also contain a total of 5 different types of shrubs or flowers.

To choose 2 shrubs from 7 possibilities, we calculate 7!/(5!2!) = 21.

Choosing bed B flowers is more tricky. We have three possible scenarios: the gardener chooses 1 annual flower (and therefore 2 perennials) OR the gardener chooses 2 annuals (and therefore 1 perennial) OR the gardener chooses 3 annuals (and therefore 0 perennials). We need to calculate the number of combinations for each and then add them together.

1 annual and 2 perennials: choosing 1 always matches the number of options, so there are 6 ways to choose the 1 annual flower. We calculated the number of possible combinations for 2 perennials when we did bed A: the number of possible combinations is 6. There are, therefore, 6 Ã- 6 = 36 possible ways to have 1 annual and 2 perennials.

2 annuals and 1 perennial: We calculated the number of possible combinations for 2 annuals when we did bed A above: the number of possible combinations is 15. For the perennials, we're choosing only 1, so there are 4 possible ways to choose a perennial. There are 15 A– 4 = 60 possible ways to have 2 annuals and 1 perennial.

3 annuals and 0 perennials: to have three annuals, we calculate 6!/(3!3!) = 20.

To have 1 OR 2 OR 3 annuals, we have 36 + 60 + 20 = 116 possible ways. In order to have this AND our 2 shrubs, we have 116 A– 21 = **2,436 possibilities for bed B.**

PASSAGE 9

d	A	
		0.56
	✓	0.62
		0.68
		0.75
✓		0.79
		0.83

Longest Area Around the spherical piece of art is its circumpherence i.e. $2\pi r$

so $2\pi r = \pi^2/4$

r comes as $\pi/8$ hence Diameter $D = \pi/4 = 0.79$

Area of Base A is D2 = 0.792 = 0.62

PASSAGE 10

Must be added to one of the groves	Cannot be added to any grove	
		Cedar (conifer)
	✓	Hemlock (conifer)
✓		Crabapple (flowering)
		Cypress (conifer)
		Fir (conifer)
		Pine (conifer)

Cedar (conifer) - It can be added in Grove 2 & 3 but it is not a Must be.

Hemlock (conifer) - It cannot be added to any groves as it has already been chosen for Grove 1 & 3. Adding it to Grove 2 will violate Condition-4

Crabapple (flowering) - It has to be added to Grove 1, so as to fulfill Condition-2. Grove 2 & 3 already has two flowering trees, so it cannot be added in these groves.

Cypress (conifer) - It can be added in Grove 1 or 3 but it is not a Must be.

Fir (conifer) - It can be added in Grove 1 or 3 but it is not a Must be.

Pine (conifer) - It can be added in Grove 1 or 3 but it is not a Must be.

Must be added to one of the groves - Crabapple (flowering)

Cannot be added to any grove - Hemlock (conifer)

PASSAGE 11

Average cost	Amount saved	
	✓	$25.00
		$35.00
		$45.00
		$55.00
✓		$65.00

Plan A has a monthly fee of $15 and a per-minute rate of $0.1, so the total cost of 500 minutes

$$= 15 + (500 \times 0.1) = 65\$$$

Plan B has a monthly fee of $30 and a per-minute rate of $0.02, so the total cost of 500 minutes

$$= 30 + (500 \times 0.02) = 40\$$$

Average monthly cost Samantha will pay for Plan A = 65$

The average amount Samantha will save per month by choosing Plan B = 65 – 40 = 25$

PASSAGE 12

Total amount with discount	Total amount without discount	
		$200
		$219
✓		$224
		$245
	✓	$250
		$304

Without discount, the customer paid the following

Dairy product $120

Fruits $80

Other items $50

Dairy product has a discount of 15%

Hence the discounted price = $120 \times 0.85 = 102$

Fruits has a discount of 10%

Hence the discounted price = $80 \times 0.9 = 72$

Total cost with discount = 102 + 72 + 50 = $224

Total amount with discount = $224

Total amount without discount = $250

PASSAGE 13

k	n	
		4
		5
✓		7
		10
	✓	12

number of board = n,

number of comittee = k (k person from n person) $\Rightarrow k < n$

each k send e-mail to board member who was not a member of the committee (n – k)

so total e-mail will be

$k \times (n - k) = 35 = 7 \times 5$

K = 7

N = 12

PASSAGE 14

C	A	
	✓	2.0
✓		2.8
		4.0
		5.7
		8.0

The sides of the plot's boundary that form the right angle of the triangle are 2 km and b km long, and the longest side is c km long. Using the Pythagorean Theorem, $c^2 = 2^2 + b^2 = 4 + b^2$ Taking the square root of each side gives $\sqrt{4+b^2}$. The area of the triangle, A km, can be found using the equation $\frac{1}{2}$ (bas)(height) $= \frac{1}{2}$(b)(2). Since A = b, A can be substituted into the previous expression:

$c = \sqrt{4+A^2}$ Using this equation, the value of c can be calculated for each possible value of A. The table below shows the calculations, rounded to the nearest tenth:

A	$c = \sqrt{4+A^2}$
2.0	2.8
2.8	3.4
4.0	4.5
5.7	6.0
8.0	8.2

The only one of these values of c that is among the options given is 2.8.

The correct answer is 2.8.

RO2

As shown in the table provided in the analysis for RO1, c = 2.8 corresponds to A = 2.0.

The correct answer is 2.0.

PASSAGE 15

Each half	Neither half	
		Bacon, artichokes, mushrooms, pepperoni, olives and sausage.
		Artichokes, mushrooms, pepperoni, peppers, spinach, and tomatoes.
		Artichokes, ham, olives, onions, peppers, sausage, spinach, and tomatoes.
	✓	Artichokes, mushrooms, olives, onions, peppers, sausage, and spinach.
✓		Artichokes, ham, mushrooms, olives, onions, pepperoni, and tomatoes.

1st Half :

Meat: Min-1; Max-2

Veg: Min-2; Max-5

2nd Half :

Meat: Min-2; Max-4

Veg: Min-3; Max-6

The Selection, which can be used for either half will contain 2 meat options (since it is the overlap) and 3/4/5 veg options.

The Selection, which can not be used for either half will have 1 meat option (as there are only 4 options available) and 6/7 veg options.

Bacon, artichokes, mushrooms, pepperoni, olives and sausage......3 meat and 3 Vegetables, Can be used only for 2nd half

Artichokes, mushrooms, pepperoni, peppers, spinach, and tomatoes......1 meat and 5 Vegetables, Can be used only for 1st half

Artichokes, ham, olives, onions, peppers, sausage, spinach, and tomatoes......2 meat and 6 Vegetables, Can be used only for 2nd half

Artichokes, mushrooms, olives, onions, peppers, sausage, and spinach......1 meat and 6 Vegetables, Cannot be used for any half

Artichokes, ham, mushrooms, olives, onions, pepperoni, and tomatoes......2 meat and 5 Vegetables, Can be used for either half

RQ2

[illegible]

Veg Min [illegible] Max [illegible]

2nd Half :

Meat Min 2 Max 4

Veg Min [illegible] Max [illegible]

